P9-CMK-294

Disability Sport

SECOND EDITION

Karen P. DePauw
*Virginia Polytechnic Institute
and State University*

and

Susan J. Gavron
Bowling Green State University

**HUMAN
KINETICS**

Library of Congress Cataloging-in-Publication Data

DePauw, Karen P.
  Disability sport / Karen P. DePauw, Susan J. Gavron.--2nd ed.
     p. cm.
  Rev. ed. of: Disability and sport. 1995.
  Includes bibliographical references and index.
  ISBN 0-7360-4638-0 (hard cover)
  1. Sports for people with disabilities.   I. Gavron, Susan J., 1947- II. DePauw, Karen P.
  Disability and sport. III. Title.
  GV709.3.D47 2005   2004022462

ISBN: 0-7360-4638-0

Copyright © 2005, 1995 by Karen P. DePauw and Susan J. Gavron

All rights reserved. Except for use in a review, the reproduction or utilization of this work in any form or by any electronic, mechanical, or other means, now known or hereafter invented, including xerography, photocopying, and recording, and in any information storage and retrieval system, is forbidden without the written permission of the publisher.

This book is a revised edition of *Disability and Sport,* published in 1995 by Human Kinetics.

The Web addresses cited in this text were current as of December 2004 unless otherwise noted.

Acquisitions Editor: Bonnie Pettifor; **Developmental Editor:** Ray Vallese; **Assistant Editor:** Derek Campbell; **Copyeditor:** Joyce Sexton; **Proofreader:** Erin Cler; **Indexer:** Sharon Duffy; **Permission Manager:** Dalene Reeder; **Graphic Designer:** Nancy Rasmus; **Graphic Artist:** Yvonne Griffith; **Photo Manager:** Kelly J. Huff; **Cover Designer:** Keith Blomberg; **Photographer (cover):** © Christian Houdek/Laserbild; **Art Manager:** Kelly Hendren; **Illustrator:** Craig Newsom; **Printer:** Edwards Brothers

Printed in the United States of America   10   9   8   7   6   5   4   3   2   1

Human Kinetics
Web site: www.HumanKinetics.com
United States: Human Kinetics, P.O. Box 5076, Champaign, IL 61825-5076
800-747-4457
e-mail: humank@hkusa.com

Canada: Human Kinetics, 475 Devonshire Road Unit 100, Windsor, ON N8Y 2L5
800-465-7301 (in Canada only)
e-mail: orders@hkcanada.com

Europe: Human Kinetics, 107 Bradford Road, Stanningley
Leeds LS28 6AT, United Kingdom
+44 (0) 113 255 5665
e-mail: hk@hkeurope.com

Australia: Human Kinetics, 57A Price Avenue, Lower Mitcham, South Australia 5062
08 8277 1555
e-mail: liaw@hkaustralia.com

New Zealand: Human Kinetics, Division of Sports Distributors NZ Ltd.
P.O. Box 300 226 Albany, North Shore City, Auckland
0064 9 448 1207
e-mail: blairc@hknewz.com

An old Hebrew saying . . .

L'Chiam (To life)
. . . and all of its ups and downs,
the people we meet,
the things we do and see and dream.

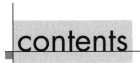

contents

Contents

preface to the second edition

We have attempted to take a good text and make it even better. In doing so, we listened to our friends, colleagues, and students express their opinions about the first edition. We consulted various resources, including the Internet, on all the current information on terminology and organizations. We kept information that is still relevant while reorganizing some of the content into different chapters, adding new chapters, deleting some chapters, and inviting colleagues to contribute to specific areas. As a result of this revision, we think that what we have is an even better text than the first edition.

We received many requests to expand the scope of the book to include more representation of other countries. Well, we listened. The status of disability sport beyond the North American borders has expanded and includes countries from which, 10 years ago, we had no way to access information. The sport bios represent people from almost every continent.

Readers will find that the disability sport movement has continued to evolve since the release of the first edition of *Disability and Sport* in 1995. As a result, some of the organizations that were instrumental in the formation of the movement have ceased to exist or merged with other organizations. This edition also points out more of the commonalities of disability sport with able-bodied sport, even the issues of blood doping, performance-enhancing drugs, and marketing.

We have kept many of the research citations intact and expanded the references to include many of the more recent papers presented at conferences around the world. But alas, there still seems to be a dearth of published research—especially field-based, real-time research—on the performance of elite athletes with disabilities. Last, we have also updated and expanded the appendixes. All of them include contact information and Web site addresses.

This book has a unique role in the realm of disability sport and adapted physical activity in general. The fact that this was the first book of the modern era to consolidate information about disability sport remains significant. Another goal of ours is to make this text more globally accepted. In the past decade, there has not been another effort to include all the information that we share with you. The publication of resources on coaching (such as wheelchair basketball and quad rugby), the availability of accessible sport equipment, and the opportunities for people with disabilities to participate in sport have increased, as has the availability of sporting clubs, organizations, periodicals, and newsletters worldwide. The fact that our readers represent diverse groups (researchers, undergraduate and graduate students, physical educators, adapted physical educators, recreation specialists, coaches, and athletes with disabilities) also makes this textbook unique.

Scope and Organization

In revising *Disability and Sport,* we maintained the original concept by organizing the material into three parts. Part I, chapters 1 to 6, presents a social construct of disability sport as well as the history, competitive opportunities, and worldview of the disability sport movement. In part II, chapters 7 to 11, you can find more of an applied component. The authors of several of these chapters offer a wealth of firsthand information. In chapter 7, new to this edition, Eli Wolff, an elite athlete in Paralympic soccer, and Dr. Mary Hums provide an in-depth view of the sports available for the serious athlete or the would-be coach. Chapter 9, by Dr. Mike Ferrara and Dr. Ron Davis, has been updated by two people who worked at the 1996 Atlanta Paralympics for an entire year. Chapter 10 is new and was written by two people with extensive knowledge of equipment design and accessibility, Patricia Longmuir and Peter Axelson, an independent businessman and former athlete.

In part III, chapters 12, 13, and 14, we go into more depth in each of the topics. Chapter 12 discusses issues in disability sport and some of the research that explores the often-contentious issues. In chapter 13, we examine the issues of females in sport. In chapter 14, we provide readers with some thoughts about the future of disability sport.

Features of the Book

This edition features some practical and creative elements:

- At the beginning of each chapter is a brief statement of what we expect you to get from the chapter.
- A chapter synopsis lists the broad subject content of each chapter.
- Key points are placed throughout the chapters to call your attention to those things that we think are significant.
- Chapter summaries are provided to synthesize the content.
- The sport bios are new to this edition and feature athletes from a variety of sports from around the world.

We hope you enjoy this book as much as we enjoyed gathering the information about the disability sport movement.

acknowledgments

Just as it takes a village to raise a child, it takes a team to write or rewrite a book. While authors are the initial moving force, the team is what gets it done. As with any team effort, it takes time and perseverance for all the parts to come together to make a high-quality product. The interactions of authors, editors, and contributing authors are an orchestrated movement that is both an exciting and sometimes pressure-filled experience. We would like to express our thanks to Bonnie Pettifor, the acquisitions editor who started us on our way; Ray Vallese for his expert, timely, and concise editing prowess; copyeditors, graphic artists, and other staff from Human Kinetics; Eli Wolff and Dr. Mary Hums for their clear descriptions of the sports; Drs. Ron Davis and Mike Ferrara for updating the sports medicine chapter; Patricia E. Longmuir and Peter W. Axelson, two outstanding practitioners and businesspeople who advocate for people with disabilities by "just doing it" time and time again; and to Antonia Dzakula-Meek for her able assistance with Internet searches.

While the professional component is necessary for completing a project of this magnitude, so too is the support of family, friends, and colleagues. For both of us, the 10 years between editions has brought joy and sadness, good health and not-so-good health, new professional opportunities, and retirement. Through all of these life events, our families, friends, and colleagues have stood by us and urged us to write this second edition. Thank you all for your support and encouragement. I (Sue) am especially grateful to people such as Karen DePauw, Dr. Gudrun Doll-Tepper, Dr. Claudine Sherrill, Dr. Jan Seaman, Dr. Betty van der Smissen, and Dr. Mary Ann Roberton for their continued support through thick and thin.

In addition to those mentioned here, I (Karen) would like to acknowledge and applaud Sue's longstanding contributions and efforts to disability sport and adapted physical activity. Thank you, Sue.

Last, but very important, both of us would like to express our appreciation to our former and current students and colleagues who are passionate about the disability sport movement and to the people with disabilities who compete in sport and participate in lifelong physical activity. We hope that this book piques your interest, stimulates your scholarly inquiry and research, and encourages you to ask questions about the past as well as the future.

In the first edition, we wrote that disability sport is a movement whose time has come. Today, we find that disability sport is alive and well. Readers of this text, we encourage you to become a part of an exciting future for disability sport. Your personal and professional contributions will keep the history alive and help promote a bright future for the generations to come.

Thank you.

Karen P. DePauw, PhD
Vice provost for graduate studies
    and dean of the graduate school
Virginia Tech
Blacksburg, Virginia

Susan J. Gavron, PED
Associate professor emeritus
Bowling Green State University
Bowling Green, Ohio

part I

Overview of Sport and Individuals With Disabilities

Introduction

Reader Goal Gain an understanding and comprehensive perspective of disability sport within a societal context

Chapter Synopsis

- Sport in Society
- Athletes With Disabilities
- Defining Terminology
- In the Context of Sport
- Concluding Comments

Individuals with disabilities have always been present in society, but for various reasons they have become more visible in the 21st century than in previous centuries. At least 10% of the population is considered to have a disability, and the legislative mandates of the late 20th century increased the accessibility and availability of services for people with disabilities. Media coverage, educational opportunities, and general information about disability have increased. As a result, we see more individuals with disabilities in society performing acts of daily living. Individuals with disabilities have become more accepted in society, including the sporting world. Athletes with disabilities have participated for at least a hundred years, but these athletes are just now beginning to receive the recognition they deserve and, more importantly, acceptance as athletes.

Sport in Society

The intersection of sport and disability into disability sport occurred initially during the 20th century; it is now a movement whose time has come. As the movement has matured, so too have the complexity of its organization, the reformation of its goals and objectives, and its visibility. And as athletic opportunities have expanded, so have the individual accomplishments of athletes with disabilities. These forgotten or invisible athletes are gaining increased recognition as athletes first and as persons with disabilities second.

Outstanding performances by elite athletes with disabilities are merely seconds or tenths of seconds behind those of elite able-bodied athletes in such sports as downhill skiing and swimming. Athletes with double-leg amputations have finished the 100-meter race in 10.85 seconds; others with less severe impairments finish in even less time. Elite male wheelchair marathoners frequently average 3.5 minutes per mile and complete marathons in approximately 90 minutes or less, while women marathoners have finished in 1:49 (www.paralympic.org). Athletes with cerebral palsy bench press 400 pounds (181 kilograms); athletes with other physical impairments bench press over 600 pounds (272 kilograms) in competition. In field events, athletes with single-leg amputations have jumped 6 feet, 8 inches (2 meters) (Atlanta Paralympic Organizing Committee, n.d.).

Thus there should no longer be a question as to the athletic ability of elite athletes with disabilities. Yet the reality is such that individuals with disabilities are still not taken seriously as athletes in terms of marketing and endorsement opportunities. Most elite able-bodied athletes (those who compete in major international competitions such as the Olympic Games) have had access to corporate sponsors throughout their competitive years, whereas elite athletes with disabilities (those who compete in major international competitions such as the Paralympic Games) typically do not. The first time an athlete with a disability attracted corporate sponsors was in 1990, when Diana Golden became the spokesperson for ChapStick and signed an agreement with Subaru (see appendix A). Since then, only selected athletes with disabilities have been able to attract corporate sponsors.

Michael Teuber of Germany demonstrates his prowess as an international-caliber athlete with a disability in cycling, sometimes without the equal benefits of able-bodied athletes.

KEY POINT

Disability sport is becoming recognized as a legitimate component of sport, although in some ways elite athletes with disabilities are still not taken as seriously as able-bodied athletes.

Athletes With Disabilities

In the 1980s and 1990s, a number of individuals with disabilities demonstrated their athletic ability in the sporting arena. Some achieved in the able-bodied sport world, while others achieved in disability sport. A few of the early examples follow, and newcomers are featured throughout the book in the form of a sport biography or "Sport Bio."

- Dr. Donalda Ammons excelled in basketball and swimming as a young woman. Her academic interests led her to pursue doctoral studies in foreign language, and she ultimately became director of foreign study programs at Gallaudet University. As a strong advocate for Deaf sport, she has served the American Athletic Association of the Deaf in many capacities, and she was the first woman to chair the U.S. World Games for the Deaf Team Committee.

- Camille Waddell Black competed in the 1992 Paralympics in Barcelona and was the first U.S. dwarf athlete to win a Paralympic gold medal. Camille set a world record in the 100-meter breaststroke.
- Distance runner Loretta Claiborne was inducted into the National Girls and Women in Sport Symposium Hall of Fame in February 1993. She has competed for a number of years with Special Olympics International.
- Running with a sighted partner, Harry Cordellos (who is blind) has run over 100 marathons; his best finish at the Boston Marathon was 2:57.42. In addition, he has competed in the Iron Man Triathlon in Hawaii and the grueling 100-mile (161-kilometer) survival run outside of San Francisco.
- Dr. Brad Hedrick is not only an elite athlete with a disability but an active professional and researcher in the field of disability sport. He has competed in wheelchair sports, including basketball and athletics (marathon time of 1:54; 10K time of 26:49). In addition, he has coached men's and women's wheelchair basketball; he has also now coached the U.S. wheelchair basketball team.
- Sharon Hedrick was the first to enter the women's wheelchair division of the Boston Marathon. She won the Olympic gold medal for the 800-meter exhibition event in the 1984 Los Angeles Olympic Games and for the 1988 Olympics in Seoul. She is a registered dietitian and works as a diabetic nutrition education specialist in Illinois.
- Duncan Wyeth, ambulatory cerebral palsy athlete, competed for the first time at the age of 32, in 1978 at the Michigan Regional Cerebral Palsy Games, in cycling and athletics. He has won gold and silver medals in regional, national, and international competitions including cerebral palsy athletes. He served as athlete and coach for the 1988 U.S. disabled sport team for the Seoul Paralympics and received the Male Athlete of the Year (Cerebral Palsy) Award from the United States Olympic Committee.

In remembering such notable athletes as these, we also look to the future when it will be possible to cite these accomplishments with the same familiarity as for able-bodied athletes.

KEY POINT

Athletes with disabilities have achieved in the sporting world, both in able-bodied arenas and in the realm of disability sport.

Defining Terminology

Before continuing, it is important to establish a common base of knowledge. Many organizations in this field are referred to by their abbreviations. See appendix B for a list of abbreviations found in this book. It is also necessary to clarify terminology. Here we define a few key terms.

Disability

Various terms have been used to describe individuals with disabilities over the years. Currently, the preferred terminology is one in which the person is mentioned first, as in "person with a disability" or "individual with a physical impairment." Throughout this text, we have attempted to use "people-first" language, such as "athletes with disabilities" or "athlete with a visual impairment." This approach acknowledges persons as individuals rather than focusing on their disability.

Disability Sport

As individuals with a disability have entered the sport world, various terms have evolved to represent their involvement as perceived by the able-bodied sport world. Among the more prevalent of these are "handicapped sports," "sport for the disabled," "adapted sport," "disabled sport," "wheelchair sport," and "Deaf sport." These terms generally imply a sport context designed for individuals with disabilities, and specify, in some instances, the type of disability. These terms do not adequately describe the broader entity of sport in which athletes with disabilities can be found: sport for athletes with disabilities specifically and sport that includes both athletes with disabilities and athletes without disabilities.

Throughout the book, when used alone, "sport" refers to the broadest context of sport; in most instances, we use the term to mean competitive sport (as conceptualized in the United States). The term "sport" as used in other countries encompasses much more than competitive sport, but its use here is intended to delimit the scope of the book.

This book deals with sport for and including individuals with disabilities (impairments)—thus the title *Disability Sport*. Much of the focus, however, is on competitive sport and athletes with disabilities (physical, sensory, and intellectual impairments)—what we call disability sport. We have adopted the term disability sport to refer to sport that has been designed for or is specifically practiced by athletes with disabilities. Disability sports might include sports that were designed for a selected disability group: goal ball for blind athletes, wheelchair basketball for athletes with physical impairments who use a wheelchair, or sitting volleyball for athletes with lower-limb impairments. Disability sport also includes those sports practiced by able-bodied individuals (e.g., athletics, volleyball, swimming) that have been modified or adapted to include athletes with disabilities (e.g., wheelchair tennis, tandem cycling), as well as those that require little or no modification to allow individuals with disabilities to participate (e.g., athletics, wrestling, swimming).

"Disabled sport" and "sport for the disabled" are the terms that have been used, and are still prevalent in the literature, to describe that which we call disability sport. "Disability sport" is preferred because sport cannot be disabled and "for the disabled" does not utilize "person-first" language. It is important to note that not all professionals agree with this terminology but that we view terminology as one component of the developmental process of a maturing movement among and between athletes and professionals.

Throughout the book, different terms are used to identify the major international competitions for athletes with disabilities. We have kept the original terminology for an accurate historical record but have added the newer term for clarification. For example, the Paralympics have been known as the International Games for the Disabled and the Olympiad for the Physically Disabled. The name for the Deaflympics has also evolved over time, from the International Silent Games to the World Games for the Deaf and now the Deaflympics.

Deaf Sport/Deaflympics

"Deaf sport is a social institution within which Deaf people exercise their right to self-determination through organization, competition, and socialization surrounding Deaf sport activities" (Stewart, 1991, p. 2). When capitalized, the term "Deaf people" refers to those who have hearing impairments or deafness and who by identifying themselves as such embrace Deaf as a cultural identity. On one level, Deaf sport can be defined as sport in which Deaf athletes compete, a parallel entity to able-bodied (hearing) sport in which individuals with hearing impairments participate. The Deaflympics may be seen as a culminating event or apex for sporting performances within this context.

On another level, Deaf sport should be viewed from a cultural perspective. Not only is Deaf sport a celebration of community among Deaf people; it is also a microcosm or subset of the larger Deaf community (Stewart, 1991).

Although some athletes with hearing impairments and deafness (Deaf athletes) typically have not considered themselves a part of disability sport, we see that they do fit within the broader context of sport for and including athletes with disabilities. Accordingly, we acknowledge fully and concur with the argument put forth by Stewart (1991) that "disability leaves the impression that a person [with a disability] has more liabilities than assets" (p. 99). Given society's traditional notion of able-bodiedness as the "norm" and the use of language that follows this tradition, we find language limiting in its ability to accurately describe individuals who present an alternative perspective to the traditional "norm," including individuals with disabilities and Deaf persons (for more information, see Davis, 1995; DePauw, 1997; Shogan, 1998). Without wishing to offend, we include Deaf athletes and Deaf sport in this book and shall discuss both not only as part of sport and disability but also within the context of disability sport. Readers unfamiliar with Deaf sport can be enlightened through such inclusion.

KEY POINT

Deaf sport is often considered a separate entity from disability sport, although it also makes sense to include Deaf athletes and Deaf sport within the context of disability sport.

In the Context of Sport

Sport is a cultural phenomenon that is often viewed as a product and a reflection of society (Donnelly, 1996; Giddens, 1977; Sage, 1987). Sport is a microcosm of the larger society; it is defined and described within the sociocultural and sociohistorical framework of the values, mores, norms, and standards of a specific society or culture.

Historically, sport has tended to be an exclusive club for the white, middle- and upper-class, Protestant, heterosexual, able-bodied male "majority" within a capitalistic society (Bonace, Karwas, and DePauw, 1992). Thus, not all persons who desired access were allowed into the sporting arena.

Women, members of ethnic minorities, and persons with disabilities have been excluded or allowed limited access to sport. Given the similarity in the patterns of exclusion or limited acceptance because of culture, gender, ethnicity, class, or disability affiliation (DePauw, 1997; Karwas and DePauw, 1990), individuals from these groupings can be considered to be "outside" of a particular culture or society, or marginalized (e.g., Hughes, 1949; Park, 1928).

Ours is a social world, "constituted and reproduced through and in human action" (Giddens, 1977, p. 166). Sport is a significant part of this world—a social construction. Not only is sport highly visible; it touches almost everyone as a participant, spectator, or consumer. Sport permeates the very fabric of society. Because sport is so pervasive in society and has been perceived by society as an equalizer and as a means of gaining acceptance, individuals with disabilities have sought access to sport.

Attitudes Toward Persons With Disabilities in Sport

As a social minority (or marginalized) group, individuals with a disability have limitations placed upon their participation in society. As sport is an integral part of society, similar sanctions and limitations have been imposed for inclusion within the sporting world.

Throughout the history of sport, individuals with disabilities have experienced exclusion and disenfranchisement. Although movement toward inclusion and acceptance is slow, it has been positive (DePauw, 1986c; DePauw and Doll-Tepper, 2000; Mastro, Hall, and Canabal, 1988). Progress, both past and future, is related directly to the attitudes held by society about sport and disability.

As we will discuss in some detail in chapter 2, the historical treatment of individuals with disabilities was focused on difference and based on fear and superstition. This perspective provided the basis for exclusion from society and lies at the heart of "exclusion" from sport. The perception of individuals with disabilities was that they were frail and thus not physically capable. As logic would have it, sport, being representative of physical prowess, could not include those who were weak or physically impaired. The traditional model of sport persisted, and those who were not "physical" or perceived as physically capable were not allowed to participate. This restriction also extended to women as a group and especially women with disability.

Medical restrictions have always been imposed on the sport participation of individuals with disabilities. Although there are still some contraindications for full, unrestricted participation, they are decreasing as a result of changing attitudes about the frailty of persons with disabilities, cutting-edge research, acceptance of their abilities, and increased socialization of people with disabilities into society.

Socialization is a process whereby individuals assimilate, or adopt, the values of a given society. Socialization is an important process of childhood in that it allows for determination of interests, aspirations, and activity selection in the future. Socialization into sport, let alone socialization via sport, is often not a part of the socialization of youth

Chris Bourne

FAST FACTS

Home Base: Ontario, Canada
Sport: Triathlon (primary), duathlon, road racing, waterskiing
Selected Accomplishments:

World Triathlon Champion 2001
Bronze medal, World Triathlon Championships
Silver medal, World Duathlon 2002

Chris Bourne runs, swims and cycles, and water-skis. He also happens to be a T-6 paraplegic as a result of a car crash with a train. His involvement in a sport such as triathlon delivers a powerful message—you can do what you want to do in sport. This hard-training athlete often goes six days a week, two sessions per day. His coaches assist him in his training. Yet Chris indicates that he had to "find" wheelchair sports on his own by observing other people having fun in this medium. This is not the way it is for nondisabled kids who are immersed in sport from an early age. Having found his niche, Chris says, "Sport defines me . . . it puts a smile on my face and makes me feel

"Sport defines me . . . it puts a smile on my face . . . makes me feel great physically . . . drains my bank account . . . inspires a mountain of self confidence. . . ."

Chris Bourne (continued)

great physically . . . it inspires a mountain of self-confidence, it challenges me and always provides me with something else to conquer."

In his capacity at Active Living Alliance for Canadians with a Disability, Chris has an opportunity to assist others and facilitate opportunities in sport and recreation for people with disabilities in Canada. Chris's formal education—he completed his undergraduate degree after his accident and his master's degree in recreation and leisure studies—along with his real-life experiences makes him an ideal role model. His enthusiasm for what he does is real. Chris wants young people with disabilities, the rehab centers, and other professionals to "get on it!"

---

with disabilities. Although sport roles and expectations tend to be socialized early in one's life, youth with disabilities have tended to be socialized to pursue different roles (e.g., spectator) and expectations (e.g., participation only, no competition). Disabled youth who deviate from these social roles or expectations have often received negative reinforcement; for example, they are rejected for participation or discouraged from continuing.

Often the attitudes of significant individuals (socializing agents) in the life of a child with a disability provide the reinforcement and modeling of appropriate sport behavior. Inasmuch as teachers, parents, schools, and community agencies are socializing agents or settings, their attitudes, behaviors, and practices serve to model or reinforce (or both model and reinforce) sporting behavior as perceived to be appropriate for individuals with disabilities. Many of the socializing agents have just begun to reflect the value of sport participation for individuals with disabilities.

Social attitudes toward sport competition by individuals with disabilities have been mixed. Because of perceived frailty and negative experience resulting from defeat, people with disabilities have often been discouraged from competing. Even though sport participation by individuals with disabilities has gained more acceptance, some continue to question the appropriateness of competition for persons with disabilities. This mixed response to sport competition appears to be related to one's perception of the type and extent of the disability, the limitations of one's ability, and the risks associated with sport competition. Individuals with disabilities have most often been perceived as physically and mentally inferior and therefore as having no cultural need for competition beyond sport for rehabilitation or therapeutic reasons (Lewko, 1979; Orr, 1979; Snyder, 1984).

Disability sport has not been viewed as legitimate sport but rather as something less. Concomitantly, opportunities, rewards, public recognition, and the like have not been afforded athletes with disabilities.

Segregated events and competitions have been somewhat acceptable but are still viewed as less valuable than sport competitions for able-bodied individuals.

Integrated participation in sporting events is slowly becoming accepted, but it is not yet routine sport practice. Individuals with disabilities who compete or are able to compete alongside nondisabled individuals are considered the exception rather than the rule. But attitudes are changing, and perhaps so is the definition of sport.

Barriers to Inclusion in Sport

Society's attitudes about individuals with disabilities in sport have led to specific barriers to participation. These barriers result from persistent social myths and alarming stereotypes held by the greater society. Many of these stem from the labels that have been created to identify the problems or impairments that characterize selected individuals in our society.

Many detrimental effects of labeling exist. Thinking about individuals in categories (e.g., categorization) by disability creates stereotypes and allows them to persist. Stereotypes also perpetuate overgeneralization and under-expectation, which have plagued persons with disabilities throughout history and have been evident in the limitations placed upon those who wish to enter sport. Persons with intellectual impairments (mental retardation, developmental disability) were not thought to understand or enjoy competition or to be capable of outstanding physical performance. Common misperceptions were that people with visual impairments could not downhill ski or run marathons, and wheelchair marathoners were never expected to complete the race in under 2 hours. In addition to promoting overgeneralization and under-expectation, labels tend to be permanent, to relieve one from responsibility for change, and to emphasize the status quo and not allow for change.

Although labeling persists, the trend within disability sport is now to place greater emphasis on classifying by ability rather than disability. Disability classifications have not been completely erased, but greater attention is being paid to functional classification. In general, the increasing athletic performances of athletes with disabilities starting in the 1980s and continuing today have done much to dispel, yet have not eliminated, the effects of labeling and the persistence of classification.

There are many parallels between women and individuals with disabilities and their desire to participate in sport. Many of the barriers to sport that exist for people with disabilities are similar to those experienced by women (Grimes and French, 1987) and other marginalized groups (individuals excluded from sport) (Karwas and DePauw, 1990). These have included

- lack of organized sport programs,
- lack of informal early experiences in sport,

- lack of access to coaches and training programs,
- lack of accessible sport facilities, and
- limiting psychological and sociological factors.

Due to recent changes, some of these barriers are being lowered. The increasing visibility of disability sport results in more sport opportunities for individuals with disabilities as well as an increasing number of role models for aspiring athletes with disabilities. But the lack of organized sport programs continues to present a barrier. Although increasing, sport opportunities for individuals with disabilities within school physical education or after-school sport programs continue to be inadequate (Gavron, 2000). Community-based recreation and sport programs have increased dramatically over the years, but they remain inadequate to fulfill the needs of the existing, let alone the potential, population of individuals with disabilities. Greater numbers of trained sport and recreation professionals and physical educators (including adapted physical education teachers) are needed. Physicians who frequently encounter or treat youth with disabilities need to be educated about the availability of physical activity and sport programs so that they can become more supportive.

Economic, psychological, and sociological factors often remain as barriers to sport participation by individuals with disabilities. The cost of necessary equipment can be especially prohibitive. Many persons with disabilities do require some additional apparatus or assistive device (e.g., wheelchair, specially designed prosthesis, sighted guide, visual cues). And because of the numerous barriers to sport participation, individuals with disabilities can face enormous psychological problems—women more so than men (Grimes and French, 1987).

Visible role models are valuable to the development of disability sport and the encouragement of sport participation by all age groups of individuals with disabilities. Since the 1980s, athletes with disabilities have been featured similarly to able-bodied athletes in commercials, on the Wheaties box, in autobiographies, as sport commentators, in media briefings, and in featured articles in the sport section of the newspaper. These forms of publicity, along with television coverage of selected events, have helped the disability sport movement become increasingly more visible. But the reality is that the level of this kind of visibility is still low, as is the comfort level of the populace at seeing these athletes featured.

KEY POINT

Physical and attitudinal barriers initially limited athletes with disabilities from meaningful participation in sport. Despite much progress and greater opportunities today for athletes with disabilities, economic, psychological, and sociological barriers remain.

"Tools of the trade"—sitting volleyball team practice results in assistive devices being removed and lying around a gymnasium, just like any warm-up clothing, sweatshirt, crutches, or wheelchair.

Accessibility

Accessibility is another key issue facing individuals with disabilities in their quest to participate in sport and recreation activities. Access to sport and adapted equipment is a necessity for full participation. Facilities that are accessible to all disability groups are still in short supply, even though laws have been passed that require accessibility. Emphasis must be placed on the local level as well as the state and federal levels to provide physical accommodation (e.g., wheelchair ramps, modifications of physical structures) and accessibility (e.g., rules, procedures, and attitudes) to those individuals with disabilities who wish to participate in sport.

Addressing accessibility issues involves identifying and eliminating common barriers. It is important to understand the legislative mandates regarding sport for individuals with disabilities.

Persons with disabilities have sometimes had difficulty in accessing opportunities in sport. Expense, fear, and distance, as well as the lack of information, skill, physician encouragement, and appropriate equipment, appear to be major contributors to this problem (Frederick, 1991;

Murphy-Howe and Charboneau, 1987). Access to information about sport programs is increasing but is not yet widespread. For information about such programs, individuals with disabilities and their families could be referred to their local parks and recreation association, chamber of commerce, schools, and sport programs. Physical educators and recreation specialists are becoming increasingly aware of sport opportunities for individuals with disabilities and can provide valuable information. For a listing of sport organizations geared toward individuals with disabilities, see appendixes D and E.

Sport as rehabilitation began after World War II. The history of the development of sport elsewhere in this text puts sport as rehabilitation in a broader context of sport. However, even today, many physicians with whom individuals with disabilities have a significant amount of contact do not recommend sport opportunities for their clients' rehabilitation or lifestyle.

Lack of skill is another variable that may affect whether an individual with a disability participates in sport. Playing standing basketball is different from playing in a wheelchair, even though the skills and the objective of the game are the same. Individuals with disabilities are encouraged to seek training through physical education in the public schools or through community recreation and youth sport programs.

Closely related to skill development is access to coaches. Like women, athletes with disabilities have been limited by the lack of coaches to help them train. Although coaches are available, many of these athletes have been self-coached. Training regimens and sports medicine programs were relatively unknown in the early development of disability sport but have increased in recent years. Later chapters present more information about sports medicine and training techniques.

Legislative Mandates for Disability Sport

Accessibility to sport programs is secured for individuals with disabilities by legal mandates in the United States. Several significant legislative mandates (e.g., Amateur Sports Act) are discussed in some detail later in this text. This section covers the Americans with Disabilities Act (ADA), a significant federal law passed in 1990 that mandates increased accessibility; removal of barriers; and promotion of economic, social, and personal independence (West, 1991).

The ADA encompasses five areas, or "titles." The first title is that of employment. The essence of this section is that "no entity shall discriminate against a qualified individual because of the disability in regard to job application procedures, the hiring, placement or discharge of employees,

Tanja Kari

FAST FACTS

Home Base: Helsinki, Finland
Sport: Cross-country skiing
Selected Accomplishments:

Medalist in four Paralympics

Medalist in world championships

Top 25 among Finnish skiers, including able-bodied

This accomplished athlete, now retired, spent 15 years competing in cross-country skiing. The loss of her right arm did not hamper her ability to be a successful athlete. In four Paralympics (Salt Lake, Nagano, Lillehammer, Albertville), she won 10 individual gold medals and one bronze relay medal. She garnered nine gold medals in world championships and was 24th out of 100 in the Finnish Championships that included able-bodied racers. In retirement, Tanja has reflected on the role of sport in her life, saying that sport was "a huge part of my identity and offered a significant opportunity to find my limits by developing myself as an athlete." Today this athlete has also earned her master's degree in sport sciences in sport management and sport sociology and works to bring some of these opportunities to others. As the manager of youth sport for the Finnish Floorball Federation, Tanja is in a position to facilitate the success of others, particularly younger athletes with disabilities. Of these young athletes Tanja says, "They will have an incredible world waiting for them. Sport can offer courage, experiences, opportunity to find the limits in many ways; it is a great way to grow."

"Sport was . . . a huge part of my identity and offered a significant opportunity to find my limits by developing myself as an athlete."

It is easy to feel Tanja's enthusiasm and commitment toward young athletes within this new arena. She has accomplished her competitive goals and will now help others to reach theirs.

employee compensation, job training and other terms, conditions and privileges of employment" (West, 1991, p. 34). Individuals with disabilities who wish to work in a sport or recreation environment cannot be generally excluded just because they have a disability, unless they are not otherwise qualified to do the job.

Title II of the ADA relates to the area of public services and has direct impact on sport for individuals with disabilities. This title provides that "no individual with a disability shall be excluded from participation in or be denied the benefits of services, programs or activities of a public entity or subjected to discrimination by any such entity" (West, 1991, p. 37). Public transportation systems need to be responsive to the needs of individuals with disabilities to travel from homes or jobs to training centers and must have the adapted equipment available.

Title III is perhaps one of the most far-reaching segments of the law. It provides that "no individual shall be discriminated against on the basis of disability in the full and equal enjoyment of the goods, services, facilities, privileges, advantages and accommodations of any place of public accommodation by any person who owns, leases or operates a place of public accommodation" (West, 1991, p. 38). This section covers places where athletes can practice, such as school or university gymnasiums, local parks, stadiums, and recreation facilities. In the late 20th century, the U.S. Olympic Training Center in Colorado Springs became physically accessible to individuals using wheelchairs. Other training sites and competition sites across the country need to follow suit. Administrators for the National Sports Festival, for example, a partially integrated sport competition, will need to make sure that housing, restaurants, spectator seating, and event venues are accessible. For buildings that are newly constructed, the law is very direct on this mandate (Munson and Comodeca, 1993).

Accessibility to programs (e.g., intramurals and teams) by individuals with disabilities is also included in the ADA. The focus in this area is on not only the removal of physical barriers but also the inclusion of an individual based upon ability. Exclusion from participation in activity is based on proving that an individual with a disability is more likely to be injured than in the "normal course of participating in a program" (Munson and Comodeca, 1993).

Concluding Comments

Sport is a social institution, a "system of social relationships or a network of positions and roles embodying the values people hold in common" (Leonard, 1980, p. 45). As a social institution and a microcosm of society, sport has evolved and has been unable to remain unaffected by political, social, and cultural changes. Sport will continue to be redefined by and in the new order of the world of the 21st century.

Disability sport has made its mark upon society. Individuals with disabilities have fought for inclusion in sport and have become recognized as athletes for their achievements and accomplishments in sport. Since the mid-20th century, attitudes toward athletes with disabilities have changed, barriers to inclusion have been lowered, and sport has become more accessible through legislative mandates. Although not complete, the trend is toward progressive inclusion and acceptance (DePauw, 1986c; DePauw and Doll-Tepper, 2000). Well into the 21st century, sport opportunities for and including individuals with a disability will continue to increase.

two

Historical Context of Disability and Sport

Reader Goal Gain a historical perspective of the treatment of individuals with disabilities and the social-political events that had an impact on their status in society, sport, and physical activity

Chapter Synopsis

- Historical Treatment of Persons With Disabilities
- Historical Perspectives of Physical Activity and Sport
- Concluding Comments

The rights of individuals with disabilities have been at issue throughout history, but they were contested particularly during the 20th century. The acknowledgment of the civil rights of individuals with disabilities evolved in response to changes in social attitudes and behaviors. Although there is now greater inclusion and acceptance of individuals with disabilities in society (DePauw, 1986c; DePauw and Doll-Tepper, 2000), this has not always been the case.

Historical Treatment of Persons With Disabilities

Individuals who did not conform to the prescribed norm of the time in appearance or behavior have always experienced differential treatment. This treatment varied from cruel to humane, and at times such persons were even revered. Historically, those who were perceived as "different" were destroyed, tortured, exorcised, sterilized, ignored, exiled, exploited, pitied, cared for, categorized, educated, and even considered divine (Hewett and Forness, 1974). The treatment was dependent on the individual, the perception of the nature of the disability, and the cultural values and norms of the time. Throughout most of history, differences in treatment have been based on a categorical distinction between those with physical impairments and those with mental impairments.

The primitive and ancient periods (3000 B.C. to 500 B.C.) were characterized by an organized society in which survival and superstition were the key elements. These societies practiced the concept of survival of the fittest. When individuals were found to be obviously physically deformed or not physically capable of hunting for food or defending themselves, they were left to face the consequences of the harsh environment, which meant death usually by starvation or predators (Davies, 1975). Often, individuals born with physical deformities were considered evil and were therefore isolated from the family unit. This attitude often resulted in the death of those with impairments, and their demise was not looked upon as a loss to the functioning of the unit (Davies, 1975). This concept of survival of the fittest permeated the early societies; for example, Indian and Asian societies often allowed the unfit to die to improve the "quality" of the unit.

During the primitive and ancient period, superstition also tended to guide social responses to persons who behaved differently. These individuals were either feared or considered possessed. Those possessed with "good spirits" were revered; those with "bad spirits" were indulged in order to prevent revenge. Also practiced during this period were exorcism and trephining, a crude operation whereby the evil spirits were released through a small hole drilled in the skull (Hewett and Forness, 1974).

In the Greek and Roman period (500 B.C. to 400 A.D.), persons born with impairments were faced with a harsh physical environment, infanticide, and eugenics (protection and further development of the species). Many physically disabled and female children were actually abandoned or exiled or literally left to die. The doctrine of the survival of the fittest was applied not only to the environmental conditions but also to the harsh discipline and punishment often inflicted upon children. The weakest were not to survive this treatment.

The Greeks and the Romans were concerned about the physical capability of their citizens, but their reasons were biased toward the safety of the state and protection from external enemies. Thus, war was the catalyst for building strong bodies and developing advanced skills for the taking of life. In this environment, those with disabilities were not valued and often were put to death. In contrast, those who became physically impaired (e.g., amputated arm) in battle were honored as heroes (Davies, 1975; Rothschild, 1968).

During this period, the treatment of those with mental impairments was based on superstition. Inasmuch as mental illness was thought to be caused by the "gods" taking away one's mind, the treatments included purification, exorcism, and other demonological practices. These practices were a continuation of early treatment of those with mental impairments.

Later in the Greek and Roman period, different conceptualizations of mental illness evolved, thanks to the efforts of such thinkers as Hippocrates and Plato. Hippocrates described mental illness as a disease of natural causes and not the result of possession by demons or the wrath of the gods. Plato advocated care, not exile, exorcism, or demonology, for those with mental impairments. For a brief period, this care included physical activity or exercise, hydrotherapy, massage, and exposure to sunshine. Although survival and superstition remained the key components of this period, the development of limited tolerance for individuals with disabilities was first realized, albeit for a brief moment of humanitarian reform (Hewett and Forness, 1974).

Onset of Judeo-Christian Influence

The early Christians (beginning around 400 A.D.) had an even greater impact on individuals with disabilities because of their strong emphasis on the concept that taking a life was a sinful act. Infanticide was no longer an accepted practice. This live-and-let-live attitude allowed such individuals to be treated with compassion, and it represented a significant change because of the large numbers of Christians (Davies, 1975). But despite the fact that infants born impaired were allowed to live, many were still not able to survive in their harsh physical and social environments.

During the Middle Ages (5th-15th centuries), individuals with disabilities, both physical and mental, were able to survive in the protective environments of monasteries and royal courts. Their status was limited, but their quality of life was much improved over that in previous periods. The religious influences of the period did much to foster acceptance, understanding, and humanitarian treatment of individuals with disabilities.

The onset of Christianity also affected treatment. Those with mental retardation were thought to be "children of God," while those with mental illness were believed to be possessed by the devil (Lilly, 1983). The mentally retarded individuals, the "blessed," were often employed in the courts of kings and queens as court jesters. Although protected and tolerated, they were denied access to the craft guilds and other forms of skilled living because they were deemed incapable (Davies, 1975). For those considered mentally ill, occasionally exorcism, torture, witch burning, and other demonological practices persisted (Hewett and Forness, 1974).

Influence of Science and Medicine

Although science and medicine were to influence the treatment of individuals with disabilities during the 16th and 17th centuries (1500s-1600s), individuals with noticeable differences were still persecuted. The demonological tradition persisted; people with mental illness were still tortured, or burned at the stake, or both.

In contrast, those with hearing impairments and mental retardation received more humanitarian treatment. Deaf children of noble birth received education afforded only to a privileged few. Primarily in institutions designed specifically for them, Deaf children were taught reading, writing, arithmetic, astronomy, Greek, and other subjects. Both oral language and finger spelling were used to educate these children. Due to their privileged status, children with hearing impairments had a high standard of living.

Individuals with mental retardation were still considered idiots and simpletons, but attempts were made to understand them from psychological and educational perspectives. They were often segregated from society, and although some were employed in workhouses, most remained unemployed and were perceived as a burden on society.

During the 18th century, the society that had been significantly influenced by belief in demons and "evil spirits" finally came under the greater influence of a movement toward the rights (and dignity) of humans. The 18th century witnessed a transition from fear, superstition, and hostility toward individuals with disabilities to compassion and a decision to educate these same individuals. Rationalism and enlightenment continued to coexist with the harsh environmental conditions and violent revolution.

In general, children were treated in a more humane manner. Although the average longevity was only 22 years when the environment and physical treatment were harsh, some babies were rescued, nursed at public expense, and placed in workhouses when old enough (Hewett and Forness, 1974). During the industrial revolution, women and children were among the labor force; because they were unskilled, this situation often led to accidents and even death.

Lukas Christen

FAST FACTS
Home Base: Switzerland
Sport: Long jump
Selected Accomplishments:

> World championship winner—gold medal
>
> Paralympic gold medals in 100 meter, 200 meter, long jump
>
> Former world record holder in 100 meter, 200 meter, 400 meter, and long jump

Lukas Christen is a man whose success in the athletic arena has led to his success as a professional who owns his own consulting company. He has not let his traumatic above-the-knee amputation dampen his dreams.

This multiple-medal winner in Barcelona (1992), Atlanta (1996), and Sydney (2000), and winner of world championships in Berlin (1994) and Birmingham (no date provided), knows what it takes to be a winner on the field and in life. A former record holder in the 100 meter, 200 meter, 400 meter, and long jump, Lukas

"You should have fun, give all you can, and . . . take care of your body."

has not let the fact that he is an above-the-knee amputee slow him down or limit his training, which he describes as "concentrated, hard, with passion and fun." Sport was his major passion for 14 years. Now that Lukas owns his own company, sport may not be a priority, but its lessons have been transferred to another venue. Lukas believes "You should have fun, give all you can, and overcome your limits, but most of all, take care of your body." When asked about issues facing the disability sport movement, Lukas says, "I don't want to be recognized as disabled only, I want to have my performance focused on, not my disability."

This young person, now a businessman, has used his sporting experiences to be successful in the business world as well. He has an established Web site and constantly makes reference to sport as a training ground. His motivational speeches are based on real-life experiences and serve as a model for others.

The French Revolution awakened the sense of individual responsibility and led to humane treatment of individuals considered to be mentally ill. They were considered "sick people" and deserving of treatment afforded to "suffering humanity." They were warehoused in large institutions with limited intervention or vocational education. Although they were cared for, housed, fed, and clothed, additional treatment was not necessarily appropriate to the impairments of these persons. Inasmuch as these institutions were usually located in the countryside, people with severe disabilities were often "out of sight and out of mind." Thus, it appears that society still was not able to accept such an individual as a functioning part of its existence (Carter, Van Andel, and Robb, 1985).

The treatment during this period involved the use of asylums, hospitals, or schools as residential institutions and even included the establishment of a humanitarian teacher. Schools for children who were blind and deaf also appeared by the end of the 18th century. However, very little systematic effort was extended on behalf of those with physical disabilities or mental retardation.

In the later years of the Age of Enlightenment, there was some movement toward accepting those who were different. This progress was achieved through the contributions of educators and philosophers. And, although their quality of life remained marginal, individuals with disabilities were allowed to survive (Davies, 1975).

Beginnings of Educational Treatment

Among the major events of the 19th century was the work of Jean Marc Itard with the "wild boy" named Victor, a young boy who grew up in the wild without human interaction. Itard was the first to show that severely retarded individuals could be taught and that improved functioning could result. Although difficult if not impossible to achieve, normal development and functioning were the goals of this training. Inasmuch as normal functioning could not be achieved for those with severe mental retardation, the view of residential schools as training institutions ultimately gave way to the idea of custodial facilities at the end of the 19th century.

Itard is credited with developing an individualized and clinical (medical) methodology as well as an initial understanding of the value of the child–teacher relationship. The work of Edouard Sequin, Itard's protégé, led to a unique educational system that stressed the physical, intellectual, and moral development of the child. In the 1890s, Maria Montessori built upon the theoretical basis provided by Itard and Sequin and extended this education and training to "normal" children.

Starting in the early 1800s, the notion of the residential institutions found in Europe crossed the Atlantic. From 1818 to 1894, residential institutions for mentally retarded persons (or, as they were called at the time, "feeble-minded" persons) as well as for Deaf and blind persons were established throughout the United States. Institutional segregation tended to be viewed as the most effective treatment for individuals with disabilities. Severely retarded persons were thought to need lifetime custodial care, but others less impaired were considered possible candidates for some level of employment. Except for the movement toward "special class" treatment that began in Germany in the late 19th century, this period was one that promoted individualized education but in a segregated setting.

KEY POINT

Throughout history, individuals with disabilities have experienced exclusion from society—the segregation or separateness taking differing forms and varying in degree from one historical period to another.

Social Reform

The 20th century can be viewed as a period of social reform, war, increased governmental concern for individuals with disabilities, and the emergence of concern about disability, especially in the fields of education, psychology, and medicine. The educational approaches developed by Itard, Sequin, and Montessori provided the basis for the developmental, individualized, and special education prevalent throughout the 20th century. During this time, the strong desire to classify disability and categorize individuals led to psychological testing specifically designed to analyze intelligence. Greater understanding of mental illness was brought to light by Freud, Pavlov, and Leo Kanner. And finally, in the 1920s and 1930s, the field of medicine began its investigation and treatment of brain injury and neurological functioning.

Although the primary care and treatment of individuals with disabilities was in residential institutions rather than in the home, in the late 19th and early 20th centuries special class education developed in Europe and spread to the United States. As a result of World War I and the Great Depression, special programs and classes for individuals with disabilities declined in the United States. After World War II, the programs and services not only resumed but increased.

Overall, the world wars had a positive effect on attitudes about and programs for persons with disabilities. First, during the course of U.S. compulsory military physical examinations, numerous men were identified who were actually physically impaired but who had led "normal" lives. This discovery contributed to a greater understanding and acceptance of physical impairments. Second, veterans who had been previously accepted in their communities and who became disabled during the war were to enjoy continued acceptance despite their physical impairments. The increased knowledge of physical impairments and acceptance of disability as found among veterans were extended unconsciously to children with physical disabilities.

The wars of the 20th and 21st centuries have continued to reinforce the role of rehabilitation and life after medical treatment. With the number of injured soldiers on the increase, it is possible that this generation of veterans will also add their mark to furthering inclusion and increasing opportunities in sport.

Three significant educational/legal events that occurred during the 20th century in the United States were to influence societal treatment of individuals with disabilities (DePauw, 1986b; Lilly, 1983).

First, with the passage of child labor laws and compulsory school attendance laws, many more children entered the classroom.

Second, children entering school late often had difficulty grasping classroom concepts. The IQ test was convenient to administer to them. Thought to be a measure of intelligence and therefore a predictor of academic success, the IQ test was used with many different types of individuals. This resulted in new classifications and special classes in which a watered-down curriculum was taught.

The third major event was the court ruling (in the 1954 decision of *Brown v. Topeka, Kansas Board of Education*) that the schools would be integrated because separate education for black children was illegal. Many black children previously educated in lesser-quality schools also experienced difficulty with education, especially with the curriculum of the time. As a result, many of these children were tested for IQ and placed in special education classes. The social movement for integration created new problems in the schools, and as a result many black children were to be labeled as "retarded."

Collectively, these events perpetuated the earlier notion that the problem of those "handicapped" children requiring special education was "in the child." Although most of these children had not been previously "handicapped in society," they became "handicapped in school" and to some extent "handicapped" by society (Lilly, 1983). Classification of the individuals by their impairments became common practice.

In response to the outcry for equality by parents of disabled children and by individuals with disabilities, federal and state legislation was enacted during the 1970s (Education of All Handicapped Children Act, Section 504 of the Rehabilitation Act) to address the issues of education, nondiscrimination, accessibility, and equal opportunity. The legislative mandates for the civil rights of individuals with disabilities reflected a change in social response to and attitudes about individuals with disabilities. Relative to legislative behavior, a change in attitude and response could be seen not only in the United States but in other Western nations as well.

The focus on impairment and limitations, otherwise referred to as the medical model, has been dominant throughout history and has helped formulate our current notions about disability as a "physical or psychological condition considered to have predominately medical significance" (Linton, 1998, p. 10); and this "medicalization of disability casts human variation as deviance from the norm, as pathological condition, as deficit" (Linton, 1998, p. 11).

The disability rights movement of the 1990s ushered in by the passage of the Americans with Disabilities Act of 1990 changed our perspectives. The belief that disability is socially constructed is at the core of this movement (DePauw, 1997; Shapiro, 1993).

Trends

Full participation by individuals with disabilities in most societies is still far from a reality. From a historical perspective, the trend has been one of progressive inclusion and acceptance (DePauw, 1986c; DePauw and Doll-Tepper, 2000). Where individuals with disabilities were once excluded from society, there is now at least partial inclusion. On a more global perspective, different societies reflect differing cultural and religious mores that have affected and continue to affect the degree of inclusion and acceptability of people with disabilities in the sporting venue.

True inclusion can come only when all persons are able to exercise their right of choice in an accessible society. Examples of such choice are to have the option to participate or not; to select one's friends, workplace, and living conditions; to choose to isolate oneself; and to have access to numerous alternatives and not be restricted in these alternatives because of one's culture, ethnicity, sex, disability, class, and so on.

KEY POINT

Progressive inclusion and acceptance of individuals with disabilities in society is the trend; what was once exclusion is now at least partial inclusion.

Historical Perspectives of Physical Activity and Sport

The roots of sport can be traced through a historical perspective of physical activity. Throughout the years, physical activity has taken many forms, including exercise, recreation, therapy, and sport. As it is conceptualized and practiced today, sport is but the outcome of the years of change. Disability sport also finds its roots in the rich history of physical activity and human movement.

Physical Activity

Physical activity has been an important component of human life throughout most of history. See table 2.1 for the historical time frame of physical activity. The roots can be traced back to antiquity, when primitive humans needed strength and endurance for basic survival, hunting, fishing, and fighting. Training one's body was simply part of one's education.

A curative use of physical activity is found in records and drawings representing life in China in approximately 2700 B.C. Additionally, exercise, massage, and baths were used by early Egyptians, Hindus, Greeks, and Romans. People exercised to prevent and alleviate physical disorders and illnesses. Specific exercises were developed for the sick, convalescent, and sedentary.

Table 2.1 Historical Periods and Physical Activity

Selected time periods	Uses of physical activity
Antiquity	Strength and endurance for survival
2700 B.C. China	Curative period for prevention and alleviation of physical disorders
Fifth century B.C. (Greek society)	Development of beautiful and harmonious body—balance of mental, social, and physical training
Reformation—16th- and 17th-century Europe	Sound mind and sound body through medical gymnastics
1850s (U.S.)	Medical gymnastics used by U.S. physicians
Early 1900s (U.S.)	Physical education to improve physical condition of youth
After World Wars I and II	Rehabilitation through physical activity
	Corrective physical education
Education perspective (1950s)	Developmental physical education
	Perceptual motor training
Civil rights and social reform (1960s and 1970s)	Separate but equal physical education
Disability rights and inclusion movement	Legislative mandates for equal opportunities in physical education, recreation, and sport
	Inclusive physical education and sport
	Sport as rehabilitation
	Sport for all
	Sport as competition

Physical activity for the development of a beautiful and well-proportioned body was prevalent in the fifth century B.C., when Athenian education contrasted with Spartan brutality (Clarke and Clarke, 1963). Greek society emphasized balance among mental, social, and physical forms of training.

After this early emphasis on physical activity, it was not until the Reformation of the 16th and 17th centuries that physical activity received serious attention again. The development of a sound mind in a sound body was promoted by English philosopher John Locke during this time.

The European influences were many and varied, and they have had a lasting effect on physical activity today. Specifically, two particular systems of medical gymnastics emerged. The German system and the Swedish system of physical education were both aimed at developing the body, mind, and character of youth using gymnastics, mass drills, and games of skill. Accordingly, exercise was thought to be the best medicine, and physicians were the main advocates for medical gymnastics.

These physical educational systems, also referred to as medical gymnastics, were transported to the United States during the 19th century. By the 1850s, American physicians had begun to use these programs. As a result, specialized programs and facilities were developed to correct postural defects, alleviate organic conditions, and improve physical strength and stamina.

Physical education evolved before, and emerged more prominently after, the world wars. The growth occurred because many of the youth were unfit for war; physical education programs were developed to address their physical condition. Physicians, who had been long involved with physical activity, became involved in physical education programs prior to World War I and remained so long after World War II. Their involvement after the wars included remedial applications of physical activity, specifically rehabilitation. Physical education continued to flourish, and corrective or remedial physical education was used to teach individuals with disabilities. Rehabilitation and therapy (recreation, physical, corrective) also remained under the medical model.

An education approach to physical activity allowed developmental physical education programs to evolve. Perceptual-motor or sensory-motor training programs became common within physical education.

Beginning with the civil rights and social reform era of the 1960s and continuing through the inclusion movement of the late 20th and early 21st centuries, physical activity programs were initially separate and supposedly equal. The civil rights era and the disability rights movement of the 1990s resulted in legislative mandates for equal opportunity in physical activity and sport and prompted inclusive physical education. Although sport maintained a rehabilitation focus into the late 20th century, sport for all, sport as recreation, and sport as competition have become prominent today.

KEY POINT

The role of physical activity in the lives of individuals with disabilities has evolved over the years. Over the centuries it has taken the form of exercise, recreation, therapy, and sport.

Recreation

Ancient or prehistoric times saw the use of physical activity and recreation as means of treatment to eliminate evil spirits and thus a part of religious beliefs (Carter, Van Andel, and Robb, 1985). The Greeks and Romans utilized recreation along with medical care and religion in the healing process. These same cultures also used people as a means of recreation or personal diversion, as in gladiator fights and contests against animals.

During the Middle Ages, the Church was the determining factor in deciding treatment for those who were different. This treatment usually consisted of confinement without the benefit of any rehabilitative services (Carter, Van Andel, and Robb, 1985).

With the advent of the industrial revolution in the 1800s, there were many uses for recreation. Nurses in hospitals utilized bowling greens, music, and rocking horses. People with disabilities were housed in large state institutions and were afforded some recreational opportunities.

The social and moral fabric of society was severely tested by the advent of war in the early 1900s. The returning veterans heightened society's sense of obligation to those perceived as heroes. For example, in the 1930s, U.S. President Roosevelt's New Deal concept fostered and promoted taking care of individuals who were less fortunate than others. As a result, recreation became a vital aspect within military hospitals again in the 1940s and 1950s because of war. It is during the 1950s that the term "therapeutic recreation" is first found in the literature. Although the term is primarily used in the United States, programs of this nature are found throughout the Western world.

Since the 1960s, there has been a tremendous growth in the recognition of the needs of individuals for recreation and outdoor pursuits. Today, it is common to find therapeutic recreation programs in hospital settings, rehabilitation centers, mental health settings, adjudicated youth environments, nursing homes, and retirement communities.

The use of the outdoors as a therapeutic modality began in the late 1800s (Gibson, 1979). Both environmental education and outdoor recreation were employed by the Europeans long before the concept reached the United States (Donaldson and Swan, 1979). One of the earliest uses of the outdoors for therapeutic purposes in the United States began in 1901, when psychiatric patients at the Manhattan State Hospital were placed

Andrea Scherney

FAST FACTS

Home Base: Austria
Sport: Track and field
Selected Accomplishments:
    World record holder in long jump
    World record holder in pentathlon
    Outstanding athlete of the 1994 World Championships
    Gold medal in javelin at Atlanta Paralympics

© Christian Houdek/Laserbild

This seasoned athlete with a below-the-knee amputation started to actively compete in 1988. Her accomplishments are awesome. She was outstanding athlete in 1994 at the World Championships; in 1995 she set world records for females in the 100 meter and long jump; she won a gold medal in 1996 at the Atlanta Paralympics and silver medals in shot and javelin in 2000 in Sydney; and in 2003 she was European champion and set a world record in the pentathlon.

> *"I had my motorbike accident during my study of sport science with the subject being rehabilitation in Vienna. So I knew it best myself."*

This all-around athlete had a motorcycle accident while studying sport science and found that she was living the topic of rehabilitation rather than just studying it. As a result, Andrea has "walked the walk." She believes that sport "is one of the best ways to come back to daily life again, if you get disabled. Sport can help to get more self-confidence in that very confusing and hard time at the beginning. If you feel new movements and learn new physical activities with your disabled/new body, you don't feel disabled. . . ."

Andrea has utilized her experiences to organize an action plan for war-torn Bosnia Herzegovina and learned that "sport for the disabled can move fixed borders, can overcome ethical crises, and bring together people with and without disabilities in a peaceful and happy way." Andrea Scherney has contributed to the disability sport movement as both an athlete and now as a facilitator. What a legacy!

in tents on the ground to relieve overcrowding. What was originally an administrative decision resulted in observations by the staff members of an improvement in the physical and mental health status of the patients (Gibson, 1979). Ten years later, another state hospital started a summer camp program.

Formalized camping for children with disabilities can be traced back to 1888 (Vinton et al., 1978). In the 1930s, school camping and wilderness programs for adjudicated youth developed rapidly (American Alliance for Health, Physical Education, Recreation and Dance, 1976). Today, we see a variety of camping and wilderness programs that specialize in meeting the unique needs of individuals with disabilities. Examples include McDonald's Camp Good Times for terminally ill youth and Easter Seals Camps across the United States for individuals who are physically impaired. Wilderness camping and adventure recreation are also available through Outward Bound, Wilderness Inquiry and Mobility International, and Cooperative Wilderness Handicapped Outdoor Group (C.W. HOG). (See appendix C.)

Therapeutic Horseback Riding

Horseback riding was first used by the early Greeks to improve the spirits of individuals considered incurable (Mayberry, 1978). During the 18th and 19th centuries, the medical profession recommended horseback riding to prevent and treat tuberculosis and neurological conditions. Improvement of posture, balance, and muscle control was reported through the active movement of the rider and the passive movement provided by the horse (DePauw, 1986a). More recently, Patterson (2000) studied the effects of a therapeutic horseback riding program on people with multiple sclerosis. Her findings, while limited, did support, overall, that a therapeutic riding program brought about both subjective and selective statistical changes in balance and walking. However, Patterson also noted that the low number of subjects in this type of research results in low statistical power and in effect makes generalization of results difficult. This has been an ongoing problem and makes it difficult for benefits of this type of activity to be widely accepted.

Specific programs of therapeutic horseback riding did not emerge until the 1950s. As with physical education and recreation, the medical profession became instrumental in developing therapeutic horseback riding programs, first in England, then in Europe, and shortly thereafter in the United States. Therapeutic horseback riding programs can be found throughout the world today. What started more as therapy (medicine) has expanded into riding as sport (riding for the disabled) and for education (remedial riding and riding as therapy) (DePauw, 1986a). For a detailed overview of therapeutic horseback riding, see Engel (1992).

Sport

The Olympic Games are among the most visible examples of sport in today's society. Although the Greek Olympic Games were instituted in 776 B.C. (the modern Olympics were revived in 1896), athletic contests were held earlier. The earliest forms were present among the peoples of the East in the second and third millennia B.C. As depicted by wall paintings of the time, wrestling, ball games, weightlifting, and other forms of exercises occurred in Egypt. The Herean Games, in which only women competed, preceded the ancient Olympics, but they soon became extinct due to the emphasis on males in athletic contests.

In Greece, sport was part of the context of man's life as a whole and formed an integral part of his education. The cultivation of the whole man included both mental and physical education. The Greeks believed that the mind could not exist without the body and that the body had no meaning without the mind. In these early years of sport, physical beauty and strength were admired and the spirit of competition remained central to the event. Since those early years, sport has been committed to the spirit of competition and fair play and the ideals of physical beauty and strength.

As in early Greek culture, sport permeates all levels of modern society. McPherson, Curtis, and Loy (1989) view sport as a social institution that reflects culture. They define sport as "structured, goal-oriented, competitive, contest-based, ludic physical activity" (p. 15). It is this context of sport into which individuals with disabilities have attempted to enter.

KEY POINT

Physical activity and competitive sport have become viable opportunities for individuals with disabilities.

Concluding Comments

A historical review of the treatment and social status of individuals with a disability reveals a pattern of neglect, followed by benign tolerance and limited acceptance. It can be argued that social status may be situational and may reflect the unique aspects of a given environment, conditions of the time, specific activity, the individual, and the interaction among these factors. In general, one may encounter these same or similar patterns of exclusion or limited acceptance because of culture, gender, ethnicity, class, or disability affiliation (DePauw, 1997). As such, these individuals are considered to be "outside" a specified society. This view comes from the sociological concept of marginality (e.g., Hughes, 1949; Park, 1928).

Marginality is not a new concept as applied to people with disabilities and sport, but people now recognize that sport and physical activity can positively affect and reduce marginality of persons with a disability (Gavron and Ullman, 2001; Mustain, 2001).

In addition to the historical inclination of humans to be physically active and to seek sport as an outlet, sport has been perceived as an equalizer and as a means of gaining social acceptance. Due to the visibility of sport and the social acceptance of athletes, groups of individuals have sought entry into sport. Athletes with disabilities are among the last groups to seek access to the sport world.

three

History of Disability Sport

Reader Goal Gain an understanding, appreciation, and knowledge of the significant history of the disability sport movement

Chapter Synopsis
- International Disability Sport
- United States Disability Sport
- Historical Perspectives on Research
- Trends and Milestones in Disability Sport
- Concluding Comments

International Disability Sport

The international disability sport movement is complex. It involves the usual growing pains of an evolving, far-flung organization. As the movement does evolve further, its history becomes important so that people will understand how it acquired its present status.

Early History

With a few notable exceptions, individuals with a disability had limited opportunities for organized sport competition prior to the mid-20th century. Two of these exceptions are Karoly Takacs, a two-time Hungarian Olympian (1948 Olympics in London, 1952 Olympics in Helsinki) who competed in Olympic shooting events left-handed after losing his right arm, and Liz Hartel from Denmark, who won a silver medal in dressage at the Olympic Games in 1952 after contracting polio in 1943 and using a wheelchair as her primary means of locomotion. For a chronology of athletes with disabilities and disability sport, see appendix A.

Deaf individuals were the first group to have access to sport. Their involvement in sport can be traced to the Sports Club for the Deaf, which was founded in Berlin in 1888. Between 1888 and 1924, six national sport federations for the Deaf emerged: in Belgium, Czechoslovakia, France, Great Britain, Holland, and Poland. These six federations came together for the first International Silent Games held August 10-17, 1924, in France. Competitors from Hungary, Italy, and Romania also participated. In conjunction with these first games, the Comité International des Sports des Sourds (CISS) (translated as the International Committee of Sports for the Deaf) became the first international organization to provide sport competition for any disability group. These first games evolved into the World Games for the Deaf and are now known as the Deaflympics, offered every two years (alternating between Summer Games and Winter Games) in the year following the Olympic Games.

In addition to Deaf individuals, amputees enjoyed early sport opportunities. The British Society of One-Armed Golfers was founded in 1932, and annual golf tournaments for amputees have since been held throughout England.

The world wars of the early 20th century significantly influenced society's view and treatment of individuals with a disability and brought rehabilitation to the forefront (Huber, 1984). Before the wars, individuals with a disability existed in the margins of society and often were considered a burden to society. Throughout the world, many veterans returned home with physical impairments and psychological needs that could not be accommodated by traditional techniques. Thus, rehabilitation programs were developed to assist these individuals to make the transition back into society.

The British government is credited with being the first to recognize these needs by opening the Spinal Injuries Centre at Stoke Mandeville Hospital in Aylesbury, England, in 1944. Sir Ludwig Guttmann, director of this center, introduced competitive sports as an integral part of the rehabilitation of disabled veterans. The competitive sports of the time included punchball exercises, rope climbing, and wheelchair polo (Guttmann, 1976). Under Guttmann's tutelage, the first Stoke Mandeville Games for the Paralyzed were held in 1948. At these games, 26 British veterans (including three women) competed in wheelchair archery.

In the late 1940s, sport as a part of medical rehabilitation spread throughout Europe and ultimately to the United States. During this same time frame, competitions and sporting events for wheelchair athletes emerged throughout former Western Europe.

In 1952, Guttmann organized the first international competition for wheelchair athletes. These games were held at Stoke Mandeville, and the British competed against a team from The Netherlands. A total of 130 athletes with spinal cord injuries competed in six wheelchair sports. To honor the social and human value derived from the wheelchair sport movement, the International Olympic Committee (IOC) recognized Guttmann's work in 1956 and awarded the Stoke Mandeville Games the Sir Thomas Fearnley Cup for meritorious achievement in service to the Olympic movement.

Since its beginnings at the Stoke Mandeville Games, wheelchair sport has expanded and become an international entity. In addition to wheelchair archery, the sports of lawn bowling, table tennis, shot put, javelin, and club throw were added to the growing list of wheelchair sports. In the 1960s, wheelchair basketball, fencing, snooker, swimming, and weightlifting were introduced. South America and the United States sent teams to the Stoke Mandeville Games competitions held in 1957 and 1960. In 1960, the International Stoke Mandeville Wheelchair Sports Federation (ISMWSF) was formed to sanction all international competitions for individuals with spinal cord injuries. Although originally sanctioned for those with spinal cord injuries, these games were expanded in 1976 at the Olympiad for the Physically Disabled in Toronto, Canada, to include other physical and visual impairments and would evolve and eventually be referred to as the Paralympics. The IOC approved the use of the term Paralympics in 1984.

During the 1960s, international sport competitions were expanded to include other disability groups not eligible for the World Games for the Deaf or the International Stoke Mandeville Games. The leadership for these additional disability sport competitions came in the form of the International Sports Organization for the Disabled (ISOD). In Paris in 1964, ISOD was officially formed to provide international sport opportunities for the blind, amputees, and persons with other locomotor disabilities (Lindstrom, 1984). Its founders intended that ISOD would become an entity parallel in structure and functions to the IOC (see appendix A).

In part due to dissatisfaction with existing competitions, the International Cerebral Palsy Society was founded in 1968 to sponsor the first international games in France for individuals with cerebral palsy. The

Iran: A Brief Case Study

The country of Iran has a young history, so to speak, with regard to disability sport. After 1979 and the end of several years of conflict with Iraq, the Iran Sports Federation was founded. A four-person delegation was sent to the Dutch World Championships to gather the necessary experience, resources, materials, and rules and regulations. The first coaching clinics across the country were conducted shortly afterward following a period of planning. The first competitions were held in 1979 in Tehran in athletics, table tennis, sitting volleyball, wheelchair basketball, and swimming. As a result of the war with Iraq, the number of injured people with disabilities had increased dramatically, and there was concern for maintaining their capabilities, physical potential, and health through sport activities. In 1981 the groundwork and training culminated in Iran's sending its first war-disabled sport delegation to the Stoke Mandeville Games. During the 1980s, additional teams followed in other international competitions—in basketball, sitting volleyball, and table tennis, among others. The representation of athletes in the Paralympics steadily increased as the athletes became more experienced. So too did their medal count. In fact, the national sitting volleyball team was a world champion six times and for four consecutive Paralympics. Currently Iran has a very successful infrastructure such that there are now 1,400 trained coaches and 14 sports available. Representatives from Iran are on the sitting volleyball world organization and that of wheelchair basketball.

"Sport is a university which turns you from immaturity to maturity." (Mr. Amrollah Dehghani)

The athletes profiled here are just a few of the many involved in the disability sport movement in Iran. Their accomplishments in such a short time are very impressive. It should be noted that women are also involved.

Mr. Ali Golkar is 34 years old and participates in sitting volleyball. Having had polio at birth, Mr. Golkar has participated since 1988 in disability sports. He has gold medals from the World Championships of 1990, the Barcelona Paralympic Games (1992), the World Championships of 1994, the Atlanta Paralympic Games (1996), the World Championships of 1998, and the Sydney Paralympic Games (2000) and a bronze from the World Championships in 2002.

Mr. Amrollah Dehghani, 40 years of age, is another medal winner. His traumatic spinal cord injury has not diminished his capacity as a powerlifter. He earned a gold medal in Sydney (2000), is a country record holder in the 100-kilogram (220-pound) category, earned a gold medal in the Great Britain World Championships (1995), a bronze medal in the Atlanta Paralympic Games, a gold medal in Belgian competitions, and silver medals in the World Championships 1998 and the Hungary World Championships 1999. Training 2 hours on a daily basis, Mr. Dehghani thinks that "sport is a university which turns you from immaturity to maturity. Sport means friendship among all. Sport means thinking and doing in a healthy way."

Mr. Aref Khosravinia is 32 and had polio. He has been involved in athletics since 1988. He earned gold medals in the Great Britain World Championships, New Zealand World Championships, Asia/Middle East Championships, and Sydney Paralympic Games and a silver medal in the France World Championships. He believes that "sport renews our lives. . . ." It is apparent by his participation in numerous competitions that he practices what he preaches.

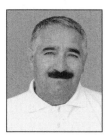

Mr. Enayatollah Bokharaei is 40 years old and has experienced a traumatic spinal cord injury. He has been in disability sport in shooting and air rifle since 1987. He was a gold medalist in the Atlanta Paralympic Games (1996) and the Sydney Paralympic Games (2000). Additionally, he has won seven gold medals, four silver medals, and three bronze medals (individual and team) in various international championships such as those in Great Britain, Austria, Denmark, Spain, and the Pacific Ocean since 1993. Mr. Bokharaei believes that "sport raises my tolerance threshold in problems and any challenges in my life." His wife and teammates assist him in his once-a-week training. It seems to have paid off!

Mr. Mohammad Sadeghimehryar, 42, is another survivor of polio and has been a part of disability sport in wheelchair basketball and athletics since 1979. His performances earned him gold medals in discus in four world championships, a gold medal in the Sydney Paralympic Games (2000), a world record in discus, and silver medals in discus and shot put at the Atlanta Paralympic Games (1996). His continuous involvement in disability sport from its inception testifies to his commitment.

(continued)

Iran: A Brief Case Study *(continued)*

Mr. Parviz Firouzi, 35, started competing in 1990 in sitting volleyball. In a very short time he won gold medals in the Barcelona (1992), Atlanta (1996), and Sydney (2000) Paralympic Games. He has also won gold medals in Germany (1994) and in the I.R. Iran (1996) World Championships. For an individual who states that this is his hobby and that it complements his life, his achievements provide a look at his philosophy of life and sport.

Ms. Nayyereh Akef, 39, is a traumatic paraplegic and is a relative newcomer to the world of disability sport. She participates in table tennis and shooting. She has won national championships in table tennis, as well as international silver and bronze medals in competitions. In air rifle she has been the air rifle national record holder since 1999 and was a bronze medalist in Sydney (2000), bronze medalist in the European Open Competitions in 2001 (Denmark), silver medalist in the World Championships in Seoul (2002), and silver medalist in the European Open Championships in 2003 (Germany). Ms. Akef is an example of how disability sport provides opportunities for all. She says that "practicing sport has a drastic effect in my life in such a way that it changes my viewpoint to human life totally and I think this matter is true for all human beings."

These athletes provide a snapshot of the success of disability sport in one emerging country. Their successes are the story for all athletes with disabilities.

Author's note: Through the courtesy of Mr. Masoud Ashrafi, General Secretary of the National Paralympic Committee of the Islamic Republic of Iran, we received a summary of the history of the formation and development of disability sport in that country.

International Cerebral Palsy Society continued this competition every two years until 1978, when the Cerebral Palsy–International Sports and Recreation Association (CP-ISRA) became recognized by ISOD as the official sanctioning body for cerebral palsy sports.

In a similar fashion, the International Blind Sports Association (IBSA) was formed in 1981 in response to increasing interest in and expanding opportunities for competitions for athletes with visual impairments including blindness. These two groups (IBSA, CP-ISRA) became the last disability sport groups to seek and attain recognition from ISOD.

Joint interest in expanding the opportunities for international sport for athletes with disabilities brought CP-ISRA, IBSA, ISMWSF, and ISOD together in 1982 to form a new umbrella organization. The International Coordinating Committee of the World Sports Organizations (ICC) was formed to coordinate disability sport worldwide and to negotiate with the IOC on behalf of athletes with disabilities. The CISS and the newly formed International Sports Federation for Persons with Mental Handicap joined the ICC in 1986.

Inasmuch as the ICC served as a fragile alliance of international sport federations and experienced an uneasy history from 1982 to 1987, representatives of 39 countries and representatives from the six international federations met to determine the future of international disability sport. This meeting, known as the Arnhem Seminar, was held on March 14, 1987, in Arnhem, The Netherlands. Seminar participants decided that a new international sport organization should be created to represent disabled sportsmen and sportswomen around the world, and they appointed an ad hoc committee to draft the constitution. As specified during the Arnhem Seminar, the new organization was to have representation from every nation with a disability sport program and was to govern itself through a council of nations. Athletes and disability sport organizations were to have a voice in the governance of disability sport on an international level. The new structure was also charged with responsibility for developmental and recreational activities in addition to international and elite sport. The existing members of the ICC were recognized and were to become an integral part of this new organization.

KEY POINT

Disability sport, in some form, has existed since the late 1800s. The world wars of the 20th century significantly influenced society's view and treatment of individuals with disabilities, and the idea of sport as rehabilitation eventually led to opportunities for persons with disabilities to participate in competitive sport.

International Paralympic Committee Era

In Dusseldorf, Germany, on September 21 and 22, 1989, the International Paralympic Committee (IPC) was created and was slated to replace the ICC officially after the conclusion of the 1992 Paralympic Games in Barcelona. At this meeting, officers were elected and the governance structure was adopted, along with a draft of the constitution. The IPC began a most significant chapter in the history of sport and disability. Initial efforts were devoted to streamlining operations, coordinating international sport, and securing communication between the IPC and IOC.

Thus, since September 1992, the IPC has been recognized as the sole international coordinating entity for athletes with disabilities. Detailed discussion of the IPC is included in chapter 4.

Recognizing the need for a professionally run organization and acknowledging the increasing growth and complexity of its operations, the IPC selected Bonn, Germany, as the site for its headquarters. The German federal government and the City of Bonn were instrumental in identifying an appropriate location and providing funding for the IPC headquarters. The early 1900s once-private residence turned office building was renovated and made wheelchair accessible, and the official opening of the headquarters was held on September 3, 1999. In attendance at the grand opening were dignitaries, officials, athletes with disabilities, coaches, and professionals from throughout the world. Then IOC President Juan Antonio Samaranch presented IPC President Robert Steadward with a sculpture depicting a wheelchair athlete in motion that is displayed prominently at IPC headquarters.

The relationship between the IPC and IOC has strengthened. The practice of holding the Olympic Games followed shortly thereafter by the Paralympic Games in the same host city has been in effect since 1988 (Summer Games—Seoul, 1988; Barcelona, 1992; Atlanta, 1996; Sydney, 2000; Athens, 2004; Beijing, 2008; Winter Games—Lillehammer, 1994; Nagano, 1998; Salt Lake City, 2002). The practice has actually become more formalized in that the formal bid process for hosting the Olympic Games in 2008 and beyond must include the hosting of the Paralympic Games. In 2000, a cooperation agreement was signed by IOC President S.E.M. Juan Antonio Samaranch and IPC President Dr. Robert D. Steadward in Sydney, Australia. The agreement acknowledged that the IPC and IOC shared a "common belief in the right of all human beings to pursue their physical and intellectual development," identified specific areas of cooperation including representation of the IPC on the IOC commissions and working groups, and co-opted then IPC President Steadward as a member of the IOC (DePauw, 2001c). Further confirmation of the solid relationship was demonstrated in the election of Phil Craven, IPC president, as the 123rd member of the IOC.

KEY POINT

The Paralympic movement has evolved into a well-organized and functional international entity with official ties to the IOC.

United States Disability Sport

While able-bodied sport in the United States has a long, organized history, the case with disability sport is a bit different. In reality, the disability sport movement in the United States, except for Deaf sport, has a rather short history.

Initial History

The earliest-known athletic event for athletes with disabilities in the United States was a wheelchair basketball game played by war veterans at Veterans Hospitals in the California and New England Chapters of the Paralyzed Veterans of America. While still in its infancy, the Flying Wheels from Van Nuys, California, toured the United States in 1946. As a result of this tour, the public became increasingly aware not only of wheelchair basketball as a sport but also of the players as capable individuals despite their impairment.

In 1947 and 1948, wheelchair basketball teams emerged: the Pioneers from Kansas City, Missouri; the Whirlaways from Brooklyn; the Gophers from Minneapolis; the Bulova Watchmakers of Woodside, New York; the Chairoteers of Queens; and the New York Spokesmen from Manhattan.

After 1946, wheelchair basketball in the United States increased so much in popularity that a wheelchair basketball tournament was desired. Tim Nugent, director of student rehabilitation at the University of Illinois, organized the first wheelchair basketball tournament in 1949 in Galesburg, Illinois. During the preparations for the tournament, it became necessary for Nugent to form a planning committee to oversee administrative aspects. This evolved into the National Wheelchair Basketball Association, the governing body for wheelchair basketball in the United States.

In the early 1950s, while Guttmann was organizing the first international competition for wheelchair athletes, Ben Lipton (from the United States) was contemplating the development of organized wheelchair sports, in addition to wheelchair basketball, on both the national and international levels. In 1957, with the cooperation of the Paralyzed Veterans of America and Adelphi College in New York, Lipton organized the first national wheelchair games. At their inaugural, these games, patterned after Stoke Mandeville, introduced several events: 60-, 100-, and 220-yard dashes and the 220- and 400-yard shuttle relays.

As a result of the successful national wheelchair games, Ben Lipton and his committee founded the National Wheelchair Athletic Association (NWAA). The prime function of this organization was to establish rules and regulations governing wheelchair sports other than basketball. Ultimately, the NWAA would expand its purpose to sponsoring various competitive sports on a state, regional, and national level.

With Lipton as director, the U.S. team entered its first international competition at the International Stoke Mandeville Games held in Rome in 1960.

Prior to 1967, the numerous wheelchair sports available were limited to summer sports. No sport association had thus far attempted to serve the winter sport interests of athletes with disabilities. As a result, the National Handicapped Sports and Recreation Association (NHSRA, later changed to National Handicapped Sports [NHS]) was formed by a small group of Vietnam veterans with amputations.

At the 1976 Olympiad for the Physically Disabled in Toronto, the U.S. team included 27 blind men and women. As a result of the successes of these athletes, a group was convened to discuss the formation of an organization to promote sport for blind athletes. In late 1976, national leaders, educators, and coaches of blind athletes formed the United States Association of Blind Athletes (USABA).

The National Association of Sports for Cerebral Palsy was founded in 1978 as the United States' governing sport organizing body for individuals with cerebral palsy and similar neurological conditions. In 1986, the National Association of Sports for Cerebral Palsy was reorganized as the United States Cerebral Palsy Athletic Association (USCPAA) to host competitions in a variety of events including archery, horseback riding, powerlifting, table tennis, soccer, bowling, swimming, and track and field events.

In 1981, a small group of amputee athletes founded the United States Amputee Athletic Association (USAAA). Although two other organizations (NHS, NWAA) served athletes with amputations, the USAAA was formed to offer these athletes another outlet. As the governing body for amputee sport, USAAA sponsored competitions for amputee athletes in events not offered by NHS and NWAA such as archery, stand-up basketball, sit-down and stand-up volleyball, swimming, weightlifting, and track and field events.

Under the auspices of the 1985 National Cerebral Palsy/Les Autres Games, dwarf athletes and physically disabled athletes with conditions other than cerebral palsy (i.e., les autres or "the others") were allowed to compete for the first time. Inasmuch as there was no organization devoted to serving either dwarf athletes or les autres athletes, two new organizations were formed (Dwarf Athletic Association of America and the United States Les Autres Sports Association).

In 1989, USAAA filed for bankruptcy and ceased to exist as an organization. With the demise of USAAA, two organizations vied for the right to coordinate and sponsor athletic events for athletes with amputations. The two groups were Disabled Sports USA (DS/USA, formerly NHS) and the National Amputee Summer Sports Association. To resolve the conflict, the United States Olympic Committee (USOC) Committee on Sports for the

Disabled (COSD) in September 1990 gave DS/USA provisional authority to conduct summer sports for amputee athletes. After months of negotiations, DS/USA and the National Amputee Summer Sports Association agreed to a transition plan that specified the manner in which DS/USA would assume responsibility for summer sport programs for amputees, allowed for significant involvement by the leaders from the National Amputee Summer Sports Association, and ensured appropriate athlete representation within DS/USA.

In addition to the disability sport associations already discussed, numerous sport-specific and recreational organizations were formed in the 1970s and 1980s in response to growing interest in sport by individuals with a disability. Examples of these are Handicapped Scuba Association (1974), National Foundation for Wheelchair Tennis (1976), and North American Riding for the Handicapped Association (1969). As the disability sport movement gathered momentum in the late 20th century, new sport organizations serving individuals with a disability emerged and continue to do so (see appendixes D and E).

Era of Committee on Sports for the Disabled

The 20th century provided most, if not all, of the legislative impetus for the development and growth of sport for and including athletes with disabilities. Although several other Western countries have utilized legislation, charters, or federally endorsed strategic planning efforts (or a combination of these) to effect change on behalf of individuals with a disability, legislative mandates have been largely American phenomena. It appears that the primary avenue for change has been in the United States through the accepted legislative process.

Legislation affecting the rights of individuals with a disability began in 1968, and the rights of disabled persons to access programs, facilities, education (including physical education), and sport have all been secured. Of specific import here are PL 90-170, the Architectural Barriers Act (1968); PL 93-112, the Rehabilitation Act (1973), which made discrimination on the basis of disability illegal; PL 94-142, the Education of All Handicapped Children Act (1975), which mandated education including physical education for disabled children (amendments and more recent legislation known as Individuals with Disabilities Education Act [IDEA '97]); and PL 95-606, the Amateur Sports Act (1978), which recognized athletes with disabilities as part of the USOC. See table 3.1. Although they did not mention disability specifically, the Civil Rights Act of 1964 and Title IX legislation of 1972 influenced the disability rights movement.

Although not directly related to sport, legislation passed in the late 1980s reaffirmed the civil rights of individuals with disabilities. The Americans with Disabilities Act of 1990 extends the broad protections offered by the Civil Rights Act of 1964 to individuals with a disability. It

Table 3.1 Significant U.S. Legislation Affecting Physical Education and Sport for Individuals With Disabilities

Year	Law number	Name and purpose
1964	PL 88-352	Civil Rights Act
		Nondiscrimination
1967	PL 90-247	Elementary and Secondary Education Act amended
		Training programs in physical education and recreation for persons with disabilities
1968	PL 90-170	Architectural Barriers Act of 1968
		Accessibility
1972	PL 92-318	Title IX
		Nondiscrimination on the basis of disability
1973	PL 93-112	Rehabilitation Act
		Nondiscrimination on the basis of disability
1975	PL 94-142	Education of All Handicapped Children Act
		Instruction in physical education required as part of special education
1978	PL 95-606	Amateur Sports Act
		Recognized athletes with disabilities as part of the United States Olympic Committee
1990	PL 101-336	Americans with Disabilities Act
		Civil rights reaffirmed for individuals with disabilities
1991	PL 102-119	Individuals with Disabilities Education Act amended
		Reaffirmed and individualized education for individuals with disabilities

provides protection against discrimination on the basis of disability in employment, public services, and public accommodations. Although not specifically mentioned, sport and recreational programs are interpreted to be included among the public services.

In 1975, President Gerald Ford formed the President's Commission on Olympic Sports to examine the structure and status of Olympic sport in the United States. The commission's 1977 report actually formed the basis for the Amateur Sports Act of 1978. The civil rights movement of the 1960s resulted in the passage of the Civil Rights Act of 1964, Title IX in 1972, and the Rehabilitation Act of 1973, setting the stage for the inclusion of ethnic minority individuals, women, and individuals with disabilities in future legislation. Inasmuch as the essence of the Amateur Sports Act was formulated during the mid-1970s, lawmakers could not help but be influenced by earlier civil rights legislation. As a result, the Amateur Sports Act included specific reference to opportunities in sport for ethnic minority individuals, women, and individuals with a disability (DePauw and Clarke, 1986).

The passage of PL 95-606, the Amateur Sports Act of 1978, was a significant event in the history of the U.S. disability sport movement. This law charged the USOC with encouraging and promoting amateur athletic activity for athletes with disabilities as follows: "To encourage and provide assistance to amateur athletic programs and competition for handicapped individuals, including, where feasible, the expansion of opportunities for meaningful participation by handicapped individuals in programs of athletic competition for able-bodied individuals" (United States Olympic Committee, 1989, p. 2). In meeting this mandate, the USOC established the COSD and a separate category of membership. Group E membership (more recently known as disability sport organizations, DSOs) was open to national amateur sport organizations serving athletes with disabilities that sponsored national athletic competitions in two or more sports included on the program of the Olympic or Pan American Games. Although the struggles were significant, disability sport has been a legally mandated part of the U.S. Olympic movement since 1979.

The COSD was established as a standing committee of the USOC. It was originally composed of two representatives from each of the then Group E members (American Athletic Association of the Deaf, USAAA, USABA, USCPAA, NHSRA, NWAA, Special Olympics) and members-at-large appointed by the USOC president. The COSD was charged with coordinating amateur athletic activity for athletes with disabilities in the United States. By law, at least 20% of the membership had to be active athletes with disabilities. At that time, members were appointed for the Olympic quadrennium (the four-year period between Olympic Games) and could be reappointed.

In its early years, the COSD advised the USOC on matters affecting the rights of athletes with disabilities. In performing its duties as outlined in the USOC constitution, the COSD met regularly, established criteria and evaluated requests by disabled sport organizations for membership in the USOC, reviewed and approved budgets for committee activities, provided financial support for developmental programs as well as elite sport programs sponsored by the DSOs, designed workshops and media productions for the dissemination of information about disability sport, resolved conflicts among groups, coordinated efforts for combined (multidisability and cross-organizational) U.S. teams for Winter and Summer Paralympics, assisted in the review of grant proposals, established criteria for evaluating membership services funds allocations, coordinated disabled athlete participation in Olympic festivals, and recommended changes to the USOC constitution.

Prior to 1992, the COSD was composed of representatives from each of the USOC-recognized DSOs. The DSOs were required to be multisport and organized around disability to the extent that at least two sports were represented. The DSOs also had to be affiliated with international sport federations serving individuals with disabilities.

At one time, eight DSOs were recognized by the USOC: American Athletic Association of the Deaf, Dwarf Athletic Association of America, USCPAA, DS/USA, NWAA, Special Olympics International (SOI), USABA, and USAAA.

Historically, sport for athletes with disabilities in the United States was organized both around disability (e.g., Special Olympics for mentally retarded individuals) and around sport (e.g., NWBA). Those associations organized around disability (and multisport) were given access to the USOC through the COSD; those organized around sport (single sport, single or multiple disability) were denied membership in the USOC as well as participation on the COSD. These associations could attempt to gain access to the National Governing Bodies (NGBs) of the USOC, and some were successful. As the USOC is organized around sport, specifically the vertical (grassroots to elite) structure sport, difficulties have ensued in attempting to integrate disability sport into the USOC. The COSD tended to function in a role for disability sport similar to the role of the USOC for Olympic sport. Much of the early effort was devoted to coordination among the DSOs and seeking access into the components of the USOC, especially the NGBs.

Although modified several times in the past 20 years, the COSD remained a critical component in the disability sport movement until the end of the 20th century. (For a comprehensive history of the COSD through 1984, see DePauw and Clarke, 1986. The activities of the COSD since 1984 have been chronicled in the COSD Forum section of *Palaestra,* a monthly magazine on sport, physical education, and recreation for individuals with disabilities.) Inasmuch as the COSD and USOC memberships were a direct result of federal legislation, the Amateur Sports Act (and its recent revisions) remains the most influential piece of legislation in regard to individuals with disabilities and their right to participate in sport.

Although a part of the USOC, the COSD tended to function outside its mainstream of elite (or Olympic) sport governance and international competition. Inasmuch as the USOC was organized around sport and the COSD effort was organized by disability, this type of organization created difficulties in the actual acceptance of athletes with disabilities within the Olympic movement, let alone the USOC.

One of the most significant changes for disability sport arose from the impasse created by the different structural organization of the USOC and disability sport within it. In January 1989, a USOC task force was appointed to examine all aspects of the USOC commitment to athletes with disabilities and to recommend appropriate policy and direction. Over the next year and a half, the task force met with representatives of the USOC NGBs, USOC staff and officers, individuals involved with writing the Amateur Sports Act, disabled sport organizations, COSD members, and athletes with disabilities. At its May 3-4, 1991, meeting, the COSD approved the following (adapted from COSD minutes, May 1991):

1. Sport for individuals with disabilities is an integral part of the Olympic movement. The USOC and NGBs have a legally mandated responsibility to provide, encourage, and support amateur athletic programs for athletes with disabilities.

2. The goals of disabled sport programs within the U.S. Olympic movement are (a) integration, where feasible, into open competition programs and (b) development of elite athletes with disabilities.

3. Amateur athletic programs for persons with disabilities should be organized around sport rather than around disability.

4. Development of athletic opportunities for all persons, including those with disabilities, should be a shared responsibility of NGBs and DSOs.

5. DSOs and athletes with disabilities should be represented through NGBs to provide for a more vertical governance structure of sport in the United States.

6. The COSD should become a regular standing committee of the USOC composed of DSO representatives, NGB representatives, and other individuals representing the interests of persons with disabilities and should coordinate and oversee the fulfillment of the responsibilities outlined herein and contained in the Amateur Sports Act of 1978.

7. USOC financial support for sports for persons with disabilities should be focused on programs for athletes and coaches.

8. USOC financial support for athletes with disabilities should continue to be made available through specific grant programs and member services funds.

9. USOC should provide, as a priority, budgeted funding for Olympic-equivalent multisport, multi-disability games.

10. Participation by elite athletes with disabilities should be ensured in USOC programs, training centers, and services.

As a result of the Task Force on Sport and Disability, disability sport within the USOC was reorganized in 1993. Specifically, the COSD was reconstituted and an office was created at the USOC headquarters. Jan

Wilson served initially as USOC liaison to the COSD and became the first coordinator of Disabled Sports Services. In 1994, Wilson resigned the position and was replaced by Mark E. Shepherd Sr.

Paralympic Sports Organizations and U.S. Paralympics Era

Throughout its tenure, the COSD assumed some responsibility for representing American athletes with disabilities on the international level. The majority if not all of this representation has been related to the Paralympic movement as opposed to efforts on behalf of Deaf athletes or athletes with mental retardation. Representation for Deaf athletes has been conducted by the American Athletic Association of the Deaf; representation for mentally retarded persons has been handled by Special Olympics.

In early 1995, the USOC assumed responsibilities as the United States' National Paralympic Committee, but it was not until October 1995 that the USOC officially became the National Paralympic Committee for the United States. In this capacity, representatives of the Disabled Sports Services staff and COSD attended the IPC general assembly and worked with the IPC for the 1996 Atlanta Paralympic Games and the Salt Lake City Winter Paralympics.

In the late 1990s, the USOC president commissioned the development of a vertical integration task force. The purpose of this commission was to examine the assimilation of elite disabled (DSO) athletes into mainstream NGB programming efforts. This task force again examined the organization and structure of disability sport within the USOC. In 1999, the Paralympic Athletes Council was formed, and provisions were made for the formation of Paralympic Sports Organizations (PSOs) to help govern disability sport within the USOC.

The COSD was officially disbanded in early 2000, and the United States Paralympic Corporation was incorporated to serve as the "sole conduit to individuals with disabilities under the USOC" (COSD forum, 2000, p. 55). Charlie Huebner was appointed as executive director, U.S. Paralympics.

U.S. Paralympics, a division of the USOC, is charged to "enhance program support and coaching expertise in collaboration with Olympic NGBs, increase Paralympic media awareness, enhance funding support for elite Paralympic athletes, and utilize the Paralympic platform to promote health and wellness for individuals with a disability" (COSD forum, 2003, p. 9).

The most recent turn of events occurred in 2003. As a result of the USOC's public crisis of governance and ethical behavior in 2002 and early 2003, USOC Acting President Bill Martin appointed the Governance and

Renata Karamonova

FAST FACTS

Home Base: Brezno, Slovakia
Sports: Skiing—alpine, slalom, giant slalom, super giant slalom, downhill
Selected Accomplishments:

Medal winner, Paralympic Winter Games (Nagano, 1998), World Championships 2000, Paralympic Games (Salt Lake City, 2002)

Renata Karamonova is a skier. She also needs assistance to ski. She is very successful at what she does. In three major international skiing competitions in 1998, 2000, and 2002, she acquired five gold medals, four silver, and two bronze. Not bad at all!

Renata has embodied the world of sport in showing that "it is a way of life." Her involvement in the competitive realm attests to her belief that she too can be an athlete first and disabled second. She expresses her belief in the value of sport in saying that she "feels great when doing sport" and that "social life is an important part of sport." As to Renata's thoughts about young people just getting involved, she says they should "go on . . . it is really worthy to overcome all failures. Nothing is easy." This successful athlete is proof of that. In the short time she has been a part of competitive sport, she has certainly made her mark.

"Nothing is easy."

Ethics Task Force to examine fundamental issues of the purpose, structure, policies, and procedures of the USOC. The task force's recommendations were approved as amendments to the constitution and by-laws in October 2003. Among the recommendations were the following:

- Return the focus of the USOC to athletes and athletic performance and refine the mission of the USOC, to emphasize the focus on United States Olympic and Paralympic athletes.

- Establish an Olympic Assembly as a mechanism for communication and cooperation and development of new initiatives involving the USOC and the diverse sport organizations involved in the Olympic movement, in order to advance and achieve the primary mission of the USOC.

- Create a cohesive, cooperative board, free of constituent loyalties and complicated weighted voting systems, with directors who do not have constituent loyalties or obligations, with no single group or class of director having the ability to control the organization.

- Empower the board to govern the USOC and increase the accountability, transparency, and performance of the organization, directed toward achieving the mission in ways that are consistent with ethical principles and the Olympic ideals.
- Introduce an entirely new structure of governance in ways that maintain compliance with the requirements of the Olympic Charter and the representation of athletes in the Olympic movement.

The task force's recommendations dramatically changed the constitution and by-laws of the USOC. Although these changes have been met with skepticism among some of the USOC constituencies including PSOs and athletes with disabilities, the result was the systematic inclusion of PSOs and Paralympic athletes as an integral component of the USOC structure, policies, and procedures. Although seemingly logical and reasonable, this inclusion is a significant victory in that fierce battles were fought and lost in the 1980s and 1990s over such matters as those identified in the following pages.

The mission of the USOC as expressed in the mission statement is "to support United States Olympic and Paralympic athletes in achieving sustained competitive excellence and preserve the Olympic ideals, and thereby inspire all Americans." The definitions now include the following:

- "Amateur athlete" means any athlete who meets the eligibility standards established by the NGB or PSO for the sport in which the athlete competes.
- "IPC" means the International Paralympic Committee.
- "PSO" means a Paralympic Sports Organization that is an amateur sports organization recognized by the corporation in accordance with Article X, Section 10.7 of these by-laws.

As a result, Paralympic athletes, PSOs, and the IPC are included in the sections of the by-laws pertaining to policies, procedures, structure, and function such as the following:

- Jurisdiction for Olympic Games, Pan American Games, and the Paralympic Games (Article I—Jurisdiction)
- Organizations eligible for membership to include those who are active in the administration of Olympic, Pan American, or Paralympic Games (Article X—Members)
- Distinct category of membership to Olympic, Paralympic, and Pan American sport organizations

- Governance of sports included on the program of the Paralympic Games to an appropriate PSO "where the designation of a NGB is not feasible or would not serve the best interest of the sport" (Section 10.6)
- Eligibility of DSOs to become PSOs or members of community-based multisport organizations (Section 10.7)
- Representation on the athletes' advisory council by athletes with disabilities (Article XII)
- Inclusion of PSOs on the NGB Council (Article XIII)
- Inclusion of Paralympic athletes in additional official functions of the USOC (official delegation and representation, team selection and tryouts, funding for U.S. teams, fielding of the U.S. teams [i.e., uniforms, medical coverage, travel], hosting of international events)

Since the passage of the original Amateur Sports Act of 1978, athletes with disabilities have struggled to gain access to sport and acceptance as athletes. Although the progress seemed very slow initially, the view from 25 years later indicates dramatic changes for disability sport and athletes with disabilities. In the late 1990s, progress was made that provided the foundation for the most recent advocacy for the rights and inclusion of U.S. athletes with disabilities.

KEY POINT

Disability sport in the United States has matured, and the USOC has assumed responsibility for athletes with disabilities.

Historical Perspectives on Research

Research about disability sport and athletes with disabilities has evolved along with the disability sport movement. The early years saw research focused on rehabilitation or on growth and development of individuals with physical and mental disabilities (DePauw, 1985a; Huber, 1984; Lindstrom, 1984; Lipton, 1970; Rarick, Dobbins, and Broadhead, 1976), whereas the post-World War II efforts focused on developing and providing physical education and sport programs for individuals with disabilities. In the 1960s, emphasis was placed upon physical fitness parameters (strength, flexibility, weight) of those with mental retardation, as well as perceptual-motor development and social development (Broadhead, 1986; DePauw, 1986b; Dunn, 1987; Pyfer, 1986; Stein, 1983).

During the 1970s, research was conducted on exercise physiology and biomechanics (DePauw, 1988; Gass and Camp, 1979; Zwiren and Bar-Or,

1975). The exercise physiology research was confined to understanding disabled athletes' levels of fitness or conditioning and their response to exercise, whereas the biomechanics research focused on wheelchair propulsion. "Subjects" included wheelchair users, individuals with post-polio, and spinal cord-injured individuals. Since the 1970s, research has increased significantly and has become sport and disability specific as well as discipline oriented and performance based (DePauw, 1988). For an excellent overview of research, see Shephard (1990).

A commitment to disability sport research was formalized in 1985 when the USOC agreed with the COSD to establish a special subcommittee concerning research on disability sport. This research subcommittee interviewed coaches, athletes with disabilities, and professionals in the field of recreation and adapted physical education and came up with seven areas of concern:

- Effects of training, competition, or both
- Selection and training of coaches, volunteers, officials
- Technological advances in sport research
- Sociological/Psychological aspects of sport
- Differences and similarities between disabled and able-bodied athletes
- Demographics of sport for the disabled
- Legal, philosophical, and historical bases for sport (DePauw, 1988, p. 293)

Although the subcommittee has long been disbanded, the research efforts have increased dramatically. The results of research on disability sport are published regularly in periodicals based in the United States such as *Adapted Physical Activity Quarterly (APAQ), Palaestra, Sports 'n Spokes,* and *Sport Sociology Journal.*

In 1993, the IPC established a sport science committee as an indication of its commitment to sport science research and the advancement of knowledge about Paralympic sport. In April 1994, a seminar on sport science and athletes with disabilities was held at the German Olympic Institute in Berlin. In attendance were the members of the IPC Sport Science Committee (IPCSSC) and representatives from the International Federation of Adapted Physical Activity. The IPC committee was chaired by Dr. Gudrun Doll-Tepper from the Free University of Berlin.

As a result of the seminar, the mission, goals, and objectives for the IPCSSC were established. In addition, guidelines for research conducted at Paralympic Games and world championships were developed; guidelines for the conduct of the Paralympic Congress and International Symposium were proposed; and a plan for preparing a Paralympic research agenda was formed. Initial efforts for setting a research agenda included the development of selected position statements, a monograph series on Paralympic sport, an international directory of sport scientists, and a database of research on disability sport.

The IPCSSC was chaired by Gudrun Doll-Tepper (Germany). Among the initial participants were Yagesh Bhambhani (Canada), Karen P. DePauw (USA), Mike Ferrara (USA), Claudine Sherrill (USA), Yves Vanlandewijck (Belgium), Gary Wheeler (Canada), Trevor Williams (England), and representatives from among Paralympic athletes. The responsibility for the IPCSSC rested initially with Michael Riding, IPC medical officer, and later with IPC headquarters staff. With the election in December 2001 of IPC President Phil Craven, a former Paralympian and president of the Wheelchair Basketball Federation, the committee was restructured and renamed the Sport Science and Education Committee. Yves Vanlandewijck became the chair in 2002. The future of sport science in the Paralympic movement rests with the collaboration among the National Paralympic Committees, the IPC sports, a network of centers counseling elite athletes, and the IPC Sport Science and Education Committee.

Research has become a prominent feature on the agenda for disability sport. Research presentations appear regularly on the scientific programs of numerous national and international conferences including the Olympic congresses, IPC Paralympic and VISTA conferences, International Federation of Adapted Physical Activity (IFAPA) symposia, American College of Sports Medicine congress, and the European College of Sport Science congresses.

Trends and Milestones in Disability Sport

Disability sport has accumulated a significant history and prominence in the sporting world. Many of the significant changes have been highlighted in this chapter (see appendix A). In addition to the identification of significant historical events, it is important to give meaning to the collective history. Thus, the following themes have been identified:

1. Wheelchair sport has been prominent throughout the history of disability sport.
2. Males had early involvement in and primary access to sport. Male athletes with disabilities compose the majority of the participants in international and national disability sport competitions.
3. The number of international umbrella sport associations serving athletes with disabilities has increased and stabilized. National and sport-specific associations continue to increase.
4. The competitive sport opportunities available to athletes with disabilities have increased in number, size, and scope. The Paralympic

Games have become the second largest sporting event in the world (see also chapter 5).

5. Increasing emphasis within disability sport is being placed on sport-specific competition and specialization in sport.

6. The athletic performances of athletes with disabilities have increased dramatically (i.e., sub-4-minute mile; decreasing times and repeat wins in the Boston Marathon; increasing height in high jump). See figure 3.1.

7. Competitions for female athletes with disabilities have evolved. The number of females with disabilities participating in sport has increased but now remains relatively constant.

8. The opportunities for athletes with disabilities to compete along-side able-bodied athletes have increased, and greater emphasis is placed upon inclusion (i.e., exhibition events in the Olympic Games, staging of Olympic and Paralympic Games sequentially, inclusion within the Boston Marathon and Commonwealth Games).

9. Athletes with disabilities have experienced increased visibility through media coverage (television, advertisements, endorsements,

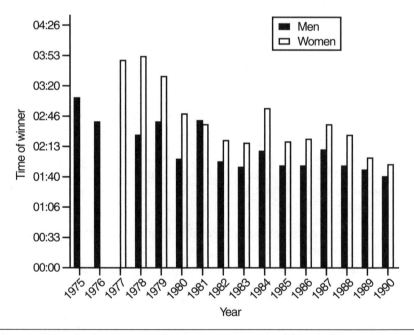

Figure 3.1 The first 15 years of Boston Marathon wheelchair division winners. Men's World Record = 1:21:23; Women's World Record = 1:34:22.

Adapted, by permission, from K.P. DePauw and S.J. Gavron, 1995, *Disability and sport* (Champaign, IL: Human Kinetics), 62.

corporate sponsorships, public relations), recognition and award ceremonies, and so on. More journals and magazines have evolved that feature athletes with disabilities.

10. There is increasing acknowledgment and acceptance of athletes with disabilities as athletes by the IOC in particular and the able-bodied sporting world in general (e.g., exhibition events at Olympic Games, development of IPC). Sport governing bodies officially recognize athletes with disabilities (e.g., IOC, USOC).

11. Research has increased and is becoming an important aspect of disability sport. More congresses, seminars, and conferences include disability sport on the scientific program.

12. Sports medicine, training of coaches, training regimens, and drugs/doping issues are a regular part of disability sport.

Concluding Comments

The history of the disability sport movement in some ways mirrors the increased acceptance and integration of persons with disabilities in society as a whole. Yet the diversity of disabilities and the numerous DSOs have increased the complexity of the movement. The survival of the stronger organizations and sport institutions, over the next several years, will give rise to a more definable movement. For now, the evolving history of the major sporting events and organizations is important to appreciate and understand. With any developing institution, there are bound to be issues and conflict as well as great strides. The disability sport movement and its evolution are no exception.

four

Structure and Organizations for Disability Sport

Reader Goal   Understand the structure and function of selected international and national disability sport organizations

Chapter Synopsis

- International Structure for Disability Sport
- International Disability Sport Organizations
- United States Structure of Disability Sport
- United States Disability Sport Organizations
- Concluding Comments

International Structure for Disability Sport

Initially the six international governing bodies for disability sport organized the International Paralympic Committee (IPC). These included the International Committee of Sports for the Deaf (CISS); International Blind Sports Association (IBSA); International Sports Organization for the Disabled (ISOD); International Stoke Mandeville Wheelchair Sports Federation (ISMWSF); Cerebral Palsy–International Sport and Recreation Association (CP-ISRA); and International Sports Federation for Persons with Mental Handicaps (INAS-FMH), now known as International Sports Federation for Persons with Intellectual Disability (INAS-FID). In contrast to their Olympic counterparts, which are organized around sport, these "international federations" are multisport and mostly organized around disability; that is, IBSA for blind, CP-ISRA for cerebral palsy, ISMWSF for spinal cord injured and wheelchair users, ISOD for amputees and les autres, CISS for Deaf, and INAS-FMH for mentally handicapped persons. Although these groups were active in the business of the IPC, only four (IBSA, CP-ISRA, ISMWSF, ISOD) participated in the Paralympics initially.

Although a member of IPC, INAS-FMH held separate world championships until 1992. With the cooperation of the International Coordinating Committee and the Barcelona Paralympics Organizing Committee, INAS-FMH scheduled the first Paralympics for Persons with Mental Handicaps for September 1992 in Madrid. These Games were identified as the "mentally handicapped sector" of the Paralympics held in Barcelona in September 1992. Unresolved in the 1990s was the status of separate or integrated international competitions for athletes competing under the auspices of INAS-FMH. After lengthy and heated discussions were held about the inclusion of the mentally handicapped among the competitors in the Paralympics in general, the organizers of the Winter Paralympics in Lillehammer, Norway, in February 1994 included two demonstration events for athletes with mental retardation.

Despite the controversy, the IPC decided that full medal events for athletes with mental retardation were to be held during the first World Championships in Athletics in Berlin in July 1994. Four events were offered for men (shot put, long jump, 200 meter, 800 meter) and two events for women (long jump, 200 meter). The World Championships in Swimming held in Malta in October 1994 also included athletes with mental retardation.

Currently, there are at least seven international sport organizations with responsibility for athletes with disabilities. Six of these are disability specific. The IPC is the only multi-disability, multisport organization. These organizations include the following:

- International Paralympic Committee (IPC)
- International Blind Sports Association (IBSA)
- Cerebral Palsy–International Sport and Recreation Association (CP-ISRA)
- International Sports Federation for Persons with Intellectual Disability (INAS-FID; originally known as the International Sports Federation for Persons with Mental Handicaps)

- International Stoke Mandeville Wheelchair Sports Federation (ISMWSF)
- International Sports Organization for the Disabled (ISOD)
- International Committee of Sports for the Deaf (CISS)

The IPC was designed to serve as the umbrella organization of athletes with disabilities. The IPC has been recognized by the International Olympic Committee (IOC) and serves as its liaison on behalf of athletes with disabilities. Five of the organizations on the preceding list are members of the IPC (IBSA, CP-ISRA, INAS-FID, ISMWSF, ISOD). As the oldest of the disability sport organizations and representing athletes who do not compete in the Paralympic Games, CISS remains an autonomous organization.

International sport for athletes with disabilities is organized in a fashion similar to that for Olympic sport. See table 4.1. For disability sport at the international level, there are the international organizations, international sport federations, international games organizing committees, national sport organizations, and a management structure that helps facilitate the work of the primary organization. Due to the added complexity of multiple categories of disability and multiple sports, there are also differences between the Olympic structure and the Paralympic structure.

Table 4.1 International and U.S. Sports Governance

Organization	Structures
International Olympic Committee	National Olympic Committees
	International Sport Federations
International Paralympic Committee	National Paralympic Committees
	International Organizations of Sport for the Disabled
	International Paralympic Committee Standing Committees, Ad Hoc Committees, and Commissions
United States Olympic Committee	National Governing Bodies—Olympic
	National Governing Bodies—Pan Am
	Paralympic Sport Organizations
	Affiliated Sport Organizations
	Community-Based Multisport Organizations
	Education-Based Multisport Organizations
	Armed forces
United States Paralympics	No structures

Although Deaf athletes did not participate in the Paralympics, CISS remained associated with the International Coordinating Committee and, later, the IPC for a few years. For most of the 20th century, the CISS hosted the World Games for the Deaf and gained recognition by the IOC as the only federation responsible for the administration of all sporting events involving Deaf athletes. In keeping with this autonomy, CISS secured a similar agreement with the IPC on July 16, 1990. Although the CISS has maintained autonomy over sporting events for Deaf athletes, the inclusion of Deaf athletes in the Paralympics has been considered and the debate has continued into the 21st century. Currently, CISS is a separate organization overseeing Deaf sport (Deaflympics) for Deaf athletes worldwide.

Special Olympics International (SOI) is not a member of IPC, nor does it participate in any of the Paralympic activities or events. On the other hand, SOI has established a link to the IOC. In 1988, SOI was formally recognized by the IOC and given permission to use the word "Olympics" in its title. This permission was granted under the condition that the word "Olympics" be used only in conjunction with "Special."

We fully acknowledge that many would also include SOI among the organizations listed earlier, while others argue that Special Olympics is really a U.S.-based organization. Because SOI has been recognized by the United States Olympic Committee (USOC) as the U.S. sport organization serving athletes with mental retardation and the IPC has recognized INAS-FID, we have chosen in this text to follow the route taken by the IPC.

KEY POINT

The organization and structure of disability sport is complex. The organization has evolved across time and by disability.

International Disability Sport Organizations

For athletes with disabilities, sport on the international level, for the most part, takes place similarly to the way it does for those without disabilities. However, some differences do exist. Some of these differences are in the structure of a particular organization or sport or in the classification system used. The term "Paralympic" is used to describe the Olympic level of sport competition for those with disabilities. Again, the similarities to able-bodied sport should be just as noticeable as aspects that make disability sport unique.

International Paralympic Committee

The IPC serves as the umbrella organization for international disability sport. The word "Paralympic" is derived from the Greek preposition "para" ("beside" or "alongside") and the word "Olympics" (the Paralympics being the parallel Games to the Olympics). The IPC was formally established on September 22, 1989, in Dusseldorf, Germany, with headquarters in Bonn.

The IPC organizes, supervises, and coordinates the Paralympic Games and other multi-disability competitions on the elite sport level. (See chapter 5 and appendix A for information about the major international sport competitions.) An international nonprofit organization, the IPC is formed and run by 160 National Paralympic Committees and five disability-specific international sport federations. The organizational structure appears in figure 4.1.

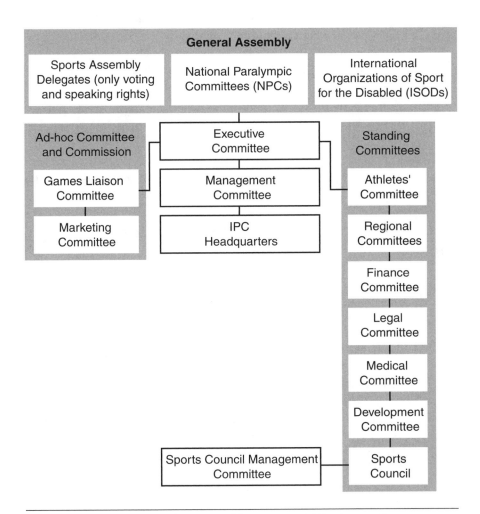

Figure 4.1 Organizational structure of the International Paralympic Committee.

Courtesy of the International Paralympic Committee. www.paralympic.org

The IPC's initial purposes included the following (taken from the IPC constitution printed in the *IPC Newsletter,* Spring 1991, p. 4):

- To organize Paralympic and Multidisability World Games and World Championships (the IPC has sole authority to do so)
- To liaise with the IOC and all other relevant international sport bodies
- To seek integration of sports for individuals with disabilities into the international sports movement for able-bodied individuals
- To supervise and coordinate the conduct of the Paralympics and other Multidisability World and Regional Games, and to coordinate the calendar of international and regional competitions
- To assist and encourage educational programs, research, and promotional activities to achieve the purposes of the IPC
- To promote sport without discrimination for political, religious, economic, gender, or race reasons
- To seek expansion of opportunities for disabled persons to participate in sports and of their access to training programs designed to improve their proficiency

Dr. Robert D. Steadward served as the first IPC president from 1989 through 2001. Phil Craven, a former Paralympian and president of the Wheelchair Basketball Federation, was elected and assumed the position of IPC president at the IPC general assembly in late 2001. Shortly after Craven's first year in office, the IPC executive committee approved the new IPC vision to "enable paralympic athletes to achieve sporting excellence and inspire and excite the world." A new Paralympic motto of "spirit in motion" and revised logo and mission and goals helped redefine the IPC. The newly developed IPC goals are as follows (www.paralympic.org):

- To guarantee and supervise the organization of successful Paralympic Games
- To ensure the growth and strength of the Paralympic Movement through the development of National Paralympic Committees in all nations and the support to the activities of all IPC member organizations
- To promote and contribute to the development of sport opportunities and competitions, from initiation to elite level, for Paralympic athletes as the foundation of elite Paralympic sport
- To develop opportunities for women athletes and athletes with a severe disability in sport at all levels and in all structures
- To support and encourage educational, cultural, research, and scientific activities that contribute to the development and promotion of the Paralympic Movement

- To seek the continuous global promotion and media coverage of the Paralympic Movement, its vision of inspiration and excitement through sport, its ideals and activities
- To promote the self-governance of each Paralympic sport either as an integral part of the international sport movement for able-bodied athletes, or as an independent sport organization, whilst at all times safeguarding and preserving its own identity
- To ensure that in sport practiced within the Paralympic Movement the spirit of fair play prevails, violence is banned, the health risk of the athletes is managed, and fundamental ethical principles are upheld
- To contribute to the creation of a drug-free sport environment for all Paralympic athletes in conjunction with the World Anti-Doping Agency (WADA)
- To promote Paralympic sports without discrimination for political, religious, economic, disability, gender, or race reasons
- To ensure the means necessary to support the future growth of the Paralympic Movement

The initial IPC logo, used at the 1988 Paralympic Games in Seoul, Korea, utilized the Tae-Geuk, a traditional Korean decorative motif. The original logo consisted of five Tae-Geuks in a configuration and in colors similar to those of the Olympic rings, that is, blue, black, red, yellow, and green. Following the 1988 Seoul Paralympic Games, the logo was adopted by the then International Coordinating Committee (ICC) of World Sports Organizations for the Disabled and later incorporated as the symbol of the IPC.

In 1991, the IOC requested that the IPC modify its logo. Although the configuration of five Tae-Geuks was allowed for use at the 1994 Paralympic Winter Games in Lillehammer, Norway, a new Paralympic logo consisting of three Tae-Geuks was officially presented to the world at the 1994 World Championships. At that same time, "Mind, Body, Spirit" was adopted as the Paralympic motto. This version of the Paralympic logo existed until 2001.

After the election of a new president, the IPC embraced a new vision of the IPC, and the Paralympic logo was redefined for the third time and approved in 2003. This logo consists of three elements in red, blue, and green—the three colors that are most widely represented in national flags around the world. The shape of the three elements (Agitos) symbolizes the new vision of the IPC, and the universality of the Paralympic movement is shown through the round shape of the entire logo, symbolizing the globe. The new Paralympic logo, created by the internationally renowned agency Scholz & Friends, was approved at the IPC executive board meeting held in Athens on April 4-6, 2003.

KEY POINT

The IPC, which organizes, supervises, and coordinates the Paralympic Games and other multi-disability competitions on the elite sport level, has become a major player in the global context of elite sport.

International Blind Sports Association

The IBSA was founded in Paris in 1981 but did not adopt its first constitution until four years later during the general assembly held in Norway in 1985. The IBSA serves as the international governing body for sport for blind and visually impaired athletes and is composed of more than 100 member nations with athletes on five continents. The IBSA was the last "disability"-specific sport organization to attain recognition by ISOD and to compete under its sanction. The IBSA is recognized as the international governing body for blind sports and is a member of the IPC.

The purposes of IBSA (www.ibsa.org) are to

- foster friendship among blind athletes;
- motivate and get as many blind people as possible involved in sporting activities on a regular basis;
- promote and disseminate the ideas underlying both competition and recreational sport for the blind;
- defend the Olympic ideal and act in accordance with its principles;
- promote the aims and ideas of IBSA at schools for the blind and among blind youngsters in general;
- plan, promote, and coordinate international events and activities with a view to stimulating greater development of sporting programs for the blind in every country, including international sports meetings, seminars, and conferences on questions related to sports for the blind;
- disseminate relevant information and arrange international exchange programs for people linked to the world of blind sport and the sport advisors and officials of those organizations;
- establish universally accepted rules for blind sports;

- establish a register of records;
- provide aid to those institutions and individuals who work in the field of blind sports; and
- act as the maximum authority in all cases, except where the decision depends on a jury at an international competition.

In the late 1990s, IBSA accomplished two of its greatest achievements in the world of disability sport. The first World Blind Sports Championships were held in July 1998 in Madrid. This multidisciplinary competition offered athletics, swimming, judo, and goal ball at the same venue. In 1999, IBSA successfully advocated for the inclusion of events for blind

Heinz Frei

FAST FACTS
Home Base: Switzerland
Sports: Track and field, cross-country sledge, basketball
Selected Accomplishments:

World record holder in 400 meter, 800 meter, 10,000 meter, and marathon in his classification

International marathon competitor

Heinz Frei has enjoyed a 25-year career as a competitive athlete. His beginnings in the 1980s resulted in several world records in athletics. Current training consists of 7 to 10 sessions per week. The impact of family and friends, both able-bodied and those with disabilities, was important to his participation. Heinz notes that his time out of work after his accident also afforded him opportunity to train. A keen perception about rehab from Heinz is that "the rehabilitation time is not over when you go home after a very short time in the center. If you can, find a new sensibility to your body. . . ." For Heinz Frei with 12 Paralympic finishes, world records, and marathon victories all over the globe, his training and patience have paid off.

"Rehabilitation time is not over when you go home . . . find a new sensibility to your body."

athletes at the International Association of Athletic Federations World Athletics Championships held in Seville, Spain.

Cerebral Palsy–International Sport and Recreation Association

Sport for individuals with cerebral palsy was initiated as a separate entity under the auspices of the sport and leisure subcommittee of the International Cerebral Palsy Society. This subcommittee sponsored the first international athletic competition for athletes with cerebral palsy in France in 1968. The activities continued, and in 1978, the subcommittee became an independent association: CP-ISRA, formalized by acceptance of the constitution at the International Games in Edinburgh, Scotland.

Also in 1978, ISOD officially recognized CP-ISRA as the international governing body for cerebral palsy sports. In that capacity, CP-ISRA soon became a member of the ICC of the World Sports Organizations for the Disabled that provided the foundation for the new organization of sport competition first seen at the Paralympics in Seoul in 1988. The Cerebral Palsy–International Sport and Recreation Association was one of the founding members of the IPC.

The Cerebral Palsy–International Sport and Recreation Association promotes and develops competitive sports and recreational sports for persons with cerebral palsy and related conditions. Over the years, it has provided sport competitions, seminars, films, demonstrations, courses and workshops, coaches' training, and recreation programs. The CP-ISRA provides opportunities for participation in 14 different sports and remains the only international sport organization to include recreation as part of its mission to promote and develop the means by which individuals with cerebral palsy throughout the world can have access to opportunities for participation in sport and recreational activities. The specific purposes are as follows (www.cpisra.org):

- To structure and regulate sports at an international level for individuals with cerebral palsy and related neurological conditions
- To plan, coordinate, and organize competitions and sporting events for individuals with cerebral palsy and related neurological conditions at a regional, continental, and world level
- To foster participation and competition in sporting events at an international level for individuals with cerebral palsy and related neurological conditions
- To foster and support close cooperation with all organizations that promote the development of sporting activities and recreation for

the physically challenged in general and for persons with cerebral palsy and related neurological conditions in particular

- To encourage and aid countries to develop sport projects and competitive sporting activities for people with the aforementioned disabilities
- To plan, set up, and organize educational and training programs that will ensure the highest level of qualifications and services of all those who facilitate the execution of the goals and purposes of the Federation
- To promote the organization of scientific meetings, seminars, conferences, and congresses for the purpose of increasing public awareness about, and promoting and developing, sports for disabled people
- To promote research and disseminate the results

International Sports Federation for Persons with Intellectual Disability

The newest disability-specific international sport organization is INAS-FID (originally formed as International Sports Federation for Persons with Mental Handicap). This group was formed in The Netherlands in 1986. Since its inception in 1986, INAS-FID has sponsored two international competitions: the first World Championships in Athletics and Swimming held in July 1989 in Sweden and the Paralympics for Persons with Mental Handicaps held in September 1992 in Madrid. A small number of athletes with intellectual disability competed in demonstration events at the 2004 Athens Paralympics.

The INAS-FID has 87 member nations and provides sport opportunities for athletes with intellectual disability in the following individual sports: athletics, cycling, Nordic skiing, swimming, tennis, and table tennis. The team sports are basketball and football. The INAS-FMH was a founding member of the IPC. As such, INAS-FID is recognized as the international governing body for sport for athletes with intellectual disability.

The general aims of INAS-FID are to enable access to international events and promote participation of all people with a mental handicap/intellectual disability in sport and recreation activities. The specific purposes of INAS-FID include the following (www.inas-fid.org):

- To promote sport activities for persons with intellectual disability
- To train coaches, trainers, officials, and so on
- To promote technical and medical research
- To disseminate information about sport for those with intellectual disability

The INAS-FID philosophy calls for the inclusion of athletes with an intellectual disability in the sport of their choice at their individual levels of ability, from local recreational activities to international elite competition. This philosophy is based on the principle of normalization such that individuals with intellectual disability should be considered as members of society entitled to the same rights, opportunities, and duties as everyone else.

Some differences exist between INAS-FID and SOI. As just noted, INAS-FID believes that persons with intellectual disability have the right to participate in the sport of their choice at the level of ability they desire. That is, athletes can choose to participate in "banded" competition (grouped by priority and ability, also known as divisioning [see chapter 7]), provided through Special Olympics or in open competition promoted by INAS-FID. Both organizations have an important role in providing international and national sport programs for persons with intellectual disability. In fact, many INAS-FID member nations offer Special Olympics programs as well.

International Stoke Mandeville Wheelchair Sports Federation

The history of ISMWSF is synonymous with the history of wheelchair sport. Sir Ludwig Guttmann is credited with the initiation of the Stoke Mandeville Games for the Paralyzed in 1948 and the establishment of the International Stoke Mandeville Games Committee that would become the ISMWSF in 1960. (See chapter 3 for detailed history.)

Although initially serving athletes with spinal cord injuries, ISMWSF sanctions all international competition for those who use a wheelchair in competition. Currently, ISMWSF includes over 70 member nations. The headquarters is still located at Stoke Mandeville where wheelchair sport was founded in 1944. The organization is managed by an executive management committee that is elected by the Assembly of Nations every four years. The ISMWSF is a member of the IPC.

International Sports Organization for the Disabled

Although the ISMWSF existed in the 1960s, it provided sport programs only for those with spinal cord injuries. This left individuals with other impairments underserved. The International War Veterans Association undertook the challenge to create alternative sport programs, and it founded the ISOD in Paris in 1964.

The ISOD historically served as the international governing body for sport programs for amputees, individuals with other locomotor disabilities, and les autres ("the others," or other physically impaired individuals). In this capacity, ISOD worked with the ICC. Although primarily responsible for sport programs for those with locomotor impairments and les autres, ISOD is also dedicated to developing sports and to uniting sport organizations for individuals with disabilities around the world. Specifically, the purposes of ISOD are as follows (adapted from ISOD pamphlet, n.d.):

1. Provide an international forum for the exchange of opinion, experiences, and resources related to sport for individuals with disabilities

2. Prepare and disseminate international principles and standards recommended for application in all programs of sports for individuals with disabilities

3. Plan, promote, and coordinate international events and activities designed to stimulate and assist the further development of sport programs for individuals with disabilities in all nations, including specifically

   a. international sports meetings,

   b. technical and education seminars and conferences,

   c. dissemination of relevant information, and

   d. international exchange of technicians and athletes with disabilities

4. Provide appropriate assistance to individuals and organizations in developing sports for individuals with disabilities

National sport organizations serving persons with a disability in each country can apply for ISOD membership.

The ISOD participates in sanctioning winter and summer quadrennial games, world championships, continental championships, and invitational tournaments. The Summer and Winter Games are the Paralympics (see chapter 5).

The world championships are held every fourth even year between the quadrennial games and are organized by single sport or multisport. In the odd years between the quadrennial games, continental championships can be held dependent on requests by continental committees for sports for the disabled. Invitational tournaments are offered by request from the member associations. The ISOD summer sports include archery, athletics, badminton, basketball, boccia, cycling, fencing, kayaking, lawn bowling, riding, sailing, shooting, swimming, table tennis, tennis, volleyball, water polo, weightlifting, and wheelchair dancing. ISOD winter sports include alpine skiing, Nordic skiing, biathlon, cross-country sledge, sledge tobogganing, ice sledge racing, and sledge hockey.

To date, ISOD continues to represent amputees, les autres, and dwarf athletes in international competition. Although once associated with the ICC, ISOD is a current member of the IPC.

International Committee of Sports for the Deaf (CISS)

A Deaf Frenchman, E. Rubens-Alcais, is credited with initiating the first International Silent Games. These were held in Paris in August 1924, with the support of the six national sport federations for the Deaf and athletes from nine countries.

Representatives from these nine countries met at the conclusion of the games to establish a union among all Deaf sporting federations and to draft the statutes for the official sanctioning of this organization. Originally called the Comité International des Sports des Sourds (CISS), the organization became known as the International Committee of Sports for the Deaf. From this beginning, the CISS established the following three purposes (adapted from CISS constitution, p. 124):

- Develop and control the physical education in general and the practice of sports in particular among the Deaf of the world
- Promote relations among countries practicing sports for the Deaf and using its influence to initiate and then give guidance to the practice of these sports in countries where it is unknown
- Supervise the regular celebration of the World Games for the Deaf, world championships, and regional championships

As specified in its constitution, CISS has sole responsibility for sports for the Deaf throughout the world. In exercising this responsibility, CISS sponsors the summer and winter World Games for the Deaf (which became identified as the Deaflympics in 2001), world championships, and regional championships. The sports included in the Summer Deaflympics are athletics, badminton, basketball, cycling, marathon, shooting, soccer, swimming, table tennis, team handball, tennis, volleyball, and water polo. Winter sports include Nordic skiing, speed skating, alpine skiing, and hockey. The technical regulations of the international federations are utilized for competition.

The Deaflympics, exclusive property of the CISS, are offered every two years, alternating summer and winter. These Games usually occur the year following the Olympics (see chapter 5).

As the oldest disability sport organization, the CISS has enjoyed a long and vibrant history. Hundreds of thousands of athletes have competed

Ellen de Lange

FAST FACTS
Home Base: The Netherlands
Sports: Swimming, basketball, and tennis
Selected Accomplishments:

Games participant in Arnhem, Stoke Mandeville, Korea, and Barcelona

Technical delegate for tennis at Atlanta (1996), Sydney (2000), and Greece (2004)

Physical educator

Sport administrator

Ellen de Lange is an achiever. She has attained her personal bests as a participant and now as an administrator in elite-level sports. Her tenacity started with her work toward her physical education degree—she was the first person with a disability to obtain this degree in The Netherlands. Her family and self-determination were the primary

"Sport was my life. . . ."

influences on her participation in disability sport. Ellen states, "I am surrounded with sport all the time, first as a participant at the highest level and now as an administrator at the highest level. As an athlete, sport was my life since I simply loved it. I loved to train and to compete and travel. When I got the opportunity to work for the ITF (International Tennis Foundation), I knew that this would mean sooner or later the end of my own career, since it is impossible to mix them at the level I was used to competing at with my newly held responsibilities. But knowing what sport, and especially tennis, meant to me at that time as an athlete motivates me to create those opportunities for others. Opportunities to simply compete (introduce tennis to juniors, developing nations, etc.) but also opportunities to be rewarded appropriately for the results—for example, prize money for our top athletes, higher profile of the game, and more professionalism of the sport." This is a woman who is giving back to disability sport and continuing her involvement after having given up her own involvement as a athlete. Her concern about the disability sport movement, its continuity, and its development and organization, as well as her personal interest in the development of athletes, is admirable.

under the CISS flag, its emblem, and its motto of "equal through sports." Recognition by the IOC came on June 15, 1955. In 1968, the CISS was awarded the Olympic Cup (created by Baron Pierre de Coubertin in 1906) for its service to sport for the Deaf.

Although the CISS has always been an autonomous organization, it became a member of the ICC of the World Sports Organizations for the Disabled in 1986, and the European Deaf Sports Organization was formally accepted as a regional confederation for Europe. During the initial development of the IPC, significant negotiations were under way regarding the governance of Deaf sports. In 1990, CISS and the IPC reached an agreement as follows:

- CISS is recognized as the supreme authority of sports for and of the Deaf.
- Deaflympics has the same status as the Paralympic Games.
- Autonomy and independence of all national Deaf sports federations are to be encouraged and respected.
- Funding for sports for the disabled is to be shared with the CISS on a proportional basis.

International Coordinating Committee of the World Sports Organizations for the Disabled

As early as March 1982, discussions were under way about the formation of a committee to coordinate the existing efforts for disability sport on the international level. Finally, in June 1984, an official agreement was signed by the four founding organizations: IBSA, ISMWSF, ISOD, and CP-ISRA. The headquarters for this coordinating committee was located in The Netherlands with funds allocated from the International Fund Sports Disabled.

The ICC served officially as the coordinating body for international sport for individuals with disabilities from June 1984 until the establishment of the IPC in 1989. The ICC remained in existence through the 1992 Summer Paralympic Games held in Barcelona. See sections on the Paralympics and International Paralympic Committee (IPC) in chapters 3 and 4.

Perhaps one of the ICC's most important functions during its short tenure as a transition organization was the negotiation with the IOC. In January 1985, a small ICC delegation was invited to meet with IOC President Juan Antonio Samaranch in Lausanne, Switzerland. At this meeting, the IOC stipulated that the ICC and disability sport organizations must refrain from using the word "Olympics." The alternative terminology selected was Paralympics, "para" meaning "attached to" and not representing paraplegic. At that time, the term "Paralympics" was officially adopted for use by the IOC and National Olympic Committees. From 1985 to 1995, only the USOC has expressed reluctance to recognize the term "Paralympics" for legal and business-related reasons.

KEY POINT

Many sport associations have formed to organize competitions and sport opportunities for athletes with disabilities—some structured by disability and others by sport.

United States Structure of Disability Sport

The USOC serves as the IOC-recognized National Olympic Committee and as such has the responsibility for Olympic sport in the United States. The roots of the USOC can be traced back to a small group that entered the first U.S. athletes into the Olympics in 1896. Since these beginnings, the USOC has undergone many structural changes as well as name changes. The most significant change occurred in 1978 with the enactment of the Amateur Sports Act, which specified that the USOC would serve as the organization for amateur athletic activity in the United States and would coordinate U.S. athletic activity related to the international Olympic movement.

Although individuals with a disability have long participated in sport and recreation activities, disability sport has rapidly become a more formalized entity in itself and a legitimate part of the U.S. sport world. The organizational structure of disability sport in the United States has evolved over the course of time since the passage of the Amateur Sports Act of 1978. For an historical overview, see chapter 3.

The governance structure of disability sport in the United States is influenced by four prominent organizations: IOC, IPC, USOC, and the U.S. Paralympics formed in 2000. Although the IOC does not have direct control over Paralympic sports, the rules governing sport, international competition, and eligibility of the IOC-related international sport federations often serve as the basis for rules and regulations governing Paralympic sport. See table 4.2.

On the other hand, the IPC plays a major role in disability sport worldwide and in its member nations including the United States. Inasmuch as the IPC governs Paralympic sport and establishes the rules for sports, eligibility, classification, and competitions, disability sport in the United States must follow the IPC rules in order to participate in the Paralympic Games. In 1995, the USOC was designated as the National Paralympic Committee for the United States. Although originally developed as a separate organization, U.S. Paralympics became an official part of the USOC as of 2000 (see chapter 3).

Table 4.2 United States and Related International Disability Sport Organizations

United States	International association
USA Deaf Sports Federation	International Committee of Sports for the Deaf
U.S. Association of Blind Athletes	International Blind Sports Association
National Disability Sports Alliance	Cerebral Palsy–International Sports and Recreation Association
Wheelchair Sports, USA	International Stoke Mandeville Games Federation
Disabled Sports USA and Dwarf Athletic Association of America	International Sports Organization for the Disabled

U.S. Paralympics

U.S. Paralympics is a division of the USOC that was created in May 2001. The purpose of U.S. Paralympics is to focus efforts on enhancing programs, funding, and opportunities for athletes with disabilities to participate in Paralympic sport. The mission is as follows (www.paralympic.org):

> To be the world leader in the Paralympic movement by developing comprehensive and sustainable elite programs integrated into Olympic National Governing Bodies. To utilize our Olympic and Paralympic platform to promote excellence in the lives of persons with disabilities.

The mandate of U.S. Paralympics is to support U.S. athletes and teams in ways that will maximize U.S. medal performances at the Paralympic Games and to ensure that U.S. Paralympics teams will be composed of athletes who have demonstrated the greatest potential to medal at their respective world championships or future Paralympic Games.

The primary way in which U.S. Paralympics plans to achieve its mandate is through the development of a performance plan for each of the 21 sports found on the program of the Paralympic Games. The purposes of these performance plans are

- to focus on the training and coaching opportunities provided to Paralympic athletes by U.S. Paralympics,
- to ensure U.S. team qualification for the Paralympic Games,
- to assess strengths and challenges in U.S. medal pursuits at the Paralympics,
- to define for athletes criteria for U.S. Paralympics support, and
- to establish procedures for the selection of U.S. teams to major international competitions.

These plans have been developed with input from athletes, volunteers, National Governing Body representatives, coaches, and other professionals in each Paralympic sport.

The capability to field a team of elite athletes with disabilities must involve a strong grassroots effort as well. To this end, U.S. Paralympics has initiated a planning process among USOC community-based member organizations to develop a nationwide network of Paralympic athlete identification and development in order to ensure the long-term success of the United States at the Paralympic Games.

KEY POINT

Disability sport in the United States has become an integral part of U.S. Olympic sport through USA Paralympics within the USOC.

United States Disability Sport Organizations

The U.S. disability sport associations are presented here in two sections. The first section highlights those current disability sport organizations (DSOs) historically associated with the USOC. The second section describes U.S. disability sport organizations that actively provide sport opportunities for individuals with a disability on a regional or national basis.

Organizations Historically Associated With the United States Olympic Committee

The USOC is the governing body for most of the major competitive sport organizations that hold national and international Olympic-caliber events. Some of these organizations are described next.

Disabled Sports USA

In 1967, a small group of Vietnam War veterans with amputations formed the National Handicapped Sports and Recreation Association (NHSRA). They did this with the belief that participation in recreation and sport activities was important for restoring self-esteem. In 1989, NHSRA changed its name to National Handicapped Sports; in 1995 it became Disabled Sports USA (DS/USA).

Initially, DS/USA was primarily involved with winter sports, especially alpine skiing. As the organization grew, local DS/USA chapters began, and continue, to promote year-round recreational activities and various levels of competitive sports. Chapters now offer nationwide sport rehabilitation programs to those with visual impairments, amputations, spinal cord injury, dwarfism, multiple sclerosis, head injury, cerebral palsy, and other neuromuscular and orthopedic conditions. Activities include snow and waterskiing, swimming, scuba diving, sailing, canoeing, river rafting, golf, tennis, hiking, biking, horseback riding, climbing, and skydiving.

The DS/USA competitions and programs are open to individuals with a wide range of physical impairments including amputations, birth defects, neurological disorders, and visual impairments. As early as the 1970s, DS/USA sponsored the National Handicapped Ski Championships and Winterfestival, the largest winter sport events for athletes with disabilities. The adaptive equipment used and the way in which one performs on skis, rather than the specific disability, determine the competition classification. In the 1980s, DS/USA established links with the United States Skiing Association to sponsor the U.S. disabled ski team. In September 1990, DS/USA was granted authority for summer amputee sports by the USOC Committee on Sports for the Disabled (COSD) when the former U.S. Amputee Athletic Association was disbanded.

Disabled Sports USA was a DSO member of the USOC and an active participant on the COSD. As a member of USA Paralympics, the DS/USA sanctions and conducts competitions and training camps to prepare and select athletes to represent the United States at the Summer and Winter Paralympic Games. Summer sports include athletics, cycling, powerlifting, sailing, swimming, and volleyball. Winter sports include cross-country skiing and downhill skiing. In addition to the Paralympic Games, DS/USA athletes have opportunities to compete in world championships and other international events sanctioned by the IPC.

Dwarf Athletic Association of America

In 1985, 25 dwarf athletes participated in the National Cerebral Palsy/Les Autres Games. At that time, these short-stature athletes and physically impaired athletes (with other than cerebral palsy) had no formal structure for organizing disabled sport opportunities. As a result, the Dwarf Athletic Association of America (DAAA) was formed shortly after the games in 1985.

Approximately a quarter-million Americans are classified as dwarfs (4 feet, 10 inches or 1.5 meters or less) due to chondrodystrophy and other related causes. It is for this population that the DAAA decided to organize sport opportunities. The purpose of the DAAA is to develop, promote, and provide quality amateur athletic opportunities for dwarf athletes in the United States. The organization is independent of Little People of America (LPA) but drew heavily from LPA for membership. The DAAA maintains ties to LPA, the Short Stature Foundation, and the Billy Barty Foundation.

The DAAA offers clinics, developmental events, and formal competitions at local and regional levels. The youth events (7 to 15 years) emphasize achieving one's personal best. Selection as a young dwarf athlete for competition at the Pan American or World Disabled Youth Games is based on one's athletic potential and demonstrated personal performance. For children under 7 years of age, the DAAA offers a noncompetitive sport program.

The DAAA oversees one winter sport, downhill skiing, and numerous summer sports including athletics, badminton, basketball, boccie, equestrian, powerlifting, soccer, swimming, table tennis, and volleyball. The DAAA sponsors a multisport national games in conjunction with the annual conference of the LPA.

The DAAA was a DSO member of the USOC and an active member of the COSD. As a current DSO member of USA Paralympics, dwarf athletes are eligible to compete in the quadrennial Summer and Winter Paralympic Games as well as world championships and other international competitions sanctioned by the IPC.

National Disability Sports Alliance

Prior to 1978, individuals with cerebral palsy and those with similar neurological conditions had no formal organization to meet their specific sport needs. As a result, the National Association of Sports for Cerebral Palsy (NASCP) was formed and sponsored its first national competition in Detroit.

Shortly after the 1979 National Games, NASCP became affiliated with United Cerebral Palsy Associations. After almost seven years as a program component of United Cerebral Palsy Associations, the majority of NASCP members fought for an independent sport organization. In November 1986, NASCP became known as United States Cerebral Palsy Athletic Association (USCPAA). In 2001, the organization changed its name to the National Disability Sports Alliance (NDSA).

The original purpose was to "provide competitive sports opportunities and support mechanisms to persons with cerebral palsy, strokes, or closed-head injuries with motor dysfunction acquired congenitally or at any age" (USCPAA pamphlet, n.d). National Disability Sports Alliance programs and competitions are designed for persons who have a diagnosis of cerebral palsy, brain injury, stroke, or other nonprogressive neurological disorders resulting in motor impairment.

Competitions for NDSA athletes are offered at local, regional, national, and international levels. The official winter sport is indoor wheelchair soccer (cross-country and downhill skiing are available through DS/USA). The summer sports include athletics, basketball, boccie, bowling, cycling, equestrian, powerlifting, soccer, and swimming.

The NDSA was a DSO member of the USOC. Cerebral palsy athletes have been represented on the COSD since its initiation under NASCP and then USCPAA. As a DSO member of USA Paralympics, National Disability Sports Alliance athletes can compete at the quadrennial Summer Paralympic Games as well as world championships and other international events sanctioned by the IPC. The CP-ISRA continues to sponsor a multisport competition called the Robin Hood Games. The NDSA conducts a multisport national games, as well as local and regional competitions in many parts of the country.

USA Deaf Sports Federation (Formerly Known As American Athletic Association of the Deaf)

The oldest U.S. disability sport organization, the American Athletic Association of the Deaf, was founded in Ohio in 1945. The original intent was to provide year-round sport and recreation opportunities to individuals with hearing impairments. In 1998, the name of the organization was changed to the USA Deaf Sports Federation (USADSF). The organization serves as the American sport organization for athletes who are Deaf; there are more than 2,000 member clubs and affiliated organizations dispersed throughout eight geographic regions. The total number of Deaf or hearing-impaired individuals represented by these associations and clubs exceeds 25,000.

Individuals with a hearing loss of 55 decibels or greater in the better ear are eligible for competition under USADSF. No classifications other than separate female and male divisions are used. Although initially focused on the three team sports of volleyball, basketball, and softball, the USADSF has national sport organizations in four winter sports (cross-country skiing, downhill skiing, ice hockey, and snowboarding) and 17 summer sports (athletics, badminton, baseball, basketball, bowling, cycling, flag football, golf, soccer, softball, swimming, table tennis, team handball, tennis, volleyball, water polo, and wrestling).

The USASDF also provides training programs for athletes and coaches and educational programs for the public. It annually inducts Deaf individuals into its Hall of Fame; selects the Deaf Athlete of the Year; and conducts competitions, clinics, and camps for Deaf athletes at the local, regional, and national levels.

The USADSF was a DSO member of the USOC and participated in the activities of the COSD; USASDF is the U.S. affiliate of CISS. The major international competition for Deaf athletes is the quadrennial multisport Deaflympics (formerly called the World Games for the Deaf).

United States Association of Blind Athletes

The United States Association of Blind Athletes (USABA) was established in 1976 as the official organization promoting athletic competition for individuals with visual impairments. The establishment of the USABA was a direct result of the success of blind athletes who competed in the

1976 Olympiad for the Physically Disabled in Toronto and the need for an organization to oversee the sport opportunities for blind and visually impaired individuals. The association has chapters in most states and more than 1,500 members throughout the United States. Since its inception, USABA has served over 100,000 blind individuals.

The mission of the USABA is to increase the number and quality of grassroots-through-competitive, world-class athletic opportunities for Americans who are blind or visually impaired through three classifications of visual impairment to totally blind. Today, USABA serves more than 3,000 athletes in nine official sports including athletics, cycling, goal ball, judo, powerlifting, swimming, and wrestling as well as cross-country skiing and downhill skiing. In 2000, four USABA athletes achieved national rankings in three sports, including 1,500-meter runner Marla Runyan, who became the first legally blind individual to qualify for a U.S. Olympic team.

The USABA was a DSO member of the USOC, participated in the activities of the COSD, and is represented internationally by the IBSA. USABA is a current DSO member of USA Paralympics. The major international competitions for USABA athletes are the quadrennial Summer and Winter Paralympic Games; world championships and other international events sanctioned by the IPC; multisport world championships conducted by the IBSA; and USABA-sanctioned competitions and camps at the local, regional, and national levels.

Wheelchair Sports, USA

With the recognition that recreational and competitive sports could play an integral part in one's rehabilitative process and daily life, the first National Wheelchair Games were held in 1957 at Adelphi College in New York. Among the competitors were disabled men from the New York-New Jersey area who expressed interest in competing in wheelchair sports other than just wheelchair basketball. What resulted was the formation of the National Wheelchair Athletic Association (NWAA) in 1956. In 1994, the NWAA changed its name to Wheelchair Sports, USA.

Wheelchair Sports, USA organizes and sponsors competitions in numerous summer sports including archery, athletics, basketball, fencing, hand cycling, pool, powerlifting, racquetball, shooting, swimming, table tennis, tennis, waterskiing, and wheelchair rugby, as well as in one winter sport—ice sledge hockey. Other winter sports such as cross-country and downhill skiing are available through DS/USA, and wheelchair dance sport is available through the IPC.

Wheelchair Sports, USA programs include publications, video rental, local and regional wheelchair games for adults and juniors, local wheelchair sports development, national training camps, road racing series, national workshops, and national wheelchair games and junior national wheelchair games. In addition, athletes competing under Wheelchair

Sports, USA are eligible for participation in the Summer and Winter Paralympic Games, world championships and wheelchair games, Pan American Wheelchair Games, and multisport Stoke Mandeville Games.

Wheelchair Sports, USA was a DSO member of the USOC and one of the original members of the COSD. Internationally, Wheelchair Sports, USA is represented by the ISMWSF. WSUSA is a current DSO member of USA Paralympics.

Special Olympics International

In 1968, Eunice Kennedy Shriver created Special Olympics and hosted the first International Special Olympic Games in Soldier Field, Chicago. Special Olympics was created by the Joseph P. Kennedy Jr. Foundation for the benefit of individuals with intellectual impairments. The mission of Special Olympics is to provide year-round sport training and athletic competition in a variety of Olympic-type sports for children and adults with mental retardation, giving them continuing opportunities to develop physical fitness, demonstrate courage, experience joy, and participate in a sharing of gifts, skills, and friendship with their families, other Special Olympics athletes, and the community. There are accredited SOI programs in more than 150 countries and in all 50 states and U.S. territories.

The goal of SOI is to help "bring all persons with mental retardation into the larger society under conditions whereby they are accepted, respected and given the chance to become useful and productive citizens" (Principles and Philosophy, specialolympics.org). Individuals with mental retardation who are 8 or more years of age, and those persons who have impairments due to cognitive delays and have significant learning or vocational problems, are eligible to participate in SOI programs.

Over the years, the programs offered by SOI have expanded. Special Olympics currently offers programs in a variety of summer and winter sports, a program for novice athletes, and an inclusive sport program for more advanced athletes. The programs are as follows:

- Winter sports include cross-country skiing, downhill skiing, figure skating, floor hockey, and speed skating.
- Summer sports include athletics, badminton, basketball, boccie, bowling, cycling, equestrian, golf, gymnastics, powerlifting, roller skating, sailing, soccer, softball, swimming, table tennis, team handball, tennis, and volleyball.
- The Motor Activities Training Program helps beginning athletes develop the skills needed for participation in these sports.
- The SOI Unified Sports Program, conducted in all 26 official sports, pairs athletes with and without mental retardation on inclusive sport teams for training and competition.

Unlike all other major DSOs, Special Olympics has established relationships with many sport organizations and other nonprofit organizations as follows:

- In February 1988, the IOC officially recognized Special Olympics and agreed to cooperate with Special Olympics as a representative of the interests of athletes with mental retardation. Special Olympics is the only organization authorized by the IOC to use the word "Olympics" worldwide.

- In April 2002, Special Olympics and World Organization of Athletes agreed to work closely together to provide opportunities for Olympians to become more involved with Special Olympics athletes, programs, and events. The initiative with Special Olympics is designed to provide Olympians with opportunities to be role models for Special Olympics athletes while increasing awareness of their many skills and achievements.

- The Joseph P. Kennedy Jr. Foundation is a private foundation that shares Special Olympics' goal of providing people with mental retardation the opportunity to reach their fullest potential. The foundation provided critical funding necessary for the establishment of Special Olympics. Although the foundation no longer provides funding to Special Olympics, it continues to provide technical assistance, guidance, and professional consultation, as well as other forms of support and assistance in expanding the Special Olympics movement.

- Special Olympics is a registered nongovernmental organization of the United Nations. As such, Special Olympics has the responsibility of working with nations throughout the world to help develop sport training and competition programs for persons with mental retardation.

The major competitions for SOI athletes are the quadrennial Summer and Winter Special Olympics World Games, held in the years preceding Olympic Games. Local/Area and state-level competitions are held annually in most areas.

Other United States Disability Sport Organizations

Numerous DSOs exist in the United States today in addition to those historically affiliated with the USOC and described so far in this chapter. Many of these are listed in appendix E. This section highlights a sampling of these organizations.

America's Athletes with Disabilities

Founded in 1985, America's Athletes with Disabilities is a consortium of five member DSOs. Its mission is to promote and sponsor sports, recreation, fitness, and leisure events for children and adults with physical disabilities. These events are held every year, across the country, under the banner of the Victory Games. In addition, the Disabled Youth Sports Training and Competition Program is a series of grants given every year to help children with disabilities uncover their unique athletic abilities.

Challenged Athletes Foundation

The Challenged Athletes Foundation, a charity, was created in the belief that people of all abilities should have the opportunity to pursue a life full of physical activity and sports. Whether for recreational purposes or in pursuit of a gold medal at the Paralympic Games, people with a physical disability are limited only by their access to funding. The Challenged Athletes Foundation has raised over $2.7 million and directly assisted 875 challenged athletes worldwide. The Challenged Athletes Foundation is a current DSO member of USA Paralympics.

National Foundation of Wheelchair Tennis

The National Foundation of Wheelchair Tennis was formed in 1976 as the governing body for wheelchair tennis in the United States. The foundation sponsors competitions, tournaments, instructional clinics and exhibitions, and multisport camps for disabled youth. The Wheelchair Tennis Players Association administers the rules and regulations that govern wheelchair tennis in the United States. Everest and Jennings sponsors the annual Grand Prix Circuit, which culminates in the U.S. Open Wheelchair Tennis.

National Wheelchair Basketball Association

The National Wheelchair Basketball Association (NWBA) is one of the oldest wheelchair sport organizations in the world and certainly the oldest in the United States. Formed in 1945, the NWBA serves as the national governing body for wheelchair basketball in the United States, sponsors regional and national tournaments for men and for women, and selects the team(s) to represent the United States in international wheelchair basketball competitions.

National Wheelchair Softball Association

Wheelchair softball in the United States has been officially governed since 1976 by the National Wheelchair Softball Association, which sponsors national tournaments each September.

North American Riding for the Handicapped Association

One of the earliest organizations for therapeutic horseback riding in the world, the North American Riding for the Handicapped Association was established in the 1970s. It promotes equine-facilitated therapy and activity programs in the United States and Canada. Currently, more than 650 program centers serve about 30,000 riders with a disability.

Paralyzed Veterans of America

The Paralyzed Veterans of America, a congressionally chartered veterans service organization founded in 1946, has developed a unique expertise on a wide variety of issues involving the special needs of its members—veterans of the armed forces who have experienced spinal cord injury or dysfunction. Since its founding, Paralyzed Veterans of America has actively encouraged sport participation among veterans with a disability.

United States Les Autres Sports Association

The United States Les Autres Sports Association (USLASA) was formed after the 1985 National Cerebral Palsy/Les Autres Games as a separate sport governing body. The association organizes and sanctions competitions for les autres. Les autres athletes include those with physical impairments not associated with any other DSO. The United States Les Autres Sports Association works closely with NDSA and DAAA in providing programs and competitions for physically impaired athletes at the local, national, and international levels.

United States Organization for Disabled Athletes

The United States Organization for Disabled Athletes was formed as a nonprofit organization in 1985. Its purpose is to bring together the various U.S. organizations serving athletes with disabilities and to provide a coordinated approach to scheduling, promotion, management, and funding for national and international sport events. Current members include USABA, NDSA, DAAA, WSUSA, and USLASA. Since 1985, the United States Organization for Disabled Athletes has sponsored numerous sport competitions including Pan Am Youth Games for the Physically Disabled, Winter Sports Festival, and Victory Games.

United States Disabled Athletes Fund

The U.S. Disabled Athletes Fund, Inc. is a direct outgrowth and legacy of the 1996 Paralympic Games held in Atlanta, Georgia. These Games, the first held on American soil, were the realization of the dreams of thousands of

Americans involved in the delivery and growth of sports for persons with physical disabilities in this country. Committed to the development of a national program that eventually makes adaptive sports in every community a reality for children and adults with physical disabilities, the Atlanta Paralympic Organizing Committee established the U.S. Disabled Athletes Fund in 1993. USDAF is a current member of USA Paralympics.

World T.E.A.M. Sports

World T.E.A.M. (The Exceptional Athlete Matters) Sports brings individuals with and without disabilities together to undertake unique athletic events throughout the world to encourage, promote, and develop opportunities in sport for all people. The team-oriented athletic events coupled with medical and educational outreach programs stimulate the power of learning through participation. The purposes of World T.E.A.M. include the following:

- Organize and host innovative and challenging sporting events that encourage all individuals, especially those with disabilities, to participate in lifetime sports
- Promote diversity and increase awareness, acceptance, and integration of those with disabilities

Concluding Comments

Disability sport is a complex social institution. Disability sport associations have evolved from their modest beginnings into efficient and effective organizations representing the interests of athletes with disabilities around the world. In particular, the IPC has been instrumental in forging a strong relationship with the IOC and creating greater visibility for athletes with disabilities. With increasing visibility and acceptance, national sport associations have formed to oversee sport opportunities for individuals with disabilities. United States disability sport associations have also developed, and selected ones enjoy the benefits of association with the USOC. Disability sport organizations not officially recognized by the USOC have also gained more prominence and are active contributors to the disability sport movement.

five

Competitions and Sport Opportunities for Athletes With Disabilities

Reader Goal Understand the historical content and development of the major sport competitions for elite athletes with disabilities

Chapter Synopsis

- Paralympic Games
- Deaflympics
- Special Olympics International
- Additional International Games for Athletes With Disabilities
- National Disability Sport Opportunities
- Intercollegiate and Interscholastic Athletic Programs
- Concluding Comments

Throughout the 20th century, sport opportunities for athletes with disabilities have increased tremendously. Today there are major international competitions for elite athletes with disabilities in addition to numerous national and regional competitions and a multitude of sport and recreation opportunities found in local and regional communities.

Multisport, multi-disability international competitions; world championships; and single-sport, single-disability international competitions are held on a regular basis. Today, world championships and regional competitions exist in virtually all sports. See chapter 7 for discussion of the sports in which athletes with disabilities compete. These can be specific to the disability type as well as to the sport—there are international wheelchair archery tournaments, world goal ball championships, international wheelchair marathons, and so on. Additional examples include, but are not limited to, the Pan American Wheelchair Games, World Cup Alpine Disabled Skiing Championships, and European championships for athletics and swimming, as well as multisport, single-disability events such as the European Special Olympics and national competitions for Deaf athletes. But perhaps the best known of the international competitions for athletes with disabilities are these three:

- The Paralympics (Summer and Winter)
- Deaflympics (formerly known as World Games for the Deaf) (Summer and Winter)
- International Special Olympics (Summer and Winter)

Paralympic Games

The Paralympics can be considered the equivalent of the Olympics for elite physically and visually impaired athletes. Both Summer and Winter Games are held every four years. Starting with Seoul in 1988, the Paralympic Games have been officially scheduled to be held in the same host country and city as the Olympics.

Summer

The Summer Paralympics include many of the sports found on the program of the Olympics and are open to athletes who have physical impairments (paraplegic and quadriplegic, amputee, cerebral palsied, and les autres) and visual impairments. Intellectually impaired athletes have participated in exhibition events as well. The history of the Paralympic Games can be traced back to the first national competition in 1948 at Stoke Mandeville, England, and the first international competition also held at Stoke Mandeville in 1952. In 1960, these Games were held in the Olympic city of Rome and would ultimately become known as the 1st Paralympic Games. See table 5.1.

Table 5.1 Summer Paralympic Games

Year	Location (Olympic Games)	Disability	Countries	Athletes	Sports
1952	Stoke Mandeville	Spinal cord injury (SCI)	2	130	6
1960	Rome, Italy (Rome)	SCI	23	400	8 (6 women)
1964	Tokyo, Japan (Tokyo)	SCI	21	375	9 (6 women)
1968	Tel Aviv, Israel (Mexico City, Mexico)	SCI	29	750	10 (8 women)
1972	Heidelberg, Germany (Munich, Germany)	SCI, visual impairment (VI) (demonstration event)	41	1,004	10 (8 women)
1976	Toronto, Canada (Montreal, Canada)	SCI, VI, les autres (LA)	42	1,657	13 (8 women)
1980	Arnhem, The Netherlands (Moscow, Soviet Union)	SCI, amputee, VI, cerebral palsy (CP)	42	1,973	12 (8 women)
1984	Stoke Mandeville and New York (Los Angeles, USA)	SCI, amputee, VI, CP	41 45	1,100 1,800	14 13
1988	Seoul, Korea (Seoul)	SCI, amputee, VI, CP, LA	61	3,053	17 (11 women)
1992	Barcelona, Spain (Barcelona)	SCI, amputee, VI, CP, LA	82	3,020	15 (11 women)
1992	Madrid, Spain	Intellectual disability (ID)	74	1,400	5 (5 women)
1996	Atlanta, USA (Atlanta)	SCI, amputee, VI, CP, LA, ID	103	3,195	17 (11 women)
2000	Sydney, Australia (Sydney)	SCI, CP, LA, ID, VI, amputee	123	3,843	18 (13 women)
2004	Athens, Greece (Athens)	SCI, amputee, CP, LA, VI, ID	130	4,000	21 (18 women)
2008	Beijing, China (Beijing)	SCI, amputee, CP, LA, ID			

The first international games for athletes with disabilities were held in 1952; the international games to be later identified as Paralympic Games were held in 1960. For historically accurate titles for each of these Games, see the text and the chronology in appendix A.

A significant milestone in Paralympic history occurred during the Summer Paralympics, held October 15-24, 1988, in Seoul. A total of 3,053 athletes from 61 countries competed in 17 sports including 732 different events. These Games utilized the same facilities, housing, competition sites, and so on as the 1988 Olympics, and the opening and closing ceremonies were identical. Competition was held in archery, athletics, basketball, boccie, cycling, equestrian events, fencing, goal ball, judo, shooting, volleyball, soccer, swimming, table tennis, weightlifting/powerlifting, lawn bowling, and snooker.

The momentum of Seoul continued into the 1992 Paralympic Games held September 3-14 in Barcelona; 3,020 athletes representing 82 countries marched into the Olympic Stadium before a crowd of 60,000 spectators (Sherrill, 1993). They competed in archery, athletics, boccie, cycling, fencing, goal ball, judo, seven-a-side soccer, shooting, swimming, table tennis, volleyball, weightlifting/powerlifting, wheelchair basketball, and wheelchair tennis. The Barcelona Paralympics have been heralded for their unparalleled success: 1,386,000 spectators attended 46 events, including spectacular opening and closing ceremonies. For a full discussion of the 1992 Paralympics, see Sherrill (1993).

The sport program for the 1996 Paralympics in Atlanta included 17 sports: archery, athletics, basketball, boccia, cycling, equestrian, fencing, goal ball, judo, lawn bowls, powerlifting, shooting, soccer, swimming, table tennis, tennis, and volleyball. In addition, demonstration events for wheelchair racquetball, wheelchair rugby, and sailing were held. More than 3,000 athletes (amputees, blind, cerebral palsy, dwarf, and spinal cord injured/wheelchair users) from 103 nations competed in the Paralympics on August 16-27, 1996 (two weeks after the close of the Olympics). The 10 days of competition allowed for more than 500 different events held in 12 to 14 different venues (also used for competitions during 1996 Olympic Games). For the first time, a Paralympic congress and expo were held in conjunction with the Games.

The Paralympics continued to gain momentum into the 21st century and held the largest Games to date in Sydney in 2000. Athletes with physical, visual, and intellectual impairments (3,800+) came from 123 nations to compete in 18 different sports (archery, athletics, basketball, boccia, cycling, equestrian, fencing, goal ball, judo, shooting, volleyball, soccer, swimming, table tennis, weightlifting/powerlifting, lawn bowling, and snooker). The athletes lived in the Paralympic Village and were accompanied by 2,300+ team officials and 800+ technical officials.

Shortly after the Games ended, the International Paralympic Committee (IPC) investigation commission found that the process of assessment and certification of athletes with an intellectual disability for the Sydney 2000 Paralympic Games had not been properly carried out. It was revealed that several athletes representing Spain in basketball, table tennis, swimming,

Louise Sauvage, Order of Australia Medal (OAM)

FAST FACTS
Home Base: Perth, Australia
Sport: Wheelchair track and distance road athlete
Selected Accomplishments:

World records
  1,500 meter, 5,000 meter
  4 × 100 meter and 4 × 400 meter
Three-time Australian Paralympian
  2000 Sydney: two gold, one silver
  1996 Atlanta: four gold
  1992 Barcelona: three gold, one silver
Dual Australian Olympian
  1996 Atlanta and 2000 Sydney
  Gold: 800-meter demonstration race
IPC World Champion
  800 meter, 1,500 meter, 5,000 meter, marathon
  4 × 100-meter and 4 × 400-meter relay
IAAF World Athletic Championships
  1993 Stuttgart, Germany: gold
  1995 Goteborg, Sweden: gold
  1997 Athens, Greece: gold
  2001 Edmonton, Canada: gold
Voted Australian Paralympian of the Year in 1994, 1996, 1997, 1998
Australian Institute of Sport Athlete of the Year in 1997
Winner of ABIGROUP National Sports Award as part of the 1998 Young Australian of the Year Awards
1999 and 2000: International Female Wheelchair Athlete of the Year

Louise is a hard worker whose results have verified her commitment to be an elite athlete. She trains 10 to 14 hours per week and, in her words, each workout is "concentrated, hard, with passion and fun." Her involvement in

"Sport is my life. I have made a career out of it. . . ."

(continued)

Louise Sauvage *(continued)*

sport has made her an independent individual who now runs her own consulting company. Born with myelodysplasia (congenital paraplegia), this 30-something athlete is known throughout Australia and the world. Her parents were a prime factor in her involvement in sport at a very young age. "Sport is my life. I have made a career out of it—I am a professional athlete. Living in Australia we are all very sport minded and I cannot see a life without it." For younger athletes, she states, "Get out there and have a go, it's so much fun; you meet some incredible people and you become fit and healthy at the same time." Her response to the question about what issues face the disability sport movement is "This is a hard one. There are a lot of issues with sport for athletes with a disability. I think one would be the whole integration with the able-bodied athletes. At an elite level it is very frustrating to know you train just as hard but do not get the rewards on many levels. As I said, there are many issues and things have changed, but unfortunately things change slowly." Louise Sauvage is representative of the knowledgeable and savvy athlete of the 21st century who plans on being noted as an athlete first and disabled as an afterthought.

and athletics were not intellectually disabled. In 2001, the International Sports Federation for Persons with Intellectual Disability (INAS-FID) was suspended from membership in the IPC and from participating in the next Paralympic Games (2002 Winter Games in Salt Lake City).

In 2004, the Paralympic Games were held in Athens in September, two weeks after the close of the Olympic Games. More than 4,000 athletes, representing 130 countries, competed in 21 different sports held at the same venues as the Olympic Games. The IPC decided to include exhibition events in athletics, swimming, basketball, and table tennis for athletes with intellectual impairments in Athens following their suspension resulting from the scandal in Sydney in 2000. Citing fiscal considerations, the IPC cancelled the Paralympic Scientific Congress. As a result, the 2004 Olympic Congress incorporated sessions on research and scientific practice for athletes with disabilities at the congress in Thessaloniki in August 2004.

Winter

Similarly to the Summer Paralympics, the Winter Paralympics are held every four years. In 1988, they were held in February in Innsbruck, Austria, and utilized the same facilities and venues as the 1984 Winter Paralympics and the 1976 Olympics. In the Winter Paralympics, competition includes a variety of alpine and Nordic events, skating, ice picking, and more. Physically impaired (amputee, cerebral palsy, les autres) athletes and visually impaired/blind athletes compete. As is the case with the Summer Paralympics, these Games are to be held in the Olympic host city near the time of the Olympics. The 1992 Winter Paralympics were held in Tigne-Albertville, France. Lillehammer, Norway, hosted both the 1994 Winter Olympics and 1994 Paralympics. See table 5.2.

The 1998 Winter Paralympic Games held in Nagano included athletes with intellectual disabilities for the first time as official competitors

Table 5.2 Winter Paralympic Games

Year	Location (Olympic Games)	Disability	Countries	Athletes	Sports[1]
1976	Omskoldsvik, Sweden (Innsbruck, Austria)	Blind, amputee	14	250	2
1980	Geilo, Norway (Lake Placid, NY)	Physical impairments (PI), visual impairments (VI)	18	350	2
1984	Innsbruck, Austria (Sarajevo, Yugoslavia)	PI, VI	22	350	2
1988	Innsbruck (Calgary, Canada)	PI, VI	22	397	2
1992	Tignes-Albertville, France (Tignes-Albertville)	PI, VI, intellectual disability (ID) (demonstration event)	24	475	2
1994	Lillehammer, Norway (Lillehammer)	PI, VI, ID (demonstration event)	31	1,000+	3
1998	Nagano, Japan (Nagano)	PI, VI, ID	32	571	5
2002	Salt Lake City, USA (Salt Lake City)	PI, VI, no ID[2]	36	416	3
2006	Torino, Italy (Torino)	PI, VI, ID			4
2010	Vancouver, Burnaby, and Whistler, British Columbia, Canada (Vancouver, BC)				

For historically accurate titles for each of these Games, see the text and the chronology in appendix A.

[1]Sports include alpine skiing, Nordic events, ice sledge hockey, and wheelchair curling. In 1998, biathlon was included.

[2]Athletes with intellectual disabilities were not included because of International Paralympic Committee suspension of International Sports Federation for Persons with Intellectual Disability.

(not demonstration events). Five hundred seventy-one athletes from 32 countries competed in five sports (alpine skiing, Nordic skiing, biathlon, sledge racing, sledge hockey).

The United States hosted the Winter Paralympic Games for the first time in 2002 following the Winter Olympics in Salt Lake City, Utah. Over 400 athletes from 36 countries participated. Andorra, Chile, the People's Republic of China, Croatia, Greece, and Hungary competed for the first time. Although athletes with intellectual disabilities had been scheduled to compete at these Games, they were suspended from the competition as a result of the scandal involving intellectually impaired athletes that had occurred during the Sydney Paralympics.

Paralympics for Persons With Mental Handicaps

In addition to competitions held under the auspices of Special Olympics International, rival competitions for mentally handicapped individuals have been held since 1985. These Games have been sponsored by the International Sports Federation for Persons with Intellectual Disability (formerly identified as mentally handicapped). In September 1992 in Madrid, the first Paralympics for Persons with Mental Handicaps were held in close proximity and timing to the Paralympics.

These "Paralympic Games" included 1,400 competitors from 74 countries (DePauw and Rich, 1993). To attend, the athletes had to be mentally retarded (mentally handicapped), at least 15 years of age, and able to meet qualifying athletics standards. The competitive events included five sports: athletics, swimming, table tennis, indoor soccer, and basketball. The competitions were open to both men and women. For more information, see DePauw and Rich (1993).

Although Special Olympics and the Paralympic Games for Persons with Mental Handicaps have sport competition in common, the emphases are quite different. Special Olympics appears to focus less on athletic competitions and more on participating; athletes who compete at international games are not selected based on standards of athletic performance. In contrast, the World Championships for the Mentally Handicapped (and as of 1992, Paralympics for Persons with Mental Handicaps) focus on athletic performance and competition.

Since 1992, athletes with intellectual impairments have been included in the Winter Paralympic Games (1992, 1994, 1998, suspended for 2002) and the Summer Paralympic Games (1996, 2000). The IPC-issued ban on competition by athletes with intellectual impairments challenged INAS-FID to demonstrate compliance with IPC international rules, thereby allowing their athletes to once again compete in the Paralympic Games. As part of the process of being reinstated with full medal status for the Paralympic Games, INAS-FID was to sponsor the 2004 Global Games, games that would showcase the six sports that are expected to be Summer Paralympic sports in the future.

Deaflympics

Athletic competition for Deaf athletes began in 1924. Since 1924, the games have been known as the International Games for the Deaf or International Silent Games (1924-1965), World Games for the Deaf (1966-1999), and now the Deaflympics. In June 2001, the International Olympic Committee approved the request from the International Committee for Sports for the Deaf to change the name of the World Games for the Deaf to Deaflympics.

International games for Deaf athletes have been held regularly since the first in 1924 in Paris. The first World Winter Games for the Deaf were held in Seefeld, Austria, in 1949. Since then, these Games have been held every four years, the year following the Olympic year, and whenever possible in the same host country or city. For example, the 1985 Games were held in Los Angeles and utilized many of the same venues as the Olympics the year before. Deaf athletes have also been able to compete in Pan American Games for the Deaf. See table 5.3.

Events on the Summer Deaflympics program include men's and women's basketball, cycling, soccer, swimming, tennis, water polo, badminton, shooting, table tennis, team handball, men's and women's athletics, men's and women's volleyball, and wrestling. For the Winter Deaflympics, athletes compete in alpine events (men's and women's downhill skiing, giant slalom, slalom, and parallel slalom), Nordic skiing events (men's 15K, 30K, and 3 × 10K relay; women's 5K, 10K, 3 × 5K relay), speed skating (500, 1,000, 1,500, 3,000 meter), and ice hockey.

The Deaflympics (Summer and Winter) are held every four years in the year following the Olympic Games. The chronology of the Summer and Winter Games is displayed in table 5.3 and included in appendix A. The first World Winter Games for the Deaf were very small, with 33 athletes from five countries in attendance. For the first seven competitions there were less than 100 participants on each occasion. The next Deaflympics are scheduled to be held in Melbourne in 2005. The 16th Winter Deaflympics are scheduled to be held in Park City, Utah, in 2007 followed by the 21st Summer Deaflympics in Taipei, Taiwan.

Perhaps somewhat unique to the Deaflympics is the concerted effort to provide an international forum for exchange of culturally relevant information (Stewart, 1990, p. 32). The Deaflympics offer participants the experience to be identified with the unique cultural identity of the

Table 5.3 Deaflympics (With Historical Event Names)

Year	Location	Summer or Winter Games
International Games for the Deaf (International Silent Games)		
1924	Paris, France	Summer (1st Summer Games)
1928	Amsterdam, Holland	Summer (2nd)
1931	Nuremberg, Germany	Summer (3rd)
1935	London, England	Summer (4th)
1939	Stockholm, Sweden	Summer (5th)
1949	Copenhagen, Denmark	Summer (6th)
1949	Seefeld, Austria	Winter (1st World Winter Games for the Deaf)
1953	Brussels, Belgium	Summer (7th)
1953	Oslo, Norway	Winter (2nd)
1957	Oberammergau, Germany	Winter (3rd)
1957	Milan, Italy	Summer (8th)
1959	Montana-Vermala, Switzerland	Winter (4th)
1961	Helsinki, Finland	Summer (9th)
1963	Are, Sweden	Winter (5th)
1965	Washington, D.C.	Summer (10th)
1967	Berchtesgaden, Germany	Winter (6th)
World Games for the Deaf		
1969	Belgrade, Yugoslavia	Summer (11th)
1971	Abelboden, Switzerland	Winter (7th)
1973	Malmo, Sweden	Summer (12th)
1975	Lake Placid, New York	Winter (8th)
1977	Bucharest, Romania	Summer (13th)
1979	Meribel, France	Winter (9th)
1981	Cologne, Germany	Summer (14th)
1983	Madonna Di Campiglio, Italy	Winter (10th)
1985	Los Angeles, CA	Summer (15th)
1987	Oslo, Norway	Winter (11th)
1989	Christchurch, New Zealand	Summer (16th)

Year	Location	Summer or Winter Games
World Games for the Deaf (cont.)		
1991	Banff, Canada	Winter (12th)
1993	Sofia, Bulgaria	Summer (17th)
1995	Yilas, Finland	Winter (13th)
1997	Copenhagen, Denmark	Summer (18th)
1999	Davos, Switzerland	Winter (14th)
Summer and Winter Deaflympics		
2001	Rome, Italy	Summer (19th)
2003	Sundsvall, Sweden	Winter (15th)
2005	Melbourne, Australia	Summer (20th)
2007	Park City, UT	Winter (16th)
2009	Taipei, Taiwan	Summer (21st)

Deaf. They are much more than athletic competition; they represent a celebration of community.

Special Olympics International

Special Olympics International (SOI) sponsors both Summer and Winter Games for individuals with intellectual disabilities. Special Olympics World Summer Games are conducted every four years in the years preceding the Summer Olympic Games.

The first Special Olympics were held at Soldier Field in Chicago; 1,000 athletes from 26 states and Canada participated. Special Olympics International competitions are held every two years, alternating Winter and Summer Games. Initially these Games were called International Special Olympics. In 1991, the name was officially changed to Special Olympics World Summer and World Winter Games. For the Summer Games, an increasing number of athletes from numerous countries have participated (see table 5.4). Official sports include aquatics, athletics, basketball, bowling, equestrian events, soccer, gymnastics, roller skating, softball, and volleyball; demonstration events include cycling, powerlifting, table tennis, team handball, and tennis. In addition to competitions held regularly in the United States, European Summer Special Olympics have been held in Belgium (1981) and Dublin (1985). In comparison to the case with the Deaflympics and the Paralympics, media coverage has been, and continues to be, more extensive for SOI events. The first television coverage occurred in 1975 as part of CBS Sports Spectacular. For the 1977 Games, CBS, ABC, and NBC all covered the events.

In March 1993, the fifth SOI World Winter Games were held in Schladming, Austria. These were the first International Special Olympics ever held outside of the United States. Approximately 1,600 athletes from 50 countries competed in alpine and cross-country skiing, figure skating, speed skating, and floor hockey (Cowan, 1993).

Since their inception, participation at the Special Olympics Games has increased for both the Summer and Winter Games. A chronology of Special Olympics World Summer and Winter Games is presented in tables 5.4 and 5.5.

KEY POINT

The three major international competitive events for athletes with disabilities are Paralympics, Deaflympics, and Special Olympics World Games.

Table 5.4 Special Olympics World Summer Games (With Historical Event Names)

Year	Location	Athletes	United States*	Other countries
International Special Olympics Summer Games				
1968	Chicago, IL	1,000	26	1
1970	Chicago, IL	2,000	50	1
1972	Los Angeles, CA	2,500	50+	n/a
1975	Mt. Pleasant, MI	3,200	50+	10
1979	Brockport, NY	3,500	50+	20
1983	Baton Rouge, LA	4,000	50+	20
1987	South Bend, IN	4,700	50+	70
Special Olympics World Summer Games				
1991	Minneapolis, MN	6,000	50+	100
1995	New Haven, CT	7,000	50+	143
1999	Raleigh, NC	7,000	50+	150
2003	Dublin, Ireland	6,500	n/a	150
2007	Shanghai, People's Republic of China			

*Includes states, Puerto Rico, and other territories.

Table 5.5	Special Olympics World Winter Games (With Historical Event Names)		
Year	Location	Athletes	Countries
International Special Olympics Winter Games			
1977	Steamboat Springs, CO	500	n/a
1981	Smuggler's Notch and Stowe, VT	600	n/a
1985	Park City, UT	n/a	14
1989	Reno, NV, and Lake Tahoe, CA	1,000	18
Special Olympics World Winter Games			
1993	Salzburg and Schladming, Austria	1,600	50
1997	Toronto and Collingwood, Canada	2,000	73
2001	Anchorage, AK	1,800	70
2005	Nagano, Japan		

Additional International Games for Athletes With Disabilities

Although the Paralympics (Summer and Winter Games) and the IPC-sanctioned world championships, Deaflympics, and International Special Olympics are the best known and frequently identified as the major international multisport disability sport competitions, additional competitive sport opportunities for athletes with disabilities have been offered, currently exist, and will continue to emerge throughout the world. The material that follows is summarized from Bell (2003), *Encyclopedia of International Games.*

African Francophone Games for the Handicapped

The African Francophone Games for the Handicapped provide international competitions for athletes with physical, visual, mental, and hearing impairments for French-speaking, primarily African nations. The games were held every two years between the years of 1994 and 2000 (Burkina Faso; Cotonou, Benin; Senegal; Ivory Coast). The fifth Francophone Games were held in 2001 in Lome, Togo, where 500 athletes from 15 countries competed.

The Arab Games for the Handicapped

The Arab Games for the Handicapped were first held in 1999 in Amman, Jordan. These games were held to allow athletes in the region to participate in regional competitions. The games were open to athletes with physical, mental, visual, and hearing impairments. Sports included athletics, wheelchair basketball, weightlifting, target ball, table tennis, and football. Seven hundred athletes from Jordan, United Arab Emirates, Bahrain, Tunisia, Algeria, Palestine, Qatar, Lebanon, Libya, Egypt, Morocco, Syria, Saudi Arabia, Sudan, Iraq, and Yemen participated in the first games. The second Arab Games for the Handicapped were originally scheduled to be held in Algeria in 2003 but were postponed due to an earthquake in the region.

The Asia Pacific Games for the Deaf

The Asia Pacific Games for the Deaf originated from the Far Eastern International Deaf Football Championships Association, which held the first international football championships in Taipei, Taiwan, in 1983. After the addition of badminton to the international competition in 1992, the name of the association was changed to reflect the broadening of the sport program. In 1996, the Asia Pacific Games for the Deaf expanded to include four sports. These games have been held in Taipei, Hong Kong, Kyoto, Melbourne, Seoul, and Kuala Lumpur and were held in Kuwait City in 2004.

The British Commonwealth Paraplegic Games

In 1962, 100 athletes from 10 countries took part in competitions similar to the Commonwealth Games, games that would become known as the British Commonwealth Paraplegic Games. These games were an outgrowth of the Paralympic Games held in Rome in 1960. The British Commonwealth Paraplegic Games were held four times (Perth, 1962; Kingston, 1966; Edinburgh, 1970; Christchurch, 1974) in conjunction with the Commonwealth Games.

Although athletes with disabilities were provided with competitions in conjunction with the Commonwealth Games, it was not until 1994 that a breakthrough occurred. The games held in Vancouver, Canada, included demonstration events for athletes with disabilities in swimming, athletics, and lawn bowls. In 1997, the Commonwealth Games Federation unanimously approved a proposal to include athletes with disabilities and disability sports as full medal sports on the program of the Commonwealth Games effective beginning in 2006. Even before the required start, the 2002 Commonwealth Games held in Manchester, England, became the first major international multisport event to include athletes with disabilities as full medal participants.

Richard Nicholson

FAST FACTS

Home Base: Canberra, Australia
Sports: Powerlifting, wheelchair racing—road and track
Selected Accomplishments:

Medal winner in powerlifting at 2002 Commonwealth Games, 2002 World Championships

Paralympic medal winner, 2000

World and European medal winner in powerlifting

Australian national track and field participant (2003): placement in 100, 200, 400, and 800 meter

Canberra Marathon (2003): first place

Administrator for Aussie Sport

A former powerlifter and now a racer, Richard Nicholson plans to compete in both events in the Paralympics in 2004. His transformation from national and international record holder in powerlifting to track and road racing came about only recently. His strength from powerlifting is a great advantage in his technique for wheelchair racing. His initial 2003 season of competition in wheelchair racing found him earning second, third, fifth, and fourth place in the Australian Track and Field Nationals in the 100, 200, 400, and 800 meter, respectively. What a debut!

> *"Sport is so much more than results."*

Richard's personal relationship to sport is intense. He states, "My sport has become my way of life. Everything I do from my work as a sports administrator working in the disability sport area to the timing of my holidays all revolves around my training and competition commitments." Richard feels that "sport is so much more than training and competing. It is any opportunity to improve your quality of life through better health and fitness, meeting new people, making new friends, and the possibility of travel. Sport is so much more than results." It seems that Richard Nicholson knows what he is talking about.

The European Special Olympic Games

As an outgrowth of the Special Olympics movement in the United States, regional European Special Olympic Games were held for the first time in Brussels, Belgium, in 1981. These Games are held every four years throughout Europe and are organized by the Special Olympics Europe-Eurasia office in Brussels.

The Far East and South Pacific Games for the Disabled

Initially developed by the British Paraplegic Commonwealth Games, the Far East and South Pacific Games for the Disabled have been held irregularly since 1975. Athletes with disabilities who live in the South Pacific and Asia are eligible to compete in these games. The games were first held in 1975 in Japan and have rotated throughout the region (Australia in 1977, Hong Kong in 1982, Indonesia in 1986, Japan in 1989, China in 1994, Thailand in 1999, Korea in 2002). The next games are scheduled for Kuala Lumpur, Malaysia, in 2006.

The International Ex-Servicemen's Wheelchair Games

The International Ex-Servicemen's Wheelchair Games were held initially in 1993 in Aylesbury, England, and Pretoria, South Africa, in 1997. These games were organized by the Royal British Legion specifically for former British servicemen.

The Pan American Games

Regional competitions among the countries of the Americas are identified as Pan American. Several examples of competitions for athletes with disabilities exist. The Pan American Games for the Blind have offered competitions since 1997. The Pan American Games for the Deaf have been held only a few times (1975, Venezuela; 1999, Havana, Cuba; 2002, Santiago, Chile; and 2003, Buenos Aires, Argentina). The Pan American Games for Patients with Asthma have been held twice (Argentina in 2000 and Mexico in 2002). The most frequent of the Pan American Games is the Pan American Wheelchair Games. Wheelchair athletes from the Pan American region were able to compete in regional competitions beginning in 1967 in Canada and continuing through 1999 in Mexico City.

Cerebral Palsy Games

The Cerebral Palsy–International Sports and Recreation Association has offered international competitions for athletes with cerebral palsy and les autres since 1989. The Robin Hood Games were started in Nottingham, England, in 1989. Competition is held in athletics, lawn bowling, cycling, powerlifting, swimming, and table tennis.

The Stoke Mandeville Wheelchair Games

The Stoke Mandeville Wheelchair Games were the first games to be held for athletes with disabilities. They were founded by Sir Ludwig Guttman, who believed in sport as part of rehabilitation for veterans of World War II. These games, originated in 1948 in Aylesbury, England, are held almost every year. The name changed in 1997 to World Wheelchair Games; and in 1999, the games were held in Christchurch, New Zealand.

Transplant Games

Transplant Games have evolved recently to provide individuals with organ transplants the opportunity to compete on regional and international levels. Several events have been held, including the following:

- Eastern European Transplant Games held in Hungary in 1996
- European Heart Lung Transplant Games held regularly beginning in 1988 ('88 in Gorsel, The Netherlands; '90 in Paris, France; '91 in London, England; '92 in Enschede, The Netherlands; '94 in Helsinki, Finland; '96 in Lausanne, Switzerland; '98 in Bad Oeynhausen, Austria; and 2000 in Sandefjord, Norway)
- European Transplant Games held in Louvain, Belgium, in 1996; Athens in 2002; and Balaton, Hungary, in 2002
- Latin American Transplant Games held in 1998 in Buenos Aires, Argentina
- Asian Transplant Games held in Chiang Mai, Thailand, in 2002
- Winter World Transplant Games, initiated in 1994—held primarily in France
- 9th European Heart and Lung Transplant Games in Austria in 2002
- World Transplant Games, held initially in 1978 in England and in 1995 in London, Ontario, Canada

Winter World Games for the Disabled

The Vastermorland Association for Disabled Sports has held winter games every two years in Sweden. Biathlon, Nordic skiing, alpine skiing, and sledge hockey are the only sports offered.

World Championship for the Blind

The Spanish Federation for Blind Sports hosted the first World Blind Sports Championships in Madrid in 1998. These games were held under the auspices of the International Blind Sports Association. Over 700+

blind athletes competed in four sports (athletics, swimming, goal ball, and judo). The second International Blind Sports Association World Championships were held in Quebec City in 2003.

The World Dwarf Games

The World Dwarf Games were established by the Dwarf Athletic Association of America in 1993. These games were the first international multi-sport games for dwarf athletes. Since 1993, the games have been held in England and Canada.

KEY POINT

Competitive sport events in addition to the Paralympics, Deaflympics, and Special Olympics are available to disabled athletes all over the world and continue to emerge.

National Disability Sport Opportunities

Throughout the world, sport opportunities and competitions exist for individuals with disabilities. Although many of these occur within the general context of sport in a given society (e.g., sport clubs, sport-specific events), there are competitions specifically designed for athletes with disabilities. In the United States and Canada, events in a number of sports are held regularly (see appendix E).

Sport events and competitions for individuals with disabilities are found at the local, state, and regional levels. These take many forms, such as local parks and recreation programs (e.g., wheelchair basketball league, Deaf softball, local Special Olympics bowling program) and even interscholastic, intramural, and intercollegiate sport programs for individuals with disabilities. Increasingly, locally organized fun runs include a wheelchair division; track meets include heats for Special Olympians; and wheelchair basketball tournaments are scheduled on a regular basis. State Games (e.g., Sunshine State Games, Empire State Games) now often include events for athletes with disabilities.

This section provides a brief overview of selected examples of the numerous sport opportunities and competitions available in the United States and Canada. Examples cover various disability groups and the wide variety of available sports. These are offered as examples only and are not intended to constitute an exhaustive or even extensive review.

Lakeshore Foundation (Official U.S. Olympic and Paralympic Training Site)

Lakeshore Foundation has a long history of serving athletes with physical disabilities. It is a not-for-profit organization that provides sport training programs as well as recreation, fitness, and outdoor adventure opportunities. It has outstanding facilities specifically designed for individuals with physical disabilities and employs a highly qualified staff. In 2003, the U.S. Olympic Committee designated Lakeshore Foundation as the first-ever official USOC Training Site for both Olympic and Paralympic sports. Lakeshore Foundation is a current DSO member of USA Paralympics.

Lakeshore Foundation provides a variety of programs including aquatics exercise programs; athletics programs for youth and adults (tennis, swimming, basketball, power soccer, marksmanship, rugby, boccia, powerlifting, track and field); fitness programs; recreation and adventure programs (hand cycling, adventure weekends, after-school programs, sport skills); and special events including Demolition Derby, Wheelchair Rugby Tournament, Pioneer Classic Wheelchair Basketball Tournament, Sporting Clays Challenge, and World Challenge Wheelchair Tennis Championship.

The National Ability Center

The National Ability Center was founded in 1985. Its purpose is to provide affordable outdoor sport and recreation experiences for individuals of all ages and abilities. The center offers a variety of activities throughout the year, including alpine and Nordic skiing, snowboarding, swimming, cycling, waterskiing, horseback riding, and rafting. Additional experiences include camping trips and challenge course activities. Participants include those with orthopedic, spinal cord, neuromuscular, visual, and hearing impairments and cognitive and developmental disabilities.

National Sports Center for the Disabled (Winter Park Disabled Skiing Program)

Located in Winter Park, Colorado, the Winter Park Disabled Skiing Program offers the largest and best-known skiing program for disabled individuals in the world. Although originally intended for fun and games, the program grew into a serious educational and sport training enterprise. The program is designed to teach skiing to visually impaired and hearing-impaired persons as well as those with physical impairments including postpolio, amputations, spinal cord injuries, cerebral palsy, muscular dystrophy, and spina bifida. Local programs run essentially once a week for eight weeks but are provided on a weekly basis for out-of-state programs.

The program includes not only ski lessons but also sessions for training volunteer ski instructors and professional certified ski instructors. Specific lessons are designed to teach two-, three-, and four-track skiing, as well as mono- and sit-skiing, and specific techniques for teaching skiing to Deaf, blind, physically impaired, and developmentally delayed persons. Lessons on adaptive equipment and safety are provided as well. Much of the instruction is conducted in conjunction with the Winter Park Ski School. In addition, races and competitions are regularly scheduled throughout the ski season. For more information, see O'Leary (1987).

Variety Village Sport Training and Fitness Center

The Variety Village Sport Training and Fitness Center, located in Scarborough, a suburb of Toronto, is hailed as North America's model of accessibility. Variety Village is a multipurpose sport training facility with no physical or psychological barriers in an integrated setting of able-bodied and disabled sport enthusiasts. Once a community service activity in the form of a residential training school for physically disabled boys, the center has become a hub of integrated sport activity. Throughout its history, Variety Village has maintained its priority on serving persons with disabilities, but it has done so with the specific purpose of integration as well.

Every attempt has been made to achieve complete accessibility. For example, flooring throughout the facility is designed for easy discrimination for visually impaired persons, with raised-square tiles in the main hallways, carpeting in the offices, and ceramic raised-square surfaces in the baths and showers. The alarm system includes both a visual alarm and an auditory alarm system to accommodate persons with visual and hearing impairments. Baseboards are actually bumper guards for the wheelchairs.

All sport areas were specifically designed for individuals with all types of impairments. Among the adaptations of the track lanes are a synthetic surface with more give for those with amputations; corners without a bank, ideal for wheelchair users; inside lanes near special railings for blind runners; and typical lanes for able-bodied runners. The lighting was designed to eliminate all shadows on the playing surfaces, and appropriate adapted equipment is available. In addition to offering a year-round training center, Variety Village sponsors competitive events, which are designed for able-bodied and disabled persons alike.

Tampa General Rehabilitation Center

Among the ongoing activities of the Tampa General Rehabilitation Center is the annual Wellness Classic, advertised as a fun-filled event for the entire family. The Wellness Classic tends to include cycling events (12.5, 25, or 50 miles [20.1, 40.2, or 80.5 kilometers]), 5K wheelchair invitational, invigorating wellness walk, 5K road race, rollerblading, and a children's fitness circuit. The Tampa General Rehabilitation Center also regularly sponsors sport clinics, Disabled Sports USA fitness workshops, ski tours, wheelchair tennis tournaments, health workshops, a triathlon for the disabled, and the annual Catch the Leisure Wave. The Leisure Wave events include exhibitions of adapted golf, adaptive racquetball, walleyball, scuba diving, and quad rugby. The program at Tampa General Rehabilitation Center is but one example of many around the country.

Training and Sport Camps

Numerous training and sport camps have been developed for children and adults with disabilities. These include the following:

- National Wheelchair Basketball Association/Paralyzed Veterans of America Wheelchair Basketball Camp
- Randy Snow Wheelchair Tennis Camp
- Wheelchair Racing Camp
- Junior wheelchair sport camps
- Paralyzed Veterans of America National Trapshoot Clinic
- U.S. Aquatic Association of the Deaf Water Polo Camp
- Canoe White Water Wilderness Experience
- Kayak the Everglades
- Float the Rio Grande
- Movement Unlimited Sports Camp at California State University at Chico

State and Local Competitive Events

Competitive events for individuals with a disability are held in the United States on a weekly basis. These vary by season, geographic location, sponsoring agency, sport, and disability. Examples of these include the following:

- Disabled Sports USA Ski Spectacular
- Ski for Light International Week (annual)

- U.S. Cerebral Palsy Athletic Association Bowling Tournament (Tucson)
- U.S. Deaf Flag Football Super Bowl (Buffalo)
- Southern Softball Association of the Deaf Basketball Tournament (Virginia)
- US Deaf Sports Federation National Men's and Women's Slow Pitch Softball Tournament (Canoga Park, CA)
- Blister Bowl Wheelchair Football Tournament (Santa Barbara)
- SportsFest (Atlanta)
- AFL-CIO International Invitational Junior Wheelchair Basketball Tournament
- Honolulu Wheelchair Marathon
- Annual Open Powerlifting Meet (Oregon)
- Can-Am World Games
- Chicagoland Regional Beep Baseball Tournament
- Pre-Paralympic Powerlifting Competitions
- Midwest Deaf Annual Golf Tournament (Minnetonka, Minnesota)
- National Disabled Waterskiing Championships
- U.S. Association for Blind Athletes Judo Paralympic Trials (Colorado Springs)
- Mitsubishi Open Wheelchair Tennis
- National Paralyzed Veterans of America Trapshoot
- Midnite Sun Wheelchair Marathon
- Florida State Cerebral Palsy Games
- Deaf Women's Bowling Tournament (Palm Beach)

KEY POINT

Competitive events for athletes with disabilities in a large number of sports are held regularly throughout the United States and Canada.

Intercollegiate and Interscholastic Athletic Programs

Recent legislation (Section 504 of Rehabilitation Act, PL 94-142, ADA) in the United States has increased access to education by individuals with disabilities. Even before the passage of these laws, individuals with disabilities participated in intercollegiate and interscholastic athletic programs on a very selective basis. A few individuals with disabilities were able to overcome the obstacles to sport competition and participate alongside able-bodied athletes (Appenzeller, 1983; D'Alonzo, 1976).

Although increasing numbers of persons with disabilities are attending colleges and universities, their access to intramurals and other extracurricular activities including intercollegiate athletics has been minimal (Hedrick and Hedrick, 1993). In 1993, only 6 of the 803 National Collegiate Athletic Association member institutions offered complementary sport opportunities for athletes with disabilities.

The earliest of these was the University of Illinois at Urbana-Champaign. In 1948, Tim Nugent created a disability sport program out of which grew the National Wheelchair Basketball Association. This program provides athletic competitions in men's and women's basketball, wheelchair track and field, and quad rugby. The University of Illinois hosted the first National Intercollegiate Wheelchair Basketball Tournament in 1977. Sixteen teams associated with the National Wheelchair Basketball Association participated. One year later, the Central Intercollegiate Conference was formed. Because of the efforts of the Central Intercollegiate Conference, intercollegiate sports for students with a disability have become a reality on many college and university campuses around the country.

Over the years, the program has gained prominence and remains the strongest collegiate sport program for individuals with a disability. Today the program is known as the University of Illinois Adapted Varsity Athletics Program. Among the program's most outstanding graduates are Jean Driscoll, eight-time Boston Marathon winner, and numerous athletes who have competed successfully at the Paralympic Games and world championships. The program also claims another prominent graduate, Chuck Graham, a state legislator for Missouri (Suggs, 2004).

In 2004, seven universities in the United States funded intercollegiate athletics for wheelchair athletics (Suggs, 2004). Intercollegiate wheelchair basketball teams were founded at Edinboro University of Pennsylvania, Oklahoma State University, Southwest Minnesota State University, University of Illinois at Urbana-Champaign, University of Wisconsin, and University of Texas at Arlington. In addition, the University of Arizona and University of Illinois at Urbana-Champaign had intercollegiate track and field teams.

Sport opportunities for individuals with disabilities in public schools are limited. For example, in 1986 Dade County public schools offered a disabled sports program that allowed students with disabilities to compete in athletics, swimming, and weightlifting sport days and gave them access to selected competitions outside the public school system (i.e., Special Olympics).

Minnesota was the first state to formally establish an interscholastic athletic program for individuals with disabilities (Hedrick and Hedrick,

1993). This competitive program was housed within the Minnesota High School League (Hanson, 1993).

KEY POINT

Interscholastic and intercollegiate athletics are available in the United States to athletes with disabilities.

Concluding Comments

Numerous sport opportunities exist for individuals with disabilities. International and national events take place on a regular basis. Among these are Paralympics, Special Olympics World Games, Deaflympics, World Championships for the Mentally Handicapped, and numerous world championships in specific sports (e.g., wheelchair basketball). Additionally, athletes with disabilities regularly participate in events such as the Boston Marathon, Bay to Breakers Race (San Francisco), Bloomsday (Spokane, WA), and wheelchair marathons held around the world.

Since the 1970s, sport opportunities and competitions for individuals with disabilities have greatly increased. But although numerous opportunities exist, they are often not widely promoted. Concerted efforts must be made to share information about the existence of disability sport organizations and the opportunities for sport participation and competitions with disabled youth through our school systems as well as our recreation departments. College and university personnel can also play a major role in sharing information about sport for and including individuals with disabilities in course work provided to physical educators, athletic trainers, physical therapists, therapeutic recreation specialists, sport management majors, and others.

six

Sport and Disability: A World View

Reader Goal   Gain an understanding of the history and various structures for disability sport on a global basis

Chapter Synopsis

- Terminology
- International Perspectives: Late 20th Century
- European Charter for Sport for All
- European Perspectives
- Canadian Perspectives
- Perspectives From Oceania
- Perspectives From Asia
- Perspectives From the African Continent
- Perspectives From the Middle East
- Concluding Comments

Sport for and including individuals with disabilities is found throughout the world. The structure and organization of disability sport have varied in relation to the societal context of a given country and its national sport structure. In addition, disability sport has varied in relation to the societal context of disability. Due to the increasing visibility of athletes with disabilities and the presence of major international sport organizations (e.g., Olympics, Deaflympics, Paralympics, Special Olympics International), the organization of regional and national disability sport has evolved and become increasingly linked around the world.

This chapter presents a sampling of the structures serving athletes with disabilities from regions around the world. The discussion is limited to selected countries and regions, reflecting the availability of information in the literature and through the Internet. The structure of international disability sport and the United States perspective are discussed in chapter 4.

Terminology

One of the greatest challenges to understanding and communicating about disability sport worldwide is the terminology and the different meanings attached to a single term. A discussion of this phenomenon has been adapted from Doll-Tepper and DePauw (1989). Within the context of the United States, the terms "physical education," "sport," and "recreation/ leisure" are used to describe separate, although related, entities; the term "sport" is used in Europe to represent that which is encompassed by all of three of those terms. Specifically, "physical education" translates into German as "Sportunterrich an Schulen" (sport instruction in the schools), "leisure" or "recreation" as "Freizeit Sport" (free-time sport), and "competitive sport" as "Wettkampf." Additionally, the term "sport for all" is commonly used in Europe and other non-Western countries to describe sport and physical activity for all persons regardless of ability or disability. This phrase is also used to some extent in the United States but is not universal. Sport and physical activity programs for individuals with disabilities are conducted under such titles as sport and physical activity for disabled individuals (Finland), disabled sport (Denmark), education physique adaptée (Belgium), Sport (The Netherlands, Norway, Austria), and Sportunterricht (sport instruction)/Bewegungserziehung (movement education) (Germany). Those professionals involved with disability sport are known as physical educators, sport teachers, trainers, coaches, and even therapists.

The historic World Health Organization's definitions of impairment, disability, and handicap were accepted throughout the world, although the actual use of these terms and others to describe individuals with a disability differed by country. For example, learning-disabled persons in

Germany are those who have learning difficulties and an IQ between 70 and 90; only those with an IQ below 70 are classified as mentally retarded. In the United States anyone with an IQ below 90 would be classified as mentally retarded. "Special populations" in the United States usually implies persons with disabilities; but in Finland, "special" groups include "the disabled, the aged, and persons suffering from long-term illnesses" (Koivumaki, 1987, p. 57).

For many years, debate has taken place about the medical model and a functional model of disability and classification. In 2002, the WHO developed an International Classification of Functioning, Disability and Health that is referred to as ICF and is described as a classification of health and health-related domains (body functions, body structures, activity, and participation) within a societal context. While the ICF is a framework for health and the experience of disability, the emphasis is on health and functioning (level of capacity and level of performance) rather than disease, impairment, and disability.

In this book, we have made every attempt to use words that are consistent in meaning and to describe any differences as they occur. Throughout, the frame of reference is sport, not physical education or leisure. In most instances, sport refers primarily to the formal organization of competitive sport and includes developmental sport opportunities. Any deviations are noted.

International Perspectives: Late 20th Century

Each country is unique in its approach to accessibility, opportunity, education, physical activity, and sport for individuals with a disability. Laws, regulations, and rules vary accordingly and are not universal. On the other hand, two organizations (United Nations and United Nations Educational, Scientific, and Cultural Organization [UNESCO]) have proclaimed the universal rights of individuals with a disability.

On December 9, 1975, the General Assembly of the United Nations adopted the following passage, Resolution 3447, as part of the Declaration on the Rights of Disabled Persons:

> Disabled persons, whatever the origin, nature and seriousness of their handicaps and disabilities, have the same fundamental rights as their fellow citizens of the same age, which implies first and foremost the right to enjoy a decent life, as normal and full as possible. (Declaration of Rights of Disabled Persons, 1975, #3)

As a direct result of this and other United Nations declarations, education of individuals with disabilities was ensured as an integral part of

cultural development; equal access to leisure activities became insepa-
rable from social integration; and the general quality of life of disabled
individuals was vastly improved (Sherrill, 1986).

In April 1976, the first International Conference of Ministers and Senior
Officials Responsible for Physical Education and Sport was held under
the auspices of UNESCO. At this conference, the right of persons with
disabilities to participate in physical education and sport was established
(Stein, 1986).

The United Nations not only enacted a "bill of rights" for persons
with disabilities but declared 1981 the International Year for Disabled
Persons. Many nations followed this lead and declared a National Year
for Disabled Persons in 1982.

KEY POINT

Disability sport is a global phenomenon, although each country is unique
in the way it approaches accessibility, opportunity, education, physical
activity, and sport for individuals with disabilities.

European Charter for Sport for All

Throughout Western Europe, sport programs for persons with a disability
are found in the schools and throughout a sport club system. Because
clubs are locally organized and developed in response to community
interests and initiatives, there are sport clubs whose members include
individuals with disabilities as well as able-bodied persons. There are
also clubs for persons with a variety of disabilities and clubs for able-
bodied persons or persons with one specific disability (e.g., Deaf). Some
of these sport clubs are associated with a rehabilitation center (e.g.,
Belgium, Austria); school; or community, town, or city (DePauw and
Doll-Tepper, 1989).

In anticipation of the "unification" of Europe (the European Union or
EU) in 1992, the Conference of European Ministers Responsible for Sport
passed a series of resolutions, titled the European Charter for Sport for
All: Disabled Persons. Although the European Charter was passed in
1987, its history can be traced back to 1980, when the Committee for the
Development of Disabled Sport commissioned a study as a contribution
to the 1981 International Year for the Disabled. During that same year, the
European Ministers Responsible for Sport adopted a resolution outlin-
ing the main priorities for European and national policies for sport for
disabled individuals. Six years later, the European Charter was finalized.
It is divided into two parts: one devoted to discussion of disability sport
and the other to the accessibility of sport and recreation facilities. The

following summarizes the major points of the European Charter (for more discussion see DePauw and Doll-Tepper, 1989):

1. Disabled persons are defined as those who are not able to participate in most sports or physical recreation without some adjustment in the form of special equipment or training. These individuals include those who are mentally retarded, physically or multiply disabled, chronically ill (diabetic, asthmatic, cardiac), blind, Deaf, or mute.

2. Sport for All is comprehensive and includes four main types of sport: top-level (elite) sport, organized sport (club sport), recreational sport, and health sport for medical reasons or for fitness purposes. In addition, sport is purported to be beneficial as therapy or rehabilitation, or both, for disabled persons.

3. Sport for All for disabled persons must be promoted because (a) disabled persons have the same right to sport as able-bodied individuals; (b) sport adds to the quality of life of participants; (c) disabled persons can achieve to the highest level of competition; and (d) disabled persons receive both the physiological and social benefits of participation.

4. Governments have the responsibility to ensure that every person, disabled or not, has the opportunity to participate in sport and physical recreation at the level one desires. Sport and recreation facilities must be accessible to disabled persons.

5. National sport organizations, public or semipublic agencies, and clubs must consider the needs of disabled persons in decisions concerning sport or policies.

6. In sport, as well as in other areas of society, integration of disabled individuals and able-bodied persons is essential. An adequate and sufficient range of appropriate sport opportunities should be provided for individuals with disabilities. Able-bodied sport federations must assume increasingly more responsibility for the sport needs and interests of disabled individuals including (a) educating trainers and coaches, (b) officiating and refereeing sport events, (c) organizing competitions for disabled individuals, (d) developing youth programs, (e) including events for disabled athletes at competitions for able-bodied athletes, and (f) organizing regular integrated activities and events.

7. Sport for disabled persons requires the coordination and cooperation of physicians, physical therapists, occupational therapists, physical education teachers, elementary school teachers, special education teachers, and sport administrators. A coordinated effort should include the provision of sport programs, accessibility to

sport facilities, transportation assistance, and technical aids for sport participation.

8. Physical education for disabled students should be provided in regular schools.

9. Research on sport for individuals with disabilities should include (a) "state-of-the-art review," (b) benefits of participation, (c) classification and integration, (d) coaching and training, and (e) professional preparation.

10. Training and education must be provided for sport personnel including (a) knowledge of impairment or disability, (b) understanding of specific disabilities and the implications for daily activities, (c) knowledge of physical activity appropriate for specific disabilities, (d) knowledge of technical and scientific research in adapted physical activity, and (e) ability to communicate with individuals with disabilities.

11. Sport for disabled persons should receive media coverage to (a) positively influence the public's attitudes toward disabled individuals, (b) recruit disabled persons into sport, and (c) create an appreciation of disabled athletes similar to that for able-bodied athletes.

12. Governments should ensure that disabled persons receive a fair share of money available to sport in general.

13. Individuals with permanent illness, chronic impairment, or mental illness must also have access to sport programs organized on their behalf.

Although the European Charter stands as the basis of Sport for All including individuals with disabilities throughout Europe, each country is unique in its application of the principles espoused.

European Perspectives

The European Paralympic Committee (EPC) serves as the coordinating body of disability sport throughout Europe, has formal relations to the International Paralympic Committee (IPC), and hosts EPC championships. The formal structure of the EPC includes a general assembly, management committee, and executive committee. The executive committee is composed of a president, secretary general, treasurer, technical officer, four members-at-large, and an athlete representative. The president of the EPC represents Europe on the IPC executive committee. The EPC works closely with the IPC, International Organizations of Sport for the Disabled (IOSDs), and the 50+ member organizations identified in appendix F.

Thomas Geierspichler

FAST FACTS

Home Base: Salzburg, Austria
Sports: Wheelchair racing and quad rugby
Selected Accomplishments:

Paralympic medal winner 2000
World record holder
European champion

This relative newcomer to the world of disability sport is a quadriplegic competing in wheelchair racing. His accomplishments since 1998 have been exceptional. He had three European championships in 2003 in the 400 meter, 800 meter, and marathon in his class. He has a world record in the 1,500 meter and 5,000 meter. He also established world champion performances in 2002 in the 800 meter, 1,500 meter, 5,000 meter, and marathon. His bronze medal finish in the marathon in the 2000 Sydney Paralympics was his first effort. Thomas is a serious athlete. He trains daily and accumulates up to 250 miles (400 kilometers) per week in a sport center with able-bodied athletes. According to Thomas, "Sport brought a new meaning into my life . . . success is my motivation. It is a feeling of deep satisfaction to push your limits, to reach your self-determined goals." Thomas's perspective demonstrates his personal growth through sport. He also states, "Moving even beyond your limits helps your personality grow. You move from one dimension into the next." Thomas sees the need for young athletes "to not be scared off by hard work, to invest in themselves because after a while it is incredibly beautiful." By his actions and accomplishments, Thomas Geierspichler has become a beacon for others to follow.

> *"Sport brought a new meaning into my life . . . success is my motivation."*

In its first years of operations, the EPC entered into a partnership agreement with the European Disability Forum and the IPC to promote 2003 as the European Year of People with Disabilities and 2004 as the European Year of Education through Sport. At the heart of this partnership is the commitment to promote and expand the opportunities for individuals with disabilities to play a more active role in society.

Denmark

Sport is reported to be the primary cultural activity in which Danish citizens participate; approximately 45% participate in clubs, which are numerous. These sport clubs are self-organized and self-governed, and many include individuals with disabilities. In addition, a few separate sport clubs are composed only of visually impaired, mentally retarded, or Deaf members.

The Danish Sport Organization for the Disabled (DSOD), formed in 1971, serves as the national governing body for disability sport. Its purpose is to promote and organize recreational as well as competitive sports for all individuals with disabilities and to promote the use of sport for rehabilitation. Inasmuch as the DSOD serves all disability groups, it is recognized as representing the national disability organizations and sport federations alike. Many of its activities are conducted conjointly with the Danish sport federations.

Four organizational levels exist: club, county, region, and national. Clubs have the primary responsibility for daily sport activities in a given community. At the county level, the primary tasks include disseminating information, recruiting new members and coaches (trainers), and assisting in forming new clubs. The primary regional responsibility is sponsoring regional sport tournaments, including the qualifying events for national tournaments. The responsibilities of the national level include sponsoring national sport events, establishing sport rules and regulations, educating and training coaches and officials, public relations, and fielding a disabled team to represent Denmark at international competitions.

The organizational structure of DSOD is similar only to that found in Sweden, Norway, and Iceland. Other European countries, and most of the rest of the world, have more than one national disability sport organization. Special Olympics International (SOI) reports an SOI chapter in Denmark, and Deaf sport is very active there. The Danish Sport Organization for the Disabled serves as the National Paralympic Committee and represents Danish athletes to the IPC.

Scandinavia (Norway, Sweden, Finland)

Norway and Sweden have structures of disability sport similar to that of Denmark. Only one national disability sport organization exists in each country: Norwegian Sport Organization for the Disabled (NSOD) and Swedish Federation for Sports for the Disabled (SHIF). In addition, the Nordsk Handicapped Sport Organization fosters communication and cooperation among Iceland, Denmark, Sweden, Finland, Faroe Islands, and Norway. These disability sport associations now serve as the National Paralympic Committees in their respective countries.

Deaf athletic associations are active in both Norway and Sweden. Autonomous associations exist for Deaf sports, but these are affiliated officially with NSOD and SHIF. Special Olympics International reports an SOI chapter in Norway but not in Sweden (the offices of International Sports Federation for Persons with Intellectual Disabilities [INAS-FID] are located in Sweden).

Disability sport in Finland is structured slightly differently and includes a broader segment of the population. In Finland, "special groups" include individuals with disabilities, the aged, and persons with long-term illnesses. Although Finnish sport clubs are prevalent, only just recently have a few begun to provide opportunities for individuals with disabilities. For the most part, the sport and physical activity needs of these individuals have been met by municipal sport offices and specific organizations serving segments of the population referred to as "special groups."

Four national sport organizations serve the disabled population in Finland: the Finnish Association of Sports for the Disabled (FASD), the Sports Committee of the Finnish Central Association of the Visually Handicapped, the Finnish Athletic Association of the Deaf, and the Disabled War Veterans Sports Association. In addition, a welfare organization meets the needs of individuals with mental retardation; this group has joined both SOI and INAS-FMH.

These organizations are responsible for providing the main sport forms including rehabilitation, physical education in the schools, sport for all, and competitive sports for the disabled. The FASD local sport offices are the most important entity for offering sport opportunities, whereas its national office has the primary responsibility for sponsoring competitive sport experiences.

In 1994 the Finnish Paralympic Committee (FPC) evolved from FASD to assume its role as the national Paralympic committee that allowed FASD to continue its specific responsibilities for disability sport in Finland. The Finnish Paralympic Committee is responsible for preparing and fielding the Finnish team to participate in the Paralympic Games. To accomplish its goals, FPC works in close cooperation with the Finnish Olympic Committee and is a member of the IPC. The Finnish Paralympic Committee has expanded its membership and is composed of the following member organizations: the Finnish Association of Sports for the Disabled, the Finnish Federation of the Visually Impaired, and the Finnish Sports Federation for Persons with Intellectual Disabilities. The Disabled War Veterans Sports Association is an honorary member of the committee, and the Finnish Athletic Association of the Deaf and the Finnish Transplant Sports Federation are candidate members of the committee.

Germany

Sport in Germany is organized around the German Federation of Sport (Deutsches Sportbund, DSB); disability sport is a part of this structure (DePauw and Doll-Tepper, 1989). The German Sport Federation for the Disabled (Deutsches Behinderten Sportverband, DBS) is the officially recognized representative of sport for individuals with a disability throughout Germany. It now serves as the National Paralympic Committee and represents German athletes with disabilities at the IPC.

Germany also utilizes a sport club system. Opportunities are organized by sport clubs at the city or community level, by state sport associations (Landessportbunde), and by the DSB. This pattern is the same for disability sport. At the national level, the DBS is responsible for all types of sport including rehabilitation, recreation, and competitive sport. Under its auspices, sport is offered for the disabled (physically, sensory, and mentally retarded) and for health-impaired persons as well. The DBS organizes national competitions and selects the team members to represent Germany in European and world competitions. The German Sport Federation for the Deaf (Deutsches Gehorlosen Sportverband) appears to have status equal to that of the DBS, and the German Wheelchair Sport Association exists under the DBS umbrella.

Since the early 1980s, a nonprofit organization (Lebenshilfe) focusing on the needs and interests of mentally retarded individuals has coordinated Special Olympics activities. The Lebenshilfe exists outside the officially recognized disability sport structure in Germany (Doll-Tepper and DePauw, 1989).

Britain

The British Sports Association for the Disabled (BSAD) was founded in 1961 as an outgrowth of the efforts of Sir Ludwig Guttmann. It was then, and is now, an association composed of national disability sports organizations. In addition, the BSAD has a network of 10 regional associations including Wales, Scotland, and Northern Ireland and more than 450 sport clubs. The BSAD organizes educational conferences and seminars, coaches' training programs, and sport events at the county, regional, and national levels. The BSAD is also responsible for representation by British disabled athletes at international sport competitions.

Many national associations exist in Britain; some are affiliated with BSAD, and some are separate and enjoy official recognition by the British Sports Council. The disability-specific associations affiliated with BSAD include British Amputee Sports Association, British Association for Sporting and Recreational Activities of the Blind, British Deaf Sports Council, British Paraplegic Sports Society, United Kingdom Sports Association for People with Mental Handicap, CP-Sports Within the Spastics Society, and British Les Autres Sports Association. Other associations include Riding for the Disabled Association, BSAD Water Sports Division, PHAB (Physically Handicapped and Able-Bodied) youth sport clubs, and Special Olympics UK.

In 1989, the British Paralympic Association (BPA) was formed. Among its responsibilities is that of preparing and fielding a team to compete at the Paralympic Games. The BPA is composed of organizations representing Paralympic Sports, national disability sport organizations, Home Country Elite Disability Sport organizations, an Athletes' Commission, and elected officers. The BPA debates and recommends policy to the General Purposes Committee, the quadrennially elected trustees/directors who plan, refine, and implement policies and future strategy for BPA.

Canadian Perspectives

The organization of sport in Canada initially revolved around the Minister of State for Fitness and Amateur Sport. This office had oversight for national sport organizations, including disability sport. Specifically, the Canadian Federation of Sport Organizations for the Disabled (CFSOD) served as the national governing body. Informally organized in 1979, CFSOD was formally incorporated in 1981. Its purpose is to facilitate, coordinate, and promote sport for athletes with disabilities through cooperative action among its member organizations.

Originial members of CFSOD include the Canadian Wheelchair Sports Association, the Canadian Association for Disabled Skiing, the Canadian Blind Sports Association, the Canadian Amputee Sports Association, the Canadian Deaf Sports Association, and the Canadian Cerebral Palsy Sports Association. The Sports Funds for the Physically Disabled is a nonprofit, federally incorporated organization whose sole purpose is to raise money to support sport competitions among disabled Canadian athletes. In 1988, it was successful in supporting the Canadian team at the 1988 Winter and Summer Games for the Disabled (now known as the Winter and Summer Paralympic Games).

In 1986, Canada undertook a collaborative effort to address the physical activity needs of its disabled citizens. This effort, known as the Jasper Talks Symposium, was sponsored by the Adapted Programs Special Interest Group of the Canadian Association for Health, Physical Education and Recreation (CAHPER); Fitness Canada; and the University of Alberta. Inasmuch as Section 15 of the Canadian Charter of Rights and Freedoms (1982) forbids discrimination on the basis of disability and calls for suitable opportunities for all to be physically active

(Wall, 1990), the Jasper Talks resulted in a strategic plan for adapted physical activity in Canada.

The CFSOD continued to serve as the coordinating body for disability sport in Canada through 1993, at which time CFSOD changed its structure and mandate and became the Canadian Paralympic Committee (CPC) with the mission to develop and grow the Paralympic movement in Canada. The CPC is a not-for-profit, charitable, private corporation recognized by the IPC as the National Paralympic Committee of Canada. CPC consists of numerous active members such as Athletics Canada; Alpine Canada; Canadian Blind Sport Association; Canadian Cerebral Palsy Sports Association; Sledge Hockey of Canada; and affiliate members such as Active Living Alliance for Canadians with a Disability, Badminton Canada, Canadian Association for Disabled Skiing, Triathlon Canada, and Water Ski Canada, to name a few.

Perspectives From Oceania

The Oceania region has increased its visibility during the past decade. The two primary countries that compose this region are New Zealand and Australia.

New Zealand

In 1962, a lone participant from New Zealand entered the first British Commonwealth Paraplegic Games held in Perth, Western Australia. Since then, a team of New Zealanders has been sent to the major international sport events for athletes with disabilities.

In cooperation with local "associations," sport competitions for disabled athletes were initiated in New Zealand: specifically, the First Inter Provincial Games in Christchurch (1966) and the First National Games for the Disabled in Auckland (1968). The New Zealand Paraplegic and Physically Disabled Federation was formed in 1968 to enable athletes to officially enter the Paralympics in Tel Aviv.

The national games continue today, but the Commonwealth Games were replaced eventually by the 1975 Far East and South Pacific International Games (FESPIC) in Japan. New Zealand has continued to send athletes to regional games, world championships, and the Summer and Winter Paralympics. In addition, New Zealand sent Neroli Fairhall to compete in archery from a wheelchair at the Los Angeles Olympics in 1984.

The New Zealand Paraplegic and Physically Disabled Federation served in the past as the national governing body and worked closely with 17 local associations and with individual members. In addition, it represented New Zealand with International Sports Organization for the Disabled (ISOD), International Blind Sports Association (IBSA), Cerebral

Maria Liduina Patricia de Souza

FAST FACTS:

Home Base: Sao Paulo, Brazil
Sports: Swimming
Selected Accomplishments:

Medal, Argentina games 2001

World championships 2001—gold medalist in regional games and silver medalist in masters

Brazilian Champion 2002

Participates in open-sea marathons as well as masters competition

This 30-something athlete experienced a traumatic amputation at age 15 and is a newcomer to disability sport. Through her family, friends, physiotherapist, and a favorite physical education teacher/coach, Maria has mastered a variety of swimming events. She has turned in medal-winning performances in the last several years in short distances and relays. Maria also swims in "aquatic sea crossing" events that are open-sea, marathon types of competitions. Her five-day-a-week training schedule for 2.5 hours each day is demanding. For young people, Maria recommends "looking for an association or sport organization and begin to practice physical activities as soon as possible. . . ." To Maria, "Sport means life . . . it benefits my body, my soul, my health. . . ." Maria Liduina Patricia de Souza is a winner in the water or out!

"Sport means life . . . it benefits my body, my soul, my health. . . ."

Palsy–International Sport and Recreation Association (CP-ISRA), and International Stoke Mandeville Wheelchair Sports Federation (ISMWSF). The federation was closely affiliated with other disability sport organizations in New Zealand, including the Royal N.Z. Foundation for the Blind, N.Z. Skiing for the Disabled, N.Z. Road Wheelers Association, N.Z. Wheelchair Basketball Association, and N.Z. Amputee Sports Association. The New Zealand Federation changed its name to ParaFed in the early 1990s and in October 1998 to Paralympics New Zealand.

Paralympics New Zealand is the national sporting organization for disability sport in New Zealand and is recognized by the IPC as the National Paralympic Committee responsible for Paralympic sports in New Zealand.

Paralympics New Zealand encourages and supports sporting opportunities for individuals with a disability, ranging from club sport to elite international competitions offered through a network of regional ParaFed Associations, National Sporting Organizations, and sport clubs. Paralympics New Zealand is responsible for the preparation and fielding of a team for the Paralympics, world championships, and other international competitions.

Australia

The first sport opportunities for individuals with disabilities in Australia were available to Deaf individuals in 1954, under the auspices of the Australian Deaf Sports Federation. Wheelchair sports in Australia began in 1972. Shortly thereafter, a group of disabled sport representatives convened to develop one organization that would speak on behalf of all disability sport groups to the Australian government (Grant and Pryke, 1987). By 1979, a constitution was adopted for the national body, the Australian Sports Council for the Handicapped. Its name was changed in 1984 to Australian Confederation of Sports for the Disabled.

The Australian Confederation provides a means whereby associations serving disabled sport can discuss matters of importance to disabled athletes. Members include the Australian Paraplegic and Quadriplegic Sports Federation, Australian Deaf Sports Federation, Ltd., Australian Cerebral Palsy Association, Riding for the Disabled Association of Australia, Amputees Sporting Association of Australia, Australian Blind Sports Federation, and Australian Disabled Skiers Federation.

Under the auspices of the Australian Paraplegic and Quadriplegic Sports Federation, the national governing body of wheelchair sports, are seven state sport organizations (e.g., New South Wales Wheelchair Sports Association, Western Australia Disabled Sports Association). Collectively and individually, these associations provide sport opportunities for wheelchair users throughout Australia. Deaf sport, cerebral palsy sport, and amputee sport are also organized by a national governing body with state associations.

Originally formed in 1990, the Australian Paralympic Committee (APC) is the national governing body for Australia's elite athletes with disabilities. Its primary mission is to facilitate success by athletes in the Paralympic Games and other IPC-sanctioned events and to encourage sport participation among individuals with a disability. The APC includes four umbrella organizations (ACT and Region Disabled Sport and Recreation Association, NSW Sports Council for the Disabled, QLD Sporting Wheelies and Disabled, Western Australian Disabled Sports Association) and the following national disability sport organizations:

- Australian Sports Organization for the Disabled Inc.
- Australian Athletes with a Disability Ltd

- Australian Wheelchair Sports
- Australian Blind Sport Federation
- Cerebral Palsy–Australian Sports and Recreation Federation
- Disabled Winter Sport Australia
- Riding for the Disabled Australia

Sport for intellectually handicapped, or mentally retarded, persons in Australia follows a different model: Sport is considered at all levels and depends upon access, awareness, attitudes, acceptance, ability, and advocacy (South Australian Sport and Recreation Association of People with Integration Difficulties [SASRAPID], 2004). This has led to the establishment of both integrated and segregated sport programs for intellectually handicapped persons at the local and state levels. The association acts as an advocate for the participation of intellectually disabled persons in sport. Many of its efforts are coordinated with the sport associations. The programs are established to integrate intellectually disabled persons into the regular club sport programs and competitions as well. The programs are unique to the club, the sport, and the persons involved. Sport for intellectually disabled persons varies across the states of Australia. State associations affiliated with SASRAPID are found in Western Australia, New South Wales, Queensland, and Victoria. Special Olympics programs are found in Tasmania, New South Wales, Australian Capital Territory, and Victoria.

Perspectives From Asia

Sport opportunities for individuals with disabilities exist in Asian countries. Disability sport is a more recent development in Asia than in Europe or North America. To date, programs are continuing to emerge. The following discussion presents but a sketch of disability sport in Asia, as it remains somewhat difficult to obtain current information from these countries.

China

Disability sport in China is a very recent phenomenon. Minimal sport opportunities existed for individuals with disabilities prior to the 1980s. The first evidence of international competition by disabled Chinese athletes was recorded at the FESPIC in 1982. The Chinese Sports Association for the Disabled was then founded on October 21, 1983, in Tianjin with the assistance of the Chinese government. The vice director of the Physical Culture and Sports Commission of the People's Republic of China not only attended the inaugural meeting but participated in the activities.

The first China National Games for the Disabled were held in Hefei, Anhui, in 1984. Over 500 athletes representing 29 provinces, municipalities, and regions including Hong Kong participated in 168 separate events.

The Third National Games were held March 18-23, 1992, in Guangzhou. Over 1,200 athletes from all over the country and Hong Kong and the Macao regions competed in six events: athletics, swimming, table tennis, shooting, weightlifting, and wheelchair basketball. Interestingly, these were the first national games after the passage of the Protection Law for the Disabled People.

The Chinese Sports Association for the Disabled has represented disabled athletes internationally in such organizations as CP-ISRA, IBSA, and ISOD. Since the 1980s, Chinese disabled athletes have been regular participants at international competitions and world championships. China sent its first official delegation to the 1984 International Games for the Disabled (now known as the Summer Paralympics) held at Hofstra University in Hempstead, New York.

In 1985, the Chinese Sports Association for the Mentally Retarded was formed and was accepted as a member of SOI one month later. China sent its first delegation to the 1987 International Special Olympics held at Notre Dame University in South Bend, Indiana.

Hong Kong

Disability sport in Hong Kong is organized around three groups: Deaf, mentally retarded, and physically impaired. Three organizations attempt to provide sport opportunities: Hong Kong Sports Association of the Deaf, Special Hong Kong Olympics, and the Hong Kong Sports Association for the Physically Disabled.

The oldest of these, the Hong Kong Sports Association for the Physically Disabled (HKSAP), was established in 1972. Its purposes are to (a) promote and encourage sport activities among physically disabled persons, (b) organize a variety of sports and training programs, (c) promote public awareness of disability sport, (d) select and organize the Hong Kong teams for all international competitions, and (e) increase athletic performances.

Sports associated with HKSAP include archery, athletics, wheelchair basketball, fencing, lawn bowls, judo, rifle shooting, swimming, table tennis, and wheelchair tennis. Training sessions are regularly scheduled. In addition, HKSAP offers special school programs, community sport programs, national team training, and participation in international competitions including Paralympics, FESPIC, world championships and games, international youth championships and games, and invitational championships and games.

In its capacity as the national governing body, HKSAP holds affiliate membership with ISMWSF, ISOD, IBSA, and CP-ISRA. The association is also recognized by the Amateur Sports Federation and Olympic Committee of Hong Kong. The organization serves as the National Paralympic Committee and represents Hong Kong at the IPC.

Korea

In response to the International Year of Disabled Persons, the annual Korean National Games for the Disabled began in 1981. In 1988, the very successful 8th Paralympics were held in Seoul, South Korea, under the auspices of the Seoul Paralympic Organizing Committee. In 1989, this committee became the Korea Sports Association for the Disabled (KOSAD). On April 28th, the Ministry of Health and Social Affairs officially approved KOSAD as the national governing body for disabled sport in Korea. The association serves in the fields of sport, culture, and art in the greatest harmony for disabled persons in Korea. Specifically its functions include promoting disability sport throughout Korea, sponsoring cultural and art events performed by disabled persons, organizing national games and other sport events, conducting research on sport and rehabilitation, operating sport facilities for disabled athletes, and providing health and recreational sport programs. The association is also the National Paralympic Committee and serves as a representative to the IPC.

In addition to KOSAD, Deaf athletes are served through the Korea Deaf Sports Federation. This federation was officially recognized as an International Committee of Sports for the Deaf (CISS) member in 1987. It is organized around a club system and offers programs in athletics, swimming, soccer, table tennis, and shooting.

Japan

Japanese athletes with disabilities have participated in sport longer than any of their Asian neighbors. The Japanese Athletic Association of the Deaf became a CISS member in 1936. Under its auspices Deaf athletes are provided with competitions and training in alpine skiing, soccer, tennis, athletics, judo, volleyball, baseball, and table tennis. The Japanese Athletic Association of the Deaf regularly fields a national team to represent Japan in the Summer and Winter World Games for the Deaf.

Japan hosted the first FESPIC in Oita in 1975 to promote the general interest and welfare of disabled persons through participation in sport events. These first games included 690 athletes with amputations, visual impairments, and other physical disabilities from 18 countries in the Far East and South Pacific region. Japan has also played a significant role in wheelchair road racing. In 1981, as part of the celebrations for the International Year for Disabled Persons, the annual Oita International Wheelchair Marathon began.

The Japanese Paralympic Committee serves as the coordinating organization for Paralympic sport in Japan. It prepares and fields teams for Paralympic Games and world championships. It is a member of the IPC.

Perspectives From the African Continent

Sport for individuals with a disability in Africa tends to be structured differently in each country. These structures include a sport society for the disabled, an "Olympic-type" sport federation for the disabled, and a government ministry office for organizing disability sport. In addition, opportunities can be found in conjunction with rehabilitation institutions. Although in these instances sport is included, medical rehabilitation is often given priority over sport.

In selected African nations a specialized federation for disability sport is organized at the local, regional, and national levels. Often the federation includes technical and sport-specific committees. In general, it is an umbrella organization serving various types of disabilities.

One example is the South African Sports Association for Physically Disabled. Established in 1962, it was originally called the South African Paraplegic Games Association (Barrish and Ndungane, 1988). It has since expanded to include other physically disabled individuals. The South African Sports Association for Physically Disabled is the only national governing body that serves without regard to race, creed, or color. It is an "autonomous amateur sport organization which conducts its affairs on a nonracial and nonpolitical basis" (Barrish and Ndungane, 1988, p. 13). The South African Sports Association held membership in ISMWSF, ISOD, IBSA, CP-ISRA, and the IPC. In 2001, the official name of the association was changed to Disability Sport South Africa.

The overarching goal of Disability Sport South Africa is to promote, manage, administer, and coordinate the competitive and recreational participation in sport activities by individuals with a disability in the Republic of South Africa. The organization works closely with the SA Commonwealth Games Association, All Africa Games, and the SA Federal Council on Disability and other national disability sport federations (SA Deaf Sports Federation, SA Sports Association for Intellectually Impaired, and SA Sports Association for Physically Disabled) to coordinate the preparation of athletes, classifiers, coaches, officials, and management for international sport competitions including the Commonwealth Games, All Africa Games, Paralympics, Deaflympics, IPC world championships, and other world championships sanctioned by ISODs.

In 1987, the African Sports Confederation of the Disabled (ASCOD) was founded in Algeria. In December 2001, ASCOD became the African Paralympic Committee (APC) as well. The purposes of ASCOD are as follows:

1. Coordinate and promote sports for persons with disabilities in Africa (locomotion disabilities [wheelchair and ambulant], sensory disabilities [deaf, blind, and visually impaired], intellectual disabilities, and cerebral palsy)
2. Coordinate and sanction the sport competitions
3. Seek the integration of sports for athletes with disabilities into the sport movements for able-bodied athletes while safeguarding and preserving the identity of sports for disabled athletes
4. Liaise with respect to these objectives and principles of the IPC and the international federations for disability groups as follows:
   - International Stokes Mandeville Wheelchair Sports Federation
   - International Sports Organization for the Disabled
   - Cerebral Palsy–International Sport and Recreation Association
   - International Sports Federation for Persons with Intellectual Disability
   - International Committee of Sports for the Deaf
   - International Blind Sport Association
   - All international sport federations and committees, Supreme Council of Sports in Africa, African National Olympic Committees Organization, Union Confederations Des Sports African

Members of the ASCOD executive committee include the president, three vice presidents, secretary general, treasurer, zone representatives (seven), athletes' representative, and a women's representative. The confederation is a membership organization (full and associate members) and holds a general assembly to conduct its business.

Perspectives From the Middle East

Disability sport opportunities are known to exist throughout the Middle East and to have existed for many years. Although sometimes with great difficulty, athletes with disabilities from the Middle East have competed in the Paralympic Games, Deaflympics, and Special Olympics as well as regional games and world championships.

It is important to note that Israel played an important role in the early history of the Paralympic Games. The 1968 Paralympic Games were held in Tel Aviv and included 750 athletes from 29 countries. Lawn bowling, women's basketball, and a 100-meter wheelchair race for men were offered for the first time at these Games.

Inasmuch as regional representation is important to the IPC, each of the IPC's six regions (Africa, Americas, Asia, Europe, Middle East, and South Pacific) has an official regional representative to the IPC. The Middle East is represented by Abdul Hakim Al-Matar from Saudi Arabia. Although many of these nations are still developing opportunities for athletes with disabilities, the following National Paralympic Committees have been formed within the Middle East:

- Afghanistan Paralympic Federation
- Bahrain Disabled Sports Committee
- Islamic Republic of Iran National Paralympic Committee
- Iraqi Paralympic Committee
- Jordan Sports Federation for the Handicapped
- Kuwait Disabled Sports Club
- Handi-Sport Lebanese Federation
- Oman National Disabled Sports Team
- Palestinian Sports Federation for the Disabled
- Qatar Sport Federation for Special Needs
- Saudi Sports Federation for Special Needs
- Syrian Sports Federation for Disabled Sport
- U.A.E. Disabled Sports Federation

KEY POINT

The structure and origins of disability sport, as well as the growth and development of the sport structure, tend to vary from one country to another.

Concluding Comments

Presenting the various structures for disability sport on a global basis makes it apparent that there are many opportunities for growth of the movement. Selected countries have been highlighted in this chapter to illustrate the similarities and differences in disability sport around the world. Some countries have very well-established programs and organizations; others are still developing these. In any case, sport for and including individuals with disabilities exists throughout the world.

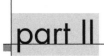

part II

Sport and Sport Performance

seven

Sports for Athletes With Disabilities

Eli A. Wolff and Mary A. Hums

Reader Goal   Gain knowledge and understanding of the competitive sport opportunities available within the prevailing major sport organizations and some of the events available for athletes with disabilities

Chapter Synopsis

- Major Competitions for Disability Sport: The Paralympic Games, Special Olympics, and the Deaflympics
- Creating Equal Playing Fields Within Disability Sport
- The Sporting Events
- Concluding Comments

This chapter focuses on describing sports for persons with disabilities as "sports." We characterize the sports in much the same way we would for persons without disabilities. Sports for people with disabilities are often described with a focus on the disabling elements and not on the athletic and sporting elements. The aim of this chapter is to help the reader understand that people with disabilities do in fact engage in sports and experience outcomes similar to those experienced by able-bodied athletes. People in disability sport compete in a discipline of the sport, specifically for people with disabilities; but these sports are no less valuable or athletic than sports for persons without disabilities. Many of the disability forms of the sport use rules identical to those of the traditional form of the sport. Often an international federation for a given sport, such as the International Tennis Federation or the World Curling Federation, governs that sport.

Specifically this chapter provides an overview of the sports offered on the official programs of the Paralympic Games, Special Olympics World Games, and the Deaflympic Games. The chapter is organized by sport, divided by summer or winter, with descriptions of variations to the sport, when applicable, with respect to each of the Games. Sport summaries present similarities and differences in the sport relative to that for persons without disabilities, as well as the use of the rules of international sport federations. Summaries discuss sport equipment, fan appeal, and athletic elements required in the sport for athletes with disabilities.

Major Competitions for Disability Sport: The Paralympic Games, Special Olympics, and the Deaflympics

The Paralympic Games are competitive sport for elite-level international athletes with various physical disabilities, including amputees, visually impaired, dwarfs, athletes with cerebral palsy, and athletes who compete in wheelchairs. The emphasis in Paralympic sport is on competition. These elite-level international athletes compete for their nations just like Olympic athletes.

Special Olympics are for athletes with cognitive and developmental disabilities and focus on participation and skill development rather than competition. Many events are similar to events for people without disabilities, but others are also adapted so that a wide range of abilities may be accommodated. The prevailing philosophy is to include participants regardless of ability at the local level and to provide "participant" ribbons as well as competitive medals. This is a worldwide organization with national- and international-level competition.

The Paralympic Games focus more on elite sport while the Special Olympics focus on grassroots involvement. The Deaflympics are similar to the Paralympics. They are the ultimate international competition for elite international Deaf athletes. The competitions are held at the state, national, and international levels. The competitions are rigorous and model the Olympics in terms of training intensity, coaching expertise, level of ability, and competitiveness. In fact, there is the occasional athlete who is Deaf who has been a member of able-bodied teams.

The U.S. Women's Sitting Volleyball Team

Photo by Sue Gavron.

FAST FACTS

Home Base: From across the United States
Sport: Women's sitting volleyball
Selected Accomplishments:

Team members received their letters of appointment on June 11, 2004

Met in Bowling Green to focus on the Greece Paralympics

Played internationally in Europe during the early spring

Ages range from 17 to 47

Won a gold medal in 2003 at the Para Pan American Games (Argentina) to secure a spot in 2004 Paralympics

Bronze medal in 2004 Paralympics

The first-ever women's sitting volleyball team trained together for the 2004 Greece Paralympics in June of that year. Their enthusiasm, focus, and intensity during two-a-day drills of 3 hours were inspiring. As volleyball players who sit on the floor during games, they serve, roll, dig, and spike just as furiously as their able-bodied counterparts. Their athletic ability was further showcased as they took on all comers in an open session and beat them all. They train two or three times per month as a team.

(continued)

The U.S. Women's Sitting Volleyball Team

(continued)

THE ASSISTANT COACH *(top row, first person from left)*

Denise Van DeWalle has been the head coach of women's volleyball for Bowling Green State University (Ohio) for over 22 years. She has coached at the high school, college, national, and international levels. This is her first experience with athletes with disabilities. Denise is the assistant coach for the team. Her practices are focused, intense, and lively. She is able to work with several athletes at a time and makes sure that each receives individual assistance. She is a motivator and is well schooled in tactics and skill progressions. Denise states that she is excited and looking forward to the three weeks in Greece even if the time frame does fall within her regular college competitive season. "This is just too good to pass up. What an honor!"

THE TEAM

Note: The team members described in the following are those who were present for the training session.

Brenda Maymon *(top row, fourth person from left)*

A 19-year-old from Indiana who is a below-the-knee amputee, Brenda says that she "was not always comfortable" with her disability. About becoming a member of the team, she states, "They have given me strength and encouragement that I very much needed. It has changed my way of thinking to a positive way of life." Her family and boyfriend have encouraged her to be active and play volleyball. Being on the team has "helped me to adapt to new things and has really helped my self-confidence," Brenda says.

Penny Ricker *(top row, sixth person from left on the end)*

Penny is a 33-year-old whose home is in Wisconsin. She has been involved in downhill skiing and golf but not competitively. Her volleyball experience is new. She trains individually three or four days a week, and the team trains together two or three times a month. What influenced Penny to become more involved in disability sport? She attended the 1996 Atlanta Paralympics and became inspired. Penny thinks her involvement allows her to "stay active and competitive despite physical limitation." As with others who experience the benefits of the disability sport movement, Penny states, "It has changed my life, improved my self-image and confidence." Penny also believes that it is important to "focus on your capabilities . . . and do whatever you put your mind to."

Erica Denae Moyers *(top row, second person from left)*

The youngest member of the team, Erica comes from Athens, Alabama. She trains six days a week without the team in addition to training each month with the team. A traumatic amputation has not halted this sport lover's participation and

138

enjoyment: "Sports, even before my accident, are a way for me to feel fulfilled and [a way] I can have a positive influence for someone." Erica says, "Take a chance; it's a feeling that no one can explain. You will never know if you will like something until you try." Not bad for a 17-year-old—who also participates in competitive karate with able-bodied folks!

Hope Lewellen (bottom row, fourth person from left on the end)

An experienced sportsperson, Hope is from Harvey, Illinois. She has experience in wheelchair tennis and wheelchair basketball. In 1996, she was a silver medalist in wheelchair tennis, and she was in the top eight in the 2000 Sydney Paralympics. She was ranked first in the United States and fourth in the world. In 2002, Hope was a member of the U.S. wheelchair basketball team that won a silver medal in Japan. This versatile athlete is "happy to be a professional athlete . . . travel the world, meet people—what can be better?" Her one concern is the lack of recognition, education, and respect surrounding the Paralympic Games.

Deborah (Deb) Lynn Vosler (bottom row, first person from left)

The senior member of the team is 47 years old and is originally from Cheyenne, Wyoming. A teacher, Deb was a volleyball player in her youth and was injured playing that sport. After 40 surgeries, amputation was the only answer to her injury. Deb states, "I was sedentary for nearly 15 years . . . now, sitting volleyball has brought sports back into my life. I never thought I'd get to play the game I love again. This has been a blessing. Out of adversity, I have achieved a nearly impossible dream." This quiet, calm, mature leader, in her first competition at a Paralympics, plays with determination and is also a role model for the younger players. Her participation as a team member is a model for all those who think they're too old to try.

Gina Jenkins McWilliams (bottom row, third person from left)

Gina, from Texas, is the captain of the team. She was a wheelchair basketball player in 1995, 1998, and 2000 for the U.S. women's team. She won a gold medal in the 1999 Pan American Games. From 1996 to 2000, she was the assistant coach of the team, and from 2000 to 2004 she was the head coach. In 2003, Gina was a member of the sitting volleyball team that won the gold medal in the Pan Am Games to qualify them for the 2004 Paralympics. A hard worker, Gina trains six days a week by herself, with support from her husband and children. Gina sums up the importance of sport: "It's not just what I do, but who I am. I am an athlete; I am competitive; I am a fighter; I am a mentor; I am a motivator; I am a teacher; I am a student; I am a survivor." Gina is certainly all of those things and more.

Kari La Raine Miller (bottom row, second person from left)

Kari Miller has been involved with disability sport for just four years. The New Jersey native has participated in wheelchair basketball in her rehabilitation center

(continued)

The U.S. Women's Sitting Volleyball Team

(continued)

and was awarded the 2002 Sportsmanship Award at the National Wheelchair Basketball Tournament. Her role model was Bill Demby, a former professional sport star well known in her area for basketball. Now involved in sitting volleyball, Kari is thankful for the opportunities she has gained from sport. "It has exposed me to new people who have contributed greatly in all aspects of my life."

Lora Jessica Webster (top row, third person from left)

Lora hails from Cave Creek, Arizona, and is new to the world of disability sport. Her involvement with the team is her first foray into international competition. Lora is excited about Athens and is practicing diligently. She is a willing and able athlete who contributes to a team effort. She is concerned about the lack of visibility for Paralympian athletes and hopes that this can be changed in the future.

Bonnie Brawner (top row, fifth person from left)

This 41-year-old hails from Texas. She has played some wheelchair basketball at the local level. Her participation on the sitting volleyball team is her first experience at the national and international level. Bonnie is a science teacher who trains five days a week. Giving her perspective on the whole experience with sitting volleyball, she says, "Competing at such a high level has changed my self-image, my self-discipline, my priorities, and my daily schedule." Go for it, Bonnie!

Author's note: June 16 to 18, 2004, at Bowling Green State University in Ohio, 9 of 13 women selected for the 2004 Paralympics to represent the United States in women's sitting volleyball conducted one of their Paralympic team trainings focused on the upcoming Paralympics in Athens, Greece, in September. This is a snapshot of that event and of the team.

People with disabilities also participate in a wide array of sports not necessarily included in these three competitions. Sports such as fishing, squash, baseball, boxing, and many others have their share of athletes with disabilities. Since the list could be endless, the Paralympics, Special Olympics, and Deaflympics were used as the groundwork for structuring this chapter.

A summary of the sports offered by each venue is presented in table 7.1, showing which organizations offer which sports. Some sports, such as soccer and swimming, are offered by all three organizations, and a few sports like badminton and sailing are offered by two organizations.

Table 7.1　Sports Offered in Paralympic Games, Special Olympics, and Deaflympics

Sport	Paralympics	Special Olympics	Deaflympics
Archery	X		
Athletics	X	X	X
Badminton		X	X
Basketball	X	X	X
Boccie	X	X	
Bowling	X	X	X
Curling	X		
Cycling	X	X	X
Equestrian	X	X	
Fencing	X		
Figure skating		X	
Goal ball	X		
Golf		X	
Gymnastics		X	
Hockey	X	X	X
Judo	X		
Orienteering			X
Powerlifting	X	X	
Roller skating		X	
Rugby	X		
Sailing	X	X	
Shooting	X		X
Skiing	X	X	X
Snowboarding		X	X
Snowshoeing		X	
Soccer	X	X	X
Softball		X	
Speed skating		X	
Swimming	X	X	X
Table tennis	X	X	X
Team handball		X	X
Tennis	X	X	X
Volleyball	X	X	X
Water polo			X
Wrestling			X

A handful of sport competitions are sponsored by just one organization, such as goal ball in the Paralympics, snowshoeing and snowboarding in the Special Olympics, and wrestling in the Deaflympics. Tables 7.2 through 7.4 at the end of the chapter present selected Paralympic Games records.

KEY POINT

The three major, prevailing sport competitions for athletes with disabilities, Paralympic Games, Special Olympics World Games, and Deaflympic Games, have different emphases on elite sport and offer different arrays of sports.

Creating Equal Playing Fields Within Disability Sport

Sport in general often uses various criteria to categorize athletes. For example, in sport for people without disabilities, we see athletes categorized for competition by gender, weight class, or age. All three of the disability sport competitions we are discussing include athletes with varying levels and forms of disability. How, then, do these competitions attempt to ensure that the "playing field is level" (Wolff and Hums, 2003)?

In the Paralympics, athletes are segmented by what is called *classification.* Athletes are categorized based on medical classification and skill level in the sport. For example, blind athletes are divided into three classification levels—B1, B2, and B3—depending on their level of vision. Athletes with cerebral palsy are classified using an 8-point scale, with a score of 1, indicating no mobility and the use of electric or motorized wheelchairs, to 8, indicating the highest level of mobility or less involvement with cerebral palsy.

In Special Olympics, the process is called *divisioning.* For individual sports, a three-step approach to divisioning is followed. First, athletes are divided by gender. Next, athletes are divided into age ranges. Finally the athletes are divided by ability level. Divisioning in team sports has the same three steps; but in the final step, dividing by ability, different sports use sport skills tests and a preliminary seeding round to group athletes into equitable playing groups. Special Olympics also organizes some sports using what is termed the "Unified Sport" approach. In Unified Sport, Special Olympic athletes are paired with one or more able-

Karolina Pelendridou

FAST FACTS

Home Base: Limassol, Cyprus
Sport: Swimming
Selected Accomplishments:

Cyprus record holder

World championship medalist (2002)

World record holder (breaststroke and backstroke, 2003)

Having competed since she was 11 years old, Karolina Pelendridou has been successful in two worlds—able-bodied and Paralympic swimming. She has been the Cyprus women's record holder and a world record holder in the breaststroke. With reduced sight, this young athlete achieved success at an early age—not so uncommon within the competitive swimming arena. Working out daily, Karolina attributes her success to the support of her coaches and her mother. To Karolina, "Sport is a way of living. I cannot imagine my life without sport. I feel more responsible as a result of being an athlete and having to respond to the difficult demands of exercising, competing, and going to school all at the same time." Karolina is an example of what can happen when children with disabilities get started early in experiencing the world of sport and competitive opportunities. Her advice about younger people with disabilities is "to get started in competing in disability sport because it makes you feel stronger, that life is no less strong, that life is no less challenging, even though you have a disability." Karolina Pelendridou has certainly provided others with a model of success that can be replicated.

"I feel more responsible as a result of being an athlete. . . ."

bodied athletes on teams or in a doubles format (Special Olympics, Inc., n.d.i).

The Deaflympics categorizes generally by gender and on a sport-specific basis by weight class. Because this particular disability is not as involved physically, the model is based on the same principles as in sport for people without disabilities whenever possible. As a result, many sports are not changed and the rules for competition are the same as for able-bodied athletes.

KEY POINT

There is a significant philosophical difference between Special Olympics and the other two sport competitions and organizations. Special Olympics reflects a more broad-based, grassroots participation focus than the Paralympic movement or Deaflympics, which emphasize competition.

The Sporting Events

The sports in this chapter are grouped as winter or summer sports. They are then arranged in alphabetical order within these categories. Note that some sports are not offered by all of the major sporting organizations.

Winter Sports

- **Curling:** Curling played by athletes using wheelchairs is currently set to make its Paralympic debut at the 2006 Winter Paralympic Games in Turino, Italy. In general, the rules of the World Curling Federation direct play. The game is played by co-ed teams, and each on-ice team must always have representation from each gender. The game itself is similar to shuffleboard, but a large stone is pushed on ice. However, there are a few basic adaptations to the game. First, sweeping (using a broom to direct the path of the stone as it glides over the ice) is not permitted. The person delivering the stone must be seated in a stationary wheelchair set at the center line. When delivering the stone, the athlete either may use the traditional hand release or is permitted to use an extender device if needed. Competitors in wheelchair curling generally have significant impairment of their lower-leg function. The Swiss team won the first Wheelchair Curling World Championships held in January 2002. This sport will be a welcome addition to the Winter Paralympic sport program (World Curling Federation, 2003).
- **Figure skating:** Figure skating, offered only by the Special Olympics, is one of the few sports in which the athletes are judged on their performance of movement, interpretation of rhythm, and tempo of movements while dancing on the ice. The Special Olympics Unified Sports allow for Special Olympic athletes to skate with a partner for both training and competition. The events include singles competitions, pairs dancing, ice dancing, guest skater dance, Unified pairs skating, and Unified ice dancing. Less skilled and experienced athletes compete in a "skills competition." Although the skills competitions do not take place at the World Games, they occur on the

local levels and serve as means to develop basic skating skills. The requirements for the routines increase in complexity as the athletes' skill levels increase. The lowest-level competitions include skills such as being able to take 10 forward steps and doing a two-foot glide the length of the body; the highest-level competition includes basic jumps and spins (Special Olympics, Inc., n.d.k)

- **Hockey:** Across the different competitions for athletes with disabilities, hockey takes different forms. In the Paralympic Games, teams compete in sledge hockey. Sledge hockey has become the biggest attraction for the Paralympic Winter Games. At the 2002 Salt Lake City Games, sledge hockey games were the "hottest ticket in town," with numerous sold-out games and a final that was decided in an overtime shoot-out. In sledge hockey, players are seated on sledges (small metal-frame sleds) with two hockey blades on the underside. Players move around on the ice using two downsized hockey sticks approximately 2 feet (0.6 meter) in length. The sticks have both a spike end and a blade end. The spike end digs into the ice so the player can propel around the rink, while the blade end is used to pass and shoot the puck. It is a very fast-paced, high-intensity, physical game. Sledge hockey is currently played only by men (International Paralympic Committee, 2003i).

  Special Olympians do not play ice hockey; rather they play floor hockey. Floor hockey is adapted from ice hockey and ringette, and allows the athletes who live in warm climates to participate in the Special Olympics winter sports. The surface for this game is either wood or concrete, not ice. The athletes use wooden poles, without blades, and sticks and pucks that are large felt disks with open centers (Special Olympics, Inc., n.d.l). In contrast to the Paralympic and Special Olympics athletes, Deaflympics competitors play ice hockey by the usual rules.

- **Skiing:** Skiing takes on many different forms, including alpine and Nordic skiing. Paralympic alpine skiing competitions include downhill, super-G, giant slalom, and slalom. Nordic skiing includes both cross-country skiing and biathlon, which combines cross-country skiing and shooting. Both alpine and Nordic skiing enable athletes with amputations and visual impairments to compete in the Paralympic Games. Alpine skiing, or downhill, includes different levels of competition with varying courses depending on the skill level of the athlete. Athletes use different adaptations of equipment ranging from single skis, to sit-skis, to stabilizers, while visually impaired athletes partner with a sighted guide. Nordic skiing athletes may use either two skis, sit-skis, or no poles in competition, while visually impaired athletes use a guide for assistance. In the biathlon events, visually impaired athletes use laser technology for the shooting portion of the competition (International Paralympic Committee, 2003b, 2003k).

Special Olympics athletes also compete in cross-country skiing. Their events are the 500-meter, 1K, 3K, 5K, 7.5K, and 10K races; the 4 × 1K relay; and the 4 × 1K Unified relay. Athletes with lower ability levels compete in 10-, 50-, and 100-meter races and the glide event (Special Olympics, Inc., n.d.g). Deaflympics has a full schedule of events similar to the Olympics.

- **Snowboarding:** Snowboarding is a relatively new sport to Olympic competition and to Special Olympics. The sport is fast paced and requires excellent coordination and balance. Special Olympics competitors are split into novice, intermediate, and advance divisions. Each division competes in super giant slalom (super-G), giant slalom, and slalom. Deaf sport has also included the sport of snowboarding. Special Olympics and the Deaf both utilize the rules of the International Ski Federation (Special Olympics, Inc., n.d.s).

- **Snowshoeing:** Snowshoeing is a sport offered only in the Special Olympics. Snowshoeing provides an excellent cardiovascular workout, similar to cross-country skiing. Individual events offered in snowshoeing range from 100-, 200-, 400-, 800-, and 1,600-meter to 5K and 10K races, and also include 4 × 100- and 4 × 400-meter relay races. Lower-level athletes compete in 25- and 50-meter races. Special Olympics, Inc. acts as the National Governing Body for snowshoeing (Special Olympics, Inc., n.d.t).

- **Speed skating:** Speed skating is a Special Olympics sport. Speed skating was first contested on an international level at the 1977 Special Olympics World Winter Games. Individual competition and Unified Sports are offered. Events are held on two different sizes of ovals. On the 100-meter ovals, athletes participate in 100-, 200-, 300-, 500-, 800-, 1,000-, and 1,500-meter races; the 4 × 20-lap relay; and Unified Sport 4 × 20-lap relay. On the 111-meter oval, competitions include 111-, 222-, 333-, 500-, 777-, 1,000-, and 1,500-meter races; 4 × 20-lap relay; and Unified Sport 4 × 20-lap relay. Athletes with lower-level abilities compete on the 100-meter oval in the 25-meter straightaway and 50-meter half lap race, and on the 111-meter oval in the 25-meter straightaway and 55-meter half lap race. Competition rules come from the International Skating Union for speed skating, except where modifications are made for Special Olympics competitors (Special Olympics, Inc., n.d.v).

KEY POINT

For some sports, adaptations and rules are unique to each sporting competition and reflect the focus of the organization on competition versus broad-based participation, as well as the physical and mental ability of the athletes involved.

Summer Sports

- **Archery:** Archery is one of the original Paralympic sports, having even been among the sports contested at the Stoke Mandeville Games in 1948. The rules, equipment, and accessories are the same as in the Olympic competition. The rules of the international archery federation, Fédération Internationale de Tir à l'Arc (FITA), govern competitions. A wheelchair of any kind may be used, or athletes can compete from a standing position. Additionally, modifications such as body supports, release aids, and compound bows are allowed. Events for men and women are held in singles, doubles, and team formats and include recurve bow and compound bow competitions. Competitions include FITA rounds, Olympic rounds, and distance rounds of 30, 50, 60, 70, and 90 meters (International Paralympic Committee, 2003c).

- **Athletics:** The term "athletics" refers to track and field events. This sport has the most competitors of all the Paralympic sports and is open to competitors of all disability types. The track events include dashes, middle distance events, long distance events, and the marathon. The field events include the usual jumping and throwing events, among them long jump, high jump, shot put, javelin, and discus. In order that there be a "level playing field," athletes compete using a classification system that matches athletes sharing similar physical and motor function levels. For example, visually impaired athletes compete against each other in the 200-meter dash. These athletes are further classified into three groups (B1, B2, B3) based on the level of vision they possess. Similarly, amputee athletes, athletes with cerebral palsy, and athletes using wheelchairs who compete against each other are classified as well. Visually impaired runners use a sighted guide during competitions (International Paralympic Committee, 2003d).

  For the Special Olympics, events are held on a very competitive basis, and athletes are placed in heats according to age, gender, and performance level (Special Olympics, Inc., n.d.b). The World

Games for the Deaf holds a full slate of track and field events and also spends extra time on clinics in which athletes develop and refine their skills.

- **Badminton:** Badminton as a sport in Special Olympics is played either as singles, doubles, mixed doubles, or Unified doubles having one Special Olympics athlete and one partner. Players of lower-level skill also compete in individual events other than traditional matches such as target serve, return volley, and return serve. Badminton players develop skills through clinics in which one Special Olympics athlete and one partner work together on skill level. The basic rules of the International Badminton Federation govern play; but there are some modifications, including using a "feeder" to pass the shuttlecock to a player, and competitions in individual skill contests such as those mentioned earlier (Special Olympics, Inc., n.d.c). The World Games for the Deaf also holds a badminton competition.

- **Basketball:** Athletes play basketball either using wheelchairs or standing. Wheelchair basketball, played by both men and women in the Paralympics, actually has more similarities in relation to the traditional standing basketball game than differences. According to the rules, the chair seat may not exceed 21 inches (0.5 meter) from the floor; the wheelchair is considered part of the player; the height of the foot platform must be no more than 4.875 inches from the floor; seat cushions are allowed; the player must wheel the chair and dribble the ball at the same time; traveling violations do occur; and there is a 30-second shot clock for offensive possessions. The three-point shot, free throws, fouls, technical fouls, court size, and general game strategy are basically the same in the wheelchair game as in the traditional standing version (International Paralympic Committee, 2003r).

For the Deaf basketball games, no modifications from the traditional game are made. Special Olympics basketball allows for variations of the game. One variation is a "Unified team" of able-bodied and Special Olympians playing on the court together. Another is co-ed team competition. Yet another aspect is the "developmental" competitions of dribbling, shooting, and passing as skills that are awarded ribbons in separate competitions (Special Olympics, Inc., n.d.d).

- **Boccie/Boccia:** Boccie/Boccia is a sport that has been played recreationally for many years. Some people refer to it as "lawn bowling," and others compare it to curling or shuffleboard. The Paralympic Games offers boccia, a slightly adapted version of boccie. Boccia is a sport for athletes with cerebral palsy. Paralympic Games competitions are offered in individual, pairs, and team competition formats. Players throw, kick, or use an assistive device such as a ramp or a chute to propel leather balls as close as possible to a small white target ball (International Paralympic Committee, 2003e). Special Olympics, for example, offers singles, doubles, and team competition in the sport of boccie. Special Olympics incorporates the traditional rules of boccie (Special Olympics, Inc., n.d.e). Boccie is not a part of Deaflympics events.

- **Bowling:** Bowling is an official sport of the Special Olympics and Deaflympics, with few modifications from the traditional game. In Special Olympics, a handle ball is permitted to provide an easier way to grasp the ball; upon release, the handle retracts, allowing for the ball to roll smoothly. Bowling sticks (extenders that allow an individual to push the ball down the lane) are permitted for those athletes who do not have the strength or balance traits needed to bowl. Bowling ramps, which allow a ball to roll down an incline that is positioned on the lane, are also permitted for athletes who cannot bowl free armed. There are individual competitions for singles, ramp assisted and ramp unassisted; doubles competitions for men, women, mixed, Unified men, Unified women, and Unified mixed; and team competitions for men, women, mixed, Unified men, Unified women, and Unified mixed. Athletes with lower skill levels may also compete in target bowling and frame bowling (Special Olympics, Inc., n.d.f).

- **Cycling:** Cycling in the Paralympic Games includes both road and track events. Athletes with visual impairments ride tandem cycles with a sighted partner, while amputees and cyclists with cerebral palsy use cycles adapted for their particular need. There are both individual and team events.

  Cycling competitions vary depending on the type of cycle being used. The competitions include time trials, track racing, road racing, tandem cycling, and hand cycling. Each competition involves a different type of bike. Variations include dual-seated bikes, tandems, hand cycles, adult tricycles, bikes for short-statured people, wheelchair attachments, and adaptations for amputees (International Paralympic Committee, 2003f).

- **Equestrian:** Equestrian events enable the rider and the horse to rely on the success of each other. Paralympic athletes compete in dressage only, and all disability types are involved. Dressage is a very old sport, with its roots in ancient Greece. Dressage involves the rider's guiding the horse with the use of leg pressure and postural shifts only. It is meant to demonstrate the unity of horse and rider. Riders who perform individually must ride a pattern incorporating various changes in pace and direction. Riders are grouped according to their functional profiles and are judged on their ability to control and maneuver the horse (International Paralympic Committee, 2003g).

- **Fencing:** Only the Paralympic Games include fencing. The athletes compete in fencing while seated in wheelchairs secured to the floor. Although the wheelchairs do not move, athletes have full upper-body movement. The traditional weapons—foil, épée, and saber—are contested at the Paralympic Games, and there are both team and individual competitions (International Paralympic Committee, 2003s).

- **Goal ball:** Goal ball is played by male and female athletes with visual impairment or those who are totally blind. The court is approximately the same size as a volleyball court. It consists of three areas—the team area directly in front of the goal; the landing area; and the neutral area, which is in the center of the court between the teams' landing areas. The markings on the court also have a string placed underneath them to help players orient themselves with their position on the court. The objective is to throw the ball into the opponent's goal while the team on defense attempts to block the shot. The goals are nets, approximately 3 feet (0.9 meter) high, extending the width of each end of the court. Each goal is worth one point. Teams consist of three players; bells inside the ball, which is approximately the size of a basketball, help the players tell the ball's location. Games consist of two 7-minute halves. Because the athletes who play have varying levels of vision, all competitors wear special eyeshades that block out all light. While the game is being played, the gymnasium is completely silent; but the cheers explode once a team scores (International Paralympic Committee, 2003h). Goal ball is on the Paralympic program only and is not played in Special Olympics or Deaflympics.

- **Golf:** In Special Olympics, the focus on golf is first the training and then the competition. The athlete first learns how to swing a golf club and how to play the game; therefore, a great deal of concentration is placed on developing skills. After the skills are developed, five levels of golf are played depending on the ability. Athletes may participate in individual skills competitions, 9-hole or 18-hole individual stroke play, Unified team play, and alternate-shot team play. The rules governing play are the rules as approved by the Royal and Ancient Golf Club at St. Andrews and the United States Golf Association. The skills competitions include short putt, long putt, chip shot, pitch shot, iron shot, and wood shot. These competitions involve earning a designated number of points for placement within a target area. The game is quite popular, and there is even a publication called the *Special Olympics Golf Newsletter* (Special Olympics, Inc., n.d.n). Golf is not a part of Deaflympics.

- **Gymnastics:** Special Olympics gymnastics tests artistic events for men and both artistic and rhythmic events for women. Both men and women can participate in all the events offered, which all combine strength, flexibility, and artistry. A wide variety of competitive categories exist for Special Olympics athletes, who compete in the following gymnastics events: (a) mixed-gender events—vaulting, wide beam, floor exercise, tumbling, all-around; (b) women's events—vaulting, uneven bars, balance beam, floor exercise, all-around; (c) men's events—floor exercise, pommel horse, rings, vaulting, parallel bars, horizontal bar, and all-around. There are also a number of similar Unified events (Special Olympics, Inc., n.d.o). Gymnastics is not a part of Deaflympics.

- **Judo:** In the Paralympic Games, visually impaired male athletes compete in judo. The only difference between judo at the Paralympic Games and other top-level judo competitions is the varied textures on the mats allowing for different zones and competition areas. The matches are governed by the rules of the International Judo Federation. The competitions are divided by weight class, with classes including extra lightweight, half lightweight, lightweight, half middleweight, middleweight, half heavyweight, and heavyweight. The intensity and power are the same as in any judo competition, which is obvious as soon as the event begins (International Paralympic Committee, 2003j). Neither Special Olympics nor Deaflympics offers this sport.

- **Orienteering:** The objective of orienteering is to either walk or run a designated course through the use of a compass and map. A series of points are shown on the maps, and the goal is to reach those points. Hopefully, the shortest routes are chosen as the runner is being timed, and the person with the fastest time back to the finish is the winner. The Deaflympics holds this event.

- **Powerlifting:** Powerlifting is a sport focusing more on the athlete's perseverance than on success or failure. It was one of the first sports in which athletes competed at the Paralympic Games, and women have been able to participate only recently (since 2000). There are 10 body-weight class divisions, and athletes perform the bench press. Rules for the athlete's position on the weight bench are relatively standard but do allow for slight variation based on disability type. In general the rules of traditional powerlifting are followed (International Paralympic Committee, 2003l).

- **Roller skating:** Roller skating allows for Special Olympic athletes to compete in artistic events, speed events, or roller hockey. Athletes may then choose to skate with in-line skates or quad skates, depending on the athlete's strength level. Much attention is placed on the development of the skill level of the athletes before the competitions. Artistic competitions include school figures, freestyle singles, freestyle pairs dance, solo and team Unified Sport dance, and team Unified Sport freestyle pairs. Speed competitions include 100-, 300-, 500-, and 1,000-meter track events; 2 × 100-, 2 × 200-, and 4 × 100-meter relay races; and 2 × 100-, 2 × 200-, and 4 × 100-meter Unified Sport relays. Hockey is played five-a-side in regular team competition and Unified Sport team competition. Athletes of lower functioning levels compete in skills competitions in school figures; freestyle singles; dance, solo, and team 30-meter straight-line race; 30-meter slalom; 15-meter ball dribble; and shoot around the goal (Special Olympics, Inc., n.d.q).

- **Rugby:** Rugby is offered in the Paralympic Games and is a highly intense and physical team sport. It combines essentials of basketball, football, and ice hockey and is played on a basketball court. A volleyball is used, and it can be carried, dribbled, or passed but may not be kicked. Athletes try to score goals by carrying the ball over the opponent's goal line. The ball is pushed via the wheelchair on the ground or on the lap of an athlete, similar to what happens in wheelchair basketball. Due to the rough nature of the sport, wheelchairs often need repair during matches. This sport has proven to be a fan favorite and draws large crowds (International Paralympic Committee, 2003t).

- **Sailing:** Sailing is a relatively new Paralympic sport, having debuted in 2000 in Sydney. Within the Paralympic Games, five factors are judged: stability, hand function, maneuverability, visibility, and hearing. The yachts used in Paralympic competition have keels, mainly because this design provides greater stability and allows more room for the sailors. The racing format is known as the fleece format, in which all yachts race the course at the same time. Points are assigned based on the order of finish in a race. The yacht with the lowest number of points, which are given for errors during the course of the competition, is declared the winner. Events are contested by teams of three using a 23-foot (7-meter) keelboat in the sonar event and by individuals piloting 7.8-foot (2.4-meter) single-handed keelboats. Sailing proves the importance of all three essentials, speed, strength, and smarts, in sport (International Paralympic Committee, 2003m). The option of combining a Special Olympic athlete with a partner also exists in sailing (Special Olympics, Inc., n.d.r).

- **Shooting:** In the Paralympic Games, the shooting competition is divided into air and .22-caliber rifle and pistol events for wheelchair and standing competitors. The rules governing the competitions for athletes with disabilities are those of the International Shooting Committee for the Disabled. Shooting utilizes a functional classification system allowing athletes from different disability classes, but with the same abilities, to compete together either individually or in teams. Men and women both compete in 10-meter air pistol, 10-meter air rifle standing, and 50-meter free rifle. Mixed teams compete in 10-meter air rifle standing, 10-meter air rifle prone, 25-meter sport pistol, 50-meter free pistol, and 50-meter free rifle prone (International Paralympic Committee, 2003n). The Deaflympics also includes the sport of shooting.

- **Soccer:** The most popular sport in the world, soccer is a part of the Paralympic Games. Athletes with cerebral palsy (cerebral palsy, stroke, and traumatic brain injury) play with seven teammates per side. In Athens in 2004, five-on-five soccer for blind and visually impaired athletes was added to the Paralympic program. Soccer for athletes with cerebral palsy is played on a slightly smaller field with smaller goals. Soccer is an eight-team competition at the Paralympic Games, where teams qualify out of a world championship. Soccer for visually impaired and blind athletes is played on a basketball court using a ball with a bell. Athletes are all blindfolded to ensure an equal playing situation for all. Soccer in the Paralympic Games is fast paced and action packed, showing excellence in balance, coordination, and teamwork (International Paralympic Committee, 2003a).

  Special Olympics accommodates several variations of the sport, including 5 versus 5 and 7 versus 7. Special Olympics has had tremendous success in its efforts working with the European Football Federation (Special Olympics, Inc., n.d.m). Deaf soccer replicates traditional 11 versus 11 soccer as seen in the Olympic Games and World Cup.

- **Softball:** Softball is offered in the Special Olympics as well as in the Olympic Games. Special Olympics provides competition in slow-pitch, T-ball, and Unified Sport competition. With teams of 10 players to a side, the games follow the basic rules of softball. In the slow-pitch version, there often is a neutral pitcher who pitches to both sides while a Special Olympic athlete fields the pitcher's position. Players are assessed in basic skills in base racing, fielding, throwing, and batting for distance. These are not skills competitions; rather they are used to assign players to the appropriate skill-level team. A player's total score is determined from these Softball Skills Assessment Tests (SAT). Teams are then grouped into divisions by their team SAT score. Softball is a very popular sport, played extensively by teams from all over the world (Special Olympics, Inc., n.d.u).

- **Swimming:** Within the Paralympic Games, large numbers of athletes compete in swimming events. All disability groups compete. Swimmers compete without use of prosthetics or assistive devices. Some adaptations are made for swimmers depending on disability. For example, swimmers generally use the starting platform; but those with balance problems, for example, may use an in-water start as long as they are in contact with the wall at the start of the race. Competitions for men and women are held in freestyle (50, 100, 200, 400, 800, 1,500 meters), backstroke (50, 100, 200 meters), breaststroke (50, 100, 200 meters), and butterfly (50, 100, 200 meters), as well as individual medley (200, 400 meters), freestyle relay (4 × 50 meters, 4 × 100 meters), and medley relay (4 × 50 meters, 4 × 100 meters). The rules of the international swimming federation, Fédération International de Natation Amateur (FINA), are used with adaptations as prescribed (International Paralympic Committee, 2003o).

  The Special Olympics allows for both strong-ability athletes and lower-ability athletes to swim in competition normally on a team of four: two Special Olympics athletes and two partners. The rule modifications include the following: The starting position, either in or out of the water, is optional; the use of a strobe light is allowed for athletes who are Deaf; and stroke judgment concerns the action of the nonimpaired limb (Special Olympics, Inc., n.d.a).

- **Table tennis:** Table tennis is an intense skill-based sport offered in the Paralympic Games, Special Olympics, and Deaflympics. Male and female Paralympians compete in standing and wheelchair divisions, and athletes from all disability groups can compete (International Paralympic Committee, 2003p). In Special Olympics, competitors face off in singles, doubles and mixed doubles, and wheelchair competition, as well as Unified Sport doubles and mixed doubles. Lower-level athletes have skill competitions in target serve, racket bounce, and return shot. Table tennis requires excellent hand–eye coordination, balance, and agility. Table tennis abides by the rules of the International Table Tennis Federation (Special Olympics, Inc., n.d.w).

- **Team handball:** Team handball is an exciting, fast-paced game of passing, dribbling, and shooting. Playing on a court approximately the size of a basketball court and using a ball the size of a volleyball, teams run the court attempting to move the ball downcourt and throw it past a goalie into a net of field hockey size. Team handball is a disability sport offered within the Special Olympics and Deaf-

© Bill Hamiter

Figure 7.1 Point, game, match, and medal. The women's sitting volleyball team in the 2004 Paralympics in Athens, Greece, when they scored the final point of the match to capture the bronze medal. U.S. players react, as does assistant coach Denise Van DeWalle in the background, to the first ever medal won in the Paralympics by a U.S. women's sitting volleyball team.

lympics. For Special Olympics, team handball is offered as team competition, five-a-side, and as Unified Sport competition (Special Olympics, Inc., n.d.x). Competitions for both Special Olympics and Deaflympics utilize the rules of the International Team Handball Federation.

- **Tennis:** Tennis is played in some form at the Paralympics, Special Olympics, and Deaflympics. In the Paralympics, where the sport takes the form of wheelchair tennis, matches are played in either singles or doubles. The only rule difference is that the ball is allowed to bounce twice before the player is obligated to return it. Between Paralympic Games, the International Tennis Federation hosts a number of events for wheelchair tennis and produces a list of national rankings for players (International Paralympic Committee,

Table 7.2 Paralympic Summer Games: Sydney 2000

Sport event (athletics)	Name	Paralympic result	Records
High jump (F20)			
Women	Llorens, Lisa (AUS)	1.54	
Men	Ben-Bahri, Wissam (TUN)	1.93	WR
Shot put (F20)			
Women	Durksa, Ewa (POL)	12.69	WR
Men	Kaczmarek, Krzysztof (POL)	13.10	WR
Javelin throw (F20)			
Women	Tiik, Sirly (EST)	39.77	WR
Men	Flavel, Anton (AUS)	52.50	PR
100 m (T12)			
Women	Santos, Adria (BRA)	12.46	
Men	Li, Qiang (CHN)	11.27	
Marathon (T54)			
Women	Driscoll, Jean (USA)	1:49.35	
Men	Neitlispach, Franz (SUI)	1:24.55	

Legend: WR = world record.

PR = Paralympic record.

2003u). In Special Olympics, matches are played in singles, doubles, and Unified Sport doubles. Players with lower skill levels have skill competitions in target stroke, target bounce, racket bounce, and return shot (Special Olympics, Inc., n.d.y). The Paralympic Games, Special Olympics, and Deaflympics use the rules of the International Tennis Federation.

- **Volleyball:** All three major disability Games incorporate some form of volleyball. In the Paralympic Games, the sport takes the form known as sitting volleyball. The court for sitting volleyball is slightly smaller than for the standing game, and the net is considerably lower—about the height of a tennis net (International Paralympic Committee, 2003q). Special Olympics has team and Unified Sport team competitions. Lower-skill-level athletes compete in the volleyball juggle, volleyball pass, and volleyball toss and hit skills competitions (Special Olympics, Inc., n.d.z). The game for the Deaf is played exactly as it is in the traditional form of standing volleyball.

Table 7.3 Paralympic Winter Games: Salt Lake City 2002

Sport event	Name	Paralympic result
Downhill (LW2)		
Women	Haslacher, Danja (AUT)	1:26.75
Men	Milton, Michael (AUS)	1:23.64
Super-G (LW2)		
Women	Billmeier, Sarah (USA)	1:18.43
Men	Milton, Michael (AUS)	1:13.76
Short-distance (5-km) sit-ski (LW12)		
Women	Myklebust, Ragnhild (NOR)	9:01.2
Men	Kryjanovski, Taras (RUS)	16:08.3
Long-distance (15-km) sit-ski (LW10+LW11+LW12)		
Women (LW12)	Myklebust, Ragnhild (NOR)	33:43.8
Men (LW10)	Shilov, Sergey (RUS)	42:03.02
Slalom (LW2)		
Women	Haslacher, Danja (AUT)	1:50.40
Men	Milton, Michael (AUS)	1:29.03

- **Water polo:** Water polo is an official sport of the Deaflympics. Water polo for the Deaf uses the rules of FINA. There are no special adjustments to the sport in the Deaflympics. The games involve teams of five in a pool who try to throw the ball into the opponent's net. This is a form of team handball in the water. It is a fast-paced game involving stamina and strength, played the same as for those without disabilities in the Olympics.

- **Wrestling:** Wrestling is a sport of the Deaflympics. The official rules of the International Wrestling Federation apply, and there are no adaptations to the sport in the Deaflympics.

KEY POINT

Many disability sports follow the same rules as sports for people without disabilities. In fact, disability sports—whether they do or do not follow the same rules—are no less valuable or athletic than sports for persons without disabilities.

Table 7.4 Composite Snapshot of One Sport (Swimming for the Blind) Over Several Games

Sport event		Name	Paralympic record	Paralympic Games
50-m freestyle				
Women	(S11)	Nilsson, Eila (SWE)	33.02	Atlanta (USA), 1996
	(S12)	Zhu, Hongyan (CHN)	28.67	Sydney (AUS), 2000
	(S13)	Hopf, Yvonne (GER)	27.38	Atlanta (USA), 1996
Men	(S11)	Kawai, Junichi (JPN)	26.37	Sydney (AUS), 2000
	(S12)	Kleynhans, Ebert (RSA)	25.79	Sydney (AUS), 2000
	(S13)	Strokin, Andrei (RUS)	24.67	Sydney (AUS), 2000
200-m backstroke				
Women	(S12)	Zorn, Trischa (USA)	2:31.13	Barcelona (ESP), 1992
Men	(S11)	Morgan, John (USA)	2:33.42	Barcelona (ESP), 1992
	(S12)	Holmes, Christopher (GBR)	2:33.14	Barcelona (ESP), 1992
	(S13)	Pedersen, Noel (NOR)	2:22.55	Barcelona (ESP), 1992
100-m butterfly				
Women	(S11)	Barret, Elaine (GBR)	1:20.50	Sydney (AUS), 2000
	(S12)	Zhu, Hongyan (CHN)	1:09.09	Sydney (AUS), 2000
	(S13)	Hopf, Yvonne (GER)	1:06.12	Atlanta (USA), 1996
Men	(S11)	Morgan, John (USA)	1:03.50	Barcelona (ESP), 1992
	(S13)	Wu, Walter (CAN)	1:00.87	Sydney (AUS), 2000
100-m breaststroke				
Women	(SB11)	Barret, Elaine (GBR)	1:30.39	Sydney (AUS), 2000
	(S12)	Font, Deborah (ESP)	1:25.42	Sydney (AUS), 2000
	(S13)	Cote, Kirby (CAN)	1:19.43	Sydney (AUS), 2000
Men	(SB11)	Bundgaard, Christian (DEN)	1:12.86	Atlanta (USA), 1996
	(S12)	Bugarin, Kingsley (AUS)	1:10.06	Sydney (AUS), 2000
	(S13)	Pedersen, Noel (NOR)	1:08.12	Barcelona (ESP), 1992

Concluding Comments

Sports for people with disabilities are sports first and foremost. These sports are physical, fast, and action packed, just like the versions of the sport for men and women without disabilities.

Athletes with disabilities want to be viewed and valued as athletes on a par with athletes without disabilities. Athletes in disability sport want their sports to be understood as sports. Views and perceptions that disability sports are not legitimate sports and should not be supported by sport organizations and sport culture are based on assumptions that people with disabilities do not hold value in sports. This reflects a belief that people with disabilities do not truly have an equal standing in all aspects of life. We need to change this way of thinking to fully recognize disability sports as sports.

Disability sport can be recognized and supported by traditional sport organizations and traditional sport culture. There are numerous opportunities for the sporting environment and all of society to learn and understand about sport for people with disabilities. Hopefully this chapter has increased awareness and made readers think about how athletes who happen to have a disability are perceived and about the sports they play.

eight

Coaching and Training Athletes With Disabilities

Reader Goal Become familiar with sport performance research in relation to disability sport as a means for better understanding the coaching and training aspects for athletes with disabilities

Chapter Synopsis

- Research and Coaching
- The Research Foundation for Disability Sport
- Summary of Selected Research Findings
- General Principles of Coaching Athletes With Disabilities
- Selected Disabilities and Specific Strategies
- Concluding Comments

The key to success for any athlete, whether able-bodied or having a disability, is training and knowledgeable coaching. While somewhat scarce in the past, coaches of athletes with disabilities are increasing in number. In addition, greater understanding of the application of scientific principles to the performance of athletes with disabilities has resulted from an integration of research and practical experience. The aspects of coaching outlined in this chapter are based upon general principles and concepts that are applicable to those with disabilities. Once again, there are more similarities than differences in coaching strategies and techniques even when appropriate modifications are utilized. This is not intended to be a "how to" chapter. Rather, readers are referred to resources on coaching for the specific sport and encouraged to use the information provided here in order to better understand appropriate modifications. Additionally, the chapter presents the foundation for the sport performance research base for disability sport. While this is not an exhaustive presentation of research, examples allow the reader to note the trends and patterns of research and the results on performance and coaching.

Research and Coaching

The impact of research on athlete performance cannot be overlooked or underestimated. A plethora of research for able-bodied athletes is disseminated via conferences and professional journals. The Olympic Scientific Congress that precedes each Olympiad provides some of the most cutting-edge research and opportunities for new information to be disseminated on an international level. The same is not necessarily true, on a consistent basis, of research on disability and sport. In the recent past the Paralympics has held a Paralympic Scientific Congress but did not do so in 2004 in Athens. However, strands were infused into the Olympic Scientific Congress in Athens for research on disability sport. Which approach is better—a separate venue or one that is integrated? Which will afford the most visibility and opportunity for disability sport research, and which will allow for the best dissemination of research? This question is not easily answered.

Research on sport and individuals with disabilities has evolved slowly, along with the disability sport movement. The early years saw research focused on rehabilitation or on growth and development of individuals with physical and mental disabilities (DePauw, 1985a; Huber, 1984; Lindstrom, 1984; Lipton, 1970; Rarick, Dobbins, and Broadhead, 1976), whereas the post-World War II efforts focused on programming. The modern era of disability sport research began in the late 1970s. Performance issues, training, and equipment came to the forefront of research interests. In the 1990s, a holistic view, which included a psychosocial and qualitative approach, developed. This approach took into consideration the "whole athlete" and the ways in which different psychological and social factors affect performance. This descriptive or qualitative approach is now used in combination with statistical analyses to form a more complete picture of athlete performance. Still, not many articles, journals, or conferences specifically focus on disability sport research. Nor, according to Bhambhani (2001), have the resources for conducting research been able to meet the growing demand by researchers, coaches, athletes, and trainers for such new information.

In the 1960s, emphasis was placed upon physical fitness parameters (strength, flexibility, weight) of those with mental retardation, as well as perceptual-motor and social development (Broadhead, 1986; DePauw, 1986b; Dunn, 1987; Pyfer, 1986; Stein, 1983). The 1970s saw research on exercise physiology and biomechanics (DePauw, 1988; Gass and Camp, 1979; Zwiren and Bar-Or, 1975). The exercise physiology research was confined to understanding disabled athletes' levels of fitness or conditioning and their response to exercise, whereas the biomechanics research focused on wheelchair propulsion. Subjects included wheelchair users, individuals with postpolio, and spinal cord-injured individuals. Since the 1970s and 1980s, research has increased. It has focused on sport- and disability-specific aspects as well as discipline-oriented and performance-based aspects (DePauw, 1988). The 1990s saw a continuance of this approach and also more psychosocial and qualitative research.

The Research Foundation for Disability Sport

A commitment to disability sport research was formalized in 1985 when the United States Olympic Committee (USOC) agreed with the Committee on Sports for the Disabled (COSD) to establish a special subcommittee concerning research on sport for the disabled.

This research subcommittee interviewed coaches, athletes with disabilities, and professionals in the field of recreation and adapted physical education and came up with seven areas of concern:

- Effects of training, competition, or both
- Selection and training of coaches, volunteers, officials
- Technological advances in sport research
- Sociological/Psychological aspects of sport
- Differences and similarities between disabled and nondisabled athletes
- Demographics of sport for the disabled
- Legal, philosophical, and historical bases for sport (DePauw, 1988, p. 293)

As a result of this survey, over 70 different topics were identified. These topics were meant to be a starting point for the next generation of researchers.

In 1993, the International Paralympic Committee (IPC) established a sport science committee as an indication of its commitment to sport science research and the advancement of knowledge about Paralympic sport. In April 1994, a seminar on sport science and athletes with disabilities was held at the German Olympic Institute in Berlin. In attendance were the members of the IPC Sport Science Committee and representatives from the International Federation of Adapted Physical Activity. The IPC committee was chaired by Dr. Gudrun Doll-Tepper from the Free University of Berlin.

As a result of the seminar, the mission, goals, and objectives for the IPC Sport Science Committee were established. In addition, guidelines for research conducted at Paralympic Games and world championships were developed; guidelines for the conduct of the Paralympic Congress and International Symposium were proposed; and a plan for preparing a Paralympic research agenda was prepared. Initial efforts for setting a research agenda included the development of selected position statements, a monograph series on Paralympic sport, an international directory of sport scientists, and a database of research on disability sport.

KEY POINT

Research is an essential aspect of the disability sport movement. Research on sport and individuals with disabilities has evolved slowly, along with the disability sport movement.

Summary of Selected Research Findings

Of value to reading and understanding the sport and disability research literature are articles and abstracts such as those in *Adapted Physical Activity Quarterly; Completed Research in Health, Physical Education, Recreation, and Dance; Abstracts of Research Presentations at the American Alliance for Health, Physical Education, Recreation and Dance Convention* featured in *Research Quarterly for Exercise and Sport; Physical Educator; Palaestra; Physician and Sportsmedicine; Research Quarterly for Exercise and Sport; Rehabilitation Yearbook; Journal of Teaching Physical Education;* and *Medicine and Science in Sport and Exercise.* Special education journals and specialized newsletters are also a source of information.

For a listing of selected periodicals about sport and disability sport, see appendix G. The Sport Information Resource Clearinghouse (SIRC) has published two comprehensive bibliographies on disability sport research (now Sport Discus). In addition, a database for research on wheelchair sport has been established by the British Wheelchair Sports Foundation and the Department of Physical Education, Sport Sciences, and Recreation Management at Loughborough University, Loughborough, England. A publication exclusively devoted to disability sport research is the edited two-volume *New Horizons in Sport for Athletes with a Disability: Proceedings of the International Vista'99 Conference in Cologne, Germany* (2001). Generalizing or applying the results of research in physical education and sport for individuals with disabilities across all disabilities and sports should be avoided or at least interpreted cautiously when applied in such a manner. The diversity of the disabled population and the small number of subjects usually found in such studies limit the ability to apply information from one study to all athletes and sports. On the other hand, a synthesis and summation of completed research showing commonalities of findings over a period of time could provide a knowledge base for and about disability sport, indicate trends, and identify further research needs.

Sport Psychology/Sport Sociology

More similarity than difference has been reported in studies comparing athletes with disabilities and able-bodied athletes on psychological parameters. Consistently, the iceberg profile (below-average tension, depression, anger, fatigue, and confusion; above-average vigor), which was first applied to able-bodied athletes, has been utilized with wheelchair athletes and athletes with visual impairments. Athletes with disabilities have also demonstrated responses to failure/success and measures of anxiety similar to those seen with able-bodied peers.

In the studies on mood states of athletes with disabilities, the majority of the samples exhibited the iceberg profile regardless of gender, type of sport, level of skill, and sport setting (Sherrill, 1990). Thus it appears that disabled athletes are more similar than different when compared to able-bodied athletes during training and competition.

Sport socialization (the process through which one enters sport) among athletes with disabilities has received some attention in the research literature. Sport socialization has been found to be different when blind and cerebral palsy (CP) athletes are compared with able-bodied athletes. In contrast to the situation with able-bodied athletes, the family and home were found not to be of primary importance for blind and CP athletes (Lugo, Sherrill, and Pizarro, 1992; Sherrill et al., 1986). Blind students tended to rate their physical education teacher and their school as more important. For wheelchair athletes in the eighth Pan Am Games, self-motivation, disabled friends, and physical educators were the three leading factors for facilitating sport participation (Gavron, 1989).

Athletes with disabilities (wheelchair user, CP, blind) were found to have the same perceptions, cognitive behaviors, and psychological profiles as able-bodied athletes. Self-concept varied depending on one's level of physical ability.

Cross-cultural comparisons regarding sport participation by athletes with disabilities are virtually nonexistent. Fung (1992) discovered significant differences among athletes with disabilities from the United States, Great Britain, and Japan in terms of motive factors of fitness, team atmosphere, and excitement and challenge. These differences were similar to those among able-bodied athletes and most likely related to the sociocultural and sociopolitical content of a given country rather than differences between able-bodied and disabled athletes. For example, in a study of Chinese disabled athletes, the physical education teacher was found to be the primary socializing agent for sport (Wang and DePauw, 1991). On the other hand, no differences were observed among Swedish athletes and their socialization into sport by disability status (with or without disability) (Johansson and DePauw, 1991).

Wheelchair Technology and Propulsion

Advances in technology over the years have greatly enhanced and contributed to the improved performances of athletes with disabilities on and off the playing field. Cycling research has been applied to wheelchairs and resulted in lighter and more efficient chairs. Various wheel sizes are available now as well as various hand rims (the portion of the wheel where a racer can grip for propulsion), adjustable cambers (the angle of the wheel in relation to the seat), and adjustable seat sizes and inclinations (Brubaker, 1984; Brubaker and McLaurin, 1982; Engel and Hildebrandt, 1974; Floyd et al., 1966; Hale, 1988; Higgs, 1983, 1992; Smith, 1990; Walsh, Marchiori, and Steadward, 1986; Wirta et al., 1990).

Wheelchair propulsion for movement efficiency has been studied in terms of rim diameter, stroke frequency, seat height, technique, speed, level of impairment, and event (sprint vs. distance) (Breukelen, 2001; Higgs, 1983, 1986; Sanderson and Sommer, 1985; Vanlandewijck et al., 2001; York and Kimura, 1986). Results are varied due to the complexity of the interaction of the variables already mentioned along with the human factor. With the decrease in the mass of the chair in addition to individual adaptations of seat height, wheel camber, and hand rim sizes, athletic performance has improved substantially over the years. Velocity for wheelchair ambulation has been found to be related to rapid stroking (pushes) on the hand rims rather than long strokes. Hand and foot propulsion techniques have been studied in relation to athletic performances of individuals with disabilities. Better training appears to result in better performances (Abel et al., 2003).

Gait Performance

Studies of gait performance of elite athletes with disabilities include those on the effect of prosthetic design on amputee performance (Enoka, Miller, and Burgess, 1982; Gandee et al., 1973; Kegel et al., 1981). Visually impaired athletes' running and walking gaits have also been studied (Arnhold and McGrain, 1985; Dawson, 1981; Gorton and Gavron, 1987; Pope, McGrain, and Arnhold, 1986). Biomechanical gait studies in running and racewalking, which describe the angles and force patterns of the body, have also been conducted in individuals with developmental disabilities and CP (Gorton and Gavron, 1987; Skrotsky, 1983). Steadward and colleagues from the Rick Hansen Centre have studied the kinematics (physics of motion) of wheelchair propulsion.

Specialized equipment such as hand and foot prostheses has improved tremendously, not only in design and functionality but also in weight and aesthetics. These improvements have allowed athletes with disabilities to perform faster and better.

Biomechanics

Biomechanics research has been conducted both in the field and in laboratory settings. There is a need to replicate studies in both environments to increase the subject pool and improve generalization of results for application for athletes and coaches. Biomechanical research has led to better-designed wheelchairs and mono-skis and to improved performance in all sport areas. An example of recent research is reported by Strike and Wells in "A Kinematic Analysis of a Trans Tibial Amputee in the Take Off of a Vertical Jump" (2003). The authors conclude that more study is needed of the skill of jumping in volleyball and the relationship/role of the prosthesis in order to clarify the impact of each component on the kinematics and mechanics that make up this very important skill in volleyball.

Classification

Classification of athletes with disabilities for competition has been a long-standing controversy. On one hand, the goal of classification seems to be to enable each competitor, regardless of severity of impairment, to compete in a fair manner with others of similar ability/disability (a more medically based classification system). On the other hand, the goal of classification based upon functional ability applied to sport is to provide for meaningful athletic competition based upon ability, not disability, thus tending to eliminate the more severely impaired from elite athletic competition. This latter goal of classification has emerged as a result of the administrative problem and logistics of numerous classes for competitions: more than seventy 100-meter races by gender and disability type—3 for blind, 8 for cerebral palsy, 9 for amputees, 6 for les autres, 7 for wheelchair users, and 42 for spinal cord (below C6)-injured males and females (Higgs et al., 1990). Even from the athlete's perspective, classification remains a difficult issue (Lorinez, 2001).

Wheelchair basketball, swimming, and track and field have been at the forefront of the classification controversy (Brasile, 1990a, 1990b; Gehlsen and Karpuk, 1992; Richter et al., 1992). Discussion of the medical versus functional issues can be found in the literature from 1979 onward (Lindstrom, 1985; McCann, 1979; Strohkendl, 2001; Thiboutot, 1986; Weiss and Curtis, 1986).

The results of research on classification have been mixed, and these investigations are often undertaken and reported based on the differing goals just identified (Brasile, 2003). Differences found in athletic performances in track and field by gender, distance, and class of athletes (Coutts and Schutz, 1988; Ridgeway, Pope, and Wilkerson, 1988; Wicks et al., 1983) have been used to support the need for classification for fairness. On the other hand, the findings reported by Higgs et al. (1990), as well as Gorton and Gavron (1987), support a reduction in the number of classifications.

Coaches and Coach Training

The number of sporting events and opportunities for athletes with disabilities has increased dramatically, and as a result there is a continuing problem of finding enough coaches (Bhambhani, 2001). DePauw and Gavron (1991) found that athletes with disabilities, for the most part, practiced on their own until the 1990s, at which time more publicity, money, and visibility increased their opportunities for more organized practices. And although the literature for able-bodied sport is replete with studies on coach role conflict, burnout, gender issues, and role modeling (Capel, Sisley, and Desertrain, 1987; Decker, 1986; Knoppers, 1987; Whitaker and Molstead, 1988), there is a paucity of research about coaches for athletes with disabilities (DePauw and Gavron, 1991). Bradbury (2001), in a study about self-coaching by elite athletes with disabilities, found that a significant degree of self-coaching still goes on and that there is a lack of guidelines and guidance for these athletes to follow.

We cannot dispute the need for the study of coaches, officials, and volunteers. DePauw (1986b) summarized the areas of needed study as identified by the research subcommittee of the COSD of the USOC. Specifically, broad topics were identified as "the training, selection, effectiveness, evaluation, and the advisability of volunteers versus paid staff" (DePauw, 1986b, p. 294). Some of the research topics put forth included

- comparing the performance of athletes when coached by volunteers, trained able-bodied coaches, and specific sport experts;
- effectiveness of various coaches' training programs;
- development of coaching certification for coaches of disability sport;
- development of training programs for coaches of youth sport; and
- profiling the background and training of current coaches.

As the sport movement for individuals with disabilities moves forward, the role of the coach becomes more significant. DePauw and Gavron (1991) studied 155 coaches of disability sport and found the following:

- Approximately 71% of the coaches were between the ages of 20 and 40.
- Only 16% of the coaches were themselves disabled.
- Over 85% of the coaches held college degrees.
- Many of the coaches indicated that they had coached able-bodied athletes longer than athletes with disabilities.
- Over 75% of the coaches had attended a workshop on coaching techniques, but only 56% had attended workshops on coaching athletes with disabilities.
- The amount of time they actually coached varied by sport and association.
- More males than females tended to be involved in coaching.

This study indicates a need for more coaches who are better trained and who have access to practice facilities and time for practice. Coaches also need more training via workshops or the certification route. Athletes with disabilities should be encouraged to become trained coaches. The importance of coaches and athletes with hearing impairments is demonstrated by the fact that initial involvement in Deaf sport usually results from contact with its coaches and athletes (Stewart, McCarthy, and Robinson, 1988).

KEY POINT

Research on coaches of athletes with disabilities is sparse, but the need for more coaches trained in working with disabled athletes is clear.

Exercise Physiology

Bhambhani (2001) has provided a salient article on the status of exercise physiology (impact of exercise on the body's systems, muscles, and bones) and Paralympic sport, presenting several premises:

- Research in this area has not kept up with the Paralympic movement.
- Many coaches utilize strategies for their athletes that are based strictly upon able-bodied athlete research.
- Many of the Paralympic sports have not been adequately researched, if at all.
- There is a lack of research on women athletes with disabilities.
- Research design, instrumentation, testing procedures, sample sizes, and makeup need to be more consistent (pp. 8-12).

Obviously, the role and understanding of exercise physiology and disability sport need to grow even more. There are currently more questions than answers.

Although differences exist, athletes with disabilities exhibit many responses to exercise similar to those of able-bodied athletes. Generally, the "true" differences found are caused by differences in functional muscle mass resulting from paralysis, amputation, or osteoporosis in paralyzed limbs and the severity of the physical impairment. Differences might be caused by difficulties of comprehension, motivation, or mechanical inefficiency related to specific types of impairment (e.g., mental retardation, CP) (Shephard, 1990). In these cases, it remains unclear whether the differences in physiological responses are caused by differences in physiological functioning or in assessment techniques.

As would be expected, wheelchair athletes who compete in track and swimming events have larger maximum oxygen intake than those who compete in strength events. Regular physical activity by wheelchair athletes can increase cardiac stroke volume; paraplegic athletes have been shown to experience greater increases than do quadriplegics (Shephard, 1990).

Training regimens for elite athletes with disabilities should include principles and practices followed by able-bodied athletes with adaptations as needed. Although a specific disability may affect the degree of intensity, duration, and frequency of exercise, there is enough evidence to suggest that physiological training effects can be achieved in individuals with disabilities (Burke et al., 1985; Cameron, Ward, and Wicks, 1978; Coutts, Rhodes, and McKenzie, 1983; Coutts and Steryn, 1987; Cowell, Squires, and Raven, 1986; Shephard, 1990). At times of practical application, it may be necessary to change or adapt body position or the number of repetitions and sets. It is also important to adjust the direction, especially for those individuals who can only propel the chair backward (e.g., person with severe CP).

Other exercise physiology studies have been conducted with below-knee and above-knee amputees (Davis, Shephard, and Jackson, 1981; Ryser, Erickson, and Calahan, 1988), hearing-impaired athletes (Lewis, Higam, and Cherry, 1985), individuals with CP (Birk et al., 1983, 1984; McCubbin and Shasby, 1985), and developmentally handicapped athletes (Rimmer and Kelly, 1991). In all instances there were not enough studies to warrant generalization, nor were the numbers of subjects robust. Additional research in this area would further benefit athletes and coaches who seek state-of-the art training regimens.

General Principles of Coaching Athletes With Disabilities

Coaching athletes with disabilities requires many of the same skills as coaching able-bodied athletes. A coach should treat athletes as individuals and understand their individual differences and their capabilities. Coaches should then maximize these qualities to the fullest so that each athlete can realize his or her potential (Australian Coaching Council, 1989).

Volleyball team assistant coach Denise Van DeWalle instructs the players.

Michael Teuber

FAST FACTS

Home Base: Germany
Sports: Cycling
Selected Accomplishments:

World champion cyclist (nine medals since 1998)

Distance and pursuit rider

European cycling records (nine gold medals)

"Impressed with the Paralympics in Atlanta in 1996 there grew a dream in my mind, the dream of winning an Olympic medal."

This young man, who has limited use of his lower legs as a result of an automobile accident, decided that he would use what he had left. Michael, in his early hospital days, redeveloped his thighs to about 65% of their original capacity. Using his newly redeveloped leg strength and assistive devices, Michael became mobile again. Then he found road racing in 1994—not quite the same as his earlier pursuits of wind surfing and snowboarding, but challenging nevertheless. This independent businessman with a degree in commerce now owns his own bike shop as well as competes. The last several years have seen him develop into a world-class cyclist. He has been an IPC world champion and European champion. He has numerous medals in road racing, trail racing, and pursuit racing. Michael's family and spouse have been with him and for him during this entire time. Their support has been invaluable. Michael found that the experience of mountain biking for rehabilitative reasons grew into a passion to compete. The rest, as they say, is history. And Michael Teuber continues to rewrite the book with his success in competitive cycling, business, and life.

Sometimes individuals with a disability are limited in their exposure to physical activity, coordination experiences, and fitness levels. However, the main problem facing most individuals with a disability has been their limited opportunity at a young age to master basic movement patterns and the resulting sporting experience (Gavron, 1999). Their confidence levels, interest, and motivation may all be affected because of this lack of participation (Australian Coaching Council, 1989; Kristen, Patriksson, and Fridlund, 2003; Sherrill, 1997).

Fitness programs are available to individuals of all abilities including those with disabilities. Researchers at the Robert D. Steadward Centre (Canada) have developed a series of three booklets (e.g., Walsh, Holland, and Steadward, 1985) that provide individuals who use wheelchairs with specific programs about aerobic fitness, muscular fitness, and flexibility. The Australian Sports Commission has various booklets and resource materials available for coaches and athletes alike (e.g., "Give It a Go," 2001; Willing and Able series, 1989-1993). Exercise videos are also available, as are sport instruction tapes. Most physical fitness training activities can be adapted to individual needs and sport. Thus, access to such publications as *Sports 'n Spokes* and *Palaestra,* which regularly provide training regimens of elite athletes with a variety of disabilities, would be helpful. Specialized equipment in the form of arm ergometers, wheelchair ergometers, wheelchair rollers, adapted treadmills, and multipurpose weight machines provides countless methods and approaches for fitness training for individuals who are ambulatory and for athletes with various levels of spinal cord injuries (Paciorek and Jones, 1989). Booklets and videos are often listed in selected issues of *Sports 'n Spokes* or *Palaestra* and are available through disability sport organizations, local sport and recreation agencies, or the public schools. Valuable resources can also be found through the Web site of the National Center for Physical Activity for Individuals with Disabilities (www.ncpad.org).

In countries around the world, various training resources are available in scientific journals, fitness magazines, rehabilitation journals, and conference proceedings. Athletes and coaches must increasingly access and utilize these resources in order to remain on the cutting edge of training and to be truly competitive. The Internet has increased access and the exchange of information and should be utilized as another tool. Ellery and Forbus (1999) describe various mechanisms such as listserves, news groups, and e-mail as they apply to our field.

Generic concepts of coaching can be applied for athletes with disabilities. Some of these concepts are similar to those for athletes without disabilities, while others call attention to special needs or concerns (Active Living Alliance for Canadians with a Disability, 1994; Australian Coaching Council, 1989; Australian Sports Commission, 2001; Bremner and Goodman, 1992; Hockey and Goodman, 1992; Nunn, 1991):

- Understand that athletes with disabilities are people first and disabled second.
- Be knowledgeable about the nature and degree of disability.
- Help athletes set realistic goals and objectives based on your knowledge of them as individuals.
- Ask athletes for information about what they can do and how to adapt activities.
- Develop reasonable skill progressions.
- Assist athletes when requested, but do not become overbearing and smother them. It is often best to anticipate when to assist.
- Modify rules as necessary, but do not lose the essence of the activity.
- Provide consistent, reliable, and timely feedback.
- Communicate in a patient, open manner. Have athletes repeat instructions to determine whether they understand them.
- Allow athletes to experience risk, success, and failure. Do not overprotect them.
- Concentrate on what athletes can do. Do not underestimate their abilities.
- Utilize smaller groups when coaching athletes with disabilities so that the ratio of coach to athlete is lower.
- Seek solutions that match an athlete's abilities and personality.
- Coach with an open mind and do not have predetermined limits of performance.

Another consideration when coaching individuals with disabilities is attending to environmental factors that may affect performance. Rich (1990) has identified several environmental concerns:

- **Sound.** Sometimes sound can distract an individual's attention from tasks and thus affect movement output quality. At other times sound can be used to set a mood for practice or for assisting an individual with location of objects or direction for running.
- **Lighting.** It is important to light a gymnasium or a field so that objects and lines may be seen easily. However, some individuals may be overstimulated by too much lighting. This factor then causes them to become hyperactive and not focus on training tasks. Likewise, lowering the lighting intensity and position can have a calming effect.
- **Temperature.** Climate control of gymnasiums or outdoor environments is important for individuals with disabilities. A cool environment is preferable to one that is hot and humid. Some individuals have allergies that are activated in a hot and humid climate. A hot

and humid climate will also result in a higher fluid loss rate and may have a quicker impact on athletes with disabilities.

- **Organization.** The training environment should be organized for optimal practice effect. The size and color of equipment are important. Colors can make an object more or less visible to an individual, and that along with size can affect performance success. A barrier-free environment is also an important consideration in organizing practices.

Adapted, by permission, from S. Rich, 1990, Factors influencing the learning process. In *Adapted physical education and sport*, (Champaign, IL: Human Kinetics), 121-130.

Gavron (1991) identified personal attributes that must be a concern of the coach when working with individuals with disabilities. One aspect is the nature, amount, and kind of medications taken. Sometimes medicines are affected by exercise. For example, diabetics may have to adjust the dosage of insulin if participating in athletic events. The sun can interact with certain antibiotics and cause severe reactions. Thus, keeping an accurate record of medications and understanding drug interactions are important for an individual's health and safety. An athlete's eating habits should also concern a coach. Eating the right kinds and amounts of food is important for performance. Skipping meals can lead to hypoglycemia and fainting episodes. A poor diet can also affect muscle strength, endurance, and coordination. In activities in which weight is a factor (e.g., gymnastics, swimming, wrestling), it is important not to encourage binge eating and purging.

The main strategy involved in coaching athletes with disabilities centers on knowledge of the sport content, the biomechanical and kinesiological applications, and one's professional and personal interaction with another human being.

Selected Disabilities and Specific Strategies

In work with athletes who have disabilities, there may be differences in coaching concepts due to the disability and the nature of the sport. Thus, it is important to be aware of specific concepts that are important to quality motor output in relation to an individual's specific disability. Coaching techniques for specific sport and recreation activities can be found in a variety of sources as previously indicated. Additionally, Special Olympics has developed coaching manuals for its sports. Disability sport groups also provide materials for their coaches and athletes (see appendix E).

The suggestions offered here are disability-specific modifications. Coaching techniques and training regimens used with able-bodied athletes should be used as the basis for training, and suggested modifications should be used only as needed. Further, athletes with disabilities should be consulted for their firsthand knowledge of effective training.

Individuals With Intellectual Impairments/ Developmental Disabilities

Although individuals with intellectual impairment have a cognitive disability, one should not infer that they are incapable of performing physically. In fact, if there are no complications other than the diagnosis of mental retardation, there should not be any limits, physiologically speaking. Thus, an individual with mental retardation has the same potential to develop physically as his or her peers. However, because of cognitive limitations and possible secondary complications, there are some specific suggestions to consider when working with individuals who are mentally retarded (Gavron, 1991; Shephard, 1990):

- Check individuals with Down syndrome for atlanto-axial syndrome prior to participation in any sport program. If this syndrome is present, then eliminate activities that place pressure on the head and neck region.
- Multiple repetitions of a task are required for mastery. Practicing a pattern, skill, or series of skills in a repetitive manner is important for these individuals.
- Allow 5 to 10 seconds for an individual to respond to directions. People may have a tendency to bombard individuals with directions. Because Down syndrome is a cognitive dysfunction, these individuals need even more time than their able-bodied peers to process information (Dunn, Morehouse, and Fredericks, 1986).
- Demonstration and manual manipulation through the range of motion are the most effective techniques for teaching movement. Physically assisting an individual through the range of motion provides kinesthetic feedback to the individual about the motion. This has been found to be very helpful for those with mental retardation.
- Use simple rather than complex sequences of instructions.
- Break tasks down into "chunks" that are sequential and have attainable goals.
- Apply behavior management strategies as needed.
- Be aware that individuals with Down syndrome are sensitive to heat and humidity.

Learning Disabilities

For individuals with learning disabilities, coaching can utilize certain adaptations:

- Keep directions short and concise.
- Break practice into small segments of high-intensity work.

- Identify the best learning channel (visual, auditory, or combination) for the individual.
- Utilize appropriate behavior management techniques and strategies as needed.
- Provide a structure or routine for practice.
- Provide for a nonthreatening practice environment.
- Develop balance, laterality, directionality, and coordination as needed.

Individuals With Sensory Impairments

Individuals with hearing or vision impairments can develop into highly skilled athletes. That one part of the sensory-motor integrative system is not functioning does not mean that everything else ceases to function or functions inefficiently. Individuals with sensory impairments can develop physiologically and in terms of strength and skill as do their able-bodied counterparts. Athletes with sensory disabilities have participated on the U.S. Olympic teams in swimming, archery, and track.

For work with individuals who have hearing impairment, suggestions include the following (Adams and McCubbin, 1991; Gavron, 1991; Shephard, 1990):

- Provide diagrams of court layouts or routes for cross country running and locations for all support services for events.
- Utilize pictures, posters, mirrors, and videotapes for skill development.
- Develop some functional signing skills.
- Do not have athletes who are lip-readers face you while the sun is in their eyes.
- Develop a system of hand signals for long-distance coaching (Australian Sports Commission, 2001; Sherrill, 2001a).
- Work on improving balance, a major factor in quality performance output and an aspect of deafness that is usually significantly impaired since the balance mechanism is located in the inner ear.

Specific considerations for working with individuals who are blind or visually impaired include the following:

- Become familiar with the sport area by walking around it, as with track and downhill skiing courses.
- Use voice, wooden clappers, or an automatic directional beeper for enhancing directional awareness.

- Count steps in activities in which approaches are important (e.g., high jump, running long jump, vaulting).
- Use a tether or partner system in running events or track and field events.
- Develop cardiovascular fitness and strength capabilities.
- Have athletes feel the shape, size, and texture of the equipment with which they will work.
- Utilize audiocassettes for instructional techniques.

Physical Impairments

Individuals with physical impairments will demonstrate variance in the amount of physical activity they can do (intensity) and in duration, frequency, and quality. Two individuals with spinal cord injuries, for example, can have a lesion at the same vertebra level and yet function in different capacities. The same is true for individuals with CP. This is what makes the issue of classification so difficult. Although research has provided generalization about the level of function, the actual level of performance is really a matter of individual functioning. For those individuals who have a physical disability and who are ambulatory, the following suggestions have been presented (Australian Sports Commission, 2001; Gavron, 1991; Shephard, 1990; Sherrill, 2001a):

- Assist individuals in and out of activity positions as needed.
- Adapt positions as needed for most effective performance.
- Have amputees and crutch walkers engage in activities in which the upper torso is the primary focus of the movement.
- Teach amputees and crutch walkers who run how to fall safely.
- Develop range of motion and strength.

For persons who have a physical disability and utilize a wheelchair for their events, one should consider the following:

- Have the correct type of wheelchair for the activity.
- Adapt the wheelchair as needed for proper balance.
- Use appropriate tie-downs for wheelchair stability.
- Develop muscular strength, range of motion, and awareness of the center of gravity for activities.
- Understand that positioning may be altered due to the functioning ability of muscles (e.g., individual with CP may push the wheelchair backward).

Roman Musil

FAST FACTS

Home Base: Czech Republic
Sport: Athletics (shot put, javelin, discus) and cycling
Selected Accomplishments:

Gold medal in 2000 Paralympics in cycling (1,500 meter)

Silver medal in 2000 Paralympics in discus, bronze in road race division

Lifelong disability sport participant

 This young man with cerebral palsy has been involved in sport since his early years. Roman trains six days a week and is assisted by family members and close friends. As a child he often went to a spa in his country and then got involved in sports with a club. Roman states, "Sports motivate me to improve my results and . . . sports keep me fit." His results speak for themselves. In the 2000 Paralympic Games, Roman won a gold medal in the 1,500-meter cycling event, a silver medal in the discus, and a bronze medal in the road race division (cycling). Roman's philosophy about sport is "Don't think about it, just start!" It appears that Roman Musil has practiced what he preaches.

"Don't think about it, just start!"

Coaching athletes with disabilities requires knowledge of the sport and the disability. Having a variety of strategies going into the coaching environment is important, but it is also important to develop strategies that fit the environment and the athlete.

KEY POINT

Coaching adaptations for sport performance may be necessary in some instances depending on the activity and the nature of the athlete's disability.

Concluding Comments

Competent coaches are critical to the continued improvement of athletic performance of athletes with disabilities. Knowledge of sport and appropriate adaptations by disability are prerequisites to success. A continuous and organized effort to develop research, both laboratory and field based, must be considered an important avenue for gaining even higher levels of performance.

nine

Sports Medicine and Athletic Training for Athletes With Disabilities

Dr. Ron Davis and Dr. Mike Ferrara

Reader Goal   Learn about the similarities and differences in sports medicine treatment, injuries, and prevention in disability sport versus sport for those without disabilities

Chapter Synopsis

- Sports Medicine
- Sports Medicine and Disability Sport
- Injuries, Incidence, Care, Prevention
- Treatment Considerations
- Training
- Exercise Considerations
- Concluding Comments

The Paralympics of Atlanta (1996), Sydney (2000), and Salt Lake City (2002) were impressive and unmatched in athletic performance, media coverage, and spectator interest. Over 3,100 athletes from 103 countries participated in the Atlanta Summer Paralympics, followed by 3,843 athletes from 123 countries competing in the Sydney Summer Paralympics (Paralympic Games, 2001).

This increase in athlete participation netted an astonishing total of more than 300 world and Paralympic records at the Games in Sydney. Jason Wening (double-leg amputee) from the United States won three gold medals in the 400-meter freestyle. American Jean Driscoll (wheelchair division) placed a close second in the women's 1,500 meter with a time of 3:48.65 (first place went to Louise Sauvage of Australia at 3:48.52). Marlon Shirley (single-leg amputee) set a new world record in the men's 100 meter with a time of 11.09 seconds, and Ross Davis (wheelchair athlete with cerebral palsy) set a new Paralympic record in the men's 100 meter with a time of 16.38 seconds.

Each new competition raised the bar of excellence, and with the 2004 Paralympic Games scheduled for Greece the world of disability sport was poised to go even further in its pursuit of excellence. The 2004 Paralympic Games would host nearly 4,000 athletes from 130 countries, with support from over 2,000 team officials, 1,000 technical officials, and 15,000 volunteers (Paralympic Games, 2001). Among those support personnel would be members of sports medicine teams assembled to provide the necessary coverage of athlete care and injury treatment.

Athletes with disabilities continue to focus on training and sports medicine as evidenced by their improvement in Paralympic performances. Accordingly the purpose of this chapter is to provide information related to sports medicine as it applies to training and athletes with disabilities. This is not a chapter on "how to" or "what is the best method." We do, however, provide general information concerning sports medicine.

Sports Medicine

What is sports medicine, and what is its background? Historically, the use of therapeutic exercises (medical gymnastics) was documented around 1000-800 B.C. (American Academy of Orthopedic Surgeons, 1991). As the popularity of sports grew over the course of time, professionals interested in the well-being of the participants organized to help provide a more effective service delivery system. Physicians were the first to become involved with sport care. With the emergence and development of interscholastic and intercollegiate programs, athletic trainers also gained prominence.

Today the term sports medicine includes, but is not limited to, the services of such professionals as athletic trainers, physicians, physical therapists, coaches, athletic administrators/directors, exercise physiologists, and nutritionists. The sports medicine professional is involved in preventing injuries and developing training schedules. Regardless of their role, sports medicine professionals have their roots in able-bodied sports.

Sports Medicine and Disability Sport

The earliest documentation of sports medicine involvement with disabled sport centered on athletic injuries. Curtis (1981a, 1981b, 1982), a physical therapist, wrote a series of articles covering exercise physiology, training, stretching routines, and athletic injuries. Curtis's work provided the foundation for other professionals in the area of sports medicine for the disabled to build upon. While Curtis's efforts were descriptive in nature, Mangus (1987) reported on injuries to disabled athletes from a prevention and treatment perspective. An athletic trainer, Mangus divided his work between athletes with sensory impairments and those with physical impairments.

Perhaps the most comprehensive study related to sports medicine and injury surveillance was a project supported by the United States Olympic Foundation under the direction of Dr. Michael Ferrara titled Athletes with Disabilities Injury Registry (ADIR). This was the first study of the causes, distribution, and occurrence of injuries in athletes with disabilities that used a cross-disability design. Ferrara's work began in 1989 and continued through 1992. The Athletes with Disabilities Injury Registry was a comprehensive injury surveillance system in which injury and exposure information was collected and analyzed. Data analysis covered location of injury (i.e., head, neck, wrist, etc.), type of injury, surface on which the injury occurred, time of injury (i.e., during training or competition), time loss due to the injury, and medical caregiver (i.e., physician, athletic trainer, therapists). Three major disability sport organizations were involved with ADIR: the National Wheelchair Athletic Association (NWAA), now called Wheelchair Sports, USA, which represents individuals with spinal cord injuries; the United States Association of Blind Athletes (USABA); and the United States Cerebral Palsy Athletic Association (USCPAA), now called the National Disability Sports Alliance (NDSA). While research on injury is continuing, field experience on the part of sports medicine professionals at disability sporting competitions is also increasing.

Davis et al. (2001) reported on the perceptions of student athletic trainers providing care to athletes competing in Special Olympic state championships. Student trainer involvement further indicates an increased involvement of sports medicine professionals in disability sport.

Kowalski and McCann (1991) reported on a unique sports medicine approach utilized at the 1991 Victory Games in New York. A mobile sports medicine center, sponsored by the Henry Ford Hospital in Detroit, Michigan, was set up on the grounds of the games. The mobile center, housed in a tractor trailer, was billed as the largest expandable athletic sports medicine facility on wheels in the world. The mobile unit had a staff of 9 physicians, 17 trainers, 12 physical therapists, 8 chiropractors, 14 nurses, and 5 emergency medical technicians. All of these professionals were ready to provide medical assistance to more than 1,200 athletes with disabilities. Another mobile unit was utilized during the 2002 Sports Festival held in New London, Connecticut. Again, sports medicine professionals were actively engaged in and supported a sporting competition for over 200 athletes with disabilities (R. Davis, personal communication, July 2003).

The 1991 International Special Olympics implemented one of the most comprehensive medical coverage systems, utilizing the latest in modern communication technology. More than 750 medical and health care personnel volunteered to serve on sports medicine teams. Each team included athletic training, nursing, first aid, and emergency medical technicians. Teams provided treatment for more than 6,000 athletes at 16 different sporting venues. Seventeen mobile medical units, housed in large recreational vehicles, were equipped with cellular phones, facsimile machines, and cellular facsimile machines to transmit medical information. "Never in the history of Special Olympics or Olympics has such a facsimile system been used" (Special Olympics medical director, personal communication, July 26, 1991).

KEY POINT

Athletes with disabilities increasingly focus on training and sports medicine. Especially as the number of these athletes continues to grow, sports medicine will become increasingly important to disability sport.

Injuries, Incidence, Care, Prevention

While it is apparent that sports medicine is becoming more actively involved with disability sport from a care and prevention standpoint, injuries still occur. This section deals with the incidence and types of injuries and treatment considerations for the athletic trainer or other medical caregiver.

Treatment, care, and prevention of athletic injuries must be documented and called to the attention of the physician, trainer, or coach (or more than one of these). Historically, physicians, athletic trainers, and physical therapists have not been alerted when athletes with disabilities are injured. Hopefully, with the increased on-site involvement of physicians and trainers at competitions, treatment will greatly improve.

Curtis (1982) documented the 10 most common wheelchair sport injuries, indicating that 33% of all injuries were classified as soft tissue (i.e., sprains, strains, muscle pulls, tendinitis, bursitis). The second and third most common injuries were blisters and lacerations, respectively. Track, basketball, and road racing were the top three sports associated with injury risk for the wheelchair athlete. According to Curtis, soft tissue injuries ranked first for the sports of road racing, basketball, and tennis. Ferrara and Davis (1990) concurred with Curtis's report of a high number of muscular injuries particularly to the shoulder.

Ferrara (1990) indicated that upper extremities suffer more chronic injuries than the lower body. Twenty-two percent of all injuries reported across disabilities occurred at the shoulder for the athlete with a spinal cord injury, cerebral palsy, or visual impairment, followed by injuries to the hand and fingers (10%). The USCPAA athletes (now NDSA) indicated a higher percentage of hand and finger injuries than NWAA (now Wheelchair Sports, USA) and USABA athletes. Ferrara's breakdown of these injuries is presented in figure 9.1.

KEY POINT

Data on sport injuries are not uniformly collected, and there is a need for more of this type of information.

Treatment Considerations

With few exceptions, treatment procedures for specific types of injuries should remain the same regardless of ability or disability. The treatment of strains, sprains, lacerations, contusions, and other injuries should not change when one is treating an athlete with a sensory or physical impairment. However, communication and follow-up management should be important considerations. Table 9.1 lists aspects of the care and prevention of some of the most common injuries. While athletes with disabilities have some unique kinds of injuries, such as pressure sores or hand problems from wheelchair racing, it is as important to note the commonalities of injury and treatment with able-bodied athletes as it is to discern the differences.

Communication with athletes with disabilities concerning injury management and follow-up treatment does require specific considerations related to individual disabilities. Athletes with sensory impairment usually have normal cognitive abilities. Comprehending treatment procedures and

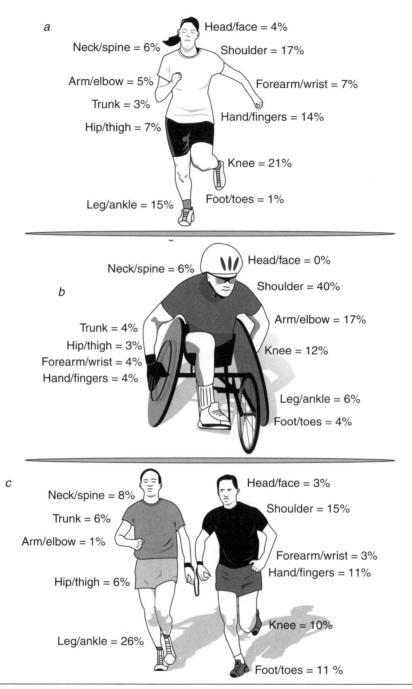

Figure 9.1 Injuries to athletes compiled from *(a)* United States Cerebral Palsy Athletic Association, *(b)* National Wheelchair Athletic Association, and *(c)* United States Association of Blind Athletes.

Adapted, by permission, from K.P. DePauw and S.J. Gavron, 1995, *Disability and sport* (Champaign, IL: Human Kinetics), 137. Data from Ferrara (1990).

Table 9.1 Care and Prevention

Injury/Concern	Prevention
Soft tissue	Stretching—warm-up/cool-down
	Protective covering for old injuries
Blisters	Taping fingers
	Protective covering (such as gloves or socks on upper arms) for wheelchair users
	Frequent inspection of footwear
Abrasions/Lacerations	Protective covering for old injuries
Pressure sores (wheelchair users)	Frequent weight shifting
	Clothing that absorbs moisture
Decreased healing time	Decubitus ulcers—account for 25% of medical costs, take time to heal
Thermal regulation	Spinal cord injury (SCI) above T6 at risk; can become poikilothermic (body assumes same temperature as the environment); adequate clothing and protection essential
Autonomic dysreflexia	Blood pressure can increase and heart rate will decrease; require all SCI to empty bladder before competition
Atlanto-axial instability	Found in athletes with Down syndrome; requires an X ray for diagnosis; if positive, restrict athlete from diving and tumbling activities

follow-up responsibilities is not a problem, but compliance may be. The individual attention has to do with the athletic trainer's ability to effectively communicate the information. In other words, choosing the appropriate mechanism for learning is key (e.g., visual, auditory, sign language).

Davis et al. (2001) reported that communication with the athlete was a great concern of student athletic trainers. The student athletic trainers indicated they had a difficult time deciding the seriousness of the injury. Several indicated that they could not understand the athlete, which made assessments difficult to complete.

Another consideration, perhaps just as important as communication, is documenting the nature, causes, and treatments of any and all injuries. Keeping individual athlete records and an overall log can identify patterns that cause injury and perhaps help prevent future occurrences.

Athletes With Hearing Impairments

Mangus (1987) suggests the following when communicating with athletes who have a hearing impairment:

- Try not to yell. Speak with a normal tone and directly to the athlete.

- Try not to speak too fast. Watch your pace.
- Be aware that the athlete might be reading your lips. Moustaches and beards might interfere. Shaving the moustache or beard might be necessary.
- Allow enough time when communicating, as the athlete might speak more slowly and need additional time. Be patient.
- Use visuals if necessary.

Athletes With Visual Impairments

Mangus (1987) suggests the following when communicating with athletes who have visual impairment:

- Realize you must work through the modalities of sense and touch.
- Use the tactile sense. Allow the athlete to feel the uninjured part and compare it to the injured part.
- Allow the athlete to follow your hands through the injury evaluation procedure.
- Physically assist the athlete through any rehabilitative exercises while under your supervision to help clarify proper procedures.

Athletes With Cerebral Palsy

The etiology or cause of cerebral palsy (CP) is often explained as a neurological impairment affecting voluntary motor control. That is, the nervous system becomes impaired, and consequently its ability to transmit signals to muscles also becomes impaired, as does motor output or movement. According to Sherrill (2001a, 2001b) less than 20% of the athletes reported by the USCPAA (now NDSA) have an associated condition related to mental retardation. Therefore, the majority of athletes with CP have normal cognitive abilities. However, greater associated dysfunctions are reported in the sensory modalities of speech, vision, hearing, and perceptual deficits. As a result of these associated disorders found in individuals with CP, communicating about the injury treatment and follow-up management do not hinge on the athletes' cognitive ability but may be unclear due to the impact of the associated complications, especially hearing.

Some considerations for communicating about injury treatment for the athlete with CP are as follows:

- Use word boards or other visuals related to the injury and follow-up treatment.
- Allow enough time to communicate. The athlete's speech might be very slow and difficult to understand. Be patient.

- Straps, slings, and wraps might be needed to appropriately position and secure ice bags/cold packs. The nature of the CP (e.g., spasticity, athetoid) might not allow the athlete the muscle control to hold treatments on the injured body part.
- Position the athlete carefully during examination, treatment, and follow-up. Incorrect positioning on a treatment table might elicit abnormal reflexive tones, which will interfere with movement.
- Avoid sudden or ballistic movements during examination. Move body parts slowly to avoid increased muscle tone or abnormal reflexive responses.

Athletes Using Wheelchairs

The following are suggestions for treatment and injury management for the athlete using a wheelchair:

- Regulate and replace fluids often. Use of spray bottles and cool towels is recommended for the quadriplegic athlete.
- Don't allow the athlete extended periods of time exposed to the sun.
- Evaluate conditions for pressure sores:
    1. Check skin frequently.
    2. Remove pressure from the site.
    3. Treat local infection with disinfectant.
    4. Keep the area clean. Use dressings to promote healing.
    5. Maintain proper nutrition and hygiene.

Decubitus ulcers are perhaps the most debilitating injury for the wheelchair athlete. A decubitus pressure sore occurs when an individual is in one position for long periods of time. The skin starts to break down and infection or ulcers may develop. Decubitus ulcers (pressure sores) do not necessarily directly relate to the athletic endeavor and may originate from causes other than training, but they may affect athletic performance and thus are a major concern. Athletes who use a wheelchair need to be conscious of this condition on a daily basis. Pressure sores can negatively affect an athlete's preparation and training for weeks or months. Constant inspection is imperative. Early signs of skin breakdown must be treated immediately, and close supervision by sports medicine professionals is vital.

Athletes With Intellectual Impairments

Platt (2001) suggests the following when one is communicating with athletes who have cognitive impairments:

- Give the athlete a primary set of instructions with simplified information. Maintain eye contact during instructions.
- Speak clearly and directly to the athlete. Use concise and age-appropriate language.
- All verbal instructions should be short and concise. All dialogues should be reviewed with the athlete to ensure comprehension.
- Demonstrate all motor patterns before asking the athlete to engage in movement.

Professional Preparation

While it is clearly documented that sports medicine professionals are becoming increasingly involved with disability sports, attention must now shift to their professional preparation. Athletic trainers and coaches should have formal training related to the etiologies of the various disabilities. A review of current professional preparation practices reveals a void in preparation for athletic trainers regarding athletes with disabilities. Course work related to athletic care and prevention for the disabled is virtually nonexistent. A survey completed at the 1991 Victory Games in New York by coaches and team leaders of disabled athletes indicated modest professional preparation. Of the 84 respondents, 33% had had an educational course in disability sport, 63% had completed a workshop/clinic on disability sport, and 50% had attended a coaching conference related to disability sport within a three-year period.

Results from Davis et al. (2001) indicated that over 65% of student athletic trainers felt that a course in disability sport would better prepare them to work with athletes with disabilities (e.g., Special Olympians).

If sports medicine professionals are to continue their involvement in disability sport, it would seem logical for them to have formal training in sport and disability. Suggestions for addressing this situation might be the inclusion of course work within the higher education curriculum, especially for degrees in physical education (kinesiology, exercise science), adapted physical education, athletic training, and coaching. Revision of coaching curricula to include a course related to sport for individuals with disabilities is another approach. Extended workshops through university continuing education programs might also be successful.

While universities have sponsored athletic programs and competitions for athletes with disabilities (see chapter 5), there is a definite lack of support on a national basis. So too with sports medicine programs for athletes with disabilities.

Historically, several universities have utilized a very effective venue for professional preparation by hosting elite training camps. Ball State University (Muncie, IN), the University of Illinois (Champaign, IL), and the University of California at Sacramento have each sponsored training

Rebecca Hart

FAST FACTS
Home Base: Erie, Pennsylvania
Sport: Equestrian—dressage
Selected Accomplishments:

Member, U.S. team at World Dressage Championships (Belgium) 2003
Bayer/USET Festival of Champions 2003—silver and bronze medals
Reserve Champion Bayer/USET Festival of Champions 2002, 2001
National Champion UPHA Exceptional Challenge Cup 2000
Scholarship to study dressage in Warendorf, Germany, 2001

This 18-year-old with familial spastic paraplegia, a genetic condition that affects balance and restricts motor functioning from the waist down, has been riding since she was about 10 years old. Her family has been a major influence, as have her coaches in Indiana and Pennsylvania. From work with her first horse, Seaweed, to her current mounts, Mr. Bingley (a.k.a. Beckon), Miss Jane, or Lord Hobbit, this young athlete is already an experienced competitor. Rebecca states, "Dressage is my passion. I feel very lucky to have discovered it at a young age. Although I love to compete, it is the training and evolution of the partnership with my horse and the partial release from my physical limitations that I love." Rebecca would tell younger children with disabilities to "find what they love to do, have faith in themselves, and get the best training possible . . . don't let anyone tell them they don't merit first-rate training because they have a disability." Rebecca, who also competes with able-bodied athletes, thinks that the lack of funding and recognition by the public of the accomplishments of athletes with a disability are a cause for concern. With young, astute, and assured people such as Rebecca Hart, disability sport is in good hands.

> *"Dressage is my passion . . . it is the training and evolution of the partnership with my horse and the partial release from my physical limitations that I love."*

camps for athletes with disabilities. These camps/clinics followed similar formats and provided the participants the opportunity to gain additional knowledge related to sports medicine and athletic preparation. The camps usually included the components of education, training, and research. Educational topics included the areas of exercise physiology, biomechanics, nutrition, sport psychology, and athletic preparation. Research investigations followed similar topic areas and were designed to minimize the time between data collection and feedback to the athlete or coach or both. Utilizing any of these camp/clinic options will help in the preservice preparation of sports medicine professionals involved with disabled sports.

New sporting organizations have been established to help coaches in their preparation for working with athletes with disabilities. The American Association of Adapted Sports Programs (AAASP) is the nation's first organization to be recognized as the governing and sanctioning body for interscholastic adapted athletics. The AAASP represents the athletic interest of students with physical disabilities or visual impairments and is an official member of the National Federation of High Schools. The association sponsors coaching certification workshops in wheelchair basketball. Coaches and sports medicine professionals are eligible to attend, participate, and increase their professional expertise in disability sport (Nash, 2002).

KEY POINT

More athletic trainers with knowledge of disability and sport are needed.

Training

This section deals with athletic preparation. It is not our intention to present a "cookbook" approach to competitive training (see chapter 8 on coaching athletes with disabilities). The section addresses the composition of a sound training program, reviews several training principles, documents training profiles of disabled athletes, and presents specific exercise considerations.

Components of Training

Before one can consider the physiological aspects of training, something must occur that is unrelated to the physical domain of a training paradigm. This component is goal setting. Without question, goal setting can be the most influential component of the training program. Without goal setting, athletes will lose focus, become increasingly difficult to motivate, and subject themselves to lower retention rates. In other words, the athlete stands a greater chance of failure and dropping out.

Goal setting is a dynamic and interactive process. Both the coach and athlete need to be actively involved with this dimension of training. A dynamic plan for goal setting requires close supervision of training. If necessary, goals need to be modified—either extended or shortened to make them attainable. Unrealistic goals will contribute to poor training habits and motivation. "Goal setting helps athletes to stay focused on relevant, attainable performance objectives that are within their control, while concurrently helping to prevent them from attending to or worrying about events or factors that are beyond their control" (Hedrick and Morse, 1991, p. 64).

Comprehensive goal setting should include behavioral and athletic performance goals. Several factors should influence goal setting: level of commitment, time available to train, and level of athletic ability. Goal setting should be multidimensional to include immediate-, intermediate-, and long-range goals. Lastly, coaches, trainers, and athletes must work together to reach the goals. Success breeds success. Setting and reaching goals will contribute to a very successful training program, although physical training is equally important.

If performance in an athletic event is dependent on the physiological factors of strength, power, flexibility, endurance, and coordination (technique), then a comprehensive training program should include these same factors. While training principles will direct the training program, the athlete must assemble these basic ingredients for optimal performance.

For the sake of clarity, let's operationally define what is meant by these basic components of training.

- **Strength:** The athlete's ability to exert a force against some form of resistance.
- **Power:** The rate at which muscular force is exerted. Anaerobic power might be measured in seconds, while aerobic power would last 5 minutes or more.
- **Flexibility:** The athlete's full range of motion around a joint. Flexibility might be specific to a functional limb or an entire body position.
- **Endurance:** Performance at a desired rate for extended periods of time. Endurance can be muscular or cardiovascular, and it can be considered anaerobic (short time period) or aerobic (longer time period).
- **Coordination:** Timing, precision, accuracy, balance, and more. Coordination brings into play the perceptual factors of training, such as in shooting free throws, drafting in a turn during a race (using the wind forces of the wheelchair in front of you, as is done in cycling), and starting techniques.

General Training Principles

Training principles remain the same for all athletes. It is the individual athlete who must make the adjustments to training based on his or her commitment, available time, outside responsibilities, and access to equipment. Training centers focus on three ingredients: frequency, intensity, and duration. Sometimes, mode of training needs to be considered. Mode of training is specific to the athlete's use of special equipment (e.g., racing wheelchair, tethered runner, beeper devices).

Frequency refers to how often the athlete applies a training overload. Several factors influence this ingredient: work or school schedules, availability of facilities, and transportation to and from the training site. Another consideration involves distance to a training site and facility accessibility. Frequency is also a function of an athlete's motivation level and may fluctuate if there is no support system, which may include friends, training partners, transportation, coaching, and finances.

Intensity is training at a set percentage of work effort (energy) over a period of time—how hard one works. For example, athletes who are weight training might train at 85% of their maximum for three days per week, then drop to 70% for two days, and then increase to 90% for one day, depending on their event. This type of training would allow the athlete's body to recover during a typical training week. Runners might train at 80% to 85% of maximum heart rate four days per week. Athletes with disabilities, like their able-bodied counterparts, can use heart rate as an indicator of their effort. However, any time athletes—whether able-bodied or disabled—are using prescribed drugs, effects on the body must be closely monitored.

Duration refers to the length of time set aside for training. Duration might be set daily, weekly, or monthly depending on the specific event. Endurance athletes will have different training durations than sprinters. Athletes with disabilities who have problems with temperature maintenance need to closely monitor their duration of exercise. For example, an athlete with a spinal cord injury who is sit-skiing may be more susceptible to the effects of cold than an able-bodied athlete.

Training must address two key principles: overload and specificity. Utilizing the principle of overload, the athlete must stress the various systems of the body (musculoskeletal, cardiovascular, and respiratory). All of these must be placed in a state of stress above the normal level. Utilizing various combinations of the ingredients of frequency, intensity, and duration will lead to overload.

Just as important as the overload principle is specificity of training. Specificity refers to matching the training sessions to the athletic performance and is critical to optimal training. The elements related to race pace, positioning, speed, cornering and starting techniques, and early-race versus late-race strategy must be included within this dimension of

Xavier Torres

FAST FACTS

Home Base: Palma de Mallorca (Balearic Islands, Spain)
Sports: Swimming, open-water swimming
Selected Accomplishments:

World record, 24 hours swimming, 58,800 meters (2002)

Total of 294 international competitions

Australian Paralympic medalist, 2000: three gold, one bronze, and three world records

Atlanta Paralympics, 1996: gold, silver, and bronze medals

Barcelona Paralympics, 1992: one gold, two silver, and two bronze medals

Numerous awards and recognitions

Local, national, and international disability sport activist

Xavier Torres is a man among men in spite of his congenital amputation of four limbs. His swimming accomplishments, awards, and recognitions go on for pages. Xavier started to compete as a junior athlete in 1990. His accomplishments in both short- and long-course swimming are extraordinary, and so is his success in life.

> *"I think sport and media are very important to afford the integration of disabled people."*

Xavier has a degree in physical education with an emphasis in sport club direction. His involvement in the disability sport movement is extensive. He is, for example, a Paralympic swimmer and a swimmer's representative to the International Paralympic Committee (since 1996), and is active nationally as a member of the Spanish Federation of Sports for the Disabled. His local involvement has included the position of Director of City Swimming Schools in Palma de Mallorca; membership in the Balearic Association, which combats drugs; and his position as a swimming coach. Xavier has also done several national and international TV commentaries.

Xavier says, "Disability sport must be next to able-bodied sport . . . maybe not in the same places . . . but we must be in the same federations." He admires "some countries like Australia, Great Britain, and Canada because they are working together. They don't talk of disability sport and able-bodied sport." As to the young person with a disability, Xavier states that it is "most important for a young person to know himself or herself and study and appreciate the possibilities." It is evident that Xavier Torres has done just that in becoming the accomplished athlete and person he has aspired to be.

training. Perhaps no other element of training requires the utilization of a coach more than this one. A coach can teach and evaluate performances during training sessions, which will allow the athlete time to implement necessary changes. Despite all we know about training and how to apply it, there is minimal documentation of training programs for elite athletes with disabilities. To help athletes document their training, a structured approach should be implemented.

The following suggestions are offered to help the athlete develop a seasonal approach to designing a training program. Written by Marty Morse at the University of Illinois, these suggestions will help the athlete document performance during training. Morse suggests that there should be four periods of preparation targeted for the specific competitive event:

- **Foundation period:** includes general conditioning, laying a solid base for future intensive training
- **Preparation period:** sport-specific training; training focused toward specific sporting activity
- **Competition period:** the peak of the training year
- **Transition period:** end of the season; active rest and relaxation; good time for recreational basketball, tennis, swimming

General Knowledge of Training and Fitness

While documentation of training is important, making sure athletes have a sound knowledge base of training and fitness is also key to their success. To help the athlete develop this knowledge base, *Sports 'n Spokes* magazine offers a series of regularly featured articles about fitness and training. These articles are written by leading experts in the areas of exercise physiology, fitness, and nutrition. Current and former athletes also contribute their expertise to the series. Table 9.2 provides a quick reference to this type of information.

Training programs must be individually designed and engineered. Athletes should strive to know as much as they can about themselves and their response to training. Athletes who learn to recognize these responses experience more successful training. Successful training is not without special considerations for specific populations.

Exercise Considerations

Everyone, regardless of disability, should be provided the opportunity to be involved with some type of exercise program. Exercise guidelines from the American College of Sports Medicine are shown in table 9.3, and

Table 9.2 Profile of Journal Articles Related to Fitness From *Sports 'n Spokes*

Title	Author(s)	Reference	Key points
Category: Fitness			
"Exercise Is for Every Body"	Brent Williams	June 2002, 28 (4)	Profiles exercise recommendations from the National Center on Physical Activity and Disability.
"Increasing Strength and Endurance"	Peter Aufsesser and Peggy Lasko-McCarthey	July 2002, 28 (5)	Highlights progressive resistive exercise. Profiles exercise programs for individuals with paraplegia, quadriplegia, and multiple sclerosis.
"Beating the Elements"	Jim Yaggie	September 2002, 28 (6)	Addresses thermoregulation during exercise and the effects of a compromised autonomic nervous system.
"Ergogenic Aids"	Amy Culp and Mark Kern	January 2003, 29 (1)	Discusses the issues of ergonomic aids versus ergonomic prospects. Provides the athlete with guidelines for appropriate selection.
"Things to Remember"	Peter Aufsesser	March 2003, 29 (2)	Provides suggestions for the beginning stages of an exercise program.
Category: Training			
"Track Practice Plans"	Martin Morse and Adam Bleakney	September 2001, 27 (6)	Offers a "skeleton" practice plan for track from the University of Illinois. Covers issues of equipment preparation, training equipment, and sample daily plan.

(continued)

Table 9.2 *(continued)*

Title	Author(s)	Reference	Key points
Category: Training (continued)			
"Circuit Training"	Martin Morse and Adam Bleakney	March 2002, 28 (2)	Covers the following related to establishing a circuit training program: prerequisites, variables within the circuit, and designing the circuit. Provides sport-specific muscular development for sports of basketball, quad rugby, tennis, hand cycling, and track/ road racing.
"Powerlifting"	Michael McDewitt	May 2002, 28 (3)	Provides a specific four-day weight training routine. Mentions considerations for athletes with spinal cord injury and cerebral palsy.
"Marathon Racing"	Martin Morse and Adam Bleakney	November 2002, 28 (7)	Provides specific training programs for wheelchair users training for marathon: starts, steady-state endurance, speed endurance, acceleration power, and speed reserve.
"The Well-Known Secret"	Martin Morse and Adam Bleakney	May 2003, 29 (3)	Provides five basic drills to be used as cross-training for any wheelchair sport: power start and stop, rollbacks, transitions, backward power start and stop, and combo power start and stop.

Table 9.3 Guidelines for Training

Disability	Component	Mode	Modification
Spinal cord injury	Aerobic	Arm ergometer	50-80% peak heart rate (HR), 3-5 days/week, 20-60 min/session; use interval approach for quadriplegics
	Strength	Weight machines, dumbbells, wrist weights	2-3 sets of 8-12 reps, 2-4 days/week
Muscular dystrophy	Aerobic	Cycling, rowing, elliptical trainer	4-6 days/week, 50-80% HR reserve, goal > 20 min
	Strength	Stretching	Daily; hold for 20 s/stretch
Multiple sclerosis	Aerobic	Cycling, walking, swimming	60-85% peak HR, 50-70% VO_2 peak, 3 days/week, 30 min/session
	Strength	Weight and/ or isokinetic machines, free weights	Avoid on endurance training days; be aware of medications; be aware of strength declines late in the day
Cerebral palsy	Aerobic	Schwinn Air-Dyne, wheelchair ergometer	40-85% HR reserve, 3-5 days/week, 20-40 min/session; emphasize duration over intensity
	Strength	Free weights or machines	3 sets of 8-12 reps, 2 days/week, resistance as tolerated

contraindications are in table 9.4. Contraindication refers to activity or exercises that are not recommended because they may have detrimental effects on an individual. Such indications for not using a specific exercise, stretch, or motion are dependent on factors like individual strength, physical condition, and nature and degree of disability.

KEY POINT

At times the uniqueness of a specific disability will affect training and increase injury or the need for medical intervention.

Table 9.4 Contraindications to Exercise

Disability	Condition	Contraindications
Down syndrome	Atlanto-axial	Forward rolls, tucking the head, diving head-first.
Spinal cord (quadriplegia)	Thermal regulation	Overheating, need to provide spray bottles, moist towels. Watch overexposure to sun; keep in shade.
	Blood pooling	Make sure to do passive range of motion for lower extremities upon completion of exercise.
	Finger contractures	Avoid hyperextension of fingers during passive range of motion.
Spinal cord (paraplegia)	Harrington rods	Avoid rotation and twisting types of activities.
Amputee	Skin breakdown	Avoid skin breakdown with frequent checks of the stump.
	Leg length	Make sure to use the type of shoe designed for the prosthesis to avoid differing leg lengths.

Concluding Comments

So, what is the message of this chapter? The profession of sports medicine is just as necessary for disability sport as it is for the able-bodied athlete, perhaps even more so because of the impact of conditions that can exacerbate dehydration or hypothermia in athletes with amputations or spinal cord injury. While sports medicine has come a long way in terms of its involvement with disability sport, there is a continuing need to further its involvement and development. Infusion of course content about disability etiology and impact on motor performance, courses on disability sport, and field experiences with athletes with disabilities are all strategies to be considered. Also, training approaches and strategies for athletes with disabilities need to be further developed. The increased participation of sports medicine professionals can only have a beneficial impact on athletes with disabilities in terms of their well-being and sport performance.

ten

Sport Equipment

Patricia E. Longmuir and Peter W. Axelson

Reader Goal Gain an appreciation and understanding of the role and function of adapted equipment within the sport and physical activity context

Chapter Synopsis

- Equipment Enhances Function
- Personal Equipment
- Activity-Specific Equipment
- Environmental Technologies
- Making Sport Technology "Fit"
- Resources for Finding the Right Equipment
- Making Equipment Adaptations
- Concluding Comments

Equipment is an essential part of virtually every sport, making it a key factor that influences sport participation for both recreational and competitive athletes. For example, water-skiers use a bathing suit, flotation device, skis, tow rope, motor boat, and gasoline. Equestrians use a horse, saddle, bridle, halter, crop, riding boots, and helmet. Technology is equally essential for sports such as swimming that initially may seem to require very little equipment. Recreational swimmers use a bathing suit, towel, and perhaps goggles, nose plugs, earplugs, or flotation devices.

Competitive swimmers use all of this equipment and additional equipment, such as starting blocks, kick boards, and pull buoys, during their training. But what is often overlooked is how a person with limitations would use these technologies. How would someone with limitations get into or out of the boat, adjust to the movement of the horse, or position and hold these devices?

Depending on the sport and the participant's purpose, recreational or competitive, the need for and sophistication of equipment will vary tremendously. Some sports, such as walking, enable participation with minimal, relatively unsophisticated equipment (e.g., shoes, clothing). Other sports, such as tennis, require the participant to have specific types of equipment (i.e., racket, balls). There are also many sports (such as scuba diving, parasailing, or rock climbing) in which the participant's safety and even survival are dependent on the use of the appropriate equipment (figure 10.1). Athletes involved in competitive sporting events must also abide by the requirements of the governing bodies.

Equipment Enhances Function

The World Health Organization developed the International Classification of Functioning, Disability and Health (ICF) as a way of documenting and categorizing the function of all individuals, both with and without disabilities (World Health Organization, 2002). Within the ICF are three major categories:

- Body function and structure (the functions that a body can perform based on its physiology and anatomy)

Figure 10.1 Equipment is essential to the survival of scuba divers.

Tools for Play, Beneficial Designs, Inc. and Veterans Health Services, US Dept. of Veterans Affairs.

- Activity and participation (the activities or skills that can be performed and how those skills can be used to participate in a sport)
- Environment and context (the influence of factors external to the individual)

The new ICF model closely parallels the major categories of equipment (Axelson, 1993; Longmuir and Axelson, 1996) that can be used for a particular sport:

- Personal equipment—something the individual essentially wears, designed to enhance body function, structure, or both
- Activity-specific equipment—designed to enhance the performance of an activity or participation in a specific sport
- Environmental technology—used to modify the facilities or environments in which the sport is played

Most people with disabilities rely on the same rackets, balls, skis, and other equipment that are used by participants without disabilities. However, modified or specialized equipment can also be used in order to compensate for changes in function that result from the disability. For example, wrapping neoprene around the legs of someone with lower-body paralysis provides additional flotation so that the swimmer can maintain a more effective body position in the water (figure 10.2).

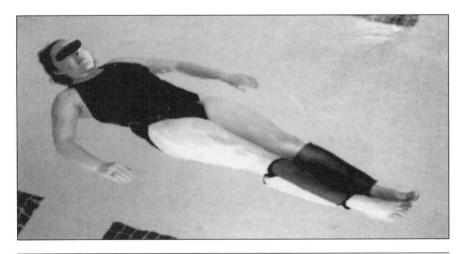

Figure 10.2 Neoprene can improve the body position of a swimmer with lower-body paralysis.

PEL Consulting.

Personal Equipment

Personal equipment encompasses things that the athlete "wears." It should be seen and treated as part of the athlete's body. Examples of personal equipment that a person with a disability may use during sport and recreation participation are

- prosthetic limbs, wheelchairs, crutches, canes, and walkers;
- hearing aids and augmentative communication systems;
- eyeglasses, navigation canes, and infrared signal detectors; and
- memory aids and symbol boards (see figure 10.3).

a

b

c

d

Figure 10.3 *(a)* Prostheses, *(b)* hearing aids, *(c)* navigation canes, and *(d)* symbol boards are personal technologies that may be used during sport and recreation.

Credit for figures 10.3a, b, and d: Tools for Play, Beneficial Designs, Inc. and Veterans Health Services, US Dept. of Veterans Affairs. Credit for figure 10.3c: Beneficial Designs, Inc.

Activity-Specific Equipment

Equipment is available for every conceivable sport in which individuals with disabilities may wish to participate. The equipment available is limited only by the type of sport or recreational activity pursued, whether the individual can purchase or otherwise obtain the equipment, and how the disability does or does not influence equipment use.

Activity-specific equipment offers the largest range of recreation and sport technologies for people with disabilities. The broadest selection of activity-specific technologies is available for individuals with amputations or those who use wheelchairs (figure 10.4). To date, much of the research to develop new recreation technologies has been supported in relation to the rehabilitation of war veterans. Sir Ludwig Guttmann, father of the Paralympic sport movement (see chapter 3), is widely believed to have

Figure 10.4 Prostheses and wheelchairs are the most common activity-specific technologies for people with disabilities.

Tools for Play, Beneficial Designs, Inc. and Veterans Health Services, US Dept. of Veterans Affairs.

been the first person to offer sport and recreational activities to people with disabilities when he incorporated exercise and recreation into the rehabilitation of Britain's veterans from World War II (Sherrill, 1993). While hospital recreation was widely used as a therapeutic tool, sport was a rather unique approach in the 1940s and 1950s. Since amputation and spinal cord injury are common disabilities that result from combat, many countries have supported the development of technologies to enhance the function of individuals with these types of injuries. As a result, a wide variety of specialized leg and arm prosthetics are available, such as hands for hockey, baseball, rock climbing, or swimming and legs for skiing, golf, scuba diving, and running. A similarly broad spectrum of wheelchairs has also been developed for activities such as road racing, track, basketball, rugby, golf, dance, hiking, cycling, and tennis.

Apart from prosthetics and wheelchairs, the diversity of activity-specific technologies is expanding rapidly. Consider the following examples:

- People who want to go skydiving but require a ventilator to breathe can use an air tank with a modified breathing valve.
- Individuals with paralysis of the legs can off-road in rugged mountains using an off-road or all-terrain vehicle operated with hand controls.
- People for whom kneeling in the garden is becoming too difficult can use a rolling garden stool or garden tools with extended handles.
- Those who wish to compose their own music but have no movement of the hands or feet can wear a head-mounted light signal connected to their computer.
- Deep-sea fishing is possible for those who have only one arm through the use of a rod holder and electrically controlled reel.
- People who rely on a power wheelchair for mobility can consider sports such as power wheelchair soccer and floor hockey.
- Those who would like to play ice hockey but have difficulty seeing can use a puck that rattles.
- People who are unable to stand but wish to do waterskiing, surfing, ice skating, or snow skiing can use the sit-ski, wave ski, ice sledge, or mono-ski.
- Adaptations for bowling include pins that beep to identify their location and bowling sticks or balls with a handle.
- For paddling a rowing scull, kayak, or canoe, adaptations include an outrigger float to enhance the boat's stability and an arm or leg paddle wheel or one-armed paddle for propulsion.

Regardless of the type of sport, someone with a disability has certainly already tried it. The biggest problem may not be figuring out whether or not it is possible (because it is) but rather finding out how it is already being done. Many adaptations to activity-specific technologies are "one of a kind." They are made to meet the needs of a single individual and are not commercially available. However, given the time and cost involved in developing new types of activity-specific equipment, it is well worth the effort to try to learn from those who have come up with a problem-solving technology rather than starting from scratch on one's own trial-and-error effort.

KEY POINT

There is a wealth of available adaptations for a variety of sports and activities.

Environmental Technologies

Environmental technologies are used to create the facilities in which a sport takes place. Gymnasiums, courts, swimming pools, playing fields, and ski hills are examples of environmental technologies that enable sport and recreation. While environmental technologies are essential components of most sport and recreation activities, the importance of their design in facilitating or limiting the participation of people with disabilities is seldom recognized. It is important to keep in mind that environmental technologies encompass not only the gym, pool, or playing field but also the changing and locker rooms, coaches' quarters, refreshment areas, therapy rooms, and so on. Is there space in the locker room for someone who uses a wheelchair? Is there a changing facility that someone who requires an adult assistant of the opposite gender (e.g., a wife helping her husband, a father helping his teenage daughter, a female support worker helping a male client) can use? Do the emergency warning and information systems provide information in both auditory and visual formats? Can participants with disabilities get water or refreshments or take a shower after their workout? All of these potential barriers to participation can be easily addressed through the use of accessible environmental technologies.

The philosophy of universal design—designing to meet the needs of the widest possible range of potential users—should be the foundation upon which all sport and recreation environments are created. The following are the seven principles of universal design (Center for Universal Design, 1997):

- Equitable use
- Flexibility in use

- Simple and intuitive use
- Perceptible information
- Tolerance for error
- Low physical effort
- Size and space for approach and use

(Copyright © 1997 NC State University, The Center for Universal Design)

Ensuring that environmental technologies are universally designed, either when initially built or during subsequent alterations, provides access for athletes with and without disabilities to a wide range of sport and recreation facilities.

KEY POINT

Equipment exists for every imaginable sport in which people with disabilities may wish to participate, but technology for equipment design is still evolving.

Making Sport Technology "Fit"

Regardless of the type of equipment, it must "fit" the athlete in terms of both size and function in order to maximize safe and effective use. For example, a poorly fitting prosthesis or wheelchair may result in soft tissue damage to the areas in contact with the device. People with disabilities often experience great difficulty in finding professionals who can provide expertise in the selection, fit, and appropriate use of recreation technologies. Personal technologies are often obtained through rehabilitation professionals who seldom have training or knowledge related to recreational activities, sport competition, and equipment. Activity-specific technologies, by comparison, are usually obtained from physical activity professionals who seldom have experience or expertise related to disability. Design recommendations for accessible recreation facilities are a recent innovation, and training materials on the safe and effective use of recreation technologies are extremely rare (e.g., manual on adapted skiing and equipment, Professional Ski Instructors of America, 1997). As a result, people with disabilities often are unaware of the recreation technologies available or have acquired technologies that are ill suited to their particular interests or skills. Later on in this chapter we provide some ideas of what is available.

Athletes continue to provide the impetus for much of the design and development work required for new and adapted technologies. Athletes, both recreational and competitive, are often performing beyond the demands that occur with daily living and as a result require optimal

Richard Orive

© Richard Julio

FAST FACTS

Home Base: San Sebastian, Spain
Sport: Swimming
Selected Accomplishments:

Sydney Paralympics (2000): four gold medals and four world records in the 50, 100, 200, and 4 × 50 freestyle relay

Atlanta Paralympics (1996): three gold medals, one silver medal, and two world records

International competitions and medals in Argentina, Sweden, and New Zealand

This young man is a swimmer, and he can go fast—very fast. The effects of cerebral palsy on his body seem to disappear when he is in the water. Starting competition at age 18 is rather late, but Richard Orive's development into an elite athlete occurred rapidly. Richard trains 2 to 4 hours per day under the watchful eyes of his club coaches. His well-being is further monitored by trainers and his family. In 2000 in the Sydney Paralympics, Richard performed perfectly. He entered four events, won four gold medals, and established four world records. This is quite an achievement for any athlete to accomplish, especially in such a short time.

> Sport is "one of the greatest schools of life . . . almost every value you gain in sport is transferable to ordinary life."

(continued)

Richard Orive (continued)

Richard states that "sport has a very significant presence in my way of life." He values the benefits of sport that "enables" one in life. Richard also is aware of the many issues that face disability sport. He is concerned about the many classification systems, the lack of social awareness, and the lack of opportunities for sport involvement and competition equal to those available to able-bodied athletes.

Richard Orive is a young man with outstanding athletic ability who is a model for those who might think that there is a place for them in the sporting arena.

---

function, fit, and aesthetics. Historically, athletes with disabilities have made changes to enhance the performance of their equipment that subsequently have been adopted by manufacturers of technologies for daily living. For example, in the 1970s, wheelchair track athletes used hacksaws to cut the arms and leg rests off their wheelchairs in order to make the chairs lighter and more maneuverable. Subsequently, wheelchair manufacturers began to produce the "lightweight" wheelchairs commonly seen today (figure 10.5).

Recently, researchers have begun to contribute to the design of recreational technologies, particularly with regard to the design of technologies that can be used by athletes both with and without disabilities. For example, Beneficial Designs is currently developing a universal design canoe seat to enhance the comfort and function of all paddlers (Siekman, Chesney, and Axelson, 1999; see figure 10.6). The project, which is funded by the National Institutes of Health (National Center for Medical Rehabilitation Research, National Institute of Child Health and Human Development), will also ensure that the canoe seat can provide the additional support that may be required by individuals with limited or no independent sitting balance. Sport researchers, from fields such as biomechanics and exercise physiology, are also contributing to the recreation and sport participation of people with disabilities by more clearly defining the skills required for participation and assisting athletes to optimize their performance. For example, changes in the helmets and wheels used by wheelchair racers parallel changes among competitive cyclists.

Standards for the design of accessible recreation environments are also being developed to supplement existing requirements for buildings used for housing or employment. Design standards for creating accessible sidewalks and shared-use paths, golf courses, swimming pools, stadiums, amusement parks, playgrounds, outdoor recreation trails, and other sporting environments have recently been published (Kirschbaum

Figure 10.5 Today's wheelchair racers use aerodynamically designed equipment.
Tools for Play, Beneficial Designs, Inc. and Veterans Health Services, US Dept. of Veterans Affairs.

Figure 10.6 A universal design canoe seat will benefit all paddlers, regardless of ability.
Beneficial Designs, Inc.

et al., 2001; U.S. Architectural and Transportation Barriers Compliance Board, 2002). New recreation facilities should be built to meet or exceed these minimum standards so that all interested individuals are able to participate. Existing facilities that are not accessible should be objectively measured to identify the existing conditions. The objective information can be used to develop a transition plan so that the facility can become accessible over time, as well as to educate participants about the existing conditions they will encounter. For example, the Universal Trail Assessment Process can be used to assess outdoor trails and other paths of travel (Longmuir and Axelson, 2002); TrailWare software can be used to summarize the data (Axelson, Mispagel, and Longmuir, 2001); and a Web site (http://trailexplorer.org) can enable people to make smart trail selections based on their specific needs and desires (Wong et al., 1998).

KEY POINT

Equipment for athletes with disabilities may or may not be fitted appropriately. Athletes themselves provide much of the inspiration for adaptations to sport equipment.

Resources for Finding the Right Equipment

Often the biggest challenge for people with disabilities wishing to become involved in a particular sport is the effort required to find and acquire the "right" equipment. In order to be "right," the equipment has to be suited to both the activity, including any standards required at competitive events, and the individual's abilities. The better the technology is at creating a match between the demands of the activity and the abilities of the individuals, the greater the probability that the individual's participation efforts will meet with success (Longmuir and Axelson, 1996).

Historically, information about sport and recreation equipment for people with disabilities was available primarily through published documents such as the following:

- Adams, R.C., and McCubbin, J.A. 1991. *Games, sports, and exercises for the physically disabled.* 4th ed. Philadelphia: Lea & Febiger; Raleigh, NC: Lippincott, Williams & Wilkins.
- Burgess, E.M., and Rappoport, A. 1992. *Physical fitness: A guide for individuals with lower limb loss.* Washington, DC: Veterans Health Administration.

- Kegel, B. 1985. Physical fitness. Sports and recreation for those with lower limb amputation or impairment. *Journal of Rehabilitation Research and Development* (Clin. Suppl. 1).

- Nesbitt, J.A., ed. 1986. *The international directory of recreation-oriented assistive diver's sources.* Marina del Ray, CA: Lifeboat Press.

- Paciorek, M.J., and Jones, J.A. 1994. *Sports and recreation for the disabled.* 2nd ed. Carmel, IN: Cooper.

While many technologies have changed dramatically over the past two decades, these documents remain excellent introductory resources to the breadth of sport and recreation opportunities available to people with disabilities. They can also provide clues as to potential sources of appropriate equipment, such as disability sport groups, commercial manufacturers, and assistive technology organizations.

Disability sport and recreation publications, such as *Palaestra, Sports 'n Spokes,* and *Active Living* magazines, continue to be an excellent source of information about existing and emerging technologies. Feature articles on existing activity opportunities often include information about the personal, activity-specific, or environmental technologies that support the participation of people with disabilities. In addition, regular features and columns often provide information about a variety of new technologies that are, or soon will be, commercially available. *Sports 'n Spokes* regularly publishes comparison articles on different types of recreation technologies (e.g., skiing [Axelson, 1995], hand cycling [Axelson, 1996]) in addition to its annual review of lightweight and sport wheelchairs [*Sports 'n Spokes,* 2003]). Many distributors of recreation technologies for people with disabilities, such as Innovator of Disability Equipment and Adaptations or IDEA (Pewaukee, WI), J.L. Pachner Ltd. (Niguel, CA), and Access to Recreation (Newburg Park, CA), publish yearly catalogs of the adapted sport equipment that they sell.

As with most fields, the emergence of the Internet has revolutionized our ability to find and disseminate information about sport and recreation technologies. Most publications provide information only on commercially available technologies since those are most readily available to all readers. One major benefit of the Internet has been the increased ability of people to share information about their own personal adaptations or technologies. In contrast to universally designed recreation equipment, which has broad marketability, most adapted sport and recreation technologies are not suitable for commercial production because of the relatively unique combination of sport interest and type of disability that they address, particularly when very specialized modifications are required. Entering the terms "disability," "equipment," and "sport" into any Internet search engine will lead to thousands of entries. There are also a growing number of online databases that anyone can search to find specific information about sport and recreation technologies. A few of the larger such databases are these:

- National Center on Physical Activity and Disability (NCPAD), available online at www.ncpad.org. This database provides recreation and sport information and equipment manufacturer information.
- ABLEDATA, available online at www.abledata.com. This database provides assistive technologies for daily living and recreation.
- AssistiveTech, available online at www.assistivetech.net. This database provides assistive technologies for daily living and recreation.

Space-age technologies are increasingly used to make assistive devices for people with disabilities lighter, stronger, and more flexible, durable, and efficient. While these technologies greatly enhance athletic performance and recreational participation in a wide variety of sports, the cost of the devices significantly limits access to this type of equipment for the majority of individuals. For example, powered wheelchairs for hiking that can safely negotiate steps and steep slopes are commercially available, but the purchase costs are often prohibitive (e.g., exceeding $10,000 US per chair). Although elite athletes with disabilities may have sponsors who subsidize their equipment costs in return for product endorsements (a relatively small number of corporations sponsor athletes with disabilities), developing athletes and recreational participants seldom have access to these technologies, which often limits their ability to participate in developmental or sanctioned competitions. Although many of these technologies, such as the power wheelchair for hiking, can also be used for day-to-day living, insurance companies and other equipment providers seldom support the acquisition of equipment that is considered "recreational." Thus, an individual who uses a wheelchair may be able to get a new folding-frame wheelchair through insurance or disability support but probably cannot get a rigid-frame wheelchair that could be used for both daily living and sport participation. Charitable organizations, such as Easter Seals or Shriners Hospitals, and service organizations (e.g., Rotary Club, Lions Club) may also help individuals with disabilities to obtain recreation technologies.

Making Equipment Adaptations

Equipment adaptations can vary from very subtle changes (e.g., a change in strap width, length, or material) to highly customized and complex designs (e.g., custom-molded racing mono-ski). "High-tech" adaptations,

Wesley Worrell

FAST FACTS

Home Base: St. Michael, Barbados
Sport: International wheelchair marathoner
Selected Accomplishments:

Pan Am Disabled Games 1999

Winner of numerous local road races in Barbados

A relative newcomer to disability sport, Wesley is a man on a mission. A T-12 paraplegic, he started racing after he became disabled. Wesley says, "Sport means a lot to me since I have become disabled. It keeps me active and in good health. It takes away the void that makes you feel sorry for yourself just because you have lost the use of your limbs." While he has not yet won any medals in the Paralympics, his progress in half-marathons and full marathons in such a short time has made him an athlete to be noticed. Within Barbados, Wesley has won many local road races and even has received a key to a city for his efforts.

"I think that many of the disabled persons who want to get involved in the sport are lacking the support and financial backing, and this is very detrimental. . . ."

Wesley is concerned about the lack of support and financial backing for athletes with disabilities, as well as the need for increased opportunities. His efforts now may well pave the way for others on his island.

such as a custom-molded tennis racket handgrip, provide optimal function but at a significant "price." The "price" is not only in the cost but also in the time and effort required to obtain the equipment. Relying primarily on "low-tech" modifications (e.g., sewing Velcro onto the palm of a glove and the racket handle; see figure 10.7) may not provide exactly the same function but often meets the broader goal of enabling relatively immediate participation and success. Most people with disabilities can successfully use "low-tech" equipment modifications (e.g., straps, sound or light signals, lighter-weight equipment, shorter distances) to enjoy a wide range of recreational activities. As an athlete develops to higher levels of competition, more "high-tech" adaptations may be required in order to optimize performance.

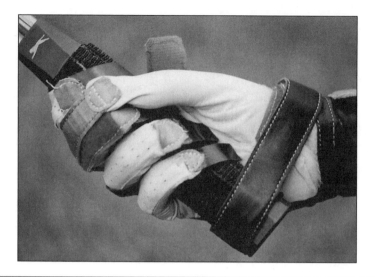

Figure 10.7 Low-tech modifications, such as these straps on a tennis racket handle, are a quick and inexpensive way to increase the range of available recreation opportunities.

PEL Consulting.

The process of adapting recreation and sport technology should be a team effort. Team members should include

- the person with the disability (who is an "expert" in his or her own abilities, interests, and needs),
- a designer (who is an "expert" in developing technologies), and
- a coach/sport professional or facility manager/designer (who is an "expert" in the demands of the activity or facility design and usability).

Creative thinking is the cornerstone of successful technology adaptations. For example, consider all of the ways in which the design or fit of a wheelchair can be adapted. One can use larger or smaller wheels with fat and knobby or thin and smooth tires. The seat position can be raised for better reach and sight lines or lowered for more stability. Increasing the camber (tilt) of the wheels can also increase stability. A longer wheel base makes tracking in a straight line easier, while a shorter wheel base increases turning capacity. An adjustable back support can be used to alter the sitting posture and gain either front-to-back or side-to-side stability (figure 10.8). The size of the hand rims can be varied to obtain benefits similar to those provided by the gears on a bicycle. Larger hand rims make it easier to start moving (as with a lower gear), while smaller hand rims require a lot of torque but enable the user to attain higher speeds (as with a higher gear). Of course, all of these adjustments are just to a wheelchair. When one considers all of the other personal, activity-specific, and environmental technologies that could be adapted for the benefit of a particular person in a particular activity, the possibilities seem almost endless (and somewhat overwhelming).

Given all of the potential variables that one may consider when making a modification to sport and recreation technology, either "low" or "high" tech, it is important to go through an effective, step-by-step design process (Longmuir and Axelson, 1996) such as the following:

- Specify the need.
- Review the existing technology and devices.
- Identify specific design criteria (including any equipment requirements for competition).
- Build a prototype.
- Have potential users evaluate the prototype.
- Use evaluation results to revise the prototype.
- Publish information on the completed design.

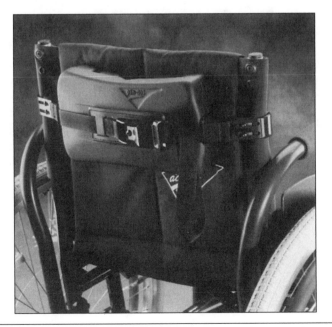

Figure 10.8 An adjustable back support can influence front-to-back or side-to-side stability.

Tools for Play, Beneficial Designs, Inc. and Veterans Health Services, US Dept. of Veterans Affairs.

These steps enable the most efficient and effective identification of technology modifications that will facilitate the participation of the person with a disability in the sport or recreation opportunity of interest to that person. Incorporating the principles of universal design when developing new technologies will make the technologies more usable by (and therefore more marketable to) a broad range of potential users (Axelson, 1993). When designing products for people with disabilities, it is also important to follow any performance standards that may exist for similar types of devices. For example, the design and production of wheelchairs can be tested using the Rehabilitation Engineering and Assistive Technology Society of North America Wheelchair Standards (McLaurin and Axelson, 1990). Finally, it is important for people to share what they find and what they try in terms of equipment modifications, whether they work or not. One person's experience may be the key to helping others realize their own dreams.

KEY POINT

Many times it is not necessary to use specialized equipment. "Low-tech" modifications often work well.

Concluding Comments

Sport and recreation opportunities abound for people with disabilities, and having the right equipment is a key component of successful participation. Equipment exists to enable people with disabilities to participate in any type of sport. However, finding out about the available technologies and acquiring the "right" equipment for each individual continue to pose significant barriers to participation. Whenever people try an equipment modification, they need to make sure they share the information with others. One never knows who is looking for exactly the type of technology that someone else has created.

eleven

Event Management

Reader Goal   Understand the subtle complexities of event management for disability sport and its similarities to and differences from that for able-bodied sport

Chapter Synopsis

- Managing the Sport Event
- Initial Planning
- Structure and Organization
- Committees and Functions
- Event Management Focal Points for Individuals With Disabilities
- Media and Athletes With Disabilities
- Planning for International Sport Events
- Concluding Comments

This chapter presents event management components for sport competitions involving individuals with disabilities. Because of the world's current geopolitical status, such issues as athlete safety, spectator safety, facility construction, and accessibility mandate that event management take on increased significance. Brief discussions of the common attributes of good sport management deal with the need for fielding a management team and strategic planning for national and international competitions, as well as the particulars of sport management components. The commonalities with sport management for able-bodied competition are also highlighted.

Managing the Sport Event

Whether a sporting event is recreational or competitive or of small or large proportions, two things are essential for its success: planning and organization. No matter the size, the location, or the ability of the participants, these two elements are critical for an event to be a success. There will, of course, be some additional needs and concerns if the population/participant focus is individuals with a disability. However, generally there are more commonalities than differences between event management for individuals with a disability and that for their able-bodied counterparts. Specifically, the professional preparation of sport management personnel surged in the 1990s (Parks and Quarterman, 2003), thus providing a cadre of well-prepared professionals to organize and manage sporting events including the Paralympics, Deaflympics, and world championships for athletes with disabilities.

Initial Planning

One of the most important initial aspects of planning a recreational or competitive sporting event is to conceptualize the idea. This aspect of planning may occur several years prior to the actual event, especially in the case of international competitions for athletes with disabilities (e.g., Paralympics, Deaflympics, Special Olympics, world championships). This means talking through the idea, its purpose, and its theme in an open, creative, and nonthreatening environment. The process may, at first, bring out a multitude of ideas that appear to conflict but in actuality serve a cleansing and focusing function. The process is the same regardless of the participants and the spectators.

A steering committee should consist of an external consultant from the business world who can objectively answer questions concerning the feasibility of sponsorship and marketing. This person may be from a major business in the community or the chamber of commerce. Other members of the steering committee should include an athlete, a representative from a sporting organization, and someone with experience in field operations for recreational or sporting events. If working with a nearby university or local parks department, a representative from that entity should also be included. But this committee should remain small and manageable.

Eli Wolff

FAST FACTS

Current Home Base: Boston, Massachusetts
Sports: Soccer
Selected Accomplishments:

Soccer World Championships (2003)

Pam Am Soccer Championships (1995, 1999, 2002)

Soccer World Cup (2001)

Paralympic soccer (1996)

Trained with Brown University varsity soccer team (1996-2000)

Founder and member, Disability Soccer Committee, U.S. Soccer Federation (2000)

Member of the 2004 U.S. Paralympic soccer team

Eli Wolff had a stroke at age 2. It did not define his life. Rather, Eli has directed his own life and has used sport as a vehicle. This articulate man is a college graduate and is now working as an advocate for disability sport

"Sport is a defining aspect of my life today, both as an athlete and in my professional work."

on a national and international basis. Using a diverse support base, Eli trains four days a week while holding down a job that allows him high visibility. He has presented at conferences of professional learned societies (e.g., National Association of Sport Sociology) and disability-specific conferences.

Sport is an integral part of Eli's life. He states, "Sport is a defining aspect of my life today, both as an athlete and in my professional work. Sport . . . serves as a powerful vehicle for inclusion, recognition, respect, and understanding in all aspects of life." Of those just starting out, Eli would say that "they are athletes [and] have athletic bodies" and that "they have a right to sports and recreation opportunities and to not let anyone tell them differently." Eli further believes that young athletes with disabilities should know that they will need to learn how to speak and stand up for themselves and to educate others about disability sport. His key point is that young people with disabilities involved in sport can change the world! The issues that face the disability sport movement can be affected by the participation of more people with disabilities so that the worldwide sporting community and the general public can become better educated and aware. Eli Wolff is an example of the young, educated, motivated, and politically active athlete with a disability who can be counted on to lead the way for others.

During the brainstorming sessions, which may last weeks or months, the steering committee should ask questions to initially provide some sort of structure for the event. Another outcome of this process would be to identify people to serve on committees. Having a theme, logo, title, and colors will convince financial backers that this is an effort worthy of their support. So, what might be some questions a steering committee needs to ask?

- Who can assist us and in what capacity?
- What kinds of events will be held, and what kind(s) of sport facilities do we need?
- When is this event to be held? Are there any other major events going on at the same time to affect sponsor opportunities?
- How are people (athletes and spectators) to be housed?
- How do we go about organizing working committees and ancillary services?

Another activity of the steering committee may be to engage a consultant to conduct a feasibility study. This study may explore the following questions (Jackson and Schmader, 1990):

- What type of event is most appropriate?
- What kind of weather is necessary?
- What is the competition in terms of established events in the nation or region?
- Does demographic research indicate that there is a target population?
- What is the attitude of the target population toward a proposed event?
- What kinds of facilities and services are needed?
- What is the nature of community support for the event?
- Has the community supported such events in the past?
- What are the history and potential for financial backing from the community?

Adapted, by permission, from R. Jackson and S.W. Schmader, 1990, *Special events: Inside and out* (Champaign, IL: Sagamore Publishing).

Financial support for a feasibility study must be considered and raised as a part of this initial step.

Additional content may be specified in the consultant's contract. That is, the feasibility study may be as in-depth as the committee specifies in view of the amount of lead time available and the cost. The cost for such an undertaking is in proportion to the degree of sophistication of the study and must be a part of the steering committee's first fund-raising efforts. An activity such as a feasibility study should be conducted with enough lead time so that fund-raising and financial backers have anywhere from three months to a year or two to commit to the event (Jackson and Schmader, 1990). The results of the feasibility study should be utilized throughout the planning and organizing process.

KEY POINT

Event planning for disability sport is more similar to event planning for able-bodied sport than different.

Structure and Organization

After the initial planning stage and when the results of the feasibility study are positive, the organization and structure for the event can be formalized. Either a steering committee of three to eight members or a board of directors consisting of 10 to 15 people may be formed. The role of each member on the steering committee or board of directors should be identified. Jackson and Schmader (1990, p. 26) suggested that a board of directors consist of the following:

- Administrative officer from a company to serve as chair and to coordinate events
- Bank officer or someone with financial acuity about borrowing or lending money
- Public relations, marketing, or advertising expert
- Certified accountant or comptroller
- Leader from the cultural arts community
- Professional tourism, travel, or leisure industry representative
- Law enforcement representative
- Attorney
- Official from the city or parks department
- Emergency medical services, local hospital, sports medicine personnel

Adapted, by permission, from R. Jackson and S.W. Schmader, 1990, *Special events: Inside and out* (Champaign, IL: Sagamore Publishing)

An individual who is experienced with the sport equipment necessary for the conduct of the event may also be appointed at this time or identified later on as the content of the event is specifically identified.

After the board of directors is appointed, the next step is to develop a specific table of organization. This is the result of thinking through and anticipating what is needed to run the event in as flawless a manner as possible. The directors must be careful not to overextend themselves by volunteering in too many other aspects of the event. Their job is to delegate to other competent people specific tasks that need to be accomplished for the event to function efficiently. In addition, directors serve as resources for problem solving and dispensing accurate information.

KEY POINT

Careful planning and anticipation—thinking through what will be needed perhaps years later when the event actually takes place—are two key elements for event success.

Committees and Functions

Jackson and Schmader (1990, pp. 27-31) identify a number of committees that are necessary for effective event management. All of the following positions need experienced people who are willing to give of their time and expertise so that the participants, coaches, and spectators may experience the best and smoothest possible running of the event. The following are suggested committees and a brief description of suggested responsibilities:

1. Event production committee—all committee chairs meet to exchange information on a regular basis and to identify insurance needs for the board of directors
2. Transportation committee—smooth routing of all participants to and from events; acquisition of donated vehicles, drivers, signs for directions; interface with law enforcement representative; special needs for specific venues (e.g., golf carts); and parking
3. Talent and program scheduling committee—entertainment programming, parades, opening and closing ceremonies, celebrities, and workshops
4. Sponsorship support committee—provides financing for the event by selling ad space or renting space to vendors
5. Accounting committee—monetary control, preparation of financial statements, IRS status
6. Vendors or concessions—food, beverages, souvenirs, licenses to conduct business, trademark patents, and logo licenses
7. Facilities, equipment, and supplies—securing facilities; purchasing disposable supplies; and purchasing, renting, or borrowing equipment
8. Maintenance committee—grounds, litter control, garbage removal, sanitary conditions

9. Human resources committee—volunteers and paid labor
10. Marketing committee—media relations, advertising, promotions, ticketing, and programs
11. Decorations committee—signs, posters, and banners

Adapted, by permission, from R. Jackson and S.W. Schmader, 1990, *Special events: Inside and out* (Champaign, IL: Sagamore Publishing)

Many of these major committees will have specific subgroups. For example, the marketing committee may have a subgroup for press credentials and one for advertising, which will interface with the sponsorship support committee and the promotions committee. The facilities, equipment, and supplies committee will be divided into the three subgroups, which all must interface with the maintenance committee. The talent and program scheduling committee will need separate subgroups for the opening and closing ceremonies and possibly another subgroup just for awards. Specific job tasks and functions should be identified for each committee and subgroup so that duplication is avoided.

Other committees suggested by Wyness (1984) may include a security committee and a medical emergencies committee, as well as security and medical emergency plans for terrorists, bioterrorism, and weather events. Millions of dollars are spent on these areas to safeguard the athletes as well as the participants. The increased profile of these aspects of any event planning makes this aspect a must for organizers.

A technical or electronic committee would be appropriate to take care of all public address system needs, lighting, and computer support needs. A housing committee is appropriate for those events lasting more than one day that involve large numbers of participants and VIPs. In many instances, a VIP or protocol committee is formed in very large events just to see to all their needs (e.g., lodging, transportation, meals, and equipment for clinics). Additionally, the International Paralympic Committee (IPC) Web page for the 2002 Paralympics in Utah included some of the following committees for that particular competition (International Paralympic Committee, 2002a, 2002b):

- General rules
- Entry procedures
- Technical arrangements
- Protocol
- Publications
- Meetings

Thus, a table of organization may become a complex integrated blueprint for the successful conduct of the event. Event management may also consist of a rules and officials committee along with a coaches committee, a uniform committee (e.g., providing hats of different colors for volunteers for different tasks), and a food services committee (American Sport Education Program, 1996). The number and nature of additional committees may add to the complexity of the organization, but this should not be seen as a detriment if such committees are needed.

Field Manager

The event venue field manager is quite possibly the key to running a smooth schedule and successful event; one should be appointed for each sporting event. In track and field this person is identified as the clerk of the course, while in swimming this person is the meet manager. These people should have extensive experience in the particular sport.

The field manager should have organizing skills and patience, be knowledgeable about the rules of the event and how it is organized, understand the organization of the entire workings and know where to refer people who have questions or complaints, and, above all, must communicate well with people so that things are resolved quickly and quietly. The event venue field manager is really the quality control inspector for running any venue. Should the event venue manager have any questions, he or she should be able to contact the head of any major committee by radio to get information quickly and accurately. This reduces confusion. Having a roving troubleshooter on the field at all times is also a good strategy. This person should be clearly identified so that coaches and venue managers may receive assistance as needed.

General Administrative Details

Once committees are organized, there are "concerns" (issues or conflicts) that need to be identified and whose scope or responsibility should be delineated. Some of these concerns, issues, or conflicts cross committee lines and necessitate legal assistance in the form of contracts. Thus, organizers should

- obtain necessary licenses and permits for the grounds;
- determine fees necessary for special events or entertainment;
- acquire appropriate insurance coverage for all, including volunteers;
- secure signed agreements for vendors (concessions) and souvenir sales;
- develop a written plan for police assistance and security measures;

- develop a list of assistants, their job assignments, and their work schedules; and
- secure contracts for health and maintenance services (Wyness, 1984).

Event Management Focal Points for Individuals With Disabilities

Several focal points need to be addressed when an integrated or segregated event for individuals with a disability is being staged. The particular areas of emphasis include (a) physical accessibility to housing, sport or activity venues, eating establishments, and transportation; and (b) medical support needs to address the effects of weather, cultural differences, the nature of a particular disability and the effects of training, and media exposure.

Physical Accessibility

The one experience that can frustrate any participant in a sporting event is that of physical barriers. When considering housing or hotel/motel accommodations, it is necessary to ascertain the specific nature of accessibility. Because housing units are built at different times, the laws governing accessibility vary. What is accessible to one person may be inaccessible to another. Acquiring a specific list of accessible features is helpful, as is a personal tour of the lodging. Some considerations in declaring a lodging accessible include the following:

- Elevators
- Entrances to bathrooms—wide enough for wheelchairs, with space to maneuver the wheelchair once in the bathroom
- Showers and bathtub—wheelchair high for easy transferability
- Ramps—available wherever there are different levels
- Signs in Braille or large print
- Emergency system (e.g., lights, horns)

Access to sport and activity venues must also be accommodating. Bleachers should have areas specifically for individuals with disabilities. The paths that lead to a venue need to be paved and free of cracks or debris that would impede a person in a wheelchair or a visually impaired person. Basketball courts should have an area set aside for individuals in wheelchairs that is within 5 feet (1.5 meters) of the end line. Fields of play for soccer, softball, or track and field should be of the highest quality

Photo by Sue Gavron.

Wheelchairs available at the entrance to a ball park.

Photo by Sue Gavron.

A wooden ramp to provide access to a ball park.

so that individuals will not step into holes or sink into mud. Additional parking space for individuals with disabilities whose vehicles are so designated via a placard should be made available. Should there be no parking within a reasonable distance, alternate means of transportation should be made available for those who need it (e.g., use of golf carts). These are little things, but they influence both participants' and spectators' impressions of an event.

Another important concern for participants and spectators alike is access to eating establishments within the community. Such accessibility issues as large-print menus, willingness to fix special diets (low fat, low salt, low cholesterol, and low sugar), accessible bathrooms, and wide doorways are important. Entering a restaurant by the back door is not accessibility! Another concern is sensitizing service personnel to speak directly to individuals with a disability. Attending to these aspects will certainly attract repeat business.

Transportation

Transportation for participants must be available. This is especially true for a multiday, large event in which athletes, coaches, and support staff are housed in dormitory settings such as those of a university campus or in motels in town. The distance from housing to sport venues must be taken into account. Contestants should not have to plan to walk for 30 minutes to get to a venue. Should long distances from housing to sport venues be a concern, alternative means of transportation must be provided. The most common method is the use of buses or vans. A daily schedule of times and stop points should be posted in conspicuous places and included in the information packet for athletes and coaches. Ramps may have to be built so that individuals in wheelchairs have access to buses. Volunteers should be recruited for major stop points to assist in off-loading people as needed. Finally, the use of golf carts for short distances and emergency troubleshooting are other ways to assist.

Information Dissemination

Another important aspect of event management concerns the organization and dissemination of information to the participants. This translates into who participates in what event, in which heat at what time, and on what day. Having the support staff to run computer programs is an absolute necessity. Getting information to venue heads is essential if a reasonable time schedule is to be met. This is particularly true if staying outside in prolonged heat or cold may be detrimental to an individual with a specific type of disability.

It is important to avoid using inappropriate methods for providing participant information and identification badges. Methods that demean an individual should be avoided. Examples are the use of a plastic wrist-band (similar to a hospital band) that lists an individual's events and the use of a participant number sign with all sorts of identifying information on the back. Using a picture ID on a chain around the neck, similar to what is done in other athletic events, is more appropriate and socially acceptable.

Spectator Care

Organizers for any sporting event, regardless of its size, must take into account the needs of the spectators as well as the athletes. Martinez (1991) has identified the needs for spectator care that planning must consider:

- Evacuation strategies in the event of sudden natural disaster or terrorism
- Disaster response structure (incident command structure), roles and responsibilities of various medical personnel
- Supply resources and storage
- Dehydration from alcohol, insect stings, cardiac and diabetic events, seizures, allergies, and pedestrian injuries
- Clear directional signs
- Adequate lighting
- Handrails to prevent falls
- Easily identifiable first aid signs
- Padding for temporary structural hazards
- Need to anticipate environmental and weather conditions
- Need for medical personnel to be familiar with stadium design (Carlson, 1992)

Martinez (1991) further recommends that an incident command system be established for handling multiple spectator injuries. Briefly, the incident command system is a system whereby a senior officer in law enforcement or a firefighter takes command of a multiple-persons injury situation by coordinating resources, site safety, security, and communications so that a command structure develops on-scene. "In particular the medical division would have four components activated: triage, treatment, morgue, and transport. Medical personnel should understand their assignments beforehand and report to a predeter-mined station in the event of a multiple injury situation" (Martinez, 1991, p. 43).

Athlete Care

The care and treatment of athletes with disabilities generally follow recommendations for able-bodied athletes (see chapter 9). That is, any event should have medical staff support in proportion to the number of participants and venues. Medical staff support can mean personnel such as certified athletic trainers, massage therapists, physical therapists, first responders, emergency medical technicians, paramedics, or physicians. Additionally, the local hospital community should be notified of the event, the number of individuals expected, and the nature of their disabilities. This linkage is necessary to assist the hospital, for example, in identifying persons who can interpret for the hearing impaired or for international competitors. A complete medical history and list of prescribed drugs should also be available for each athlete. The local fire department should also be notified and involved in the planning inasmuch as their ambulance service may play a role in transporting people to the hospital. The input from the fire department is especially critical in establishing entrance points and exit points from various parts of the games site.

The overall planning for medical support services should be overseen by a physician, preferably one who is familiar with emergency medicine and with individuals with disabilities. It is preferable that this physician work with the facility manager (Carlson, 1992, p. 142). The plan for medical services should be established so that all participants, coaches, and medical support staff know where to go for assistance. This is also true for those who run the sport venues and organize volunteers. Knowing where to go in an emergency saves time, which can be critical in treatment. Thus, clear signs for first aid stations are an absolute necessity. It is also helpful if all medical support personnel wear a distinctive color, hat, or uniform. Medical information in the form of where first aid stations are located, how to obtain assistance during the day and after hours, and where hospitals are located should be made available to all coaches, participants, and parents in the coaches' handbook and other materials routinely distributed to all prior to the event.

Medical supplies should include various kinds of insulin for individuals with diabetes, anti-seizure medications, and allergy medications. Various straps for positioning individuals with spinal cord injuries or cerebral palsy may also be helpful. A current *Physicians Desk Reference (PDR)* for drugs is another useful item to have available to key first aid stations because many individuals with disabilities are taking several kinds of medication at once.

Information about each athlete and the specific nature of the disability, along with any medications or allergies, should be with every coach at all times or entered into a computerized system to ensure instant access. Because of the interactions of certain drugs or allergies with certain substances, it is important that this information be available to medical support staff. This is especially true for those individuals who are speech impaired or nonverbal. Another concern from a medical point of view is the effect of climate and cultural changes on international athletes. Sometimes extreme changes in either can trigger seizures or allergic reactions.

When one is working with athletes with disabilities, there is a possibility that all are not equally trained in terms of physiological conditioning or are "in shape." This factor may cause some problems at the conclusion of an event rather than during it. For example, a runner who collapses at the end of an event may not have had sufficient training and may suffer from leg cramps as a result. It is therefore helpful to find out the exact nature of the event a person was participating in and whether the person had trained adequately, as this information may affect the nature of the medical crisis. Other aspects that may cause problems include the weather (in cold, rainy weather, for example, persons with asthma may have trouble breathing and amputees may develop hypothermia more easily) and prostheses, which may need repair and may cause blistering or other soft tissue types of injury. Thus, including prosthesis and wheelchair repair resources as part of the medical support team is recommended.

From an administrative standpoint, some aspects of medical support services will interface with other areas. For example, a communications system is needed strictly for medical support services. Communications must be available from the field to a central point (e.g., hospital or physician in charge) and to the fire department for transportation needs. Transportation must be established not only during the day for events but also during the evening if participants are housed in university dorms. Emergency evacuation routes must be identified by law enforcement agencies and emergency personnel. Supplies and access to supplies must be arranged so that all aid stations are well stocked. The medical support staff need to have a system of command established for each shift and to identify the roles and responsibilities of various personnel. All of this planning should occur prior to the event and should be evaluated after its conclusion (Martinez, 1991).

The physical safety and security of athletes and spectators at state, regional, national, and international events must be attended to. Because of the threat of individual or extremist groups to "make a statement" at highly visible events, the use of security guards, fencing, barriers, and identification systems for access to specific areas must be a part of the planning process. The incorporation of technology will continue to grow in this regard and be a major financial cost for events (Parks and Quarterman, 2003). The feeling of being safe is an important aspect for spectators and athletes at large events.

KEY POINT

Security and medical needs for athletes and spectators are a significant aspect of event planning. Particularly with respect to medical issues, athletes with disabilities may have some specific and unique needs that event managers must address.

Media and Athletes With Disabilities

Media exposure is another important aspect of event management. Any event should have a public relations specialist or a complete press center, although one or two people may handle smaller events. A press center should be large enough to hold press representatives, phone lines, computers, tables, food, and preassembled press kits. However, even the best-equipped media center cannot make sure that events involving individuals with disabilities are treated as hard news or sport stories. Often the stories are classified as human interest rather than as legitimate sport stories. The only avenue open is to present the most professional press releases possible and run the media operations as if the event were for able-bodied athletes. The atmosphere of the press center imparts a sense of what is going on to the media, and media people will take their cue from it. Emphasize that these individuals are athletes first and disabled second.

Planning for International Sport Events

In planning and implementing a sport event for athletes with disabilities it is important to be cognizant of, and perhaps model, the programs provided at the major international competitions for athletes with disabilities (e.g., Paralympics, world championships, Deaflympics, Special Olympics) as well as those for able-bodied athletes. Although these are very complex undertakings, the information in this section comprises examples of those components that can be included as an integral part of a sport event for athletes with disabilities. These components are not all-inclusive but can serve as a guide for those who may not have access to or be familiar with the aspects of hosting a large competition. Because of the plethora of books and research now available on sport management, sport marketing, and sport finance and promotions, the realm of possibilities for elite athletes with disabilities to experience more similarities related to the sport experience and its components (e.g., marketing, finance, research) with their able-bodied counterparts is available.

Marsha Wetzel

FAST FACTS

Home Base: Rochester, NY
Sports: Basketball, softball, mini-marathoner, cyclist
Selected Accomplishments:

Two-time Deaflympics gold medalist in Women's Basketball (1985, 1989)

Four time National Deaf Softball Championships

NCAA Division I Women's Basketball Official

Courtesy of Chuck Solomon.

Marsha Wetzel is by her own admission "a natural athlete." Born deaf, Marsha, with the support of her deaf parents, never let profound hearing loss stop her. During her senior year in high school she was captain of the soccer, basketball, and softball teams. During her college years and matriculation from Gallaudet College, she played varsity basketball and softball. Marsha was a two-time gold medal winner in the 1985 and 1989 Deaflympics along with being a member of a national Deaf basketball champion team. She was also a four-time national Deaf softball champion participant. So what does this say about this seasoned athlete? Well there's more. Marsha has cycled cross-country from Oregon to Virginia and from Vancouver, B.C., to San Diego. Her parents, who were also athletic, fostered this independent spirit. Her father was a participant in the 1953 Deaflympics.

"Be proud of one's deaf identity and of Deaf Culture."

Currently Marsha has the distinction of being the only certified female referee who is deaf. She has officiated for 14 years and 3 years in both the Patriot League and the Atlantic 10 Women's Basketball Conference. According to Marsha, being involved in sport has "taught me a lot about the importance of commitment, hard work, stability in fitness, teamwork, perseverance. . . ." She further states, "Sports have also helped me to become a better and stronger character in life and prepared me to deal with the world challenges and struggles. . . ." Marsha does not consider her hearing loss to be a disability. Her modeling for Deaf younger athletes is important to her. Marsha can say, "Look at me—you can do it too!"

All of the competitions mentioned include impressive opening and closing ceremonies. Opening ceremonies have typically included

- colorful displays of logos and mascots;
- official welcomes by host country government officers and official representatives of sport organizations (e.g., International Olympic Committee, IPC, international federations);
- official anthems and other musical presentations;
- lighting of the torch or flag raising; and
- various forms of entertainment including fireworks, celebrities, and the like.

With similar activities, closing ceremonies tend to continue this festive aspect of the competition and the celebration of athletic performance, and include

- the passing on of the games to representatives from the site of the next games;
- extinguishing of the "Olympic" flame;
- comingling of athletes rather than a parade of nations;
- entertainment consisting of song, dance, and other elaborately staged events; and
- fireworks.

Opening and closing ceremonies are held in large arenas that can accommodate (tens of) thousands of spectators, athletes, coaches, officials, and so on. (Souvenir books are usually produced to commemorate the games.)

In addition to the sport program offered at each of these international competitions, social and cultural programs are provided for spectators as well as athletes and coaches. These often include

- game rooms;
- social tents;
- evening dances and performances;
- collector pin trading centers;
- food booths;
- sales of T-shirts, pins, buttons, pens, sportswear, postcards, commemorative stamps and postmarks, hats, visors, and so on; and
- official photographers to make pictures of competitors and events available for purchase.

Usually a "newspaper" about the games is published daily. In such papers are the results of competitions held the day before, medal count standing, feature articles on selected athletes or sport leaders, and so on. For these international competitions, a media center is centrally located. Reporters from around the world are provided with press credentials and given space, typewriters, and phones to facilitate media coverage. In addition, official press releases are written daily. Often representatives of the media (news reporters for print and visual media, reporters for sport magazines like *Palaestra* or *Sports 'n Spokes*) are supplied with pertinent written information about the games, profiles of selected athletes, list of contacts, and so on, as well as gifts, film, and free development.

These competitions require that attendees receive appropriate credentials primarily for security reasons and logistics. Among the categories used for badges are the following: athletes, coaches, officials, press, invited guests (VIPs), officers, national delegates, medical staff, organizing committee, and volunteers. The type of badge obtained often carries with it restrictions on access to the various venues of the games.

Medical services for athletes and spectators at major international competitions are provided in a variety of ways. For example, an area for prosthesis and wheelchair repair is provided at the Paralympics. This area is not only staffed by experts but also includes space and equipment necessary for self-repair. In addition, first aid stations and medical emergencies areas are dispersed throughout the grounds. These facilities and services are accessible to all.

In addition to the athletic competitions and social programs, opportunity and space for classification, athlete certification, official meetings, coach and athlete training workshops, and drug testing are commonly provided. Scientific congresses may also be included before the games (e.g., the Paralympic Scientific Congress preceding the 1996 Paralympic Games in Atlanta). While the IPC ruled out a scientific congress before the Athens Paralympics (2004), sessions on disability sport were incorporated in the scientific congress preceding the Olympic Games.

The athletes and coaches are housed in an athletes' village (e.g., Paralympic Village). Included in these villages are restaurants, residences, religious services, television, library, cinema, information centers, discotheque, game rooms, and commercial services such as public telephones, post office, hairdressers, travel agency, bank and automatic tellers, photographic services, and florist (Atlanta Paralympic Organizing Committee, 1996; Salt Lake 2002 Organizing Committee, 2002).

KEY POINT

Integrating social and cultural events into a sport competition is important.

Concluding Comments

The most important aspect of event management is planning and anticipation (Wyness, 1984). A plethora of books written on event management detail the kinds of committees needed and the functions of each. This chapter has provided an overview of event management and highlighted those aspects necessary to consider when planning and implementing a sport event for athletes with disabilities. The emphasis is on many of the similarities with able-bodied events as well as the specific needs for elite athletes with disabilities.

Event planning is both an art and a science. There are people and organizations that specialize in aspects of the process, from conducting feasibility studies to directing events from one major competition to another. There is no reason disability sport competitions cannot have the same chances of success as those for persons without disabilities.

part III

The Changing Landscape of Disability Sport

twelve

Challenges and Controversies in Disability Sport

Reader Goal   Gain an understanding of the numerous challenges and controversies that exist in and affect the disability sport movement

Chapter Synopsis

- Inclusion and Integration
- Classification
- Ethics Issues
- Doping in Disability Sport
- Media Representation
- Youth Sport Development
- Marketing Disability Sport
- Concluding Comments

Disability sport has faced a number of challenges and controversies in its evolution to a maturing social institution. Classification, the system by which athletes with disabilities are organized into competitive classes, is one of the most visible and controversial aspects. Similarly to sport in general, disability sport has faced challenges with ethics, doping and performance-enhancing drugs, lack of media coverage and adequate representation, the development of youth sport, and opportunities to market disability sport. This chapter provides an overview of selected issues that confront the disability sport movement.

Inclusion and Integration

Throughout history, and especially in the 20th century, individuals with disabilities have experienced increasingly greater inclusion and acceptance within society (DePauw, 1986c; DePauw and Doll-Tepper, 2000). As a result, they have also been able to experience selective inclusion and acceptance in the sport world. Although doors are opening, they have not been opened without resistance. In the United States and Canada in particular, these openings have occurred as a result of federal legislation, political pressures, or both (Allard and Bornemann, 2001; Stevens, 1998). However, in other countries around the globe, both political and cultural mores have paved the way.

Throughout the world, disability sport programs have been shaped by the interaction of given societal factors (e.g., political, economic, sociohistorical, sociocultural). The trend is one of inclusion. Internationally, athletes with disabilities have experienced selected inclusion within the Olympic arena. Examples of inclusion are exhibition events at the Summer and Winter Olympics, approval to use the term Paralympics, and full medal events for the Commonwealth Games. In keeping with this trend, athletes with disabilities will find themselves with increasingly more opportunities to compete alongside able-bodied athletes.

Given the assumption of progressive inclusion, disability sport must address at least three major issues:

- Whether to group sport by ability or by disability
- Whether sport is for participation or for competition
- Whether sport competitions should be integrated or separate (DePauw, 1990a)

It is best to think of each of these issues as representing a continuum rather than a simple dichotomy—that is, the position one takes on each is a matter of degree. On one end of the disability/ability grouping continuum, the emphasis is on classifying sport competition by disability (e.g., visual impairment, level of amputation, severity of cerebral palsy, level of spinal cord lesion); on the other end, emphasis is on grouping by ability (e.g., without regard to disability, cross-disability classification). The participation/competition continuum has to do with the perceived primary purpose of the sporting event (e.g., Special Olympics for participation, Paralympics for competition). On the integration/separation continuum, at one end is competition with able-bodied persons as well as with other persons with disabilities (cross-disability); at the other end is separate competitions for those with disabilities (Paralympics) or by specific disability grouping (Special Olympics International, World Games for the Deaf). In addition, this continuum includes the notion of separate events for athletes with disabilities within a competition for able-bodied athletes.

Over the years, a number of initiatives have been launched to include athletes with disabilities within sport. One instance was the formation of the International Paralympic Committee (IPC) International Committee on Integration of Athletes with a Disability in November 1990 by a group of Canadians who envisioned the inclusion of selected full medal events for athletes with disabilities in major international competitions (Merklinger, 1991, p. 8). Specifically targeted were the Olympic Games and the Commonwealth Games. This committee was later renamed the Commission for Inclusion of Athletes with a Disability (CIAD). Rick Hansen, a Canadian who completed the Man in Motion World Tour to raise money for research, accepted the IPC invitation to chair the committee. (Hansen wheeled 24,855 miles [40,000 kilometers] through 34 countries on four continents in two years, two months, and two days and raised $26.1 million for spinal cord injury research.) The CIAD's goals were identified in its June 1993 report as follows:

1. Develop a lobbying strategy for the inclusion of selected full medal events for athletes with disabilities initially within the Olympic Games and Commonwealth Games

2. Increase the awareness and understanding of the appropriateness of the inclusion of selected full medal events for athletes with disabilities into major international competitions

3. Facilitate the successful conduct of selected full medal events included into major international competitions

4. Develop a model process for the inclusion of selected full medal events for athletes with disabilities into major international events

5. Establish formal linkages and effective liaisons with appropriate entities

6. Gain interest in and financial support for the CIAD and its objectives

The CIAD concentrated its efforts on the 1994 Commonwealth Games in Victoria, British Columbia. In April 1991, the Commonwealth Games Federation agreed to include six exhibition events in the 1994 games. The events finally selected were men's open wheelchair marathon, men's open 800-meter wheelchair race, men's 100-meter freestyle class S9, women's 100-meter freestyle class S9, men's visually impaired lawn bowling singles, and women's visually impaired lawn bowling singles.

In the summer of 1992, the Commonwealth Games Federation granted athletes with disabilities greater inclusion in the 1994 games. Athletes received distinctive medals, were allowed to live in the Athletes' Village, received full athlete accreditation, participated fully in the opening and closing ceremonies, and wore their countries' national team uniforms.

In 1997, the Commonwealth Games Federation, in consultation with the National Paralympic Committees and the international sports governing bodies, decided to make selected events for athletes with disabilities full medal events. This action was intended to be effective for the Commonwealth Games in 2006, but the Manchester Organizing Committee decided to include disability sport events in the 2002 Commonwealth Games. As a result, 160 athletes with disabilities from 20 countries competed in five sports (swimming, athletics, lawn bowls, weightlifting, and table tennis) (Commonwealth Games Federation, 2003).

Although progress has been made toward integrating athletes with disabilities into major international sport competitions, the efforts will continue. It is likely that discussions between the IPC and the International Olympic Committee (IOC) as well as within the IPC will continue for a number of years until the issues surrounding inclusion are resolved.

Closer ties between the IOC and the IPC have been established in the late 20th and early 21st centuries. International Paralympic Committee President Robert Steadward (who served from 1989 to 2000) represented the IPC on the IOC. International Paralympic Committee President Phil Craven (whose term began in 2001) was elected as a member of the IOC in 2003. The bidding process for future Olympic Games includes a bid for the Paralympic Games (see chapter 3).

The question of integrating athletes with disabilities into international competitions can be answered only as the issues facing athletes with disabilities—identified throughout this book—are not only acknowledged but specifically addressed. For example, disability sport could not have made the progress noted previously if it had not been viewed as being for competition, not participation, and if the primary emphasis had not been on sport by ability, not disability. Inasmuch as disability remains an important factor (for both the IPC and the Olympic Games organizers), the events chosen will be limited to selected athletes with disabilities, and specific disabilities in particular.

While the focus on integration or segregation has been on the athletes, Fay (2001) makes a good case for a look at how organizations can strategically plan for the vertical integration of athletes with disabilities (that is, including athletes from the grassroots level through elite competition). His study addresses sport managers and leadership within organizations from a sport management perspective. In this distinctive study, Fay takes on the problems with integration of athletes with disabilities and provides some measures to perhaps tackle this problem and others of discrimination.

Kuniko Obinata

FAST FACTS

Home Base: Shibuya, Tokyo, Japan
Sport: Skiing
Selected Accomplishments:

Medalist in 1998 and 2002 Winter Paralympic Games

World rank in Alpine Cup Skiing (third place)

Kuniko Obinata is a hard worker as a skier with an amputation, and in life. Her training is five days a week in-season and three days a week off-season. During the competitive season the head of the Japanese National Ski Team for the Handicapped coaches Kuniko. A coach and a chair ski mechanic were influential in

"Sports make me grow . . . as well as challenge my own limits."

getting Kuniko started in her very successful endeavors. Kuniko was a gold, silver, and bronze medal winner in alpine skiing at the 1998 Nagano Winter Paralympic Games. At the 2002 Salt Lake City Winter Games she was a bronze medal finisher. In 2003 she ranked third in the World Cup Alpine Skiing events. Her 14 years of involvement in disability sport speak of a committed athlete.

Kuniko believes that "sports make me grow in various ways as well as challenge my own limits." She is also a quiet activist in that she regards sport as "an important means of presentation to call upon the interests from the public to realize the universal society, which is my lifelong theme." Her strong feelings are also directed to younger athletes with a disability. She suggests that they "find something that they can be totally absorbed" in. Kuniko also focuses on the social status and standing of athletes with disabilities. In her perception, the need for all countries to accept athletes with disabilities as athletes first and to provide them with equal opportunities for training is paramount. Kuniko is both an athlete and a role model whose work ethic and success pave the way for others to also succeed.

In support of inclusion (integration), Hedrick and Hedrick (1993) questioned the current organizational structure of disability sport as one that promotes segregation. They proposed instead that the current segregation model must be gradually replaced by one in which adapted sports become legitimate member organizations affiliated with the mainstream National Governing Bodies (pp. 14-15). Landry (1992) also called for integrating and streamlining the various structures of the disability sport movement into one international governing body (e.g., IPC) as the means for accepting athletes with disabilities and disability sport throughout the world. As McCrae (2001) has noted, inclusion does not occur in any one singular fashion. His perspective reinforces that there may be a multitude of ways and means to achieve this objective. Whether or not a single model can be developed is yet to be seen.

KEY POINT

Inclusion and integration remain a priority for the disability sport movement.

Classification

Classification of athletes with disabilities for competition has been a long-standing controversy. On one hand, the goal of classification seems to be to enable each competitor, regardless of severity of impairment, to compete in a fair manner with others of similar ability/disability (a more medical-based classification system). On the other hand, the goal of classification based on functional ability applied to sport is to provide for meaningful athletic competition based upon ability, not disability. Given this increased emphasis on ability and less on adaptation/modification of the sport, the more severely impaired tend to be eliminated from elite athletic competition. This latter goal of classification has emerged partly because of the administrative problem and logistics of having numerous classes for competitions (e.g., currently more than fifty 100-meter races by gender and disability type—three for blind, eight for cerebral palsy, nine for amputee, six for les autres, seven for wheelchair users).

According to Sherrill (1993), sport classification theory has been consistently ranked as a sport topic in which research is greatly needed. She suggested that the current issues of classification include the following:

- Should sport classifications be medical or functional?
- Should sport classifications be specific to each disability (e.g., cerebral palsy, spinal cord injury), or should there be one system broad enough to include all?
- Should there be a classification system for each sport or a general system encompassing several sports? (p. 176)

The results of research on classification have been mixed, and these studies are often undertaken and reported based upon the differing goals identified earlier. Differences found in athletic performances in track and field by gender, distance, and class of athletes (Coutts and Schutz, 1988; Ridgeway, Pope, and Wilkerson, 1988; Wicks et al., 1983) have been used to support the need for classification for fairness. On the other hand, the findings reported by Higgs et al. (1990), as well as Gorton and Gavron (1987), seem to support a reduction in the number of classifications.

Strohkendl (2001) states that "there is a growing interest in sports classification issues in science and research" (p. 281). He acknowledges that there is controversy between medical and functional classification systems. He further notes that while the functional system (based upon functional ability of the athlete rather than the specific type and extent of impairment) implemented in Barcelona did result in decreasing the number of events, there is still a need for development and implementation of a classification theory. Strohkendl identifies three major areas for discussion and research:

- "The purpose and provisions for a fair, equitable and adequate classification system for the disabled
- the significance of classification systems in the context of sport for the disabled
- design and application of a sports and athlete oriented classification system" (p. 283)

Note that Strohkendl is proposing a systematic and organized scientific inquiry into the subject rather than putting out systems on a trial-and-error basis.

Throughout the 1990s and into the 21st century, integrated or functional classification systems have continued to be examined and refined for use in international competitions. These same systems will also permeate the national competitions, especially those for qualifying for international competitions. But when, if ever, will they become universally accepted?

KEY POINT

Classification of athletes with disabilities for competition is a long-standing issue.

Classification: Integration and Segregation

Classification is primarily a concern for the fairness of competitions among athletes with disabilities. But central to sport and disability in the broader context is the issue of competition with able-bodied athletes.

This issue manifests itself in two distinct ways: the inclusion of disability sport events within competitions for able-bodied athletes, and competition between athletes with disabilities and able-bodied athletes.

A growing number of athletes with disabilities advocate the inclusion of events for athletes with disabilities within major international competitions such as the Olympic Games, Pan American Games, World University Games, Commonwealth Games, and world championships (Clarke, 1986; Daignault, 1990; Labanowich, 1988). But although this type of competition has been advocated, the classification issues have yet to be identified fully.

Also virtually ignored in the sport and disability literature is discussion of athletes with disabilities competing alongside able-bodied athletes. Except for notable examples during the Olympic Games (such as Karoly Takacs, who won gold medals in shooting in 1948 and 1952; Liz Hartel, who despite polio won a silver medal in dressage in 1952; and Neroli Fairhall, who represented New Zealand in 1984 and competed in archery from a wheelchair), this type of competition exists at the regional or local level. As the future of sport and disability unfolds, it is important to consider all facets of integration/inclusion and related classification issues.

Classification has always been a major component of disability sport, particularly for international competitions. In the 1990s, the medical classification system gave way to the functional classification system as utilized in the Paralympic movement. Although classification issues are themselves controversial, they are related to the underlying philosophies of disability sport.

Classification and the Future of the Paralympic Games

The Paralympic Games has utilized several classification systems to place athletes in appropriate classes (including three for blind/visually impaired athletes and numerous classes for physically impaired athletes). There has been pressure to reduce the number of classes in major competitions, as well as considerable disagreement on the current system and who is advantaged and disadvantaged. The able-bodied world with 90% of the population crowns two Olympic 100-meter champions (male, female), and the disability sporting world has "crowned so many I can't keep count" (Higgs, 2003).

For the 2004 Athens Paralympics, the pressure was great to reduce the number of athletes and therefore the number of classes for competition, as is the case also with respect to all future Paralympic Games. To do so equitably requires a new approach. Higgs (2003) argues for a system that is fair, transparent, easy to comprehend, gives immediate knowledge of the results, and yet provides for meaningful competitions. For track events, he proposes that all classes compete in the same race with different starting times or at different points along the track. This would result in retaining more classes but fewer events, with class forming the basis for starting position and not the individuals. Higgs also argues for indexing in sports like shot put or table tennis so that the starting classification point score is based upon disability classification. Inasmuch as time and distance can be divided into an infinite number of units, this means that athletes with disabilities can be provided with a starting score for the event (for example, one athlete starts with 8 points and another starts with 3). The system is similar to the handicap system used in golf.

"Our current approach to integrated classification is hurting those with the most severe impairments and those at the lower end of their classification. It is unfair, and exclusionary. A fair, inclusionary, and practical method has to be found . . . this might just work." (Higgs, 2003)

Ethics Issues

It would be naive to believe that disability sport is immune to the ethical dilemmas that are found in able-bodied Olympic sport. Performance-enhancing efforts through banned means (such as boosting and doping) have become important considerations in team and athlete management and have also resulted in disqualifications of athletes and teams (Riding, 2001). Equipment specifications for wheelchair and other assistive devices are also ripe for manipulation.

One example of ethical issues for Paralympians was the scandal that occurred after the 2000 Sydney Paralympic Games. Athletes from Spain who competed in events for intellectually impaired athletes were later found not to have intellectual impairments. This resulted in expulsion of those athletes who competed under the auspices of the International Sports Federation for Persons with Mental Handicap and a ban against its athletes from participating in the Paralympic Games.

As an earlier example, a scandal occurred in 1992 when a team misrepresented itself at the Barcelona Paralympics. The U.S. men's basketball team was stripped of its gold medal because one of the players, David Kiley, tested positive for Darvocet, a banned painkiller.

In terms of medications, a significant difference and need may be inherent for athletes with disabilities versus able-bodied athletes. For example, certain medicines may be needed to inhibit neurological responses from a condition causing pain or muscular contractions. Yet these same drugs may also be a factor in helping an athlete to ignore pain and train well above his or her capacity, and may result in death if taken to the extreme (Riding, 2001). The role anabolic steroids play in performance may be clearly delineated with an able-bodied athlete, but what if the same steroid is essential for the life functioning of an athlete with a disability? Should the drug protocols for the Olympics be adopted in totality? If there is a difference between the Paralympics and Olympics protocols, will it be accepted by the IOC?

Athletes have not only ethical dilemmas to face. Because of the rapid and competitive nature of the sport business, managers and coaches also have to face choices. Endorsements mean money. Endorsements enhance visibility. Thus the business of sport means trying to earn these. How one goes about getting endorsements may affect training, use of drugs, and manipulation of equipment.

Wheeler (2001) refers to the concept of ethical relativism as a means of describing the status of ethics in the (disability) sporting world. The premise is that a decision-making process and code for athletes and administrators, officials, coaches, institutions, and nations are dependent on the society and the individuals within it. Thus we have differential treatment of athletes, payoffs, and other unethical behaviors that are a part of the sporting environment, able-bodied or Paralympian.

Is there a way to solve the ethical issues? Wheeler (2001) promotes a standardized code of ethics for all Paralympic athletes in all phases of the sporting experience (e.g., youth, competition, and retirement phases). While this may be viewed as a simplistic approach, it is necessary.

Boosting due to autonomic dysreflexia can result in enhanced performance and has been reported to have occurred during competitions. Individuals with cervical or high thoracic spinal injuries can have an abnormal sympathetic reflex called autonomic dysreflexia. Although this reflex happens spontaneously, it can be deliberately caused through boosting. This reflex is considered a health hazard and is caused by painful stimuli to the lower part of the body, particularly distension or irritation of the bladder. According to the IPC, athletes who show signs of being dysreflexic are eliminated from the competition.

Doping in Disability Sport

The fight against doping (the use of performance-enhancing drugs) is important for Olympic athletes and Paralympic athletes. The IOC and the IPC have taken a strong stance against doping and put policies and procedures in place to prevent the use of performance-enhancing drugs. Specifically, the IPC Medical and Anti-Doping Code prohibits the use of certain substances and methods intended to enhance or having the effect of enhancing athletic performance. A list of the prohibited substances and methods is identified in the IPC code along with the penalties. Disqualifications and suspension are common penalties. In 2003, the IPC revised the IPC Medical and Anti-Doping Code to comply with the World Anti-Doping Code and its standards.

The prevalence of doping among athletes with disabilities is not well documented, but many believe that the problem is not any different from elsewhere in the sporting world. The first attempt at doping controls in disability sport occurred in 1983, and the effort continues to date. The following is a chronology of drug testing at the Paralympic Games:

- Samples were taken but not analyzed at the first International Sports Organization for the Disabled Games in Oslo, Norway, in 1983.

- Samples were also taken at the Paralympic Games for wheelchair athletes in Stoke Mandeville in 1984.

- In 1986, 100 samples were taken and analyzed during the world championships in athletics, swimming, and archery in Gothenburg, Sweden. Four samples were found to be positive—one amphetamine case and three cases with less severe stimulant drugs. Because the sampling procedure was questioned and the International Coordinating Committee had no doping policy, the results were declared invalid.

- At the Seoul 1988 Paralympics, 50 tests were conducted and one person tested positive.

- An anti-doping policy for disability sport was developed under the auspices of the IPC through the work of its medical commission. The IPC has identified the same list of banned drugs as the IOC.

- Since the Barcelona 1992 Paralympics, drug testing has been conducted in IPC-sanctioned international events. From Barcelona 1992 through Sydney 2000, a total of 12 positive cases have been reported. The athletes were disqualified and the medals redistributed.

- Precompetition drug testing was implemented for the Sydney 2000 Paralympics. Of 128 precompetition tests, 9 were found to be positive. Two additional athletes tested positive in approximately 500 competition tests. All of these cases were major doping offenses involving the use of anabolic steroids or diuretics that led to disqualification and four years' suspension.

KEY POINT

Banned performance-enhancing substances (e.g., doping and boosting) have been used by athletes with disabilities despite anti-doping efforts of the IPC.

Media Representation

Why is it that the Paralympic movement and disability sport movement cannot garner the necessary coverage from the media? After all, more than 3.5 million people attended Paralympic Games in the 1990s. The opening and closing ceremonies for the 1996 Paralympic Games were attended by 66,257 and 57,640, respectively. Over 2,000 media representatives were accredited for the Games. This compares quite well with other large-venue sport events such as the 1998 World Cup, the 1998 World Series (baseball), the Super Bowl, and the 1999 Women's World Cup (Wanzel, Gibeault, and Tsarouhas, 2001, p. 854).

The reasons for a lack of coverage are diverse. Perhaps the one that is foremost is society's perspective and lack of understanding about disability; in effect, people's fear of the unknown turns them off from even considering watching, attending, or reading about an event. This implies that a societal change is needed. Perhaps newspapers and magazines can use the "power of the press" to change attitudes (Howe, 2001). If they can cover disability sport as a sport event first and the disability as a distant second, then and only then can the disability sport movement be perceived as real. Location of stories should be on the sport page and not in the human interest section. Coverage should be objective and professional and as critical as for any other athlete or event.

The continuing struggle for equitable coverage by the media is not a new phenomenon. The coverage of Paralympic sport has been at best inconsistent and unremarkable. In a study conducted at the 1996 Paralympic Games in Atlanta, Schantz and Gilbert (1997) examined coverage of the Games in the French and German press over a month and a half. Their conclusions, which were not at all unexpected, showed that the French and German press sport scene had little interest in the event. What interest did exist was expressed in terms of respect for how athletes handled their disability rather than their sport performance. Additionally, the sport most covered was wheelchair events; and then, most often the nature of the disability was not mentioned.

Golf, while not a Paralympic sport, received extensive coverage in the 1990s because of the lawsuit in which Casey Martin sought the right to play at the professional level while using a cart as necessitated by his impairment, which was specifically prohibited by the rules. Casey won the decision, but no positive benefit in terms of increased media coverage has resulted. Maas and Hasbrook (2001) analyzed several golf magazines during the time of the Casey Martin trial and found that "golfers with disabilities are absent from advertisements and photographs and are given minimal attention in the articles" (p. 21). The authors further contended that golf magazines continued to maintain their neglect of women golfers and older golfers, although both groups are on the rise.

The curriculum in media must include training in coverage of disability sport. Students should have the opportunity to attend, cover, write about, or photograph events in their community or in their region. The greater the exposure to these events, the more acceptable such events may become to the public.

While sport may be considered a common denominator across people, cultures, genders, or races, in reality it is not. Pearce and Kane (2001) analyzed the content of two popular sport magazines for people with disabilities. They found that representations of race and gender in these magazines followed the trends of the mainstream press; that is, more males than females were featured, as were more white athletes in comparison to any other race. Again, the findings indicated that the power of the press, real or imagined, follows a similar pattern for people with disabilities even in their own media formats as regards race and gender.

KEY POINT

For many reasons, perhaps most importantly society's lack of understanding about disability, media representation is lacking for disability sport.

Youth Sport Development

Our youth are our future. But young athletes with disabilities who become involved in competitive sport and recreational activities are still the exception, not the rule. While it is acknowledged that there are opportunities, wholesale participation of young athletes is not a significant factor (Sherrill, 2001a). They are not visible. And when they do compete, their participation is placed within a human interest context or in the closing story of a newscast. Yet youth with disabilities (for example, amputees, intellectually challenged athletes, and hearing-impaired athletes) have participated in football at all levels.

DeFrantz (2000), whose focus was on gender-equal opportunities for all (which can be seen to include sport for all), states that "sport belongs to us all . . . it is a powerful force for community throughout the world . . . but sadly there are fewer and fewer opportunities for sport to exist within the curricula of primary and secondary schools. . ." (p. 17). Without appropriate physical education content in the early, developing years, the lack of opportunity to learn fundamental movement and skills will limit the ability of youth with disabilities to enter the competitive sporting world sooner rather than later.

Gavron (2000, p. 26) also noted the impact of the decline of physical education content (in the United States) along with (1) a lack of available

Junichi Kawai

FAST FACTS

Home Base: Shizouka, Japan
Sport: Swimming
Selected Accomplishments:

Paralympic silver and bronze medalist in Barcelona, 1992

First winner of a gold medal in the 1,000-meter freestyle in Barcelona

Two gold, a silver, and a bronze in the Atlanta Paralympics, 1996

Two gold and three silver medals in Sydney, 2000

World record holder established in 50-meter freestyle and 400-meter medley relay in Sydney

This young man is on a mission. His main point to any young athlete with a disability is "set a goal and do your best." It appears that Junichi Kawai has done just that. He has medalled in every Paralympics he has entered. In 1992 he was the first gold medalist in the 1,000-meter freestyle for blind swimmers. In

"Set a goal and do your best."

the Atlanta Paralympic Games (1996) he won two gold medals, a silver, and a bronze in his events. In Sydney in 2000 he won two gold and three silver medals and established world records in the 50-meter freestyle and the 400-meter medley relay. Junichi, who is congenitally blind, trains by himself six days a week for 2 to 3 hours. The coach he had as a high school student was instrumental in his involvement in disability sport.

Junichi is representative of an athlete who is focused and disciplined. He feels that "sports give me a full life." He is concerned that public understanding of disability sport is lacking in the world, and that the financial basis of many athletes with disabilities is unstable and does not provide a means to make a living. It appears, however, that Junichi Kawai is able to set his goals and do very well in spite of these concerns.

offerings for competitive sport competition; (2) lack of desire to participate or knowledge that they can participate among children and youth with disabilities; (3) lack of knowledge, interest, or support on the part of adults to facilitate the process; (4) a lack of funding and other support mechanisms in the public school arena to support the process; and (5) lack of a definitive lifelong inclusive sport model and philosophy within the public school environment (at least in America).

While the concept of sport for all (physical activity and sport for all persons) is common on the European continent, parallel to the Aussie Willing and Able program in Australia and the Active Living approach in Canada, there is no such common, uniting philosophy in America. Special Olympics does have Unified teams, but this is not a concept that is highly visible or is covered by the media on a regular basis.

Marketing Disability Sport

Some might think that having a major competition such as the Paralympic Games should result in marketing success. This is not the reality. The social acceptance and public comfort level with regard to disability sport is not great (Lienert, Malone, and Yilla, 2003; Moeller, 2001; Schantz, 2003; Wanzel, Gibeault, and Tsarouhas, 2001) in spite of its growth over the last decade. Some limited success has been seen in the inclusion of athletes with disabilities in Nike ads, on the Wheaties box along with other celebrated athletes, and in awards given by major companies such as Sudafed, to mention a few.

The Paralympic sport movement can be seen as "underdeveloped property with excellent potential" (Wanzel, Gibeault, and Tsarouhas, 2001) in regards to corporate sponsorship. Corporate sponsorship is the key to global development and consequently better visibility. But can corporate sponsorship change people's attitudes?

Schantz (2003), in a field study at the 2000 Paralympics, found that "attitudes towards sport competition for people with disabilities are often ambivalent and that freak show behaviors still abound, depending on the sport" (p. 85). Will corporate partners buy into such an undertaking when these kinds of attitudes still exist?

Concluding Comments

The evolution of the disability sport movement continues. Throughout its struggle to obtain legitimacy, disability sport has faced challenges similar to those confronting able-bodied sport: use of illegal performance-enhancing practices by athletes, ethics issues, and the desire to develop youth sport. Unique to the disability sport movement are the inclusion or integration efforts and lack of media attention. The evolution of disability sport will continue and so will the issues and controversies.

thirteen

Female Athletes With Disabilities in Sport

Reader Goal Acknowledge the athletic achievements of girls and women with disabilities in sport and understand the experience of women with disabilities in society and the sporting world

Chapter Synopsis

- Historical Perspectives
- Female Athletes in the Olympic Games
- Female Athletes in Marathons
- Equity Issues
- Concluding Comments

Throughout history, various segments of society have experienced exclusion from the activities found in the mainstream of society and available to those of the dominant culture. Included among these "marginalized" groups are women; specific racial and ethnic groups; individuals with disabilities; those from lower socioeconomic classes; and gays, lesbians, and bisexuals. Because of marginalization, women with a disability have often found themselves in double jeopardy (Holcomb, 1984). The sporting world for female athletes with disabilities is no exception.

The first books written about disability sport (e.g., Guttmann, 1976; Paciorek and Jones, 1989; Sherrill, 1986; Stewart, 1991; van Hal, Rarick, and Vermeer, 1984; Vermeer, 1986) made little or no mention of diversity with regard to race, ethnicity, or gender, for example. The first writers to include women with disabilities were authors of women-in-sport books (e.g., Cohen, 1993; Hult and Trekell, 1991) and Stewart (1991), who discussed gender and race issues in Deaf sport. Since then, some of the disability sport books have provided some coverage of female athletes with disabilities (e.g., Doll-Tepper, Kroner, and Sonnenschein, 2001; Driscoll, Benge, and Benge, 2000; Steadward, Nelson, and Wheeler, 1994; Steadward and Peterson, 1997; Steadward, Wheeler, and Watkinson, 2003). Inasmuch as this book provides a comprehensive overview of sport and disability, this chapter is intended to describe the progress and detail the accomplishments of girls and women with a disability in the context of sport.

Although the disability sport literature contains very little reference to gender, let alone to differing ethnic backgrounds or issues of class, sexual orientation, religion, or cultural context, it is a well-acknowledged fact that one's sport experience varies dependent on one's specific frame(s) of reference (e.g., Birrell, 1988; Boutilier and SanGiovanni, 1983; Theberge, 1985). This chapter explores gender as one of the various interacting factors influencing sport participation by individuals with a disability.

Researchers have recently included female athletes with disabilities in their studies, but research on female athletes as well as studies of gender and sport are very limited. The only known comprehensive survey of females with disabilities and their participation in sport and physical activity was conducted in Canada in the late 1980s. With support from the Fitness Canada women's program, the Canadian Federation of Sport Organizations for the Disabled surveyed girls and women with physical disabilities throughout Canada between 1986 and 1988. The results indicated the following (excerpted from *Physical Activity and Women With Disabilities: A National Survey,* n.d.):

- Current levels of physical activity were insufficient.
- Physical activity was at least somewhat important or very important.
- Awareness of the physical activity opportunities available was limited.
- The respondents preferred participating in organized noncompetitive or recreationally competitive activities.

- Very few were satisfied with the type of activities available.
- Participation in physical activity was mostly self-initiated but also influenced by family and friends.
- Respondents participated for pleasure and fun, to feel better, to relax and reduce stress, and to improve or maintain fitness.
- Barriers to participation included time constraints, inaccessible facilities, transportation problems, and lack of available information; disability and medical concerns were not primary barriers.
- Increased participation could occur through facilities closer to home, accessible facilities, knowledgeable instructors, partners for participation, and more information on programs for women with disabilities.
- The respondents did not prefer participation segregated by gender, disability, or both; integrated settings were fine.

Historical Perspectives

Although little known and mostly unrecognized, the history of girls and women with disabilities in competitive sport dates back to the early 1900s and continued to evolve throughout the 20th and into the 21st century. For the most part, this history is somewhat difficult to trace separately from the history of disability sport because until recently, it has been devoid of specific reference to gender, race, ethnicity, and specific type of impairment. In a general sense, female athletes with disabilities (including hearing impairments) have been present not only throughout the evolution of disability sport but also in the history of able-bodied sport. But their stories have not been told; their voices have not been heard.

Women with disabilities had to fight for their right to be included in the arena of sport (Hedrick and Hedrick, 1991). Given that disability sport is actually relatively young (DePauw, 1986c, 1990a; Steadward and Walsh, 1986), it follows that girls' and women's participation in sport is an even newer phenomenon. Much of the history of disability sport has been written since the 1960s. Female athletes with disabilities have gained greater visibility and acceptance as athletes alongside their male counterparts.

The detailed chronology of disability sport presented in appendix A incorporates the involvement and accomplishments of female athletes with disabilities. This chronology is admittedly not all-inclusive and represents primarily a Western society perspective. The following subsections present an overview and highlights.

KEY POINT

Female athletes with disabilities have participated in sport, including disability sport, for more than 100 years.

Deaf and Hard of Hearing

Under the auspices of the CISS (International Committee of Sports for the Deaf), Deaf males and females were given the opportunity to compete in the first International Games for the Deaf in 1924. Since then, participation at the international and national competitions for the Deaf has remained at approximately one-fourth to one-third female.

The governance structure of Deaf sport has been male dominated in the United States as well as internationally. Specifically, all CISS presidents have been men, and the prominent leadership positions have also been held by men. In the late 1980s, CISS elected a woman to its executive committee before the International Olympic Committee saw fit to do so (Stewart, 1991, p. 7).

In the United States, two Deaf women assumed leadership positions in the late 1980s. The American Athletic Association of the Deaf elected its first woman to serve as secretary-treasurer, Shirley Platt from Utah; and Dr. Donalda Ammons from Washington, D.C., became the first woman to chair the United States World Games for the Deaf Team Committee.

Physical Impairments

In 1944, organized sport opportunities for individuals with physical impairments emerged in conjunction with the creation of the Spinal Injuries Centre of the Stoke Mandeville Hospital in England. Its development marked the beginning of wheelchair sports as part of the rehabilitation of war veterans by hospital administrator Sir Ludwig Guttmann. Four years later, 13 men and 3 women (all patients at the hospital) competed in wheelchair archery at what would become the first Stoke Mandeville Games.

In contrast to the inclusion of females in Stoke Mandeville, the early days of wheelchair basketball around the world provided opportunities for men only. After the initiation of wheelchair basketball in the mid-1940s, it took over 20 years for women to be included. In 1968, the Paralympics in Tel Aviv formally introduced women's wheelchair basketball; and since then, women's wheelchair basketball has been included on the program of the International Stoke Mandeville Games (1970), the Pan American Wheelchair Games (1971), the European Championships (1974), and the World Cup Championships (1990).

Anne-Mette Bredahl

FAST FACTS

Home Base: Denmark
Sports: Cross country and biathlon, goal ball
Selected Accomplishments:

Gold medal, Paralympics 1994

Clinical psychologist

Anne-Mette Bredahl thought of herself as a clumsy, awkward child who did not especially like sports. Her vision was completely lost at age 22, and she was not even a winter sportsperson, let alone "athletic." This same individual won the first-ever gold medal for Denmark at a winter games—for either disabled or able-bodied athletes—in biathlon at the 1994 Paralympics in Lillehammer. She became a champion! Her training was intense, one or two times per day. A sighted guide was the single most important person to Anne, assisting her and teaching her to believe in herself and her abilities. Her family was there for moral support as well.

> *"Sport can challenge the way people perceive us."*

It is often stated that sport is a metaphor for life. Anne has felt that the training, discipline, and rigor of being a world-class athlete have helped her "to have the energy to master my busy life. I am a clinical psychologist and have been practicing for 10 years. I have written books and articles and give lectures to people working with disabled people, [give] courses for people with disabilities themselves, teach at a university and high schools, and give talks at business conferences." The focus Anne recommends for young athletes is to understand that being an athlete means being fit and that being fit is a way "to master life as independently as possible." An ancillary thought is that being involved in sport competition will perhaps "challenge the way people perceive us." As for integration and classification issues, Anne notes that there are pros and cons to each that need to be addressed. The complexity of the issue makes it difficult to solve in a quick or easy manner that is universally acceptable. This athlete has been a champion both personally and professionally because of her involvement in sport and continues to be a mentor to others.

Although U.S. women participated in the 1968 Paralympics, the National Wheelchair Basketball Association did not end its discriminatory practice of prohibiting women from participating until 1974 (Hedrick and Hedrick, 1991). The next year, the first women's national tournament was held.

As international competitions for athletes with disabilities prior to the 1960s were only for individuals with hearing impairments and wheelchair users (primarily spinal cord injured), additional sport associations were formed and competitions organized to include individuals with other physical impairments. Inasmuch as women had already broken through, the newly developed organizations, such as the International Sports Organization for the Disabled, Cerebral Palsy–International Sports and Recreation Association, International Blind Sports Association, International Coordinating Committee, and International Paralympic Committee (IPC), provided opportunities for both men and women from the outset.

Today, approximately one-third of the athletes in international competitions are women. Similar to the situation in the able-bodied sport world and the CISS, men hold the leadership positions. A notable exception is Elizabeth Dendy from Great Britain, who served as the first and only president of Cerebral Palsy–International Sports and Recreation Association and in that capacity presided over the International Coordinating Committee's last meeting. In addition, Dendy has the distinction of being the first female to serve as a member of the IPC.

Mental Impairments

Special Olympics International and the International Sports Federation for Persons with Intellectual Disabilities have always provided sport opportunities for mentally retarded males and females. A fairly equitable distribution of male and female athletes participate in their national and international competitions.

Female Athletes in the Olympic Games

Male and female athletes with disabilities competed in their first exhibition events at the 1984 Winter Olympics in Sarajevo and the 1984 Summer Olympics in Los Angeles. The two exhibition events selected for the Summer Olympics were the 800-meter wheelchair race for women and the 1,500-meter wheelchair race for men. These events were continued in Seoul in 1988 and Barcelona in 1992. As for the Winter Olympic Games, alpine and Nordic skiing events for blind and physically disabled athletes were offered in Sarajevo (1984) and Calgary (1988) but not in Albertville (1992). Diana Golden, a single-leg amputee, became the most celebrated female disabled skier in Calgary.

Few female athletes with disabilities have participated in the Summer Olympic Games. One example is Liz Hartel (postpolio), who won a silver medal in dressage in 1952. Neroli Fairhall, representing New Zealand, competed in archery during the 1984 Olympics in Los Angeles. As a fully accepted Olympian, she competed in her wheelchair.

Two women successfully competed in both the Olympic and Paralympic Games. In 1996, Paola Fantato entered the stadium to compete in archery from her wheelchair at the Olympic Games as part of the Italian delegation (Mascagni, 1996). Two weeks later, she would defend her title at the Atlanta Paralympic Games as well. Marla Runyan, legally blind middle distance runner and heptathlete, qualified and competed in the Olympic Games in Sydney in 2000. She has earned medals in both the Olympic and Paralympic Games. Runyan also ran and finished fifth in the 2003 Boston Marathon.

Female Athletes in Marathons

The Boston Marathon, which included wheelchair athletes as early as 1974, is considered the premier road racing/marathon event for athletes with disabilities. The first female wheelchair competitor was Sharon Rahn Hedrick. She entered the race in 1977 and finished with a time of 3:48.51.

Photo by Sue Gavron.

USA sitting volleyball team members practice setting and movement.

Since then, the times have decreased dramatically (see figure 3.1 on p. 58). The gap between the winning times for women and men has narrowed over the years; in 1990 the time for the men's division was 1:29.53 and for the women's division, 1:43.17. Although the performances have improved, the number of female competitors remains relatively low (only three or four each year). Jean Driscoll holds the record of winning the women's push rim division of the Boston Marathon eight times, more than any other individual (male or female, able-bodied or with disability) in the history of the Boston Marathon. In 2003 Cheri Blauwet set a new course record for the New York City Marathon wheelchair division with a time of 1:59.30 and broke her own course record set in 2002 by 15 minutes. She also won the Los Angeles Marathon with a time of 1:50.06 (Women's Sports Foundation, 2003).

Since the first running (wheeling) of the Boston Marathon, wheelchair divisions for competition in other marathons (e.g., Montreal, Japan, Los Angeles, Long Beach) and other road races (e.g., Lilac Bloomsday Run, Wheels of Fire, Gasparilla) have been developed. Male and female athletes with disabilities have been able to compete professionally, earning cash prizes on the circuit.

KEY POINT

The athletic achievements of female athletes with disabilities rival those of able-bodied women and of men with disabilities.

Equity Issues

Equity issues in disability sport involve more than gender and race. They include the intersection of gender, type and severity of impairment, and even the sport.

Female athletes participated in the first competitions (i.e., Stoke Mandeville Games in 1952, International Games for the Deaf in 1924), and the major international competitions have included competitive events for women (see table 5.1 on p. 91). But female athletes have been underrepresented in the Paralympic Games (DePauw, 1994; Sherrill, 1997). According to Sherrill (1997), the gender ratio (male to female) for the Barcelona Paralympic Games was 3:1, increasing to 4:1 at the 1996 Atlanta Paralympic Games. In Atlanta, 49 of the 103 participating countries (47%) brought no female athletes, and most countries brought less than nine female athletes (Sherrill, 1997).

Given this trend and growing concern, the IPC Sports Council established the Women's Initiative to address the issue of female representation and participation in future Paralympic Games. In recognition of

Lori Miller

FAST FACTS

Home Base: Warsaw, Indiana
Sport: Multi-athlete in dressage, cycling, goal ball, alpine skiing
Selected Accomplishments:

Medals and high placements in cycling, goal ball, skiing at national and international level

Undergraduate degree in history and American studies

Master's degrees in blind rehabilitation and orientation and mobility

Author, mentor, and volunteer

"Don't let anyone else set your limitations," says Lori Miller. With this philosophy Lori has managed to live with her blindness and survive cancer three times. Her tenacity is the basis for her success personally, professionally, and athletically. Her sport ability is phenomenal. As a multisport athlete she has been highly successful in dressage, goal ball, cycling, and alpine skiing, among others. Her willingness to learn new sports and apply herself is indicative of a focused athlete.

> "Don't let anyone else set your limitations."

Lori Miller has another side to her. She is a writer of articles on blindness and speaks to audiences about her experiences and successes. She is a community volunteer and assists younger people with disabilities who are entering the sport arena. She is also a mentor and motivator for the DeNe Dogrib Indian tribe, Northwest Territory, Canada. Approximately 23% of the population have a degenerative visual impairment and are not accepting of blindness (Lori Miller, personal communication, June 18, 2003). Lori Miller is an elite athlete, an outstanding citizen, and above all a survivor.

the importance of increasing the participation of girls and women with disabilities in sport, the first principle of the Brighton Declaration on Women and Sport (1994) called for equity and equality in society and sport. Specifically, it stated that "equal opportunity to participate in sport whether for the purpose of leisure and recreation, health promotion or high performance, is the right of every woman, regardless of race, color, language, religion, creed, sexual orientation, age, marital status, disability, political belief or affiliation, national or social origin." This was affirmed again in the Wyndhoek Call for Action in 1998, and progress was reported at the 2002 World Conference on Women and Sport in Montreal.

Sport opportunities for athletes with disabilities in the United States have been expanded beyond selected community recreation and sport programs into intercollegiate programs. Individuals with physical impairments at the University of Illinois and Wright State University, and Deaf athletes at Gallaudet University, have been provided with collegiate sport experiences, including athletic scholarships (see also chapter 5). Although these sport opportunities have been available to women, the numbers favor men.

KEY POINT

Equity issues and adequate representation of girls and women in sport are a relatively recent concern of the disability sport movement.

Concluding Comments

Although much progress appears to have been made, women and individuals with a disability have long been excluded from sport (Birrell, 1988; DePauw, 1997, 2003). Parallels between the women's and disability sport movements have been identified. The parallels include specific cultural and attitudinal similarities (Mastro, Hall, and Canabal, 1988), medical restrictions to participation in sport, legal mandates for nondiscrimination and equal opportunity, socialization via and into sport, involvement of professional organizations (e.g., American Alliance for Health, Physical Education, Recreation and Dance; United States Olympic Committee), basketball as the first sport for women and disabled athletes, the Boston Marathon as the setting for breaking into the able-bodied sport world, and common barriers to sport participation. Among these barriers are the lack of school or community programs, role models, coaches, and accessibility (Grimes and French, 1987).

Perhaps the single greatest barrier to equity in sport for female athletes with disabilities is the traditional and historical model of sport. As the domain of the elite and the masculine, sport has played a significant role in preserving the patriarchal social order (Hall, 1985) and the gender segregation and inequality found in other realms of social life (Theberge, 1985, p. 193). The "masculinity" of sport has had the effect of excluding women from full participation (e.g., Birrell, 1988; Felshin, 1974; Theberge, 1985). Similarly, the "physicality" of sport has tended to exclude individuals with disabilities (DePauw, 1997, 2003; Hahn, 1984). Traditional notions of body and objectification of one's body, as topics within both the disability and women's movements, gain greater significance within the context of sport.

In opposition to the "exclusive" nature of sport, the disability sport movement championed the inclusion of athletes with disabilities in the sporting world. Even though disabled women did not initially have to fight their battle alone, their struggle is not yet over. The additional barriers faced by women with a disability who actively seek sport competitions can, and will, be overcome so that women of tomorrow will have greater opportunities than their foremothers. As the future of sport including and for athletes with disabilities unfolds, women with a disability will be found not only among the athletes but as coaches, administrators, trainers, officials, and spectators. In turn they will serve as role models for aspiring youth. As barriers are eliminated, sport programs will become increasingly more available and accessible.

fourteen

The Future of Disability Sport

Reader Goal Understand the trends for the future of disability sport

Chapter Synopsis

- Trends
- Inclusion
- Images of Disability Sport
- Sport, Society, and Disability
- Concluding Comments

Societal attitudes toward sport participation and competition by athletes with disabilities have changed significantly over the past half-century. This is due in part to the impact of the disability rights movements of the 1990s and the fact that the medical model of disability has been challenged by the social model of disability that implies "difference" rather than "less than," identifies social stigma as a shared experience, and utilizes graphic representations for disability that are active (view of a wheelchair in motion) instead of passive (the common upright stationary wheelchair logo) (Shapiro, 1993; Sherrill, 1997).

Trends

The future of disability sport will not only be shaped by the political, social, and economic factors of a given cultural context but will continue to be influenced by the elite sport movement. Classification issues, drug testing, technological advances, improved training techniques, and sports medicine will continue to be factors in the development of elite disability sport. Disability sport in the 21st century will be described by the following (adapted from DePauw, 1990a, 2001c; DePauw and Gavron, 1995):

- A vertical structure of sport with extensive developmental sport programs for individuals with a disability leading toward a national- and international-level competitive structure for elite athletes with disabilities
- Establishment of multi-disability national and international sport organizations as the governing bodies for disability sport with strong links to and within the national and international sport structure (organized more by sport than by disability)
- Increasing emphasis on high levels of athletic excellence and high standards for performance
- Increasing specialization within sport among athletes with disabilities and a decrease in the number of athletes participating in multiple events
- Classification and competitions becoming more sport specific and ability oriented than disability specific
- Increasing numbers of individuals with a disability (adults, youth, seniors) seeking sport programs
- Increasing concern for equity in sport opportunities for girls and women with a disability, and increasing attention to issues of race and socioeconomic status
- Inclusion of athletes with disabilities within the sport world, including major international competitions such as the Olympic Games and world championships
- Greater inclusion of persons with a disability within the structure of disability sport as well as among coaches, officials, and administrators
- Increased public awareness and acceptance of athletes with disabilities and of sport as a viable option for youth

KEY POINT

Society's view of disability sport and athletes with disabilities has evolved to the point that we accept individuals with disabilities as athletes.

Inclusion

If the trend of "progressive inclusion and acceptance" is accurate, we will see more integration of persons with a disability into sport. Critical to acceptance of this trend or assumption is an understanding of what is meant by integration or inclusion. What is advocated here is "true" accessibility to sport or the reconstruction of sport as an institution that allows individuals with a disability (e.g., as a marginalized group) an informed choice about sport participation (DePauw, 1994, 1997).

Inclusion (integration) means that individuals from marginalized groups (e.g., persons with disabilities, persons of racial or ethnic minority backgrounds, women) have choices similar to those afforded persons of the dominant culture (e.g., white, male, able-bodied). Having access to sport should not imply that all individuals with a disability will opt for, or desire, sport participation (and competition) or participation with able-bodied persons. It means having opportunities. Inclusion of individuals with a disability in sport means having "choice" and not being excluded solely because of a condition of one's physical being or body (DePauw, 2003). Integration or inclusion does not mean that competition and participation with able-bodied individuals is preferred; rather it means having the option to choose to participate, compete in a segregated setting, or participate/compete alongside able-bodied individuals.

Images of Disability Sport

The original purpose of disability sport as rehabilitation through sport has expanded to sport for sport's sake and competition for competition's sake. The Scandinavian sociologist Soeder (1995) suggested that the images of disability sport comprise sport as rehabilitation, sport as freak show, and sport as empowerment. For many, the historical, if not predominant, image of disability sport is that of rehabilitation. This image tends to focus on disability, places emphasis on overcoming limitations, and encourages viewers to see athletic achievements as measures of successful rehabilitation. The freak show image focuses on sport as exceptional for the sake of exceptionality and allows the viewer to become fascinated by

Sarah Reinertsen

FAST FACTS

Home Base: California
Sports: Running and triathlon
Selected Accomplishments:

Participated in Carlsbad Triathlon, San Diego International Triathlon, Pendleton Olympic Triathlon (2003)

Participated in London Marathon (2002); Millennium Marathon, New Zealand (2000); New York Marathon (1997, 1998)

Paralympics: Barcelona, 1992

Numerous records in sprints and marathons

Activist, program manager for Challenged Athletes Foundation

Photo courtesy of www.kreutzphotography.com

At the age of 7, Sarah went through an above-the-knee amputation due to a congenital tissue problem. Four years later she had learned to run and has never looked back. Starting out in sprints, Sarah held national and world records. Sarah next took up distance road running and has competed in named half-marathons and full marathons on a regular basis nationally and internationally. As if that were not enough, Sarah graduated into triathlons on a global basis. While doing all of this, she received both an undergraduate and a master's degree in communications and has been a broadcast journalist for NBC-TV in various capacities. In addition to her athletic achievements—she was the first above-the-knee amputee to compete in a 5,000-foot (1,524-meter) mountainous trail run and was the first physically challenged athlete inducted into the Suffolk County Sports Hall of Fame—Sarah has also been an activist. Using the 2002 London Marathon, Sarah and her teammates raised enough money to clear a minefield in Vietnam. Her current position with the Challenged Athletes Foundation in California is one of fund-raising and providing and promoting opportunities for athletes with disabilities.

"Sports have always been central to my life, a driving force in all that I do."

Sarah's success in athletics was due to her ability to focus and also due to various mentors along the way—another amputee friend, a physical therapist, and other athletes with disabilities. Sarah still trains five to six times a week with local running clubs, marathon clubs, and by herself. Sarah states, "Sports have always been central to my life, a driving force in all that I do." Sarah Reinertsen has always looked forward and will continue to go forth toward new frontiers.

the performance, not to identify with the performers. The third image is of disability sport as empowerment. This image focuses on the athlete as a competent individual capable of running his or her life in a meaningful way and allows the viewer to see athletic performance as not associated primarily with a disability. The image of disability sport as empowerment is key and will be instrumental to the future of disability sport.

Sport, Society, and Disability

Convergence of the sport movement for athletes with disabilities with the Olympic sport movement was inevitable (Landry, 1992). As a result of international competitions for athletes with disabilities (e.g., Paralympics, Deaflympics, Special Olympics), sport is no longer the sole prerogative of able-bodied athletes.

What once were exclusively the domain of those free of physical impairments—sport and society's view of sport—have been altered and now include different sport forms and differing ways of athletic expression (DePauw, 1997). Although sport remains a forum for the expression of physical prowess, strength, endurance, and grace, society's view has been expanded to include athletes using wheelchairs and those with other physical, mental, or sensory impairments.

KEY POINT

Disability sport has become a genuine part of the broader perspective of sport.

Throughout history, sport has remained a somewhat exclusive or elite social institution. As such, sport is socially constructed. Sport has been, and will continue to be, changed by the inclusion of women and individuals of racial/ethnicity minority groups as well as the most recent entrance into sport by individuals with a disability. Access is a critical first step. With access (inclusion) come change and adaptation. Moving beyond adaptation to transformation requires that sport, as a social institution, undergo fundamental change (DePauw, 1997, 2003).

This fundamental change is under way. This is exemplified through the connectedness of the Olympic and the Paralympic sport movements by means of enhanced working relations between the International Olympic Committee (IOC) and the International Paralympic Committee (IPC). Stronger connections would include the following (Wolff, 2004, personal correspondence):

- Opportunities for training Paralympic athletes, coaches, and officials
- Education and financial support for the Paralympic movement

- Inclusion of the Paralympics and Paralympic athletes among Olympians
- Promotion of interest in and understanding of the Paralympic Games and the Paralympic movement by the IOC in its operations and media efforts

In the early 21st century, the International Olympic Academy has regularly included athletes with disabilities among the participants at its events, IPC Presidents Robert Steadward and Phil Craven among its speakers, and disability sport among the topics. A summary of relevant discussions at the 2004 International Olympic Academy (Wolff, 2004, personal correspondence) included the following points:

- Paralympics and Special Olympics have the potential to influence attitudes and raise awareness of disability issues.
- Social change will have been achieved only when individuals with disabilities are treated as equal and active members of society. The Paralympic and Special Olympic Games athletes definitely have the potential to act as catalysts for this kind of social change.
- Greater media coverage is key to increased awareness.
- The Games are an avenue for change to occur through the education of the global community, erosion of stereotypes, the integration of people with disabilities into society, and the promotion of acceptance of what all human beings can accomplish.

KEY POINT

The positive working relationship of the IPC and IOC has enhanced the elite athletic experience for individuals with disabilities.

In addressing the question of sport as a platform for people with disabilities to showcase their abilities to the world, the following points were articulated (Wolff, 2004, personal correspondence):

- "Through sport, athletes with a disability can demonstrate their prowess and highlight their capabilities and determination to reach personal goals.
- Sport brings about self-confidence and self-fulfillment while fostering courage and promoting an independent and determined character.
- Acceptance and equality of opportunity can be promoted through sport sending a strong and inspirational message across society.

- The recognition of athletes with a disability increases participation across the spectrum and this generates awareness and understanding within many cultures. In addition, it can change attitudes within society.
- Sport allows the application of the Olympic Charter in the sense that everyone can participate without any discrimination whatsoever. It promotes values such as tolerance, acceptance and diversity.
- Athletes with a disability exemplify the Olympic values of unity and harmony. They demonstrate that all deserve an opportunity to aspire to and to attain excellence.
- An increase in media coverage which results in exposure and equality in society may lead to more public financial support.
- Sport can encourage technological progress and advances which in the long term would assist individuals with a disability."

Concluding Comments

Disability sport has come a very long way since its modest beginnings more than 100 years ago. Athletes with disabilities today have a far greater number of opportunities for sport participation and competitions than in the past. Sport of tomorrow will be an avenue of socialization for youth with a disability in the same way that sport serves the youth of today. Sport for and including individuals with disabilities is a movement whose time has come.

appendix A

Chronology and Significant Milestones of Disability Sport

Year	Event
1888	First Sports Club for the Deaf founded in Berlin.
1924	1st International Games for the Deaf (also referred to as International Silent Games) (now Deaflympics) held in Paris (sponsored by Comité International des Sports Silencieux, or CISS).
1928	2nd International Games for the Deaf (Deaflympics) held in Amsterdam.
1931	3rd International Games for the Deaf (Deaflympics) held in Nuremberg.
1932	British Society of One-Armed Golfers founded.
1935	First U.S. participation in 4th World Games for the Deaf.
1939	The first textbook on disability sport published; George Stafford publishes *Sports for the Handicapped*.
	5th International Games for the Deaf (Deaflympics) held in Stockholm.
1944	Sir Ludwig Guttmann establishes the Spinal Injuries Centre at the Stoke Mandeville Hospital in Aylesbury, England.
1945	American Athletic Association of the Deaf founded.
1946	First wheelchair basketball game in the United States played by war veterans at Veterans Administration Hospitals in the California and New England chapters of Paralyzed Veterans of America.
1948	1st Stoke Mandeville Games for the Paralyzed (Aylesbury, England).
	Karoly Takacs, competing on the Hungarian Olympic team at the Olympics in London, wins the gold medal in rapid-fire pistol event, using his left hand after loss of his right hand.
	The Flying Wheels of California win the 1st National Paralyzed Veterans of America Wheelchair Basketball Championships.

1949   1st Annual Wheelchair Basketball Tournament at the University of Illinois (U.S.).

6th International Games for the Deaf (Deaflympics) held in Copenhagen.

1st World Winter Games for the Deaf (Seefeld, Austria).

National Wheelchair Basketball Association founded.

1952   Liz Hartel (postpolio) wins silver medal in dressage at Summer Olympics, representing Denmark.

First international wheelchair athlete tournament (became identified as the International Stoke Mandeville Games).

1953   7th International Games for the Deaf (Deaflympics) held in Brussels.

2nd World Winter Games for the Deaf (Winter Deaflympics) held in Oslo.

1955   CISS officially recognized by the International Olympic Committee (IOC) in June.

1956   First athletic scholarships in the United States for athletes with a disability (blind wrestlers).

Stoke Mandeville Games (Sir Ludwig Guttmann) awarded the Sir Thomas Fearnley Cup for meritorious service to the Olympic movement.

National Wheelchair Athletic Association founded (later to become Wheelchair Sports, USA).

1957   1st U.S. National Wheelchair Games (Adelphi College, New York).

8th International Games for the Deaf (Deaflympics) held in Milan.

3rd World Winter Games for the Deaf (Deaflympics) held in Oberammergau, Germany.

1959   4th World Winter Games for the Deaf (Deaflympics) held in Montana, Switzerland.

1960   9th Annual International Stoke Mandeville Games (would become known as the 1st Paralympic Games; also referred to as 1st International Games for Disabled) in Rome.

United States sends a team to participate in these games for the first time.

International Stoke Mandeville Wheelchair Sports Federation founded.

1961   9th International Games for the Deaf (Deaflympics) held in Helsinki.

1964   International Sports Organization for the Disabled founded.

5th World Winter Games for the Deaf (Deaflympics) held in Are, Sweden.

2nd International Games for the Disabled (2nd Paralympics) held in Rome.

1965   10th International Games for the Deaf (Deaflympics) held in Washington, DC.

1967   1st Pan American Games for spinal cord-injured athletes.

National Handicapped Sports and Recreation Association formed to govern U.S. winter sports for athletes with disabilities.

6th World Winter Games for the Deaf (Deaflympics) held in Berchtesgaden, Germany.

1968   International Special Olympics founded by Eunice Kennedy Shriver; first competition held in Soldier Field, Chicago (1st Special Olympics World Summer Games).

3rd International Games for the Disabled (3rd Paralympic Games) held in Tel Aviv.

Women's wheelchair basketball included in Tel Aviv Paralympic Games.

International Cerebral Palsy Society founded; sponsors the first international games for individuals with cerebral palsy in France.

CISS awarded the Olympic Cup, created by Baron Pierre de Coubertin in 1906, for its service to sport for the Deaf.

1969   11th World Games for the Deaf (Deaflympics) held in Belgrade.

North American Riding for the Handicapped Association formed in Virginia.

1970   2nd Special Olympics World Summer Games held in Chicago.

1971   7th World Winter Games for the Deaf (Deaflympics) held in Adelboden, Switzerland.

1972   3rd Special Olympics World Summer Games held in Los Angeles.

4th International Games for the Disabled (4th Paralympic Games) held in Heidelberg; first quadriplegic competition added.

1973   12th World Games for the Deaf (Deaflympics) held in Malmo, Sweden.

1974   1st National Wheelchair Marathon held in Ohio.

U.S. women's basketball team competes against another U.S. team for the first time.

1975   First women's National Wheelchair Basketball Tournament held.

1st Gold Cup Tournament/World Championship (wheelchair basketball) held in Bruges, Belgium.

Bob Hall, first wheelchair entrant in Boston Marathon; finishes in 2:58.

First meeting of U.S. cerebral palsy athletes at Springfield College, Massachusetts.

8th World Winter Games for the Deaf (Deaflympics) held in Lake Placid, New York.

4th Special Olympics World Summer Games held in Mt. Pleasant, Michigan; games broadcast nationwide on CBS-TV's Sports Spectacular.

Sports 'n Spokes magazine founded.

1976   The Olympiad for the Physically Disabled (5th Paralympic Games in Toronto) includes blind and amputee athletes.

1st International Winter Games for the Disabled (1st Winter Paralympic Games) held in Omskoldsvik, Sweden.

United States Association of Blind Athletes (USABA) formed.

UNESCO conference establishes right of individuals with a disability to participate in physical education and sport.

National Foundation of Wheelchair Tennis founded.

1977   First female wheelchair entrant to the women's division of Boston Marathon (3:48).

First national championships of USABA held in Macomb, Illinois.

University of Illinois hosts the 1st Intercollegiate Wheelchair Basketball Tournament.

13th World Games for the Deaf (Deaflympics) held in Bucharest, Romania.

1st Special Olympics World Winter Games in Steamboat Springs, Colorado. CBS, ABC, and NBC cover the Games.

1978   PL 95-606, the Amateur Sports Act of 1978, passed by Congress.

National Association of Sports for Cerebral Palsy (NASCP) founded, now known as U.S. Cerebral Palsy Athletic Association.

Cerebral Palsy–International Sports and Recreation Association organized.

Connie Hansen and Candace Cable become the only two women to compete in all Summer Olympic exhibition events to date.

Tanni Grey (Great Britain) named the Sunday Times Sportswoman of the Year by Her Majesty The Queen.

Tricia Zorn (USA) wins 12 medals (10 gold, 2 silver) at the Summer Paralympic Games in Barcelona (also had won 12 in 1988 Paralympics in Seoul).

1993   The COSD reorganized, with USOC allowing for greater participation of athletes with a disability in governance of disability sport.

IPC establishes the Sport Science Committee.

17th World Games for the Deaf (Deaflympics) held in Sofia, Bulgaria.

5th Special Olympics World Winter Games held in Salzburg and Schladming, Austria.

1994   6th Winter Paralympic Games held in Lillehammer, Norway.

Brighton Declaration on Women and Sport calls for equity and equality in society and sport including women with disabilities.

Monique Kalkman (The Netherlands) earns the title of Amsterdam's Sportswoman of the Year.

Mark E. Shepherd Sr. becomes the second coordinator, USOC Disabled Sport Services.

1995   The USOC officially becomes the designated organization to the IPC and, therefore, the official U.S. National Paralympic Committee.

13th World Winter Games for the Deaf (Deaflympics) held in Rovaniemi, Finland.

9th Special Olympics World Summer Games held in New Haven, Connecticut.

1996   The IPC officially hosts the 10th Summer Paralympic Games in Atlanta, Georgia, and assumes responsibility for the Games in the future. First Paralympics to attract worldwide sponsors.

Jean Driscoll (USA) becomes the first person to win the Boston Marathon for the seventh time (all divisions).

1997   18th World Games for the Deaf (Deaflympics) held in Copenhagen.

6th Special Olympics World Winter Games held in Toronto and Collingwood, Canada.

1998   7th Winter Paralympic Games held in Nagano, Japan.

1st World Blind Sports Championships held in July in Madrid.

1999   Official opening of the IPC headquarters in Bonn, held September 3. IOC President Samaranch attends.

14th World Winter Games for the Deaf (Deaflympics) held in Davos, Switzerland.

10th Special Olympics World Summer Games held in Raleigh, North Carolina.

USOC forms the Paralympic Athletes Council and the Paralympic Sport Organizations.

2000   Cooperation agreement signed by IOC President S.E.M. Juan Antonio Samaranch and IPC President Dr. Robert D. Steadward in Sydney.

11th Summer Paralympic Games held in Sydney.

Marla Runyan (legally blind) competes in the Paralympics and the Olympics in Sydney.

The COSD is reorganized again, allowing for the formation of the U.S. Paralympic Corporation as the representative body for athletes with a disability in the United States.

Jean Driscoll wins a record-breaking eighth Boston Marathon.

2001   19th Deaflympics held in Rome.

7th Special Olympics World Winter Games held in Anchorage, Alaska.

Phil Craven elected as the second president of the IPC, the first athlete with a disability to serve in this capacity.

Laureus World Sports Awards includes Sportsperson with a Disability award to Vinny Lauwers, an Australian paraplegic yachtsman. Tiger Woods is Sportsman of the Year and Cathy Freeman, Sportswoman of the Year.

The International Sports Federation for Athletes with Intellectual Disability suspended from membership in the IPC after an IPC investigation commission finds that the process of assessment and certification of athletes with an intellectual disability for the Sydney 2000 Paralympic Games had not been properly carried out (athletes without intellectual disabilities competed and received medals in events for athletes with intellectual disability).

2002   8th Winter Paralympic Games held in Salt Lake City, Utah.

Commonwealth Games in Manchester includes official disability sport events (160 athletes from 20 countries and five sports).

2003   IPC President Phil Craven elected as a new IOC member (#123) at the 115th session of the IOC in Prague.

The IPC signs the World Anti-Doping Code and revises the IPC Anti-Doping Code to comply with the World Anti-Doping Code and WADA's standards.

15th Deaflympics held in Sundsvall, Sweden.

11th Special Olympics World Summer Games held in Dublin (first time the Games are held outside the United States).

European Commission designates 2003 the European Year of People with Disabilities; IPC introduces International Paralympic Day 2003.

International Association of Athletics Federation (IAAF) 2003 Athletics World Championships includes IPC exhibition events.

Marla Runyan finishes fifth among sighted runners in the Boston Marathon.

Jean Driscoll serves as commentator for the official coverage of the Boston Marathon.

Paralympic athletes Scott Hollonbeck, Tony Iniguez, and Jacob Heilveil file major discrimination lawsuit against the USOC.

2004   12th Summer Paralympic Games held in Athens.

Randy Snow, wheelchair tennis player, inducted into the U.S. Olympic Hall of Fame; first Paralympian to be honored. Paralympian category to continue as a permanent class of the Hall of Fame.

The Isabel Ferrer Prize "International Sportswomen of the Year" awarded to five-time Paralympian Ljiljana "Lilo" Ljubisic, competing in athletics for Canada.

U.S. women's goal ball team becomes the first disability sport team to move into the Olympic Training Center resident program.

2005   20th Deaflympics scheduled for Melbourne.

8th Special Olympics World Winter Games scheduled for Nagano, Japan (first time for the Games to be hosted in Asia).

2006   9th Winter Paralympic Games scheduled for Torino, Italy.

2007   16th Winter Deaflympics scheduled for Park City, Utah.

12th Special Olympics World Summer Games scheduled for People's Republic of China.

2008   13th Summer Paralympic Games scheduled for Beijing.

2009   21st Deaflympics scheduled for Taipei, Taiwan.

2010   10th Winter Paralympic Games scheduled for Burnaby and Vancouver, Canada.

appendix B

List of Abbreviations

Note: This listing is not meant to be all-inclusive. Rather, this listing represents the more commonly and frequently used acronyms in disability sport as a whole. Some of the abbreviations may or may not have been used in this textbook, while others may appear on the Internet on specific sites or general disability sport sites.

AAASP	American Association of Adapted Sports Programs
ADA	Americans with Disabilities Act
ADIR	Athletes with Disabilities Injury Registry
AK	above-knee amputation
APC	Asian Paralympic Committee
ASCOD	African Sports Confederation of Disabled
B-1, B-2, and B-3	Standard classifications used for athletes with visual impairments
BK	below-knee amputation
BPA	British Paralympic Committee
BSAD	British Sport Association for the Disabled
CAHPER	Canadian Association for Health, Physical Education, and Recreation
CFSOD	Canadian Federation of Sport Organizations for the Disabled
CIAD	Commission for Inclusion of Athletes with a Disability
CISS	International Committee of Sports for the Deaf
COSD	Committee on Sports for the Disabled
CP	cerebral palsy
CPC	Canadian Paralympic Committee
CP-ISRA	Cerebral Palsy–International Sport and Recreation Association
DAAA	Dwarf Athletic Association of America

DBS	Deutsches Behinderten Sportverband (German Sport Association for the Disabled)
DSB	Deutscher Sportbund (German Sports Association)
DSO	disability sport organization
DSOD	Danish Sport Organization for the Disabled
DS/USA	Disabled Sports USA
EPC	European Paralympic Committee
FASD	Finnish Association of Sports for the Disabled
FESPIC	Far East and South Pacific International Games
FINA	Federation International de Natation Amateur
FITA	International Archery Federation
FPC	Finnish Paralympic Committee
HKSAP	Hong Kong Sports Association for the Physically Disabled
IAAF	International Association of Athletics Federations
IBSA	International Blind Sport Association
ICC	International Coordinating Committee
ICF	International Classification of Functioning, Disability and Health
IF	international federation (international sport governing body)
INAS-FID	International Sport Federation for Persons with Intellectual Disability
INAS-FMH	International Sports Federation for Persons with Mental Handicap
IOA	International Olympic Academy
IOC	International Olympic Committee
IPC	International Paralympic Committee
IPCSSC	International Paralympic Committee Sport Science Committee
ISMWSF	International Stoke Mandeville Wheelchair Sports Federation
ISOD	International Sports Organization for the Disabled
KOSAD	Korean Sports Association for the Disabled
LA	les autres
LPA	Little People of America

NASCP	National Association of Sport for Cerebral Palsy
NDSA	National Disability Sports Alliance
NFWT	National Federation of Wheelchair Tennis
NGB	National Governing Body (category of member in USOC)
NHS	National Handicapped Sports
NHSRA	National Handicapped Sports and Recreation Association
NOC	National Olympic Committee
NSOD	Norwegian Sport Organization for the Disabled
NWAA	National Wheelchair Athletic Association
NWBA	National Wheelchair Basketball Association
OOC	Olympic Organizing Committee
PSO	Paralympic Sport Organization
SCI	spinal cord injury
SHIF	Svenska Handikappidrottsforbundet (Swedish Sports Organisation for Disabled)
SOI	Special Olympics International
UNESCO	United Nations Educational, Scientific and Cultural Organization
USAAA	United States Amputee Athletic Association
USABA	United States Association of Blind Athletes
USADSF	United States of America Deaf Sports Federation
USCPAA	United States Cerebral Palsy Athletic Association
USLASA	United States Les Autres Sports Association
USOC	United States Olympic Committee
USOTC	United States Olympic Training Center
WC	wheelchair
WGD	World Games for the Deaf

appendix C

Outdoor Recreation Activities for Individuals With Disabilities

Accessible Camping in Selected National Parks

Alaska

Denali National Park and Preserve
Denali Park
Accessible sites near accessible toilets are reserved for use by disabled campers at Riley Creek, Savage, Teklanika, and Wonder Lake campgrounds.
www.nps.gov/dena

Arizona

Grand Canyon National Park
Grand Canyon
Six accessible tent/RV sites near wheelchair-accessible rest rooms are available at Mather. Wheelchair-accessible rest rooms are provided at Desert View.
www.nps.gov/grca

Organ Pipe Cactus National Monument
Ajo
Wheelchair-accessible rest rooms are available.
e-mail: orpi_information@nps.gov
www.nps.gov/orpi

California

Death Valley National Park
Death Valley
The Sunset area has 16 accessible sites near wheelchair-accessible rest rooms.
Furnace Creek and Mesquite Springs have wheelchair-accessible rest rooms.
www.nps.gov/deva

Sequoia National Park
Three Rivers
Lodgepole has accessible rest rooms, and Potwisha has an accessible site near accessible rest rooms.
www.nps.gov/seki

Colorado

Mesa Verde National Park
Six accessible campsites are located near wheelchair-accessible rest rooms.
www.nps.gov/meve

Rocky Mountain National Park
Estes Park
Moraine Park, Glacier Basin, and Timber Creek have wheelchair-accessible rest rooms. An accessible back-country site, Handi-camp, has an accessible rest room.
www.nps.gov/romo

Florida

Everglades National Park
Homestead
Each campground has one site reserved for people with disabilities, next to a wheelchair-accessible rest room. One back-country site, Pearl Bay Chickee, is accessible.
www.everglades.national-park.com

Gulf Islands National Seashore
Gulf Breeze
Several campsites near a wheelchair-accessible rest room are held for disabled campers until at least noon each day.
www.nps.gov/guis

Georgia

Chickamauga and Chattanooga
National Military Park
Fort Oglethorpe
One accessible group campground is located near an accessible toilet.
www.nps.gov/chch

Kentucky

Mammoth Cave National Park
Mammoth Cave
Two accessible sites at Headquarters Campground, located near accessible rest rooms, are held until 6:00 P.M. each day during the camping season for disabled campers.
www.nps.gov/maca

Maine

Acadia National Park
Bar Harbor
Both campgrounds have a few wheelchair-accessible sites near accessible rest rooms.
www.nps.gov/acad

North Carolina

Blue Ridge Parkway
Asheville
All campgrounds have at least two wheelchair-accessible sites near accessible rest rooms.
www.blueridgeparkway.org

Virginia

Prince William Forest Park
Triangle
Both campgrounds have wheelchair-accessible sites and rest rooms. One whole section of accessible cabins and rest rooms in the group-camping area is available.
www.nps.gov/prwi

Accessible Outdoor Recreation and Wilderness Experiences

The following programs offer outdoor recreation and wilderness experiences for individuals with disabilities. The groups served are identified in parentheses; PI—physical impairment, VI—visual impairment, D/HI—Deaf and hearing impairment, MR—mental retardation. The abbreviation Integ stands for integrated programs (with able-bodied persons).

Copyright, 1992, Paralyzed Veterans of America, by permission of Sports 'N Spokes.

Adventures Without Limits
1341 Pacific Ave.
Forest Grove, OR 97116
Phone/Fax: 503-359-2568
e-mail: jill@awloutdoors.com
www.awloutdoors

Western PA, BOLD (Blind Outdoor Leisure Development)
Box 2574
Pittsburgh, PA 15230
Phone: 412-882-3965
e-mail: info@wpabold.org or www.wpabold.org

Boy Scouts of America (scouting for the handicapped) (all)
Irving, TX
www.seascout.org

Bradford Woods Outdoor Center
5040 State Rd. 67 North
Martinsville, IN 46151
Phone: 765-342-2915
Fax: 765-349-1086
www.indiana.edu/~bradwood

Breckenridge Outdoor Education Center (Integ, PI, VI, D/HI, MR)
Breckenridge, CO
www.boec.org

Capable Partners (Integ)
Golden Valley, MN
www.capablepartners.com

Cooperative Wilderness Handicapped Outdoor Group (C.W. HOG) (PI, VI, D/HI)
Pocatello, ID
www.isu.edu/cwhog

Courage Center (PI, VI, D)
Minneapolis, MN
www.courage.org

Environmental Traveling Companions (all)
San Francisco, CA
www.etctrips.org

Girl Scouts of the USA (girls with disabilities) (all)
New York, NY
www.girlscouts.org

Maine-Niles Association of Special Recreation (all)
Morton Grove, IL
www.desplainesparks.org/mnasr.html

Northeast DuPage Special Recreation Association (PI, Integ)
Addison, IL
www.nedsra.org

Veterans on the Lake (PI)
Ely, MN
www.veterans-on-the-lake.com

Vinland National Center (all)
Loretto, MN
www.vinlandcenter.org

Voyageur Outward Bound (PI, D/HI, VI)
Minnetonka, MN
www.vobs.com

Wilderness Inquiry (Integ)
Minneapolis, MN
www.wildernessinquiry.org

Ski Programs

Alaska

Challenge Alaska
Anchorage, AK
www.challenge.ak.org

California

Disabled Sports USA Orange County Chapter (DSUSA-OC)
www.dsusa.org

Colorado

Adaptive Sports Center of Crested Butte
Crested Butte, CO
e-mail: asc@rmi.com
www.adaptivesports.org

Aspen Handicapped Skiers Association
Snowmass Village
Challenge Aspen
Aspen, CO
www.challengeaspen.com

Breckenridge Outdoor Education Center
Breckenridge, CO
www.boec.org

Cuchara Mountain Sports Center for the Disabled
La Junta, CO
e-mail: RoycethePT@juno.com

Durango/Purgatory Adaptive Sports Association
Durango, CO
www.asadurango.org

ESRP (Eldora Special Recreation Program)
Boulder, CO
e-mail: WJHEAD@yahoo.com

Foresight Ski Guides, Inc.
Denver, CO
www.foresightskiguides.org

National Sports Center for the Disabled
Winter Park, CO
www.nscd.org

Telluride Adaptive Sports Program
Mtn. Village Blvd.
Telluride, CO
www.skitasp.org

VIBeS
(Visually Impaired & Blind Skiers)
Colorado Springs, CO
Phone: 719-597-5241

Connecticut

Connecticut Disabled Ski Association
Milford, CT
e-mail: edusick@aol.com

Sports Association, Gaylord Hospital
Wallingford, CT
Phone: 203-284-2772

Illinois

RIC-Skiers
(Rehabilitation Institute of Chicago)
Chicago, IL
www.richealthfit.org

The American Blind Skiing Foundation
Elmhurst, IL
www.absf.org

Maryland

Baltimore Adapted Recreation and Sports
(BARS)
Baltimore, MD
www.barsinfo.org

Nation's Capital Handicapped Sports
(District of Columbia)
Olney, MD
Phone: 301-208-8949

Nation's Capital Handicapped Sports
Sunny Spring, MD
e-mail: lerche0001@msn.com

Massachusetts

Ability Plus, Inc.
Sterling, MA
e-mail: kcability@mediaone.net

New England Handicapped Sports Association
P.O. Box 2135
Newbury, NH 03255-2135
e-mail: info@nehsa.org

Michigan

Cannonsburg Challenged Ski Association
Rockford, MI
e-mail: ski_ccsa@hotmail.com

Michigan Handicapped Sports & Recreation Association
P.O. Box 569
Keego Harbor, MI 48320
Contact: Carol Roubal
Phone: 248-988-0156
Fax: 248-362-1702
e-mail: cmroubal@comcast.net
www.michiganadaptivesports.org

Minnesota

Courage Alpine Skiers
Golden Valley, MN
www.courage.org

Courage Center
Duluth, MN
www.courage.org

Montana

Dream Adaptive Recreation Programs, Inc.
Whitefish, MT
Phone: 406-862-1817

Eagle Mount-Billings
Billings, MT
e-mail: Imullowney@eaglemountbillings.org

Eagle Mount-Bozeman
Bozeman, MT
Phone: 406-586-1781

Eagle Mount-Great Falls
#93rd Street N., Suite 1
Great Falls, MT 59401
Phone: 406-454-1449 (Office) or 406-771-4829 (Arena)
Fax: 406-454-1780
e-mail: eaglemount@eaglemount.net

Nevada

Tahoe Adaptive Ski School
Incline Village, NV
www.tahoesbest.com/Skiing/alpine.htm

New Mexico

Adaptive Ski Program
Santa Fe, NM
www.adaptiveski.org

Lovelace/Sandia Peak Ski Program
Albuquerque, NM
www.sandiapeak.com/skiing.html

New York

Disabled Ski Program at Ski Windham
Adaptive Sports Foundation
Windham, NY
www.adaptivesportsfoundation.org

Greek Peak Ski Area
Cortland, NY
e-mail: greekpeak@lightlink.com
www.greekpeak.net

Lounsbury Adaptive Ski Program
East Aurora, NY
http://members.rogers.com/lounsbury-program/

Ohio

The Adaptive Adventure Sports Coalition
Westerville, OH
www.taasc.org

Three Tracker of Ohio
Cleveland, OH
Phone: 216-556-0787
e-mail: MD1053@aol.com

Oregon

Challenge Oregon Adaptive Ski Program
Bend, OR
www.adaptive-skiing.org

Utah

National Ability Center
Park City, UT
www.nac1985.org

Vermont

Vermont Adaptive Ski and Sports Association
Brownsville, VT
www.vermontadaptive.org

Virginia

Wintergreen Adaptive Skiing
Batesville, VA
e-mail: michaelzuckerman@hotmail.com

Washington

Disabled Sports USA Northwest–Team USAble (Washington)
Issaquah, WA
e-mail: klanning@dsusa.org

Skiforall
Seattle, WA
www.skiforall.org

West Virginia

Challenged Athletes of West Virginia
Snowshoe, WV
www.cawvsports.org

Wisconsin

SEWASP (SouthEastern Wisconsin Adaptive Ski Program)
Germantown, WI
www.sewasp.org

International Disability Sport and Recreation Programs

International Ski and Sport Associations

Afghanistan	Blindenistitut Kabul
Area in Pyrénées, Andorra	Pas de la Casa/Grau Roig
Australia	Australian Paralympic Federation
Australia	Disabled WinterSport Australia
Austria	Osterr. Behindertensportverband
Austria	Osterr. Paralympisches Komitee
Austria	Osterreichischer Skivrband
Belgium	R.F.S.S. Belgique

Belgium	Vlaamse Liga Gehandicaptensport
Canada	Canadian Association for Disabled Skiing
Canada	Canadian Federation of Sports for the Disabled
Czechia	Tschechischer Behindertensportverband
Denmark	Dansk Handicap Idraetsforbund
Finland	Finnish Associations of Sports for the Disabled
France	Fédération Française de Ski Alpin Handisport
Germany	Deutscher Behindertensportverband
Germany	International Paralympic Committee
Great Britain	British Disabled Alpine Ski Team
Great Britain	British Paralympic Association for Disabled
Great Britain	National Handicapped Skiers Association
Italy	Federazione Italiana Sport Disabili
Japan	Japanese Sports Association for the Disabled
Lichtenstein	Lichtensteiner Behindertensportverband
Luxemburg	Federation sportive Lux. des Handicapes Phys.
Netherlands	Nederlande Ski Uereniging
Netherlands	Nederlandse Ski Vereniging
New Zealand	Disabled Skiing New Zealand
Norway	Norges Funksjonshemmedes Idrettsfourbund
Poland	Polski Zwiazek S.N.
Poland	Start, Rada Glowna Zreszenie Sporttowe
Russia	Russian Federation for Disabled
Slovakia	Slovak Sports Association for the Disabled
Slovenia	Slowenisches Versehrtenskireferat
Slovenia	Sports Federation for the Disabled of Slovenia
Spain	Federacisn Espanola de Deportes de Minusvalidos Fisicos
Spain	Spanish Sports Federation for Physical Disabled
Sweden	Swedish Sports Organisation for the Disabled
Switzerland	Swiss Disabled Ski Team
Switzerland	Swiss Paralympic Committee
United States	National Sport Center for the Disabled
United States	U.S. Ski and Snowboard Association (+disabl.)

World Cup Committee for Alpine Skiing for the Disabled

Canada Quebec	Eastern Townships Disabled Skiers Foundation
Netherlands	Poly-Aktief
Norway	Sitski
Sweden	Totalskidskolan
Switzerland	Handisport
Switzerland	Isi Handisport Geneve
Switzerland	Waterski

You can find an electronic version of this table at www.spokesnmotion.com/
program_links/index.asp. To see full contact information for each country,
just click on "View Details."

appendix D

Selected International Disability Sport Organizations

Cerebral Palsy–International Sport and Recreation Association (CP-ISRA)
P.O. Box 16
6666 ZG Heteren
The Netherlands
Phone: +31 26 47 22 593
Fax: +31 26 47 23 914
e-mail: Cpisra_NL@Hotmail.com
www.cpisra.org

Deaflympics
7310 Grove Rd., Suite #106
Frederick, MD 21704
Fax: +1 301 620 2990 (USA)
e-mail: info@deaflympics
www.deaflympics.com

Fédération Equestre Internationale (FEI)
Avenue Mon Repos 24
P.O. Box 157
1000 Lausanne 5
Switzerland
Phone: 41 21 310 47 47
Fax: 41 21 310 47 60
www.horsesport.org

Fédération Internationale de Basketball (FIBA)
8, Ch. de Blandonnet
1214 Vernier
Geneva
Switzerland
Phone: (+41-22) 545.00.00
Fax: (+41-22) 545.00.99
e-mail: info@fiba.com
www.fiba.com

FIBA Europe
Widenmayerstrasse 18
80538 Munich
Germany
Phone: (+49-89) 78 06 08 –0
e-mail: info@europe.fiba.com

Fédération Internationale de Canoe (FIC)
Calle de la Antracita, 7 4 floor
E 28045 Madrid
Spain
Phone: +34-91 506 11 50; +34-91 506 11 51
Fax: +34-91 506 11 55
e-mail: message@canoeicf.com
www.canoeicf.com

Fédération Internationale d'Escrime (FIE)
Avenue Mon-Repos 24
Case postale 128
CH-1000 Lausanne 5
Switzerland
Phone: +41 21 320 31 15
Fax: +41 21 320 31 16
e-mail: contact@fie.ch
www.fie.ch

Fédération Internationale de Football Association (FIFA)
Hitzigweg 11
Postfach 85
CH-8030 Zurich
Switzerland
www.fifa.com

Fédération Internationale de Gymnastique (FIG)
10, rue des Oeuches
Case postale 359
CH-2740 Moutier 1
Switzerland
Phone: +41 32 494 64 10
Fax: +41 32 494 64 19
e-mail: webmaster@fig-gymnastics.org
www.fig-gymnastics.com

Fédération Internationale de Handball (FIH)
Peter Merian-Strasse
CH-4002 Basle
Switzerland
Phone: +41 61 228 90 40
Fax: +41 61 228 90 55
e-mail: ihf@magnet.ch
www.ihf.info

Fédération Internationale des Luttes Associées (FILA)
3, ave. Ruchornet
CH-1003 Lausanne
Switzerland
www.fila-wrestling.com

Fédération Internationale de Natation Amateur (FINA)
Av. de l' Avant-Poste 4
1005 Lausanne
Switzerland
Phone: 41-21 310 4710
Fax: 41-21 312 6610
www.fina.org

Fédération Internationale de Roller Skating (FIRS)
Rambla Catalunya, 121, 2-3
08008 Barcelona
Spain
e-mail: info@rollersports.org
www.rollersports.org

Fédération Internationale de Ski (FIS)
Blochstr. 2
CH-3653 Oberhofen
Switzerland
www.fis-ski.com

Fédération Internationale de Softball (ISF)
1900 So. Park Rd.
Plant City, FL 33563
USA
Phone: 813-864-0100
Fax: 813-864-0105
e-mail: isf@internationalsoftball.com
www.internationalsoftball.com

Wheelchair Tennis Department
International Tennis Federation (ITF)
Bank Lane
Roehampton, London SW15 5XZ
England
Phone: +44 392 208 878 6464
Fax: +44 392 208 392 4741
e-mail: wheelchairtennis@itftennis.com
www.itfwheelchairtennis.com

Fédération Internationale de Volleyball (FIVB)
12, ave. de la Gare
CH-1001 Lausanne
Switzerland
Phone: +41 21 345 35 35
Fax: +41 21 345 35 45
www.fivb.org

Handicapped Scuba Association (HSA) International
1104 El Prado
San Clemente, CA 92672-4637
Phone: 949-498-4540
Fax: 949-498-6128
www.hsascuba.com

International Association of Athletics Federations (IAAF)
17, rue Princesse Florestine
BP 359
MC-98007 Monaco Cedex
Monaco
www.iaaf.org

International Blind Sports Association (IBSA)
Street: José Ortega y Gasset, 18
28006 Madrid
Spain
www.ibsa.es

International Sports Federation for Persons with Mental Handicap (INAS-FID)
Box 1002
S-821 11 Bollnäs
Phone: +46 278 62 60 67
Fax: +46 278 244 56
e-mail: anna.olsson@inas-fid.org

International Skating Union (ISU)
Chemin de Primerose 2
1007 Lausanne
Switzerland
Phone: +41 21 612 66 66
Fax: +41 21 612 66 77
www.isu.org

International Sport Organization for the Disabled (ISOD)
Ferrez 16
28008 Madrid
Spain
Phone: 34-91-547-17-18
Fax: 34-91-541-99-61
www.is-od.com

International Stoke Mandeville Wheelchair Sports Federation (ISMWSF)
ISMWSF Secretariat
Olympic Village
Guttmann Rd.
Aylesbury, Bucks HP21 9PP
United Kingdom
Phone: +44 (0) 01296 436179
Fax: +44 (0) 01296 436484
e-mail: info@ismwsf.powernet.co.uk

International Table Tennis Federation (ITTF)
Avenue Mon Repos, 30
1005 Lausanne
Switzerland
Phone: 41 21 340 7090
Fax: 41 21 340 7099
e-mail: ittf@ittf.com
www.ittf.com

The International Tennis Federation (organization for Paralympic Tennis)
Bank Lane
Roehampton, London
SW15 5XZ
United Kingdom
Phone: +44 (0)20 8878 6464
Fax: +44 (0)20 8392 4744
www.itftennis.com

International Weightlifting Federation (IWF)
Rosenburg HP.U.L.
Postafiok 614
1374 Budapest
Hungary
Phone: +36.1.353 0530
Fax: +36.1.353 0199
e-mail: iwf@iwf.net
www.iwf.net

International Wheelchair Road Racers Club, Inc.
c/o Joseph M. Dowling
30 Myano Ln., Box 3
Stamford, CT 06902
Phone: 203-967-2231

International Wheelchair Aviators
Mike Smith, President
P.O. Box 2799
Big Bear City, CA 92314
Phone: 909-585-9663
Fax: 909-585-7156
e-mail: IWAviators@aol.com
www.wheelchairaviators.org

**Recreational Sports Development
 and Stimulation Disabled International (RESPO DS-DI)**
P.O. Box 263
8440 AG Heerenveen
The Netherlands

International Wheelchair Rugby Federation
Pawel Zbieranowski
67 Riverside Blvd.
Thornhill, ON L4J 1H8
Canada
Phone: 905-886-1252
e-mail: Pawel.Zbieranowski@sbe.scarborough.on.ca

appendix E

Selected U.S. and Canadian Disability Sport Organizations

National Sport Associations: United States

Access to Sailing
e-mail: info@accesstosailing.org
www.access2sailing.org

ActiveAmp
P.O. Box 9315
Wilmington, DE 19809
Phone: 302-683-0997
e-mail: rgh@activeamp.org
www.activeamp.org

Aircraft Owners and Pilots Association (AOPA)
421 Aviation Way
Frederick, MD 21701
e-mail: inforequest@aopa.org
www.aopa.org

Amateur Softball Association (ASA)
2801 N.E. 50th St.
Oklahoma City, OK 73111
www.softball.org

American Amateur Racquetball Association (AARA)
1685 W. Uintah
Colorado Springs, CO 80904-2921
www.racquetball.org

American Amputee Soccer Association
e-mail: rgh@ampsoccer.org
www.ampsoccer.org

American Blind Bowling Association
e-mail: abbapres@aol.com
www.geocities.com/blindbowlers/abba

American Blind Golfers Association
300 Carondelet St.
New Orleans, LA 70112
Phone: 504-891-4737

American Bowling Congress (ABC)
www.bowl.com/bowl/abc/index.html

American Canoe Association (ACA)
7432 Alban Station Blvd., Ste. B-232
Springfield, VA 22150
Phone: 703-451-0141
Fax: 703-451-2245
e-mail: aca@acanet.org
www.acanet.org

American Horse Shows Association (AHSA)
220 E. 42nd St., Ste. 409
New York, NY 10017-5876
www.usef.org

American Water Ski Association (AWSA)
1251 Holy Cow Rd.
Polk City, FL 33868
Phone: 863-324-4341
Fax: 863-325-8259
e-mail: usawaterski@usawaterski.org
www.usawaterski.org/pages/HQemail.html

American Wheelchair Bowling Association (AWBA)
Earle Annis, Executive Secretary/Treasurer
2912 Country Woods Lane
Palm Harbor, FL 34683-6417
Phone/Fax: 727-734-0023
e-mail: bowlawba@aol.com
www.awba.org

American Wheelchair Table Tennis Association (AWTTA)
Affiliated with Wheelchair Sports USA
1668 320th Way
Earlham, IA 50072
Phone/Fax: 515-833-2450
e-mail: wsusa@aol.com
www.wsusa.org/Sports/table_tennis

Breckenridge Outdoor Education Center
P.O. Box 697
Breckenridge, CO 80424
Phone: 970-453-6422
Fax: 970-453-4676
e-mail: boec@boec.org
www.boec.org

Disabled Sports USA (DS/USA)
451 Hungerford Dr., Ste. 100
Rockville, MD 20850
Phone: 301-217-0960
Fax: 301-217-0968
www.dsusa.org

Dwarf Athletic Association of America (DAAA)
c/o Janet Brown
418 Willow Way
Lewisville, TX 75067
www.daaa.org

National Amputee Golf Association (NAGA)
Bob Wilson, Executive Director
P.O. Box 1228
Amherst, NH 03031-1228
email: info@nagagolf.org
www.nagagolf.org

National Archery Association of the United States (NAA)
1 Olympic Plaza
Colorado Springs, CO 80909-5778
Phone: 719-866-4576
Fax: 719-866-4733
e-mail: info@usaarchery.org
www.usarchery.org

National Beep Baseball Association (NBBA)
Jeanna Weigand
5568 Boulder Crest St.
Columbus, OH 43235
Phone: 614-442-1444
e-mail: info@nbba.org
www.nbba.org

National Sports Center for the Disabled
P.O. Box 1290
Winter Park, Colorado 80482
Phone: 970-726-1540 or 303-316-1540
Fax: 970-726-4112
e-mail: info@nscd.org
www.nscd.org

National Strength and Conditioning Association (NSCA)
1955 N. Union Blvd.
Colorado Springs, CO 80909
Phone: 719-632-6722
Fax: 719-632-6367
e-mail: nsca@nsca-lift.org
www.nsca-lift.org

National Wheelchair Athletic Association
3595 E. Fountain Blvd., Ste. L-1
Colorado Springs, CO 80910
Phone: 719-574-1150

National Wheelchair Basketball Association (NWBA)
110 Seaton Building
University of Kentucky
Lexington, KY 40506
www.nwba.org/rules.html

National Wheelchair Racquetball Association
c/o American Amateur Racquetball Association
National Commissioner—John Faust
815 North Weber
Colorado Springs, CO 80903
Phone: 719-635-5396

National Wheelchair Shooting Federation (NWSF)
P.O. Box 18251
San Antonio, TX 78218

National Wheelchair Softball Association (NWSA)
P.O. Box 22478
Minneapolis, MN 55422
Phone: 612-437-1792
www.wheelchairsoftball.com

North American Riding for the Handicapped Association (NARHA)
Box 33150
Denver, CO 80233
Phone: 303-452-1212
Fax: 303-252-4610
www.narha.org

Professional Association of Diving Instructors (PADI)
1251 E. Dyer Rd., No. 100
Santa Ana, CA 92705
www.padi.com

Skating Association for the Blind and Handicapped (SABAH)
1200 East and West Rd.
West Seneca, New York 14224
Phone: 716-675-7222
e-mail: sabah@sabahinc.org
www.sabahinc.org

Special Olympics, Inc
1325 G St., N.W., Ste. 500
Washington, DC 20005
Phone: 202-628-3630
Fax: 202-824-0200
www.specialolympics.org

Turning POINT (Paraplegics On Independent Nature Trips)
403 Pacific Ave.
Terrell, TX 75160
Phone: 972-524-4231
e-mail: pointntl@aol.com
www.turningpointtexas.com

United States Association of Blind Athletes (USABA)
33 N. Institute St.
Colorado Springs, CO 80903
Phone: 719-630-0422
Fax: 719-630-0616
www.usaba.org

United States Blind Golf Association
3094 Shamrock St. North
Tallahassee, FL 32308
Phone/Fax: 850-893-4511
www.blindgolf.com

United States Cerebral Palsy Athletic Association (USCPAA)
34518 Warren Rd., Ste. 264
Westland, MI 48185
www.uscpaa.org

United States Cycling Federation (USCF)
1 Olympic Plaza
Colorado Springs, CO 80909
Phone: 719-866-4581
Fax: 719-866-4628
www.usacycling.org

United States Deaf Ski and Snowboard Association (USDSSA)
www.usdssa.org

United States Deaf Tennis Association (USDTA)
3607 Washington Blvd., No. 4
Ogden, UT 84403-1737
e-mail: info@usadsf.org
web@usadsf.org

United States Disabled Ski Team (USDST)
P.O. Box 100
Park City, UT 84060
Phone: 801-649-9090
www.ussa.org

United States Fencing Association (USFA)
1750 East Boulder St.
Colorado Springs, CO 80909
e-mail: info@USFencing.org
www.usfencing.org

United States Figure Skating Association (USFSA)
20 First St.
Colorado Springs, CO 80906
Phone: 719-635-5200
Fax: 719-635-9548
e-mail: info@usfigureskating.org
www.usfsa.org

U.S.A. Gymnastics (USA Gym)
Pan American Plaza, Ste. 300
201 S. Capitol Ave.
Indianapolis, IN 46225
Phone: 317-237-5050
Fax: 317-237-5069
e-mail: webmaster@usa-gymnastics.org
www.usa-gymnastics.org

United States Les Autres Sports Association (USLASA)
Dave Stephenson
Les Autres Sports
1475 West Gray, Ste. 166
Houston, TX 77019-4926
Phone: 713-521-3737
www.fsma.org

United States Parachute Association (USPA)
1440 Duke St.
Alexandria, VA 22314
Phone: 703-836-3495
Fax: 703-836-2843
e-mail: uspa@uspa.org
www.uspa.org

United States Powerlifting Federation (USPF)
1013 S. Fayetteville St.
Asheboro, NC 27203-6809
e-mail: uspf_news@att.net
www.uspf.com

United States Quad Rugby Association (USQRA)
Kevin Orr
101 Park Place Circle
Alabaster, AL 35007
Phone: 205-868-2281
Fax: 215-868-2283
e-mail: supersports@mindspring.com
www.quadrugby.com

U.S. Rowing Association
201 S. Capitol Ave., Ste. 400
Indianapolis, IN 4622
www.usrowing.org

United States Ski Association
P.O. Box 100
Park City, UT 84060
www.ussa.org

United States Soccer Federation (USSF)
1801-1811 S. Prairie Ave.
Chicago, IL 60616
www.ussoccer.com

United States Swimming (USS)
1 Olympic Plaza
Colorado Springs, CO 80909
Phone: 719-866-4578
www.usswim.org

U.S.A. Table Tennis Association (USATT)
1 Olympic Plaza
Colorado Springs, CO 80909
Phone: 719-866-4583
Fax: 719-632-6071
e-mail: usatt@usatt.org
www.usatt.org

United States Taekwondo Union (USTU)
1 Olympic Plaza, Ste. 104C
Colorado Springs, CO 80909
Phone: 719-866-4632
Fax: 719-866-4642
e-mail: feedback@ustu.org
www.ustu.org

United States Tennis Association (USTA)
1212 Ave. of the Americas
New York, NY 10036
www.usta.com

United States Volleyball Association (USVBA)
3595 E. Fountain Blvd.
Colorado Springs, CO 80910-1740
www.volleyball.org

United States Weightlifting Federation (USWF)
1 Olympic Plaza
Colorado Springs, CO 80909
www.usaweightlifting.org

United States Wheelchair Weightlifting Federation (USWWF)
Bill Hens
39 Michael Pl.
Levittown, PA 19057

U.S. Sailing Association
15 Maritime Dr.
Portsmouth, RI 02871-0907
Phone: 401-683-0800
www.ussailing.org

USA Basketball
5465 Mark Dabling Blvd.
Colorado Springs, CO 80918-3842
www.usabasketball.com

USA Gymnastics (USA Gym)
e-mail: webmaster@usa-gymnastics.org
www.usa-gymnastics.org

USA Karate Federation (USAKF)
1300 Kenmore Blvd.
Akron, OH 44314
Phone: 330-753-3114
Fax: 330-753-6967
e-mail: usakf@raex.com
www.usakarate.org

USA Track and Field
201 S. Capitol Ave., Ste. 400
Indianapolis, IN 46225
www.usatf.org

USA Wrestling (USAW)
6155 Lehman Dr.
Colorado Springs, CO 80918
www.usawrestling.org

National Sport Associations: Canada

Alpine Canada
Ste. 200, 505-8th Ave. SW
Calgary, AB T2P 1G2
Phone: 403-777-3200
Fax: 403-777-3213
e-mail: info@canski.org
www.canski.org

Athletics Canada
Ste. 300-2197 Riverside Dr.
Ottawa, ON K1H 7X3
Phone: 613-260-5580
Fax: 613-260-0341
e-mail: athcan@athletics.ca
www.athleticscanada.com

Canadian Association for Disabled Skiing
www.disabledskiing.ca

Canadian Cerebral Palsy Sports Association
305-1376 Bank St.
Ottawa, ON K1H 7Y3
Phone: 613-748-1430
Fax: 613-748-1355
e-mail: ccpsa@bellnet.ca
www.ccpsa.ca

Canadian Curling Association
1660 Vimont Ct.
Cumberland, ON K4A 4J4
Phone: 613-834-2076
Toll free: 800-550-2875
Fax: 613-834-0716
e-mail: info@curling.ca
www.curling.ca

Canadian Cycling Association
702-2197 Riverside Dr.
Ottawa, ON K1H 7X3
Phone: 613-248-1353
Fax: 613-248-9311
e-mail: general@canadian-cycling.com
www.canadian-cycling.com

Canadian Electric Wheelchair Hockey Association
www.geocities.com/cewha

Canadian Federation of Sports for the Disabled
333 River Rd.
Otawa, ON K1L8B9
Canada

Canadian Fencing Federation
2197 Riverside Dr., Ste. 301
Ottawa, ON K1H 7X3
Phone: 613-731-6149
Fax: 613-731-6952
e-mail: cff@fencing.ca
www.fencing.ca

Canadian Table Tennis Association
2800-1125 Colonel By Dr.
Ottawa, ON K1S 5R1
Phone: 613-733-6272
Fax: 613-733-7279
e-mail: ctta@ctta.ca
www.ctta.ca

Canadian Wheelchair Basketball Association
Ste. B2-2211, Riverside Dr.
Ottawa, ON K1H 7X5
Phone: 613-260-1296
Fax: 613-260-1456
www.cwba.ca

Canadian Wheelchair Sports Association
#200-2460 Lancaster Rd.
Ottawa, ON K1B 4S5
Phone: 613-523-0004
Fax: 613-523-0149
e-mail: info@cwsa.ca
www.cwsa.ca

Canadian Yachting Association
Portsmouth Olympic Harbour
53 Yonge St.
Kingston, ON K7M 6G4
Phone: 613-545-3044
Fax: 613-545-3045
e-mail: sailcanada@sailing.ca
www.sailing.ca

Cross-Country Canada
CCC National Office
Bill Warren Training Centre
1995 Olympic Way, Ste. 100
Canmore, AB T1W 2T6
Phone: 403-678-6791
Fax: 403-678-3644
e-mail: info@cccski.com
http://canada.x-c.com

Equine Canada Hippique
National Office
2460 Lancaster Rd.
Ottawa, ON K1B 4S5
Phone: 613-248-3433
Toll free: 866-282-8395
Fax: 613-248-3484
e-mail: webmaster@equestrian.ca
www.equestrian.ca/EC/index.shtml

Federation of Canadian Archers
2460 Lancaster Rd., Ste. 200
Ottawa, ON K1B 4S5
Phone: 613-260-2113
Fax: 613-260-2114

Judo Canada
226-1725 St. Laurent
Ottawa, ON K1G 3V4
Phone: 613-738-1200
Fax: 613-738-1299
www.judocanada.org

Ontario Wheelchair Sports Association (OWSA)
www.disabledsports.org/owsa.htm

Ottawa-Carleton Sledge Hockey and Ice Picking Association
www.ncscd.ca/OCSledgeIcePick.html

Shooting Federation of Canada
45 Shirley Blvd.
Nepean, ON K2K 2W6
Phone: 613-727-7483
Fax: 613-727-7487
Contact persons: Sandra Deeks and Ann Deavy
e-mail: SFC@ncf.ca
http://sfc.ncf.ca

Sledge Hockey of Canada
P.O. Box 20063
Ottawa, ON K1N 9N5
Phone: 888-857-8555 (toll free)
Ottawa area: 613-723-5799
Fax: 613-723-5463
e-mail: shoc@shoc.ca
www.shoc.ca/welcome.htm

Swimming Natation Canada
2197 Riverside Dr., Ste. 700
Ottawa, ON K1H 7X3
Phone: 613-260-1348
Fax: 613-260-0804
e-mail: natloffice@swimming.ca
www.swimming.ca

Tennis Canada
www.tenniscanada.com

Volleyball Canada
5510 Canotek Rd., Ste. 202
Gloucester, ON K1J 9J5
Phone: 613-748-5681
Fax: 613-748-5727
e-mail: info@volleyball.ca or beach@volleyball.ca
www.volleyball.ca

Affiliate Members

Active Living Alliance for Canadians with a Disability
720 Belfast Rd., Ste. 104
Ottawa, ON K1G 0Z5
Phone: 800-771-0663 or 613-244-0052
Fax: 613-244-4857
e-mail: info@ala.ca
www.ala.ca

Badminton Canada
e-mail: bmiller@badminton.ca
www.badminton.ca

Canadian Association for Disabled Skiing
P.O. Box 307
Kimberly, BC V1A 2Y9
Phone: 250-427-7712
Fax: 250-427-7715
e-mail: cads@rockies.net
www.disabledskiing.ca

Canadian Wheelchair Sports Association
Gloucester, ON K1B 5N4
Phone: 613-748-5685
Fax: 613-748-5722

Gymnastics/Gymnastique Canada
#203-5510 Canotek Rd.
Ottawa, ON K1J 9J4
Phone: 613-748-5637
Fax: 613-748-5691
www.gymcan.org/content/index.php

Racquetball Canada
www.racquetball.ca

Rowing Canada Aviron
www.rowingcanada.org

Triathlon Canada
#704-1185 Eglinton Ave. E.
Toronto, ON M3C 3C6
Phone: 416-426-7180
Fax: 416-426-7294
e-mail: Info@TriathlonCanada.com
www.triathloncanada.com

Water Ski and Wakeboard Canada
304-2197 Riverside Dr.
Ottawa, ON K1H 7X3
Phone: 613-526-0685
www.waterski-wakeboard.ca

Sport Specific Organizations and Organizations by Disability

Archery

Wheelchair Archery, USA
c/o Wheelchair Sports, USA
3595 E. Fountain Blvd, Ste. L-1
Colorado Springs, CO 80910
Phone: 719-574-1150
Fax: 719-574-9840
www.wsusa.org/Sports/archery.htm

Basketball

National Wheelchair Basketball Association
Charlotte Institute of Rehabilitation
c/o Adaptive Sports/Adventures
1100 Blythe Blvd.
Charlotte, NC 28203
Phone: 704-355-1064
Fax: 704-466-4999
e-mail: nwba@carolinas.com
www.nwba.org

Billiards

National Wheelchair Pool Players Association
30872 Puritan
Livonia, MI 48154
Phone: 734-422-2124

Bowling

American Wheelchair Bowling Association
6264 North Andrews Ave.
Fort Lauderdale, FL 33309
Phone: 954-491-2886
www.awba.org

Flying

Freedom's Wings International
1832 Lake Ave.
Scotch Plains, NJ 07076
Phone: 908-232-6354
www.freedomswings.org

International Wheelchair Aviators
P.O. Box 2799
Big Bear City, CA 92314
Phone: 909-585-9663
Fax: 909-585-7156

Football

Universal Wheelchair Football Association
UC Raymond Walters College
Disability Services Office
9555 Plainfield Rd.
Cincinnati, OH 45236-1096
Phone: 513-792-8625
Fax: 513-792-8624
http://home.nyc.gov/html/sports/html/uwfa.html

Golf

Association of Disabled American Golfers
P.O. Box 280649
Lakewood, CO 80228-0649
Phone: 303-922-5228
Fax: 303-922-5257
www.golfcolorado.com/adag

National Amputee Golf Association
P.O. Box 23285
Milwaukee, WI 53223-0285
Phone: 800-633-6242
Fax: 414-376-1268
www.amputee-golf.org

Hand Cycling

Crank Chair Racing Association
3294 Lake Redding Dr.
Redding, CA 96003-3311
Phone: 916-244-3577

United States Handcycling Federation
Phone: 207-443-3063
e-mail: info@ushf.org
www.ushf.org

Hockey

American Sled Hockey Association
10933 Johnson Ave. S.
Bloomington, MN 55437
Phone: 612-881-2129

Multisport

Bay Area Outreach Recreation Program (BORP)
830 Bancroft Way
Berkeley, CA 94710
Phone: 510-849-4663
Fax: 510-849-4616

Casa Colina Wheelchair Sports and Outdoor Adventures
2850 North Garey Ave.
Pomona, CA 91767
Phone: 909-596-7733
Fax: 909-593-0153

Disabled Sports USA
451 Hungerford Dr., Ste. 100
Rockville, MD 20850
Phone: 301-217-0960

United States Cerebral Palsy
Athletic Association, Inc.
200 Harrison Ave.
Newport, RI 02840
Phone: 401-848-2460
Fax: 401-848-5280

Wheelchair Sports, USA
3595 E. Fountain Blvd., Ste. L-1
Colorado Springs, CO 80910
Phone: 719-574-1150
Fax: 719-574-9840

World T.E.A.M. Sports
2108 S. Blvd., Ste. 101
Charlotte, NC 28203
Phone: 704-370-6070
Fax: 704-370-7750
www.worldteamsports.org

Quad Sports

United States Quad Rugby Association
101 Park Place Cir.
Alabaster, AL 35007
Phone: 205-868-2281
Fax: 205-868-2283
www.quadrugby.com

Racket Sports

International Wheelchair Tennis Federation
Bank Lane, Roehampton
London SW15 5XZ
England
Phone: (011) 44 181 878 6464
Fax: (011) 44 181 392 4741
www.itftennis.com

United States Tennis Association
70 West Red Oak Lane
White Plains, NY 10604
Phone: 914-696-7000
Fax: 914-696-7029
www.usta.com

Recreation

**American Competition Opportunities
for Riders With Disabilities (ACORD) Inc.**
5303 Felter Rd.
San Jose, CA 95132
Phone: 408-261-2015
Fax: 408-261-9438

National Handicap Motorcyclist Association
404 Maple St.
Upper Nyack, NY 10960
Phone: 914-353-0747

North American Riding for the Handicapped Association
P.O. Box 33150
Denver, CO 80233
Phone: 800-369-RIDE

Turning POINT (Paraplegics On Independent Nature Trips)
4144 N. Central Expy., Ste. 130
Dallas, TX 75204
Phone: 214-827-7404
Fax: 214-827-6468

Road Racing

Crank Chair Racing Association
3294 Lake Redding Dr.
Redding, CA 96003-3311
Phone: 530-244-3577

Wheelchair Athletics of the USA
2351 Parkwood Rd.
Snellville, GA 30278
Phone: 770-972-0763
Fax: 770-985-4885

Shooting

National Wheelchair Shooting Federation
102 Park Ave.
Rockledge, PA 19046
Phone: 215-379-2359
Fax: 215-663-9662

NRA Disabled Shooting Services
11250 Waples Mill Rd.
Fairfax, VA 22030
Phone: 703-267-1495

Skiing

Ski For Light, Inc.
1400 Carole Lane
Green Bay, WI 54313
Phone: 920-494-5572
Fax: 920-492-5821
e-mail: pagsj@aol.com

Softball

National Wheelchair Softball Association
1616 Todd Ct.
Hastings, MN 55033
Phone: 612-437-1792

Table Tennis

American Wheelchair Table Tennis Association
23 Parker St.
Port Chester, NY 10573
Phone: 914-937-3932

Track and Field

Wheelchair Athletics of the USA
2351 Parkwood Rd.
Snellville, GA 30039
Phone: 770-972-0763
Fax: 770-985-4885

Water Sports and Water Recreation

Access to Sailing
6475 East Pacific Coast Hwy.
Long Beach, CA 90803
Phone: 562-499-6925
Fax: 562-437-7655

Aqua Sports Association for the Physically Challenged
9052-A Birch St.
Spring Valley, CA 91977
Phone: 619-589-0537
Fax: 619-589-7013

Handicapped Scuba Association
1104 El Prado
San Clemente, CA 92672
Phone: 714-498-6128
e-mail: hsahdq@comp.com

U.S. Rowing Association
201 S. Capitol Ave., Ste. 400
Indianapolis, IN 4622

Water Skiers With Disabilities Association
American Water Ski Association
799 Overlook Dr.
Winter Haven, FL 33884
Phone: 800-533-2972

appendix F

Paralympic Committees by Region

The information in this appendix was last updated on June 30, 2004. We've provided each committee's e-mail, Web site, and/or full contact information.

Source: www.paralympic.org

National Paralympic Committees: Africa

Algeria

Algerian Sports Federation for Disabled
Contact: Mr. Djamel Belaboid
4 Rue Youcef Meliani
Château Neuf, El Biar
Alger 16030
Algeria
Phone: +213 (2192) 8248
Fax: +213 (2192) 3974

Angola

Comite Paralimpico Angolano
e-mail: cpa@nexus.ao

Benin

Fed. Handisport du Benin-Comité National Paralympique
e-mail: sgeorges27@hotmail.com

Botswana

Paralympic Association of Botswana
e-mail: rathedirr@mopipi.ub.bw

Burkina Faso

National Paralympic Committee Burkina Faso
e-mail: yameogojean_s@hotmail.com

Burundi

Féd. Sportive des Handicapés du Burundi
e-mail: ndenzabel@yahoo.fr

Cape Verde Islands

Comité Caboverdeano Desp. Para Deficientes
e-mail: cedeficientes@cvtelecom.cv

Central African Republic

Federation Centrafricaine Handisports
e-mail: dameca.intnet@caramail.com

Congo

Fédération Congolaise des Sports des Personnnes Handicapées
e-mail: jmboyo@yahoo.fr

Côte d'Ivoire

Fédération Handisport Côte d'Ivoire
e-mail: jeanmarcromain@yahoo.fr

Egypt

African Sports Confederation of Disabled
e-mail: info@ascod.org
Web: www.ascod.org

Ethiopia

Ethiopian Paralympic Committee
e-mail: mysc@telecom.net.et

Gabon

Fed. Gabonaise Omnisports pour Personnes Handicapées
e-mail: bakita_lionel@yahoo.fr

Gambia

Gambia Assn. of the Physically Disabled
e-mail: sulcolley@hotmail.com

Ghana

National Paralympic Committee of Ghana
e-mail: npcghana2004@yahoo.com

Guinea

Guinea Sports Federation for Disabled
e-mail: handicapgui@mirinet.net.gn

Kenya

Kenya National Paralympic Committee
e-mail: npckenya@hotmail.com

Lesotho

National Paralympic Committee of Lesotho
e-mail: mnkuatsana@hotmail.com

Libya

Libyan Federation of Sports for Disabled
e-mail: libyanfsd@yahoo.com

Madagascar

Fédération Malagasy de Handisport
e-mail: sabinb@simicro.mg

Mali

Mali Federation of Sport for the Disabled
e-mail: amaldeme@afribone.net.ml

Mauritania

Federation Handisport of Mauritania
e-mail: femhandis@hotmail.com

Mauritius

Mauritius National Paralympic Committee
e-mail: udadim@intnet.mu

Morocco

Royal Moroccan Fed. of Sports for the Disabled
e-mail: H.federation@caramail.com

Mozambique

Inst. Nac. para Deficientes Visuals e Ciegos
Contact: P.O. Box 364
Beira
Mozambique
Phone: +258 (3) 323999
Fax: +258 (3) 328549

Namibia

Namibia Sports Fed. of the Disabled
e-mail: utev.maltzahn@webmail.co.za

Niger

Fédération Nigérienne Sports pour Personnes Handicapés
e-mail: baroseyni@yahoo.fr

Nigeria

Special Sports Federation of Nigeria
e-mail: wsc_disabled@yahoo.co.uk

Portugal (Gui-Bi)

Federacao de Desportos Para Deficientes da Guiné-Bissau
Contact: Dr. José Manuel Vaz Fernandes
c/o Rua Braancamp
no 12-r/ch. Dto
1250 Lisboa
Portugal (Gui-Bi)
Phone: +351 (21) 3861673
Fax: +351 (21) 3860657

Rwanda

Federation Rwandaise Handisport
e-mail: sporthand@yahoo.fr

Senegal Republic

CNP Handisport
e-mail: hagne@metissacana.sn

Sierra Leone

Association of Sports for the Disabled
e-mail: olympic@sierratel.sl

South Africa

Disability Sport South Africa
e-mail: burchell@mweb.co.za
Web: www.dissa.co.za

Sudan

National Paralympic Committee of Sudan
Contact: Dr. Ali Mohamed Ahmed El Fadl
P.O. Box 3071
Khartoum
Sudan
Phone: +249 (11) 781461
Fax: +249 (13) 318966

Tanzania

Sports Assn. for Disabled Persons of Tanzania
e-mail: iddi_ok@yahoo.com

Togo

Federation Togolaise de Sports pour Personnes Handicapées
e-mail: fetospha2002@yahoo.fr

Tunisia

Federation Sports pour Handicapés
e-mail: ftsh@planet.tn

Uganda

Uganda National Paralympic Committee
e-mail: apcpd@infocom.co.ug

Yaounde

Cameroonian Paralympic Committee
e-mail: cpc_fecash@yahoo.fr

Zambia

Zambia Federation of Sports for the Disabled
Contact: Mr. Keshi Chisambi
P.O. Box 37071
10101 Lusaka
Zambia
Phone: +260 (1) 264893
Fax: +260 (1) 261241

Zimbabwe

Zimbabwe Paralympic Committee
e-mail: 105121.314@compuserve.com

National Paralympic Committees: Americas

Argentina

Comité Paralimpico Argentino
e-mail: hramirez@cvtci.com.ar

Bahamas

Bahamas Assn. for the Physically Disabled
Contact: Ms. Marcela Inés Abascal
Ramsay 2250
1428 Buenos Aires
Argentina
Phone: +54 (9611) 47941785
Fax: +1 (242) 3227984

Barbados

Paralympic Association of Barbados
e-mail: PAB18@hotmail.com

Bermuda
Bermuda Sports for Disabled
e-mail: southern@ibl.bm

Bolivia
Federacion Nacional de Ciegos de Bolivia
e-mail: fenaciebo@bolnet.bo

Brazil
Brazilian Paralympic Committee
e-mail: cpb@urbi.com.br
Web: www.brasilparaolimpico.org.br

Canada
Canadian Paralympic Committee
e-mail: brian@paralympic.ca
Web: www.paralympic.ca

Chile
Federacion Paralimpica de Chile
e-mail: chile_paralimpico@latinmail.com

Colombia
Federacion Paraolimpica Colombiana
e-mail: comiteparalimpicocolombiano@hotmail.com

Costa Rica
Assn. Costarricense de Deportes para Ciegos
e-mail: chupis@amnet.co.cr

Cuba
Federacion de Deportes y Recreacion
e-mail: chang@inder.co.cu

Dominican Republic
Organ. Dominicana de Ciegos Inc.
e-mail: pedropablo86@hotmail.com

Ecuador
Federedis "Mitad del Mundo"
e-mail: momentum@ccia.com

El Salvador
Instituto Nacional de Deportes de El Salvador
e-mail: siresa2004@yahoo.com

Guatemala, C.A.

Comité Paralimpico Guatemalteco
e-mail: copag_guatemala@yahoo.com

Haiti

**Fédération Haitienne des Associations
& Institutions des personnes han**
e-mail: jean_chevalier_sanon@hotmail.com

Honduras

Comité Paralimpico Honduras
e-mail: comiteparalimpicohon@hotmail.com

Jamaica

Paraplegic Association
e-mail: monarehab@jamweb.net

Mexico

Comité Paralimpico Mexicano (COPAME)
e-mail: durandz@servidor.unam.mx

Nicaragua

Comité Paraolimpico Nicaraguense
Contact: Ms. Sandra López Gomez
Apartado Postal 383
Antigua Hacienda El Retiro
Managua
Nicaragua
Phone: +505 (266) 35162224042
Fax: +505 (266) 3704

Panama

Asociacion Nacional de Deportes para Ciegos
e-mail: mmcdeb@hotmail.com

Peru

Centro de Rehabilitación Profesional (Cerp IPSS)
Contact: Dra. Gabi Curi Jaramillo
Prolong. Cangallo CDRA.
3 S/N La Victoria
Lima 13
Peru
Phone: +51 (1) 3242983
Fax: +51 (1) 3239331

Puerto Rico

Comité Paralimpico de Puerto Rico
e-mail: quilesma1@aol.com

Suriname

Stichting Suriname Para Olympisch Comite
e-mail: frankcameron65@hotmail.com

United States

U.S. Paralympics
e-mail: charlie.huebner@usoc.org
Web: www.olympic-usa.org

Uruguay

Uruguayan Paralympic Committee
e-mail: RLong@latu.org.uy

Venezuela

Comité Paralimpico Venezolano
e-mail: fevesruedas@cantv.net

National Paralympic Committees: Asia

Bangladesh

National Games for Disabled Association
e-mail: makasem@bdonline.com

Cambodia

National Paralympic Committee of Cambodia
e-mail: ncdp_dir@online.com.kh
Web: www.ncdpcam.org

China (People's Rep.)

China Sports Association for Disabled Persons
e-mail: npcchina@cdpf.org.cn
Web: www.cdpf.org.cn

Chinese Taipei

Chinese Taipei Paralympic Committee
e-mail: fouhwan@ctsod.org.tw
Web: www.ctsod.org.tw

Hong Kong

Hong Kong Sports Association for the Physically Disabled
e-mail: admin@hksap.org
Web: www.hksap.org

India

Paralympic Committee of India
e-mail: npc_india2001@yahoo.com

Indonesia

**Indonesian Body for the Promotion
of Sports for the Disabled**
e-mail: bpocpusat@yahoo.com

Japan

Japan Paralympic Committee
e-mail: kunio@jsad.or.jp
Web: www.jsad.or.jp

Korea

Korea Sports Association for the Disabled
e-mail: jaejinpark@hanmir.com
Web: www.kosad.or.kr

Kyrgyz Republic

Invalid Sport Fed. of the Kyrgyz Republic
Contact: Mr. Klimentiy Epelman
P.O. Box 1949, Glavpochtamt
720000 Bishkek
Kyrgyz Republic
Phone: +7 (996) 312210685
Fax: +7 (996) 312210672

Lao PDR

Lao Paralympic Committee
e-mail: olympicl@laotel.com

Macao, China

Assn. Recreativa dos Deficientes de Macau
Contact: Mr. Antonio Fernandes
Torreao Do Jardin de S. Francisco
P.O. Box 571
Macao
Macao, China
Phone: +853 (563) 214
Fax: +853 715169

Malaysia

Malaysian Paralympic Council
e-mail: mparacou@tm.net.my

Mongolia

Mongolian Paralympic Committee
e-mail: UBTDS@magicnet.mn

Myanmar

Myanmar Disabled Sports Federation
e-mail: Y.swe@mptmail.net.mm

Nepal

National Para Sports Association–Nepal
e-mail: npsanepal@hotmail.com

Pakistan

National Paralympic Committee of Pakistan
e-mail: imran_shami@hotmail.com

Philippines

Philippine Sports Assn. of the Differently Abled
e-mail: pspada@skyinet.net

Singapore

Singapore Disability Sports Council
e-mail: info@sdsc.org.sg
Web: www.sdsc.org.sg

Sri Lanka

National Federation of Sports for the Disabled
e-mail: slfrd@mail.ewisl.net
Web: www.nfsd.wb.gs

Tajikistan

Disability Sport Federation of Tajikistan
e-mail: DSF_Tajik@mail.ru

Thailand

Paralympic Committee of Thailand
e-mail: sadt@lox1.loxinfo.co.th

Vietnam

The Vietnam Sports Association for the Disabled
e-mail: vsad@hn.vnn.vn

National Paralympic Committees: Europe

Albania

Albanian National Paralympic Committee
e-mail: koksh@albaniaonline.net

Andorra

Fed. Andorrana d' Esports per Minusvalids
e-mail: fadem@andorra.ad

Armenia

Armenian National Paralympic Committee
e-mail: rsarg@mail.com

Austria

Austrian Paralympic Committee
e-mail: office@oepc.at
Web: www.oepc.at

Azerbaijan

Paralympic Committee of Azerbaijan Republic
e-mail: azenpc@azintex.com

Belarus

Paralympic Committee of the Republic of Belarus
e-mail: typhlo-bel@mail.ru

Belgium

Belgian Paralympic Committee
e-mail: Nico.Verspeelt@skynet.be

Bosnia and Herzegovina

Paralympic Committee of Bosnia & Herzegovina
e-mail: npcbih@bih.net.ba

Bulgaria

Bulgarian Paralympic Association
e-mail: disabled@olympic.bg

Croatia

Croatian Sports Federation for the Disabled
e-mail: ticijan.komparic@hssi-hpo.hr
Web: www.hssi-hpo.hr

Cyprus

Cyprus National Paralympic Committee
e-mail: paralympic@cytanet.com.cy

Czech Republic

Czech Paralympic Committee
e-mail: cpvpha@mbox.vol.cz
Web: www.paralympic.cz

Denmark

Dansk Handicap Idraets-Forbund
e-mail: handicapidraet@dhif.dk
Web: www.dhif.dk

Estonia

Estonian Paralympic Committee
e-mail: paralympic@paralympic.ee
Web: www.paralympic.ee

Faroe Islands

Itrottasamband Fyri Brekad
e-mail: isb@post.olivant.fo
Web: www.isb.fo

Finland

Finnish Paralympic Committee
e-mail: maria.laakso@paralympia.fi
Web: www.paralympia.fi

France

Federation Française Handisport
e-mail: international@handisport.org

Georgia

Georgian Paralympic Committee
e-mail: ligadzneladze@mail.ru

Germany

National Paralympic Committee Germany
e-mail: keuther@dbs-npc.de
Web: www.paralympics.de or www.dbs-npc.de

Greece

Hellenic Paralympic Committee
e-mail: npc_greece@hotmail.com

Hungary

Hungarian Paralympic Committee
e-mail: h.paralympic@acenet.hu
Web: www.hparalimpia.hu

Iceland

Icelandic Sports Association for the Disabled
e-mail: if@isisport.is
Web: www.isisport.is/if

Ireland

Paralympic Council of Ireland
e-mail: info@pcireland.ie

Italy

Italian Paralympic Committee
e-mail: fisd.tecnica@libero.it
Web: www.fisd.it

Kazakhstan

Association for Phys. Culture and Sports for the Disabled
e-mail: mvrozhkov@host.kz

Latvia

Latvian Paralympic Committee
e-mail: ld@labklajiba.rcc.lv

Liechtenstein

Liechtensteiner Behinderten Verband
e-mail: lbv@supra.net

Lithuania

Lithuanian Paralympic Committee
e-mail: vidas@kksd.lt

Luxembourg

Federation Sportive des Handicapés
Contact: Mr. Marc Schreiner
47, rue de Luxembourg
7540 Berschbach
Luxembourg
Phone: +352 44905516
Fax: +352 329181

Macedonia (FYROM)

Federation for Sport and Recreation for Disabled of Macedonia
e-mail: ssrim@mt.net.mk

Malta

Malta Federation of Sports Associations for Disabled Persons
e-mail: info@razzett.org

Moldova

Paralympic Committee of Moldova
e-mail: paralympic@mail.ru

Netherlands

Netherlands Paralympic Committee
e-mail: e.de.winter@nebasnsg.nl
Web: www.nebasnsg.nl

Norway

Norges Funksjonshemmedes Idrettsforbund
e-mail: funksjh@nif.idrett.no
Web: www.nfif.no

Poland

Polish Paralympic Committee
e-mail: mail@pkpar.com.pl
Web: www.pkpar.com.pl

Portugal

Federacao Portuguesa de Desporto para Deficientes
e-mail: fpddpor@mail.telepac.pt

Romania

Romanian Sport Federation for Disabled People
e-mail: frsph@mcit.ro

Russian Federation

Paralympic Committee of Russia
e-mail: oms@vos.org.ru

Serbia and Montenegro

Paralympic Committee Serbia and Montenegro
e-mail: pulago@beotel.yu

Slovakia

Slovak Paralympic Committee
e-mail: spcoffice@paralympic.sk
Web: www.spv.sk

Slovenia

Sports Federation for the Disabled of Slovenia
e-mail: zsis@siol.net
Web: http://sport.si21.com/sport-invalidov

Spain

Spanish Paralympic Committee
e-mail: cpe@csd.mec.es
Web: http://paralimpicos.sportec.es

Sweden

Swedish Sports Organization for the Disabled
e-mail: stig.carlsson@shif.rf.se
Web: www.handikappidrott.se

Switzerland

Swiss Paralympic Committee
e-mail: mail@swissparalympic.ch
Web: www.swissparalympic.ch

Turkey

National Paralympic Committee of Turkey
e-mail: info@paralimpik.org.tr

Turkmenistan

National Paralympic Committee of Turkmenistan
e-mail: npc_tkm@mail.ru

Ukraine

Ukrainian Natl. Com. of Sport for Disabled
e-mail: npc_ukraine@sport.kiev.ua

United Kingdom

British Paralympic Association
e-mail: info@paralympics.org.uk
Web: www.paralympics.org.uk

Uzbekistan

Invalid Sport Association of Rep. of Uzbekistan (ISA)
e-mail: umidm@albatros.uz

National Paralympic Committees: Middle East

Afghanistan

Afghanistan Paralympic Federation
e-mail: manager@afghanparalympic.org

Bahrain

Bahrain Disabled Sports Federation
e-mail: GCCOC@batelco.com.bh

Iran

Islamic Republic of Iran National Paralympic Committee
e-mail: info@npc.ir
Web: www.npc.ir

Iraq

Iraqi Paralympic Committee
e-mail: khatan_inpc@yahoo.com

Israel

Israel Sports Association for the Disabled
e-mail: isad1@barak-online.net

Jordan

Jordan Sports Federation for the Handicapped
e-mail: JSFH@go.com.jo

Kuwait

Kuwait Disabled Sports Club
e-mail: disabled@kuwait.net
Web: www.kuwait.net/~disabled/

Lebanon

Handi-Sport Lebanese Federation
e-mail: lwah@lwah.org.lb

Oman

Oman National Disabled Sports Team
e-mail: salam@omantel.net.om

Palestine

Palestinian Sport Federation for the Disabled
e-mail: psfd@gawab.com

Qatar

Qatar Sport Federation for Special Needs
e-mail: qsfsn@qatar.net.qa

Saudi Arabia

Saudi Sports Federation for Special Needs
e-mail: nasserr_99@hotmail.com

Syria

Syrian Federation for Disabled Sport
e-mail: syrdisabled@shuf.com
Web: www.sport-sy.com

United Arab Emirates

U.A.E. Disabled Sports Federation
e-mail: uaedsf@emirates.net.ae

National Paralympic Committees: South Pacific

Australia

Australian Paralympic Committee
e-mail: darren.peters@paralympic.org.au
Web: www.paralympic.org.au

Fiji Islands

Fiji Sports Association for the Disabled
e-mail: samv@tfl.com.fj

New Zealand

Paralympics New Zealand
e-mail: chobbs@paralympics.org.nz
Web: www.paralympics.org.nz

Papua New Guinea

Papua New Guinea Disabled Sports Association
e-mail: takale_tuna@treasury.gov.pg

Samoa

Samoa Paralympic Committee
e-mail: m_tuala@hotmail.com

Tonga

Tonga Sports & Recreation Assn. for People with a Disability
e-mail: tasanoc@kalianet.to
Web: http://kalianet.to/tasanoc

Vanuatu

VandiSports
e-mail: vanuatudisable@vanuatu.com.vu

appendix G

Periodical and Journal Resources

This list provides names and contact information for periodicals on physical education, sport, and recreation for individuals with disabilities. Note that newsletters are available from many disability sport organizations as well.

Ability Magazine
www.abilitymagazine.com

Able Data
www.abledata.com

Active Living
www.cripworld.com

Adapted Physical Activity Quarterly
www.humankinetics.com/products/journals

American Journal of Art Therapy
www.arttherapy.org/aboutaata/journal.htm

American Journal of Health Education
www.aahperd.org

American Journal of Physical Medicine and Rehabilitation
www.amjphysmedrehab.com

American Journal of Sports Medicine
www.sportsmed.org

American Rehabilitation
www.ed.gov/pubs/AmericanRehab

Archives of Physical Medicine and Rehabilitation
www.physiatry.org/publications/aboutaj.html

Athletic Therapy Today
www.humankinetics.com/products/journals

Bulletin of Prosthetics Research
Prosthetics Research Study
www.prs-research.org

Canadian Abilities Foundation
www.enablelink.org/about_abilities.html

Clinics in Sports Medicine
www.medicine.ucsd.edu

Disabled Sports USA
Challenge Magazine
www.dsusa.org/challmag-current.html

Exceptional Child (Council for Exceptional Children)
www.cec.sped.org

Exceptional Parent Magazine
www.eparent.com

Exercise and Sports Science Reviews
www.acsm-essr.org

International Journal of Rehabilitation Research
www.intjrehabilres.com

inMotion
www.amputee-coalition.org

Journal of Leisurability
www.lin.ca/resource/html/jofl.htm

Journal of Physical Activity and Health
www.humankinetics.com/products/journals

Journal of Physical Education, Recreation and Dance
www.aahperd.org

Journal of Prosthetics and Orthotics
www.oandp.org/jpo

Journal of Rehabilitation
www.nationalrehab.org

Journal of Sport Rehabilitation
www.humankinetics.com/products/journals

Journal of Sports Science and Medicine (JSSM)
http://jssm.uludag.edu.tr

Medicine and Science in Sports and Exercise
www.ms-se.com

National Wheelchair Athletic Association Newsletter
www.herlpitt.org/bobby/publications.htm

New Mobility
www.newmobility.com

No Limits
www.nolimitstahoe.com

Palaestra
www.palaestra.com

Paraplegia News
www.pvamagazines.com/pnnews

Pediatric Exercise Science
www.humankinetics.com/products/journals

Physical Therapy
www.apta.org/PTmagazine

Physician and Sportsmedicine
www.physsportsmed.com/journal.htm

Rehabilitation Gazette
www.post-polio.org/gini

Research Quarterly for Exercise and Sport
www.aahperd.org

Sit Down Sports
www.sitdownsports.com

Sit Ski
www.sitski.com

Ski Racing Magazine
www.skiracing.com

Sports Medicine Reports
www.biomedcentral.com/currsportsmedrep

Sports 'n Spokes
www.sns-magazine.com

Strategies
www.aahperd.org

Teaching Exceptional Children
www.unlv.edu/Colleges/Education/ERC

Therapeutic Recreation Journal
http://scolar.vsc.edu:8005/VSCCAT/ABP-0759

Update
www.aahperd.org

bibliography

Abel, T., Kroner, M., Bleicher, I., Rojas, S., Kupfer, A., and Platen, P. 2003. Comparison of physical responses to synchronous and asynchronous arm cranking on a handbike. In *Proceedings, 13th international symposium in adapted physical activity,* July 3-7, 2001, ed. M. Dinold, G. Gerber, and T. Reinelt (pp. 350-354). Vienna: Manz Verlag Schulbuch.

Active Living Alliance for Canadians with a Disability. 1994. *Moving to inclusion.* Ottawa, ON: Author.

Adams, R.C., and McCubbin, J.A. 1991. *Games, sports and exercises for the physically disabled.* 4th ed. Philadelphia: Lea & Febiger.

Adelson, E., and Fraiberg, S. 1974. Gross motor development in infants blind from birth. *Child Development* 5: 114-126.

Adeoja, T.A. 1987. Psychological and social problems of physical disability: State of the art and relevance to physical education. In *International perspectives on adapted physical activity,* ed. M.E. Berridge and G.R. Ward (pp. 25-31). Champaign, IL: Human Kinetics.

Alexander, M.J. 1984. Analysis of the high jump technique of an amputee. *Palaestra* 1: 19-23, 44-48.

Allard, R., and Bornemann, R. 2001. Inclusion—the Canadian experience. In *New horizons in sports for athletes with a disability, proceedings of the international Vista '99 conference,* Cologne, Germany, August 28-September 1, 1999, ed. G. Doll-Tepper, M. Kroner, and W. Sonnenschein (pp. 534-582). London: Meyer & Meyer Sport.

American Academy of Orthopedic Surgeons. 1991. *Athletic training and sports medicine.* Park Ridge, IL: Author.

American Alliance for Health, Physical Education, Recreation and Dance. 1975. *Annotated bibliography in physical education, recreation, and psychomotor function of mentally retarded persons.* Reston, VA: Author.

American Alliance for Health, Physical Education, Recreation and Dance. 1976. *Involving impaired, disabled, and handicapped persons in regular camping programs.* Reston, VA: Author.

American College of Sports Medicine. 1990. The recommended quantity and quality of exercise for developing and maintaining fitness in healthy adults. *Medicine and Science in Sports and Exercise* 22: 265-274.

American College of Sports Medicine. 1997. *ACSM's exercise management for persons with chronic diseases and disabilities.* Champaign, IL: Human Kinetics.

American College of Sports Medicine. 2003. *Exercise management for persons with chronic diseases and disabilities.* Champaign, IL: Human Kinetics.

American Sport Education Program. 1996. *Event management for sport directors.* Champaign, IL: Human Kinetics.

Ammons, D. 1986. World games for the deaf. In *Sport and disabled athletes,* ed. C. Sherrill (pp. 65-72). Champaign, IL: Human Kinetics.

Anderson, S.C. 1980. Effectiveness of an introduction to therapeutic recreation courses on students' attitudes toward the disabled. *Leisurability* 7: 13-16.

Andrew, G.M., Reid, J.G., Beck, S., and McDonald, W. 1979. Training of the developmentally handicapped young adults. *Canadian Journal of Applied Sport Sciences* 4: 289-293.

Appenzeller, H. 1983. *The right to participate.* Charlottesville, VA: Michie.

Arnhold, R.W., and McGrain, P. 1985. Selected kinematic patterns of visually impaired youth in sprint running. *Adapted Physical Activity Quarterly* 2: 206-213.

Asken, M.J. 1990. The challenge of the physically challenged: Delivering sport psychology services to physically disabled athletes. *Sport Psychologist* 5: 370-381.

Asken, M.J., and Goodling, M.D. 1986a. Sport psychology I: An undeveloped discipline from among the sport sciences for disabled athletes. *Adapted Physical Activity Quarterly* 3: 312-319.

Asken, M.J., and Goodling, M.D. 1986b. Sport psychology II: The basic concepts of readiness and concentration. *Sports 'n Spokes* 12: 22-24.

Asken, M.J., and Goodling, M.D. 1986c. Sport psychology III: Techniques for performance enhancement and competitive stress management. *Sports 'n Spokes* 12: 27-29.

Atlanta Paralympic Organizing Committee. n.d. *The triumph of the human spirit.* Atlanta: Author.

Atlanta Paralympic Organizing Committee. 1996. *Guide to the Games.* Atlanta: Author.

Aufsesser, P.M. 1982. Comparison of the attitudes of physical education, recreation, and special education majors toward the disabled. *American Corrective Therapy Journal* 36: 35-41.

Australian Coaching Council. 1989. Coaching athletes with disabilities. *Sports Coach* 12 (4): 6-8.

Australian Sports Commission. 1989. *Intellectual disabilities: Coaching athletes with disabilities.* Canberra, NSW: Author.

Australian Sports Commission. 1993. *Coaching athletes with disabilities: General principles.* Canberra, NSW: Author.

Australian Sports Commission. 2001. *Give it a go.* Canberra, NSW: Prime Printers Pty Limited.

Axelson, P. 1993. Design beyond the norm. *International Design Magazine,* 46-47.

Axelson, P. 1995. Snow show. *Sports 'n Spokes* 21: 23-44.

Axelson, P. 1996. Geared for action: 1996 handcycle survey. *Sports 'n Spokes* 22: 26-29.

Axelson, P., and Castellano, J. 1990. Take to the trail . . . everything you wanted to know about off-road wheelchairs. *Sports 'n Spokes* 16: 20-24.

Axelson, P.W., Mispagel, K.M., and Longmuir, P.E. 2001. Trailware: Technology for the universal design of outdoor environments. In *Proceedings of the RESNA 2001 annual conference,* ed. R. Simpson (pp. 118-120). Arlington, VA: RESNA Press.

Barker, R.G., Wright, B.A., and Gonick, H.R. 1983. Adjustment to physical handicap and illness: A survey of the social psychology of physique and disability. *Social Science Research Council Bulletin* 5 (55): 5.

Barrish, M.B., and Ndungane, E. 1988. Sport for the physically disabled in South Africa. *Journal of the International Council for Health, Physical Education, and Recreation* 25: 13-15, 27.

Beal, O.P., Glaser, R.M., Petrofsky, J.S., Smith, P.A., and Fox, E.L. 1981. Static components of handgrip muscles for various wheelchair propulsions. *Federation Proceedings* 40: 497.

Beasley, C.R. 1982. Effects of a jogging program on cardiovascular fitness and work performance of mentally retarded adults. *American Journal of Mental Deficiency* 86: 609-613.

Bell, D. 2003. *Encyclopedia of international games.* Jefferson, NC: McFarland & Company.

Berg, K. 1970. Effect of physical training of school children with cerebral palsy. *Acta Paediatrica Scandinavica* (Suppl. 244): 27-33.

Beuter, A.C. 1983. Effects of mainstreaming on motor performance of intellectually normal and trainable mentally retarded students. *American Corrective Therapy Journal* 37: 48-52.

Bhambhani, Y. 2001. Bridging the gap between research and practice in paralympic sport. In *New horizons in sports for athletes with a disability, proceedings of the international Vista '99 conference,* Cologne, Germany, August 28-September 1, 1999, ed. G. Doll-Tepper, M. Kroner, and W. Sonnenschein (pp. 5-25). London: Meyer & Meyer Sport.

Bicknell, J. 1972. Riding for the handicapped. *Outdoors* 3 (3): 33.

Biering-Sorensen, F. 1980. Classification of paralyzed and amputee sportsmen. In *Proceedings of the first international medical congress on sports and the disabled,* ed. H. Natvig (pp. 44-54). Oslo, Norway: Royal Ministry of Church and Education, Office of Youth and Sport.

Birk, T.J., and Birk, C.A. 1987. Use of ratings of perceived exertion for exercise prescription. *Sports Medicine* 4: 1-8.

Birk, T., Gavron, S., Ross, S.E., Hackett, K., Boullard, K., and Olson, R. 1984. Relationship of perceived exertion and heart rate response during exercise testing in wheelchair users. Paper presented at American Alliance of Health, Physical Education, Recreation and Dance, April 8, 1983, Minneapolis.

Birk, T., Gavron, S., Ross, S.E., Hackett, K., Boullard, K., Olson, R., and Gosling, R. 1983. Physiological profiles of three women from the 5th International Cerebral

Palsy Games. Paper presented at the 4th International Symposium in Adapted Physical Activity, London.

Birrell, S.J. 1988. Discourses on the gender/sport relationship: From women in sport to gender relations. In *Exercise and sports science reviews,* ed. K.B. Pandolf (pp. 459-502). New York: Macmillan.

Birrer, R.B. 1984. The Special Olympics: An injury overview. *Physician and Sports-medicine* 12: 95-97.

Blair, S., Kohl, H., and Goodyear, N. 1987. Rates and risks for running and exercise injuries: Studies in three populations. *Research Quarterly for Exercise and Sport* 58: 221-228.

Bloomquist, L.E. 1986. Injuries to athletes with physical disabilities: Prevention implications. *Physician and Sportsmedicine* 14: 96-105.

Bobath, B. 1971. Motor development: Its effect on general development and application to the treatment of cerebral palsy. *Physiotherapy* 57: 526-532.

Bonace, B., Karwas, M.R., and DePauw, K.P. 1992. Sport and marginalized individuals. Paper presented at the National Girls and Women in Sport Symposium, October 1992, Slippery Rock, PA.

Boutilier, M.A., and SanGiovanni, L. 1983. *The sporting woman.* Champaign, IL: Human Kinetics.

Boyd, J. 1967. Comparison of motor behavior in deaf and hearing boys. *American Annals of the Deaf* 112: 598-605.

Bradbury, T. 2001. Athletes doing it for themselves: Self-coaching guidelines for elite athletes. In *New horizons in sports for athletes with a disability, proceedings of the international Vista '99 conference,* Cologne, Germany, August 28-September 1, 1999, ed. G. Doll-Tepper, M. Kroner, and W. Sonnenschein (pp. 81-96). London: Meyer & Meyer Sport.

Brandmeyer, G.A., and McBee, G.F. 1985. Social status and athletic competition for the disabled athlete: The case of wheelchair road racing. In *Sport and disabled athletes,* ed. C. Sherrill (pp. 181-188). Champaign, IL: Human Kinetics.

Brasile, F.M. 1986. Wheelchair basketball skills proficiencies versus disability classification. *Adapted Physical Activity Quarterly* 3: 6-13.

Brasile, F.M. 1990a. Performance evaluation of wheelchair athletes: More than a disability classification level issue. *Adapted Physical Activity Quarterly* 4 (7): 289-297.

Brasile, F.M. 1990b. Wheelchair sports: A new perspective on integration. *Adapted Physical Activity Quarterly* 4 (7): 3-11.

Brasile, F.M. 1992. Inclusion: A developmental perspective—a rejoinder to examining the concept of reverse integration. *Adapted Physical Activity Quarterly* 9: 293-304.

Brasile, F. 2003. A decade of skills-testing results and their implications for wheelchair basketball classification. In *Proceedings, 13th international symposium in adapted physical activity,* July 3-7, 2001, ed. M. Dinold, G. Gerber, and T. Reinelt (pp. 350-354). Vienna: Manz Verlag Schulbuchr.

Brattgard, S.O. 1970. Energy expenditure and heart rate in driving a wheelchair ergometer. *Scandinavian Journal of Rehabilitation and Medicine* 2: 143-148.

Bremner, A., and Goodman, S. 1992. *Coaching deaf athletes.* Canberra: Australian Sports Commission.

Brenes, G., Dearwater, S., Shapera, R., LaPorte, R.E., and Collins, E. 1986. High-density lipoprotein cholesterol concentrations in physically active and sedentary SCI patients. *Archives of Physical Medicine and Rehabilitation* 67: 445-450.

Breukelen, K. 2001. Wheelchair & performance. In *New horizons in sports for athletes with a disability, proceedings of the international Vista '99 conference, Cologne, Germany, August 28-September 1, 1999,* ed. G. Doll-Tepper, M. Kroner, and W. Sonnenschein (pp. 171-179). London: Meyer & Meyer Sport.

Brighton Declaration on Women and Sport. 1994. www.sportsbiz.bz/womensportinternational/conferences/brighton_declaration.htm.

Broadhead, G.D. 1986. Adapted physical education research trends: 1970-1990. *Adapted Physical Activity Quarterly* 3: 104-111.

Brubaker, C. 1984. Determination of the effects of mechanical advantage on propulsion with hand rims. *Wheelchair Mobility* 1982-3: 1-3.

Brubaker, C., and McLaurin, C. 1982. Ergonomics of wheelchair propulsion. *Wheelchair III,* 22-42.

Brud, R., and Grass, K. 1987. Strapping to enhance athletic performance of wheelchair competitors with C.P. *Palaestra* 3: 28-32.

Buell, C. 1979. Association for blind athletes as seen by a blind sportsman. *Journal of Visual Impairment and Blindness* 73: 412-413.

Bulbulian, R., Johnson, R., Bruber, J., and Darabos, B. 1987. Body composition in paraplegic male athletes. *Medicine and Science in Sports and Exercise* 19: 195-210.

Burgess, E.M., and Rappoport, A. 1992. *Physical fitness: A guide for individuals with lower limb loss.* Washington, DC: Veterans Health Administration.

Burke, E.J., Auchinachie, J.A., Hayden, R., and Loftin, J.N. 1985. Energy cost of wheelchair basketball. *Physician and Sportsmedicine* 13 (3): 99-105.

Burkett, L.N., Chisum, J., Cook, R., Norton, B., Taylor, B., Ruppert, K., and Wells, C. 1987. Construction and validation of a hysteresis brake wheelchair ergometer. *Adapted Physical Activity Quarterly* 4: 60-71.

Butterfield, S.A. 1991. Physical education and sport for the deaf: Rethinking the least restrictive environment. *Adapted Physical Activity Quarterly* 8: 95-102.

Byrens, D.P. 1983. Analysis of the competitive wheelchair stroke. Unpublished master's thesis, University of Alberta.

Cameron, B.J., Ward, G.R., and Wicks, J.R. 1978. Relationship of type of training to maximum oxygen uptake and upper-limb strength in male paraplegic athletes. *Medicine and Science in Sports and Exercise* 9: 58.

Canabal, M., Sherrill, C., and Rainbolt, W. 1987. Psychological mood profiles of elite cerebral palsied athletes. In *International perspectives on adapted physical activity*, ed. M.E. Berridge and G.R. Ward (pp. 157-163). Champaign, IL: Human Kinetics.

Canadian Association for Health, Physical Education and Recreation/l'Association canadienne pour la sante l'education physique et le loisir. 1988. Jasper talks: Strategies for change in adapted physical activity in Canada. Ottawa, ON: Author.

Capel, S.A., Sisley, B.L., and Desertrain, G.S. 1987. The relationship of role conflict and role ambiguity to burnout in high school basketball coaches. *Journal of Sport Psychology* 9: 106-117.

Carlson, L. 1992. Spectator medical care. *Physician and Sportsmedicine* 20 (1): 141-142, 144.

Carter, M.J., Van Andel, G., and Robb, G. 1985. *Therapeutic recreation: A practical approach.* St. Louis: Times Mirror/Mosby.

Cauette, M., and Reid, G. 1985. Increasing the work output of severely retarded adults on a bicycle ergometer. *Education and Training of the Mentally Retarded* 20: 296-304.

Ceccotti, F.S. 1984. Wheelchair sport injuries: An athletic training approach. *Paraplegia News,* 29-30.

Center for Universal Design. 1997. *The principles of universal design.* Version 2.0. Raleigh, NC: North Carolina State University.

Chappell, A.L. 1992. Towards a sociological critique of the normalization principle. *Disability, Handicap & Society* 7 (1): 35-50.

Chawla, J.C., Bar, C., Creber, I., Price, J., and Andrews, B. 1977. Techniques for improving the strength and fitness of spinal cord injured patients. *Paraplegia* 17: 185-189.

Clark, G., French, R., and Henderson, H. 1985. Teaching techniques that develop positive attitudes. *Palaestra* 2: 14-17.

Clark-Carter, D.D., Heyes, A.D., and Howarth, C.I. 1986. The efficiency and walking speed of visually impaired people. *Ergonomics* 29: 779-789.

Clark-Carter, D.D., Heyes, A.D., and Howarth, C.I. 1987. The gait of visually impaired pedestrians. *Human Movement Science* (Amsterdam) 3 (6): 277-282.

Clarke, H.H., and Clarke, D.H. 1963. *Developmental and adapted physical education.* Englewood Cliffs, NJ: Prentice Hall.

Clarke, K.S. 1966. Caloric costs of activity in paraplegic persons. *Archives of Physical Medicine and Rehabilitation* 47: 429-435.

Clarke, K. 1984. The Amateur Sports Act of 1978 and the athlete with disabilities. *Rehabilitation World* 8: 19-20.

Clarke, K.S. 1986. Perspectives for the future of the disabled in sport. *Adapted Physical Activity Quarterly* 3: 152-155.

Clinkingbeard, J.R., Gersten, J.W., and Hoehn, D. 1964. Energy cost of ambulation in traumatic paraplegia. *American Journal of Physical Medicine* 43: 157-165.

Coaching disabled athletes: The role of NSA. 1985. *Coaching Director* 1 (2): 7-10.

Cocoran, P.J. 1980. Sports medicine and the physiology of wheelchair marathon racing. *Orthopedic Clinics of North America* 11: 697-716.

Cohen, G.L. 1993. *Women in sport.* Newbury Park, CA: Sage.

Comité International des Sports des Sourds. 1975-1985. *CISS handbook.* Washington, DC: Gallaudet University.

Commonwealth Games Federation. 2003. Post games report. www.thecgf.com.

Cooke, R.E. 1984. Atlantoaxial instability in individuals with Down's syndrome. *Adapted Physical Activity Quarterly* 1: 194-196.

Cooper, M.A. 1988. The computer as a tool in coaching disabled athletes. *Palaestra* 4: 30-32, 35.

Cooper, M.A., Sherrill, C., and Marshall, D. 1986. Attitudes toward physical activity of elite cerebral palsied athletes. *Adapted Physical Activity Quarterly* 3: 14-21.

Copeland, R., and Sherrill, C. 1986. Colors seen best by visually impaired athletes: Implications for coaching. *Abstracts of research papers,* 1986 AAHPERD convention. Reston, VA: American Alliance of Health, Physical Education, Recreation and Dance.

Cordellos, H. 2002. *No limits: Legendary blind athlete leads the way to hew horizons.* Waco, TX: WRS.

COSD forum. 2000. *Palaestra* 16: 55.

COSD forum. 2003. *Palaestra* 19: 9.

COSD minutes. 1991, May.

Coutts, K.D. 1988. Heart rates of participants in wheelchair sports. *Paraplegia* 26: 43-49.

Coutts, K.D., Rhodes, E.C., and McKenzie, D.C. 1983. Maximal exercise responses of tetraplegics and paraplegics. *Journal of Applied Physiology* 55: 479-482.

Coutts, K.D., Rhodes, E.C., and McKenzie, D.C. 1985. Submaximal exercise responses of tetraplegics and paraplegics. *Journal of Applied Physiology* 59: 237-241.

Coutts, K.D., and Schutz, R.W. 1988. Analysis of wheelchair track performances. *Medicine and Science in Sports and Exercise* 20 (2): 188-194.

Coutts, K.D., and Steryn, J.L. 1987. Aerobic and anaerobic power of Canadian wheelchair athletes. *Medicine and Science in Sports and Exercise* 19: 62-65.

Cowan, J. 1993. Brave in the attempt. *Olympian* 19: 23.

Cowell, L.L., Squires, W.G., and Raven, P.B. 1986. Benefits of aerobic exercise for the paraplegic: A brief review. *Medicine and Science in Sports and Exercise* 18: 501-508.

Coyle, C.P., and Kenney, W.B. 1990. Leisure characteristics of adults with physical disabilities. *Therapeutic Recreation Journal* 24 (4): 64-73.

Crews, D., Wells, C.L., Burkett, L., and McKeenman-Hopkins, V. 1982. A physiological profile of four wheelchair marathon racers. *Physician and Sportsmedicine* 10: 134-143.

Crocker, P.R.E. 1993. Sport and exercise physiology and research with individuals with physical disabilities: Using theory to advance knowledge. *Adapted Physical Activity Quarterly* 10: 324-335.

Curtis, K.A. 1981a. Wheelchair sports medicine: Part 1. Basics of exercise physiology. *Sports 'n Spokes* 7 (1): 26-28.

Curtis, K.A. 1981b. Wheelchair sports medicine: Part 2. Training. *Sports 'n Spokes* 7 (2): 16-19.

Curtis, K.A. 1981c. Wheelchair sports medicine: Part 3. Stretching routines. *Sports 'n Spokes* 7 (3): 16-18.

Curtis, K.A. 1982. Wheelchair sports medicine: Part 4. Athletic injuries. *Sports 'n Spokes* 8 (1): 20-24.

Curtis, K.A. 1991. Sport-specific functional classification for wheelchair athletes. *Sports 'n Spokes* 17 (2): 45-47.

Curtis, K.A., and Dillon, D.A. 1985. Survey of wheelchair athletic injuries: Common patterns and prevention. *Paraplegia* 23: 170-175.

Daignault, L. 1990. Integration battle heats up at Commonwealth Games. *Abilities* 1: 6-7.

Dal-Monte, A., Faina, M., Maglio, A., Sardella, G., and Guide, G. 1982. Cardiotelemetric and blood lactate investigations in paraplegic subjects during several sports activities. *Journal of Sports Medicine and Physical Fitness* 22: 172-184.

D'Alonzo, B.J. 1976. Rights of exceptional children to participate in interscholastic athletics. *Exceptional Children* 43: 86-92.

Davies, E. 1975. *Adapted physical education.* 3rd ed. New York: Harper & Row.

Davis, G.M., Kofsky, P.R., Shephard, R.J., and Jackson, R.W. 1981. Classification of psycho-physiological variables in the lower-limb disabled. *Canadian Journal of Applied Sport Sciences* 6 (3): 141.

Davis, G.M., Shephard, R.J., and Jackson, R.W. 1981. Cardiorespiratory fitness and muscular strength in the lower-limb disabled. *Canadian Journal of Applied Sport Sciences* 6: 159-165.

Davis, G.M., Shephard, R.J., and Ward, G.R. 1984. Alterations of dynamic strength following forearm crank training of disabled subjects. *Medicine and Science in Sports and Exercise* 16: 147.

Davis, L.J. 1995. *Enforcing normalcy: Disability, deafness, and the body.* London: Verso.

Davis, R. 2002. *Inclusion through sports: A guide to enhancing sport experiences.* Champaign, IL: Human Kinetics.

Davis, R., and Ferrara, M. 1991, November. Training profiles of elite wheelchair athletes. Paper presented at the 8th International Symposium of Adapted Physical Activity, Miami.

Davis, R., Ferrara, M., Woodard, R., and Campbell, A. 2001, September. Perceptions of student athletic trainers caring for Special Olympic athletes. Paper presented at the World Congress and Exposition on Disabilities, Atlanta.

Dawson, M. 1981. A biomechanical analysis of gait patterns of the visually impaired. *American Corrective Therapy Journal* 35: 66-71.

Decker, J.I. 1986. Role conflict of teacher/coaches in small colleges. *Sociology of Sport Journal* 3: 356-365.

Declaration of Rights of Disabled Persons. 1975. UN Resolution #3447. www.un.org/issues/docs/d-disabl.asp.

DeFrantz, A. 2000. School sport and competition: Commentary. *Perspectives* 1: 17-20.

Dendy, E. 1978. Recreation for the disabled people—what do we mean? *Physiotherapy* 64: 290-297.

DePauw, K.P. 1985a. History of sports for individuals with disabilities. *Able Bodies* 4: 1, 3.

DePauw, K.P. 1985b. USOC's commitment to sports for individuals with disabilities. *Palaestra* 1: 6.

DePauw, K.P. 1986a. Horseback riding for individuals with disabilities: Programs, philosophy, and research. *Adapted Physical Activity Quarterly* 3: 217-226.

DePauw, K.P. 1986b. Research on sport for athletes with disabilities. *Adapted Physical Activity Quarterly* 3: 292-299.

DePauw, K.P. 1986c. Toward progressive inclusion and acceptance: Implications for physical education. *Adapted Physical Activity Quarterly* 3: 1-6.

DePauw, K.P. 1988. Sport for individuals with disabilities: Research opportunities. *Adapted Physical Activity Quarterly* 5: 80-89.

DePauw, K.P. 1990a. Sport, society and individuals with disabilities. In *Problems in movement control,* ed. G. Reid. New York: North-Holland.

DePauw, K.P. 1990b. PE and sport for disabled individuals in the United States. *Journal of Physical Education, Recreation and Dance* 61: 53-57.

DePauw, K.P. 1990c. Teaching and coaching individuals with disabilities: Research findings and implications. *Physical Education Review* 13: 12-16.

DePauw, K.P. 1994. A feminist perspective on sport and sports organizations for persons with disabilities. In *Vista '93—the outlook,* ed. R.D. Steadward, E.R. Nelson, and G.D. Wheeler. Edmonton, AB: Rick Hansen Centre.

DePauw, K.P. 1997. The (in)Visibility of DisAbility: Cultural contexts and "sporting bodies." *Quest* 49: 416-430.

DePauw, K.P. 2000. Women with disabilities. In *Encyclopaedia of sports medicine: Women in sport,* ed. B. Drinkwater (vol. 8, pp. 301-310). London: Blackwell Science.

DePauw, K.P. 2001a. Disability sport. In *International encyclopedia of women and sport* (vol. 1, pp. 326-330). Great Barrington, MA: Berkshire Reference Works.

DePauw, K.P. 2001b. Equity issues in disability sport. In *New horizons in sport for athletes with a disability, proceedings of the international Vista '99 conference,* Cologne, Germany, August 28-September 1, 1999, ed. G. Doll-Tepper, M. Kroner, and W. Sonnenschein (pp. 619-630). Oxford, England: Meyer & Meyer Sport.

DePauw, K.P. 2001c. The Paralympic movement: Past, present & future. *ICHPER-SD Journal* 37: 43-47.

DePauw, K.P. 2003, July. Challenging limits and expectations: Sport and athletes with a disability. European College of Sport Science, Salzburg, Austria.

DePauw, K.P., and Clarke, K.C. 1986. Sports for disabled U.S. citizens: Influence of amateur sports act. In *Sport and disabled athletes,* ed. C. Sherrill (pp. 35-50). Champaign, IL: Human Kinetics.

DePauw, K.P., and Doll-Tepper, G. 1989. European perspectives on adapted physical activity. *Adapted Physical Activity Quarterly* 6: 95-99.

DePauw, K.P., and Doll-Tepper, G.M. 2000. Toward progressive inclusion and acceptance: Myth or reality? The inclusion debate and bandwagon discourse. *Adapted Physical Activity Quarterly* 17: 135-143.

DePauw, K.P., and Gavron, S.J. 1991. Coaches of athletes with disabilities. *Physical Educator* 48: 33-40.

DePauw, K.P., and Gavron, S.J. 1995. *Disability and sport* (pp. 6, 7, 9). Champaign, IL: Human Kinetics.

DePauw, K.P., and Rich, S. 1993. Paralympics for the mentally handicapped. *Palaestra* 9: 59-64.

DePauw, K.P., and Sherrill, C. 1994. Adapted physical activity: Present and future. *Physical Education Review* 17: 6-13.

Doll-Tepper, G., and DePauw, K.P. 1989. COSD forum: Sport for the disabled in the Federal Republic of Germany. *Palaestra* 5 (6): 13.

Doll-Tepper, G., Kroner, M., and Sonnenschein, W., eds. 2001. *New horizons in sport for athletes with a disability* (vols. 1 and 2). Cologne: Meyer & Meyer Verlag.

Donaldson, G.W., and Swan, M.D. 1979. *Administration of eco-education.* Reston, VA: American Alliance of Health, Physical Education, Recreation and Dance.

Donnelly, P. 1996. Approaches to society inequality in the sociology of sport. *Quest* 48: 221-242.

Dreisinger, T.E., and Londeree, B.R. 1982. Wheelchair exercise: A review. *Paraplegia* 20: 20-34.

Driscoll, J., Benge, J., and Benge, G. 2000. *Determined to win.* Colorado Springs, CO: Shaw Books.

Dummer, G., Ewing, M., Halbeck, R., and Overton, S. 1986. Cognitive reactions of athletes with cerebral palsy to success and failure in sports competition. *Abstracts of research papers, 1986 AAHPERD convention* (p. 219). Reston, VA: American Alliance for Health, Physical Education, Recreation and Dance.

Dunn, J.M. 1987. The state-of-the-art of research concerning physical education for handicapped children and youth. In *Proceedings of the CIVITAN-I-M SPECIAL NETWORK International Conference on Physical Education and Sport for Disabled Persons,* ed. L. Bowers, S. Klesius, and B. Price. Tampa: University of South Florida.

Dunn, J.M., Morehouse, J.W., and Fredericks, H.D. 1986. *Physical education for the severely handicapped.* Austin, TX: Pro-Ed.

Durstine, L. 1997. *ACSM's exercise management for persons with chronic diseases and disabilities.* Champaign, IL: Human Kinetics.

Ellery, P.J., and Forbus, W.R. 1999. Technology in adapted physical education, using internet technology in adapted physical education. In *Proceedings 11th international symposium in adapted physical activity,* May 3-7, 1997, ed. D. Drouin, C. Lepine, and C. Simard (pp. 106-113). Quebec, PQ: Institut de readaptation en deficience physique de Quebec, Canada.

Ellis, M.K., and Darby, L.A. 1993. The effect of balance on the determination of peak oxygen consumption for hearing and nonhearing athletes. *Adapted Physical Activity Quarterly* 10: 216-225.

Ellis, W.K. 1992. Accessible camping in national parks. *Sports 'n Spokes* Jan./Feb.: 47-50.

Emes, C. 1978. Physical work capacity of wheelchair athletes. *Research Quarterly* 48: 209-212.

Engel, B.T. 1992. *Therapeutic riding programs: Instruction and rehabilitation.* Durango, CO: Barbara Engel Therapy Services.

Engel, R., and Hildebrandt, G. 1974. Wheelchair design: Technological and physiological aspects. *Proceedings of the Royal Society of Medicine* 67: 409-411.

Enoka, R.M., Miller, D.I., and Burgess, E.M. 1982. Below-knee amputee running gait. *American Journal of Physical Medicine* 62 (2): 66-84.

European charter for sport for all: Disabled persons. 1987. Strasbourg, France: Council of Europe.

Fay, T. 2001. Strategic approaches to vertical integration and equity for athletes with disabilities: An examination of critical factors. In *New horizons in sport for athletes with a disability, proceedings of the international Vista '99 conference,* Cologne, Germany, August 28-September 1, 1999, ed. G. Doll-Tepper, M. Kroner, and W. Sonnenschein (pp. 499-528). Oxford, England: Meyer & Meyer Sport.

Felshin, J. 1974. The triple option . . . for women in sport. *Quest* 21: 36-40.

Ferrara, M. 1990. Sports injuries to disabled athletes. Paper presented at the USODA meeting, February 1990, Tampa.

Ferrara, M., and Davis, R. 1990. Injuries to elite wheelchair athletes. *Paraplegia* 28: 335-341.

Floyd, W.F., Guttmann, L., Noble, C.W., Parks, K.R., and Ward, J. 1966. A study of the space requirements of wheelchair users. *Paraplegia* 4: 24-37.

Frederick, K.L. 1991. A comparison of rural and urban parent perceptions of elementary multihandicapped students' leisure activities. Unpublished master's thesis, Bowling Green State University, Bowling Green, OH.

French, R., Henschen, K., and Horvat, M. 1985. The psychological characteristics of female wheelchair basketball players. *Abstracts of research papers.* Reston, VA: American Alliance of Health, Physical Education, Recreation and Dance.

Fung, L. 1992. Participation motives in competitive sports: A cross-cultural comparison. *Adapted Physical Activity Quarterly* 9: 114-122.

Gandee, R., Datta, S.R., Chatterjee, B.B., and Roy, B.N. 1973. Performance evaluation of amputee prosthesis systems in below-knee amputees. *Ergonomics* 16: 797-810.

Gandee, R., Winningham, M., Deitchman, R., and Narraway, A. 1980. The aerobic capacity of an elite wheelchair marathon racer. *Medicine and Science in Sports and Exercise* 12: 142.

Gass, G.C., and Camp, E.M. 1979. Physiological characteristics of trained Australian paraplegic and tetraplegic subjects. *Medicine and Science in Sports and Exercise* 11: 256-259.

Gavron, S. 1989. Early play and recreational experiences of elite athletes with disabilities of the VII Pan Am Games. Paper presented at the 7th International Symposium in Adapted Physical Activity, June 1989, Berlin.

Gavron, S.J. 1991. Track and field for all persons. In *Sport instruction for individuals with disabilities,* ed. S. Grosse, C. Cooper, S. Gavron, J. Huber, and J. Stein (pp. 217-234). Reston, VA: American Alliance of Health, Physical Education, Recreation and Dance.

Gavron, S.J. 1999. Role of disability sport specialist: Addressing serious disabilities. In *Psychomotor domain training and serious disabilities,* 5th ed., ed. P. Jansma (pp. 75-86). Lanham, MD: University Press of America.

Gavron, S.J. 2000. School sport and competition: Adapted physical activity. *Perspectives* 1: 21-31.

Gavron, S., and DePauw, K. 1989. National coaches of disabled skiing: A background survey. *Journal of Applied Research in Coaching and Athletics* 4 (1): 17-34.

Gavron, S.J., and Ullman, D. 2001. Athletes and cancer: Stigma or role model? *North American Society for the Sociology of Sport conference abstracts* (p. 71), October 31-November 3, 2001, San Antonio, TX.

Gehlsen, G.M., and Karpuk, J. 1992. Analysis of the NWAA swimming classification system. *Adapted Physical Activity Quarterly* 9: 141-147.

Gessaroli, M.E., and Robertson, D.G.E. 1980. Comparison of two wheelchair sprint starts. *Canadian Journal of Applied Sport Sciences* 5 (4): 202.

Gibbons, S.L., and Bushakra, F.B. 1989. Effects of Special Olympics participation on the perceived competence and social acceptance of mentally retarded children. *Adapted Physical Activity Quarterly* 6: 40-51.

Gibson, P.M. 1979. Therapeutic aspects of wilderness programs: A comprehensive literature review. *Therapeutic Recreation Journal* 3 (3): 21-33.

Giddens, A. 1977. *Studies in social and political theory.* New York: Basic Books.

Gilstrap, T., and Sherrill, C. 1989. Personality profiles of elite blind female athletes. *Palaestra* 6: 21-23, 31-33.

Glaser, R.M., and Collins, S.R. 1981. Validity of power output estimation for wheelchair locomotion. *American Journal of Physical Medicine* 60: 180-189.

Glaser, R.M., Foley, D.M., Laubach, L.L., Sawka, M.N., and Suryaprasad, A.G. 1979. Exercise test to evaluate fitness for wheelchair activity. *Paraplegia* 16: 341-349.

Glaser, R.M., Laubach, L.L., Foley, D.M., Barr, S.A., and Suryaprasad, A.G. 1978. Interval training program for wheelchair users [abstract]. *Medicine and Science in Sports* 10: 54.

Glaser, R.M., Sawka, M.N., Brune, M.F., and Wilde, S.W. 1980. Physiological responses to maximal effort wheelchair and arm crank ergometry. *Journal of Applied Physiology* 48: 1060-1064.

Goodbrand, S. 1987. A comparison of the psychological mood profiles of elite cerebral palsied athletes and cerebral palsied nonathletes. Unpublished master's thesis, McGill University, Montreal.

Gorton, B., and Gavron, S. 1984. A biomechanical analysis of the running patterns of mentally retarded boys and girls in the 50-meter dash. In *Adapted physical activities: Proceedings of the fourth international symposium in adapted physical activity,* ed. A. Brown (pp. 98-114). Bodmin, Cornwall: Hartnoll.

Gorton, B., and Gavron, S.J. 1987. A biomechanical analysis of the running pattern of blind athletes in the 100-m dash. *Adapted Physical Activity Quarterly* 4: 192-203.

Grant, J., and Pryke, G. 1987. The organization of disabled sport. In *Physical education and disability,* ed. R. Lockwood (pp. 209-213). Parkside, Australia: Australian Council for Health, Physical Education, and Recreation.

Greenwood, C.M., Dzewaltowski, D.A., and French, R. 1990. Self-efficacy and psychological well-being of wheelchair tennis participants and wheelchair nontennis participants. *Adapted Physical Activity Quarterly* 7 (1): 12-21.

Gregson, I. 1998. *Irresistible force: Disability sport in Canada.* Victoria, BC: Polestar Book.

Grimes, P.S., and French, L. 1987. Barriers to disabled women's participation in sport. *Journal of Physical Education, Recreation and Dance* 58: 24-27.

Grosse, S., Cooper, C., Gavron, S., Huber, J., and Stein, J.U., eds. 1991. *Sport instruction for individuals with disabilities: The best of practical pointers.* Washington, DC: American Alliance of Health, Physical Education, Recreation and Dance.

Guttmann, L. 1971, July 16. Sport for the disabled. *Times Educational Supplement,* 31-32.

Guttmann, L. 1976. *Textbook of sport for the disabled* (p. 13). Oxford: HM & M.

Hahn, H. 1984. Sports and the political movement of disabled persons: Examining nondisabled social values. *ARENA Review* 8: 1-15.

Hale, S. 1988. Dynamic analysis of the above the knee amputee swing phase during speed walking under varying prosthetic conditions. Unpublished master's thesis, Dalhousie University, Halifax, NS.

Hall, M.A. 1985. Knowledge and gender: Epistemological questions in the social analysis of sport. *Sociology of Sport Journal* 2: 25-42.

Hamilton, N., and Adrian, M. 1987. A kinematic analysis of the wheelchair javelin throw. *Abstracts of research papers,* 1987 AAHPERD convention. Reston, VA: American Alliance for Health, Physical Education, Recreation and Dance.

Hanrahan, S.J., Grove, J.R., and Lockwood, R.J. 1990. Psychological skills training for the blind athlete: A pilot program. *Adapted Physical Activity Quarterly* 7: 143-155.

Hansen, R., and Taylor, J. 1987. *Rick Hansen: Man in motion.* Vancouver, BC: Douglas & McIntyre.

Hanson, B. 1993. Minnesota Association for Adapted Athletics. In *Proceedings of achieving a balance: National Adapted Physical Activity conference,* ed. D. Beaver (pp. 10-15). Macomb, IL: Western Illinois University.

Hedrick, B. 1979, December. A look at disabled sports. *Parks & Recreation,* p. 54.

Hedrick, B. 1984. The effects of wheelchair tennis participation and mainstreaming upon the perceptions of competence of physically disabled adolescents. Unpublished doctoral dissertation, University of Illinois at Urbana-Champaign.

Hedrick, B. 1985a. The effect of wheelchair tennis participation on adolescents. *Therapeutic Recreation Journal* 14: 34-36.

Hedrick, B. 1985b. Women's wheelchair basketball: A perspective on the U.S. program. *Sports 'n Spokes* 11: 14-17.

Hedrick, B., Byrnes, D., and Shaver, L. 1989. *Wheelchair basketball.* Washington, DC: Paralyzed Veterans of America.

Hedrick, B., Byrnes, D., and Shaver, L. 1994. *Wheelchair basketball.* 2nd ed. Washington, DC: Paralyzed Veterans of America.

Hedrick, B., and Hedrick, S. 1991. Women's wheelchair basketball. In *A century of women's basketball,* ed. J. Hult and M. Trekell (pp. 367-378). Reston, VA: American Alliance for Health, Physical Education, Recreation and Dance.

Hedrick, B., and Hedrick, S. 1993. The undiscovered athlete: A perspective on collegiate sports for persons with disabilities. Paper presented at CESU conference, July 1993, Buffalo, NY.

Hedrick, B., and Morse, M. 1991. Setting goals in wheelchair basketball. *Sports 'n Spokes* 17 (4): 64-65.

Hedrick, B., Morse, M., and Figoni, S. 1988. Training practices of elite wheelchair roadracers. *Adapted Physical Activity Quarterly* 5: 140-153.

Hedrick, B., Wang, Y.T., Moeinzadeh, M., and Adrian, M. 1990. Aerodynamic positioning and performance in wheelchair racing. *Adapted Physical Activity Quarterly* 7: 41-51.

Henschen, K., Horvat, M., and French, R. 1984. A visual comparison of psychological profiles between able-bodied and wheelchair athletes. *Adapted Physical Activity Quarterly* 1: 118-124.

Hetzler, R.K., Knowlton, R.G., Hammill, J., Noakes, T., and Schneider, T. 1986. A physiological and biomechanical comparison of able-bodied persons to wheelchair-dependent persons during wheelchair ergometry. *Abstracts of research papers,* 1986 AAHPERD convention. Reston, VA: American Alliance for Health, Physical Education, Recreation and Dance.

Hewett, F.M., and Forness, S.R. 1974. *Historical origins.* Boston: Allyn & Bacon.

Heyward, S. 1992. *Access to education for the disabled. A guide to compliance with Section 504 of the Rehabilitation Act of 1973.* Jefferson, NC: McFarland.

Higger, Y. 1984. Biomechanical analysis of stand-up and wheelchair basketball set shooting. Unpublished master's thesis, University of Alberta.

Higgs, C. 1983. An analysis of racing wheelchairs used at the 1980 Olympic Games for the Disabled. *Research Quarterly for Exercise and Sport* 54: 229-233.

Higgs, C. 1986. Propulsion of racing wheelchairs. In *Sport and disabled athletes*, ed. C. Sherrill (pp. 165-172). Champaign, IL: Human Kinetics.

Higgs, C. 1990. Wheelchair racquetball: A preliminary time motion analysis. *Adapted Physical Activity Quarterly* 7: 370-384.

Higgs, C. 1992. Wheeling in the wind: The effect of wind velocity and direction on the aerodynamic drag of wheelchairs. *Adapted Physical Activity Quarterly* 9 (1): 74-87.

Higgs, C. 2003. Classification and the future of the Paralympic Games. Paper presented at the 2003 ISAPA, Seoul.

Higgs, C., Babstock, P., Buck, J., Parsons, C., and Brewer, J. 1990. Wheelchair clarification for track and field experts: A performance approach. *Adapted Physical Activity Quarterly* 7 (1): 22-40.

Hildebrandt, G., Voigt, E.D., Bahn, D., Berendes, B., and Kroger, J. 1970. Energy cost of propelling a wheelchair at various speeds: Cardiac responses and effect on steering accuracy. *Archives of Physical Medicine and Rehabilitation* 51: 131-136.

Hockey, K., and Goodman, S. 1992. *Coaching athletes with vision impairments.* Canberra: Australian Sports Commission.

Holcomb, L.P. 1984. Disabled women: A new issue in education. In *Perspectives on disability*, ed. M. Nagler (pp. 381-388). Palo Alto, CA: Health Markets Research.

Hooper, C.A. 1982. Socialization of wheelchair athletes in sport. Abstract in *Dissertation Abstracts International* 43: 1976A. University Microfilms No. 84-235, 7242.

Horvat, M., French, R., and Henschen, K. 1986. A comparison of the psychological characteristics of male and female able-bodied and wheelchair athletes. *Paraplegia* 24: 115-122.

Horvat, M., French, R., and Henschen, K. 1988. Special Olympics training programs around the world . . . a survey. *Palaestra* 5: 28-31.

Horvat, M., Golding, L., Beutel-Horvat, T., and McConnell, T. 1984. A treadmill modification for wheelchairs. *Research Quarterly for Exercise and Sport* 55: 297-301.

Howe, P.D. 2001. Read all about it! Representation of a distinctive community: The printed media, sport and disability. In *2001 North American Society for the Sociology of Sport, 22nd conference, Marginality, power and sport, abstracts* (p. 60). October 31-November 3, 2001, San Antonio, TX.

Huber, C.A. 1984. An overview and perspective on international disabled sport: Past, present, future. *Rehabilitation World* 8: 8-11.

Hughes, E. 1949. Social change and status protest: An essay on the marginal man. *Phylon* 10: 58-65.

Hullemann, K.D., List, M., Matthes, D., Wiese, G., and Zika, D. 1975. Spiroergometric and telemetric investigations during the XXI International Stoke Mandeville Games. *Paraplegia* 13: 109-123.

Hult, J.S., and Trekell, M. 1991. *A century of women's basketball: From frailty to Final Four.* Reston, VA: American Alliance for Health, Physical Education, Recreation and Dance.

International Paralympic Committee. 2002a. Handbook. www.paralympic.org (accessed March 7, 2002).

International Paralympic Committee. 2002b. Results, summer sports. www.paralympic.org (accessed May 23, 2002).

International Paralympic Committee. 2003a. 7 a-side football. www.paralympic.org (accessed November 1, 2003).

International Paralympic Committee. 2003b. Alpine skiing. www.paralympic.org (accessed November 4, 2003).

International Paralympic Committee. 2003c. Archery. www.paralympic.org (accessed November 5, 2003).

International Paralympic Committee. 2003d. Athletics. www.paralympic.org (accessed November 1, 2003).

International Paralympic Committee. 2003e. Boccia. www.paralympic.org (accessed November 2, 2003).

International Paralympic Committee. 2003f. Cycling. www.paralympic.org (accessed November 5, 2003).

International Paralympic Committee. 2003g. Equestrian. www.paralympic.org (accessed November 3, 2003).

International Paralympic Committee. 2003h. Goalball. www.paralympic.org (accessed November 7, 2003).

International Paralympic Committee. 2003i. Ice sledge hockey. www.paralympic.org (accessed November 5, 2003).

International Paralympic Committee. 2003j. Judo. www.paralympic.org (accessed November 1, 2003).

International Paralympic Committee. 2003k. Nordic skiing. www.paralympic.org (accessed November 2, 2003).

International Paralympic Committee. 2003l. Powerlifting. www.paralympic.org (accessed November 5, 2003).

International Paralympic Committee. 2003m. Sailing. www.paralympic.org (accessed November 3, 2003).

International Paralympic Committee. 2003n. Shooting. www.paralympic.org (accessed November 6, 2003).

International Paralympic Committee. 2003o. Swimming. www.paralympic.org (accessed November 4, 2003).

International Paralympic Committee. 2003p. Table tennis. www.paralympic.org (accessed November 4, 2003).

International Paralympic Committee. 2003q. Volleyball. www.paralympic.org (accessed November 3, 2003).

International Paralympic Committee. 2003r. Wheelchair basketball. www.paralympic.org (accessed November 2, 2003).

International Paralympic Committee. 2003s. Wheelchair fencing. www.paralympic.org (accessed November 6, 2003).

International Paralympic Committee. 2003t. Wheelchair rugby. www.paralympic.org (accessed November 3, 2003).

International Paralympic Committee. 2003u. Wheelchair tennis. www.paralympic.org (accessed November 3, 2003).

International Paralympic Committee Constitution. 1991. *IPC Newsletter,* Spring.

International Sports Organization for the Disabled (ISOD). n.d. *A brief presentation of ISOD.* Pamphlet available from ISOD.

Jackson, R.W., and Davis, G.M. 1983. The value of sports and recreation for the physically disabled. *Orthopedic Clinics of North America* 14 (2): 301-315.

Jackson, R.W., and Frederickson, A. 1979. Sports for the physically disabled: The 1976 Olympiad (Toronto). *American Journal of Sports Medicine* 7: 293-296.

Jackson, R., and Schmader, S.W. 1990. *Special events: Inside and out.* Champaign, IL: Sagamore.

Jochheim, K.A., and Strohkendl, H. 1973. Value of particular sports of the wheelchair-disabled in maintaining health of the paraplegic. *Paraplegia* 11: 173-178.

Johansson, J.O., and DePauw, K.P. 1991. Sport socialization of Swedish disabled athletes. Paper presented at 1991 ISAPA, Miami.

Johnson, R.E., Sundheim, R., and Santos, J. 1989. An outcome study of Special Olympics training techniques on athletes in track and field. *Palaestra* 5: 9-11, 62.

Jones, J. 1988. *Training guide to cerebral palsy sports.* 3rd ed. Champaign, IL: Human Kinetics.

Jones, J., ed. 1990. Focus on training. *Palaestra* 6 (4): 57-58.

Jones, J., ed. 1991. Focus on training. *Palaestra* 7 (4): 56-57.

Jones, J., ed. 1992. Focus on training. *Palaestra* 8 (1): 60-61.

Joukowsky, A.A.W., and Rothstein, L. 2002. *Raising the bar: New horizons in disability sport.* New York: Umbrage Editions.

Karwas, M.R., and DePauw, K.P. 1990. Parallels between the women's and disabled sport movements. *Abstracts of research papers,* 1990 AAHPERD convention. Reston, VA: American Alliance for Health, Physical Education, Recreation and Dance.

Kegel, B. 1985. Physical fitness. Sports and recreation for those with lower limb amputation or impairment. *Journal of Rehabilitation Research and Development* (Clin. Suppl. 1): 1-125.

Kegel, B., Burgess, E.M., Starr, T.W., and Daley, W.K. 1981. Effects of isometric muscle training on residual limb volume, strength, and gait of below-knee amputees. *Physical Therapy* 61: 1419-1426.

Kelly, J., and Frieden, L. 1989. *Go for it: A book on sport and recreation for persons with disabilities.* Orlando, FL: Jovanovich.

Kennedy, M.J. 1980. Sport role socialization and attitudes toward physical activity of wheelchair athletes. Unpublished master's thesis, University of Oregon, Eugene.

Kennedy, S.O. 1988. Flexibility training for wheelchair athletes. *Sports 'n Spokes* 13: 43-46.

Kenyon, G., and McPherson, B. 1973. Becoming involved in physical activity and sport: A process of socialization. In *Physical activity: Human growth and development,* ed. G.L. Rarick (pp. 303-332). New York: Academic Press.

Kirschbaum, J.B., Axelson, P.W., Longmuir, P.E., Mispagel, K.M., Stein, J.A., and Yamada, D.A. 2001. *Designing sidewalks and trails for access part II of II: Best practices design guide.* Washington, DC: Federal Highway Administration.

Knaus, R.L. 1987. Physiological and psychological benefits of exercise for athletes with disabilities: An interview with George Murray. *Journal of Osteopathic Sports Medicine* 4 (1): 7-9.

Knoppers, A. 1987. Gender and the coaching profession. *Quest* 39: 9-22.

Knowlton, R.G., Fitzgerald, P.L., and Sedlock, D.A. 1981. Mechanical efficiency of wheelchair-dependent women during wheelchair ergometry. *Canadian Journal of Applied Sport Sciences* 6: 187-190.

Kobberling, G., Jankowski, L.W., and Leger, L. 1989. Energy cost of locomotion in blind athletes. *Adapted Physical Activity Quarterly* 6: 58-67.

Koivumaki, K. 1987. Sports and physical activities for special groups. In *Sports and physical education in Finland.* Helsinki: Finnish Society for Research in Sport and Physical Education.

Kowalski, E., and McCann, H. 1991. The Victory Games: Milestone on the road to Barcelona. *Palaestra* 8 (1): 24-29.

Kristen, L., Patriksson, G., and Fridlund, B. 2003. Benefits of sport activities for disabled children and youth. In *Proceedings, 13th international symposium in adapted physical activity,* July 3-7, 2001, ed. M. Dinold, G. Gerber, and T. Reinelt (pp. 394-398). Vienna: Manz Verlag Schleicher.

Kruimer, A., Hoeberigs, J.H., and Vorteveld, H. 1985. Classification system for wheelchair basketball. *Workshop on sport for disabled (proceedings)* (pp. 111-117). The Netherlands: Amersfoot.

Labanowich, S. 1978. Psychology of wheelchair sports. *Therapeutic Recreation Journal* 12: 11-17.

Labanowich, S. 1988. A case for the integration of the disabled into the Olympic Games. *Adapted Physical Activity Quarterly* 5: 264-272.

Labanowich, S., Karman, P., Veal, L.E., and Wiley, B.D. 1984. Principles and foundations for the organization of wheelchair sports. *Sports 'n Spokes* 2: 26-32.

Lakomy, H.K.A., Campbell, I., and Williams, C. 1987. Treadmill performance and selected physiological characteristics of wheelchair athletes. *British Journal of Sports Medicine* 21: 130-133.

LaMere, T., and Labanowich, S. 1984a. The history of sport wheelchairs: 1. Background of wheelchair basketball. *Sports 'n Spokes* 2: 6-11.

LaMere, T., and Labanowich, S. 1984b. The history of sport wheelchairs: 2. The racing wheelchair. *Sports 'n Spokes* 2: 12-16.

Landry, F. 1992. Olympism, Olympics, Paralympism, Paralympics: Converging or diverging notions and courses on the eve of the third millennium? Paper presented at the 1st Paralympic Congress, August 31, 1992, Barcelona.

Lenskyj, H. 1991. *Women, sport and physical activity: Research and bibliography.* Ottawa, ON: Minister of Supply and Services Canada.

Leonard, J. 1980. *A sociological perspective of sport.* Minneapolis: Burgess.

Lewallen, R., Quanbury, A.O., Ross, K., and Letts, R.M. 1985. A biomechanical study of normal and amputee gait. In *Biomechanics IX-A,* ed. D.A. Winter, R.W. Norman, R.P. Wells, K.C. Hayes, and A.E. Patla (pp. 587-593). Champaign, IL: Human Kinetics.

Lewis, S., Higam, L., and Cherry, D. 1985. Development of an exercise program to improve the static and dynamic balance of profoundly hearing impaired children. *American Annals of the Deaf* 4 (130): 278-283.

Lewko, J. 1979. Significant others and sport socialization of the handicapped child. In *Psychological perspectives in youth sports,* ed. F. Smoll and R. Smith (pp. 249-277). New York: Wiley.

Lienert, C., Malone, L., and Yilla, A. 2003. Attitudes towards disability sport: Results of a study using the disability sport survey. In *14th international symposium in adapted physical activity, abstracts* (p. 83). August 4-7, 2003, Seoul.

Lilly, M.S. 1983. Divestiture in special education: An alternative model for resource and support services. Unpublished manuscript.

Lindstrom, H. 1984. Sports for disabled: Alive and well. *Rehabilitation World* 8: 12-16.

Lindstrom, H. 1985. An integrated classification system. *Palaestra* 2 (1): 47-49.

Lindstrom, H. 1986. Sports classification for locomotor disabilities: Integrated versus diagnostic systems. In *Sport and disabled athletes,* ed. C. Sherrill (pp. 131-136). Champaign, IL: Human Kinetics.

Lindstrom, H. 1990. The dramatic birth of a new international body for the disabled. *Palaestra* 6: 12-15.

Linton, S. 1998. *Claiming disability: Knowledge and identity.* New York: NYU Press.

Lipton, B.H. 1970. Role of wheelchair sports in rehabilitation. *International Rehabilitation Review* 21 (2): 25-27.

Lockette, K.F., and A.M. Keys. 1994. *Conditioning with physical disabilities.* Champaign, IL: Human Kinetics.

Longmuir, P.E., and Axelson, P. 1996. Assistive technology for recreation. In *Evaluating, selecting, and using appropriate assistive technology,* ed. J.C. Galvin and M.J. Scherer (pp. 162-197). Gaithersburg, MD: Aspen.

Longmuir, P., and Axelson, P. 2002. *Universal Trail Assessment Process training guide: Assessing outdoor paths, access routes, and trails to collect access, mapping, and maintenance information.* Minden, NV: PAX Press.

Lorinez, N. 2001. The classification of the elite athlete in disability sport—an athlete's "holistic" perspective. In *New horizons in sports for athletes with a disability, proceedings of the international Vista '99 conference,* Cologne, Germany, August 28-September 1, 1999, ed. G. Doll-Tepper, M. Kroner, and W. Sonnenschein (pp. 303-317). London: Meyer & Meyer Sport.

Lugo, A., Sherrill, C., and Pizarro, A. 1992. Use of a sport socialization inventory with cerebral palsied youth. *Perception and Motor Skills* 74: 203-208.

Lundberg, A. 1980. Wheelchair driving evaluation of a new training outfit. *Scandinavian Journal of Rehabilitation Medicine* 12: 67-72.

Lussier, L., Knight, J., Bell, G., Lohmann, T., and Morris, A.F. 1983. Body composition in two elite female wheelchair athletes. *Paraplegia* 21: 16-22.

Maas, K., and Hasbrook, C.A. 2001. Media promotion of the paradigm citizen/golfer: An analysis of golf magazines' representations of disability, gender, and age. *Sociology of Sport Journal* 18: 21-36.

MacGowan, H.E. 1983. The kinematic analysis of the walking gait of sighted and congenitally blind and sighted children. Abstract in *Dissertation Abstracts International* 44: 703a.

Madorsky, J.B., and Curtis, K.A. 1984. Wheelchair sports medicine. *American Journal of Sports Medicine* 12: 128-132.

Madorsky, J.B., and Kiley, D.P. 1984. Wheelchair mountaineering. *Archives of Physical Medicine and Rehabilitation* 65: 490-492.

Madorsky, J.B., and Madorsky, A. 1983. Wheelchair racing: An important modality in acute rehabilitation after paraplegia. *Archives of Physical Medicine and Rehabilitation* 64: 186-187.

Mangus, B. 1987. Sports injuries, the disabled athlete, and the athletic trainer. *Athletic Training* 22 (7): 305-308.

Martinez, R. 1991. Catastrophes at sporting events. *Physician and Sportsmedicine* 19 (11): 40, 43-44.

Mascagni, K. 1996. Paola Fantato: Sports as a means of social integration. *Olympic Review* 26: 75.

Mastenbroek, A.C. 1979. Delta and net muscular efficiency in wheelchair athletes during steady rate exercise in two types of wheelchairs. Unpublished master's thesis, University of Oregon, Eugene.

Mastro, J.V., Canabal, M., and French, R. 1986. Mood profiles of visually impaired and sighted beep baseball players. *Abstracts of research papers,* 1986 AAHPERD convention. Reston, VA: American Alliance for Health, Physical Education, Recreation and Dance.

Mastro, J.V., and French, R. 1986. Sport anxiety and elite blind athletes. In *Sport and disabled athletes,* ed. C. Sherrill (pp. 203-208). Champaign, IL: Human Kinetics.

Mastro, J.V., French, R., Henschen, K., and Horvat, M. 1985. Use of the State-Trait anxiety inventory for visually impaired athletes. *Perceptual and Motor Skills* 61: 775-778.

Mastro, J.V., French, R., Henschen, K., and Horvat, M. 1986. Selected psychological characteristics of blind golfers and their coaches. *American Corrective Therapy Journal* 40: 111-114.

Mastro, J.V., Hall, M.M., and Canabal, M.Y. 1988. Cultural and attitudinal similarities: Female and disabled individuals in sport and athletics. *Journal of Physical Education, Recreation and Dance* 59: 80-83.

Mastro, J.V., Sherrill, C., Gench, B., and French, R. 1987. Psychological characteristics of elite visually impaired athletes: The iceberg profile. *Journal of Sport Behavior* 10: 39-46.

Mayberry, R.P. 1978. The mystique of the horse is strong medicine: Riding as therapeutic recreation. *Rehabilitation Literature* 39: 192-196.

McCann, C.B. 1979. Wheelchair medical classification system. *Proceedings of the first international conference on sport and training of the physically disabled athlete* (pp. 25-35). University of Alberta, Edmonton.

McCann, C.B. 1980. Medical classification: Art, science, or instinct? *Sports 'n Spokes* 5: 12-14.

McCann, C.B. 1981. Does the track athlete need medical classification? A possible effect of wheelchair design. *Sports 'n Spokes* 7: 22-24.

McCann, C.B. 1984. Classification of the locomotor disabled for competitive sports: Theory and practice. *International Journal of Sports Medicine* (Suppl. 5): 167-170.

McCann, C.B. 1987. The structure and future of sport for the disabled: The Arnhem seminar. *Palaestra* 3: 9-40.

McCormick, D. 1985. Injuries in handicapped alpine ski racers. *Physician and Sportsmedicine* 13: 93-97.

McCrae, D. 2001. The integration and inclusion of world class disability sports programs. In *New horizons in sports for athletes with a disability, proceedings of the international Vista '99 conference,* Cologne, Germany, August 28-September 1, 1999, ed. G. Doll-Tepper, M. Kroner, and W. Sonnenschein (pp. 499-528). London: Meyer & Meyer Sport.

McCubbin, J.A., and Shasby, G.B. 1985. Effects of isokinetic exercise on adolescents with cerebral palsy. *Adapted Physical Activity Quarterly* 2: 56-64.

McLaurin, C.A., and Axelson, P. 1990. Wheelchair standards: An overview. *Journal of Rehabilitation Research and Development* 2: 100-103.

McPherson, B.D., Curtis, J.E., and Loy, J.W. 1989. *The social significance of sport.* Champaign, IL: Human Kinetics.

Merklinger, A. 1991. Committee on integration of athletes with a disability. *International Paralympic Committee Newsletter* 2: 8-9.

Miles, D.S., Sawka, M.N., Wilde, S.W., Durbin, R.J., and Gotshall, R.W. 1982. Pulmonary function changes in wheelchair athletes subsequent to exercise training. *Ergonomics* 25: 239-246.

Miller, D.I. 1981. Biomechanical considerations in lower extremity amputee running and sports performance. *Australian Journal of Sport Medicine* 13 (3): 55-87.

Miller, P. 1995. *Fitness programming and physical disability.* Champaign, IL: Human Kinetics.

Moeller, R. 2001. Perspectives of marketing and sponsoring in disability sports: A different approach. In *New horizons in sports for athletes with a disability, proceedings of the international Vista '99 conference,* Cologne, Germany, August 28-September 1, 1999, ed. G. Doll-Tepper, M. Kroner, and W. Sonnenschein (pp. 863-873). London: Meyer & Meyer Sport.

Monnazzi, G. 1982. Paraplegics and sports: A psychological survey. *International Journal of Sports Psychology* 13: 85-95.

Morris, A.F. 1984. A philosophy of sports and recreation at a comprehensive rehabilitation center. *Rehabilitation World* 8: 30-31, 60-61.

Morris, A.F. 1986. A case study of a female ultramarathon wheelchair road racer. *Paraplegia* 24: 260-264.

Morris, J. 1992. Personal and political: A feminist perspective on researching physical disability. *Disability, Handicap, & Society* 7: 157-166.

Munson, A.L., and Comodeca, J.A. 1993. The act of inclusion. *Athletic Management* 5 (4): 14-17.

Murphy-Howe, R., and Charboneau, B. 1987. *Therapeutic recreation intervention: An ecological perspective.* Englewood Cliffs, NJ: Prentice Hall.

Mustain, K. 2001. Exercise as a complementary therapy for breast cancer [abstract]. *North American Society for the Sociology of Sport Conference abstracts* (p. 33). October 31-November 3, 2001, San Antonio, TX.

Myers, K. 1991. Pushing a wheelchair . . . fast! *Sports 'n Spokes* 16: 51-54.

Nash, S. 2002. Youth force. *Sports 'n Spokes* 28 (6): 54-57.

National Center on Physical Activity and Disability (NCPAD). www.ncpad.org.

National Disability Sports Alliance (NDSA). www.ndsaonline.org.

National Wheelchair Basketball Association (NWBA). www.nwba.org.

Nesbitt, J.A., ed. 1986. *The international directory of recreation-oriented assistive diver's sources.* Marina del Rey, CA: Lifeboat Press.

Nilsen, R., Nygaard, P., and Bjorholt, P.G. 1985. Complications that may occur in those with spinal cord injuries who participate in sport. *Paraplegia* 23: 52-58.

Nixon, H. 1988. Getting over the worry hurdle: Parental encouragement and sports involvement of visually impaired children and youths. *Adapted Physical Activity Quarterly* 5 (1): 29-43.

Nixon, H.L. 1989. Integration of disabled people in mainstream sports: Case study of a partially sighted child. *Adapted Physical Activity Quarterly* 6 (1): 17-31.

Nugent, T.J. 1964. Let's look beyond. *Recreation in Treatment Centers* 3: 3-42.

Nunn, C. 1991. *Coaching amputee athletes.* Canberra: Australian Sports Commission.

Ogilvie, B.C. 1985. Sports psychologists and the disabled athlete. *Palaestra* 4 (1): 36-40, 43.

O'Leary, H. 1987. *Bold tracks: Skiing for the disabled.* Evergreen, CO: Cordillera Press.

Orr, R. 1979. Sport, myth and the handicapped athlete. *Journal of Physical Education, Recreation and Dance* 50: 33-34.

Owen, E. 1982. *Playing and coaching wheelchair basketball.* Urbana, IL: University of Illinois Press.

Pachner, J.L. 1993-1994. *Products to assist the disabled sportsman.* Laguna Niguel, CA: Author.

Paciorek, M.J. 1993. Technology only a part of the story as world records fall. *Palaestra* 9: 14-19.

Paciorek, M.J., and Jones, J.A. 1989. *Sports and recreation for the disabled: A resource handbook.* Indianapolis: Benchmark Press.

Paciorek, M.J., and Jones, J.A. 1994. *Sports and recreation for the disabled.* 2nd ed. Carmel, IN: Cooper.

Pacioreck, M.J., and Jones, J.A. 2001. *Disability sport and recreation resources.* Traverse City, MI: Cooper.

Paralympian. 2000. IOC-IPC cooperation agreement signed. www.paralympic.org/paralympian/20004/2000405.htm (accessed May 23, 2002).

Paralympic Games. 2001, August 24. Paralympic Summer Games Sydney 2000. www.paralympic.org/games/2000/01 (accessed July 2003).

Pardine, P., Napoli, A., and Eustace, A. 1985. Personality profiles of world-class disabled athletes. *Abstracts of research papers,* 1985 AAHPERD convention. Reston, VA: American Alliance for Health, Physical Education, Recreation and Dance.

Park, R. 1928. Human migration and the marginal man. *American Journal of Sociology* 33: 881-893.

Parks, J.B., and Quarterman, J. (2003). *Contemporary sport management.* 2nd ed. Champaign, IL: Human Kinetics.

Parks, W. 1986. A model program: The journal wheelchair sports camp program. *Palaestra* 3 (2): 16-19.

Patrick, D.L. 1997. Rethinking prevention for people with disabilities, part I: A conceptual model for promoting health. *American Journal of Health Promotion* 11: 257-260.

Patrick, G.D. 1986. The effects of wheelchair competition on self-concept and acceptance of disability in novice athletes. *Therapeutic Recreation Journal* 4 (20): 61-71.

Patterson, T.S. 2000. The effects of a therapeutic horseback riding experience on selected behavioral and psychological factors on ambulatory adults diagnosed with multiple sclerosis. Unpublished master's thesis, Bowling Green State University, Bowling Green, OH.

Pearce, K., and Kane, M.J. 2001. Disability, sport and media. In *2001 North American Society for the Sociology of Sport, 22nd conference, Marginality, Power and Sport, abstracts* (p. 60). October 31-November 3, 2001, San Antonio, TX.

Physical activity and women with disabilities: A national survey. n.d. Ottawa, ON: Fitness Canada.

Pitetti, K.H. 1993. Introduction. Exercise capacities and adaptations of people with chronic disabilities: Current research, future directions, and widespread applicability. *Medicine and Science in Sports and Exercise* 25 (4): 421-422.

Pitetti, K.H., Jackson, J.A., Stubbs, N.B., Campbell, K.D., and Battar, S.S. 1989. Fitness levels of adult Special Olympic participants. *Adapted Physical Activity Quarterly* 6: 354-370.

Platt, L. 2001. Medical and orthopaedic conditions in Special Olympic athletes. *Journal of Athletic Training* 36 (1): 74-80.

Pope, C.J., McGrain, P., and Arnhold, R.W. 1986. Running gait of the blind: A kinematic analysis. In *Sport and disabled athletes,* ed. C. Sherrill (pp. 173-179). Champaign, IL: Human Kinetics.

Pope, C.J., Sherrill, C., Wilkerson, J., and Pyfer, J. 1993. Biomechanical variables in sprint running of athletes with cerebral palsy. *Adapted Physical Activity Quarterly* 10: 226-254.

Principles and philosophy. www.specialolympics.org (accessed July 1, 2004).

Professional Ski Instructors of America. 1997. *Adaptive manual.* Lakewood, CO: Author.

Pyfer, J.L. 1986. Early research concerns in adapted physical education. *Adapted Physical Activity Quarterly* 3: 95-103.

Rarick, G.L., Dobbins, D.A., and Broadhead, G.D. 1976. *The motor domain and its correlates in educationally handicapped children.* Englewood Cliffs, NJ: Prentice Hall.

Renwick, R., and Friefield, S. 1996. Quality of life and rehabilitation. In *Quality of life in health promotion and rehabilitation,* ed. R. Renwick, I. Brown, and M. Nagler. Newbury Park, CA: Sage.

Rich, S. 1990. Factors influencing the learning process. In *Adapted physical education and sport,* ed. J. Winnick (pp. 121-130). Champaign, IL: Human Kinetics.

Richardson, D.B. 1986. Movement purpose values among wheelchair athletes. *Abstracts of research papers,* 1986 AAHPERD convention. Reston, VA: American Alliance of Health, Physical Education, Recreation and Dance.

Richter, K.J., Adams-Mushett, C., Ferrara, M.S., and McCann, B.C. 1992. Integrated swimming classification: A faulted system. *Adapted Physical Activity Quarterly* 9 (1): 5-13.

Ridgeway, M., Pope, C., and Wilkerson, J. 1988. A kinematic analysis of 800-meter wheelchair racing techniques. *Adapted Physical Activity Quarterly* 5: 96-107.

Riding, M. 2001. Doping—a Paralympic perspective. In *New horizons in sports for athletes with a disability, proceedings of the international Vista '99 conference,* Cologne, Germany, August 28-September 1, 1999, ed. G. Doll-Tepper, M. Kroner, and W. Sonnenschein (pp. 273-277). London: Meyer & Meyer Sport.

Riggen, K., and Ulrich, D. 1993. The effects of sport participation on individuals with mental retardation. *Adapted Physical Activity Quarterly* 10 (1): 42-51.

Rimmer, J.H. 1994. *Fitness and rehabilitation programs for special populations.* Dubuque, IA: Wm. C. Brown.

Rimmer, J.H. 1999. Health promotion for people with disabilities: The emerging paradigm shift from disability prevention to prevention of secondary conditions. *Physical Therapy* 79: 495-502.

Rimmer, J.H., Braddock, D., and Pitetti, K.H. 1996. Research on physical activity and disability: An emerging national priority. *Medicine and Science in Sports and Exercise* 28: 1366-1372.

Rimmer, J.H., and Kelly, L.E. 1991. Effects of a resistance training program on adults with mental retardation. *Adapted Physical Activity Quarterly* 8 (2): 146-153.

Road racing training. 1986, Spring. *National Wheelchair Athletic Association Newsletter,* 18-19.

Roeder, L.K., and Aufsesser, P.M. 1986. Selected attentional and interpersonal characteristics of wheelchair athletes. *Palaestra* 2: 28-32.

Roper, P.A., and Silver, C. 1989. Regular track competition for athletes with mental retardation. *Palaestra* 5: 14-16, 42-43, 58-59.

Roswal, G.M. 1988. Coaches' training the Special Olympics way. *Palaestra* 5: 36-37, 41.

Roswell, G., Jacobs, D., and Horvat, M. 1986. Psychological make-up and self-concept of the junior wheelchair athlete. *NCPERH Newsletter* 15: 6.

Rothschild, C.S. 1968. Prejudice against the disabled and the means to combat it. In *Social and psychological aspects of disability: A handbook for practitioners,* ed. J. Stebbins (pp. 261-267). Baltimore: University Park Press.

Ryser, D.K., Erickson, R.P., and Calahan, T. 1988. Isometric and isokinetic hip abductor strength in persons with above-knee amputations. *Archives of Physical Medicine and Rehabilitation* 10 (69): 840-845.

Sage, G.H. 1987. Pursuit of knowledge in sociology of sport: Issues and prospects. *Quest* 39: 255-281.

Salt Lake 2002 Organizing Committee. 2002. *Salt Lake 2002 Paralympic media guide.* Salt Lake City: Author.

Sanderson, D.J., and Sommer, H.J. 1985. Kinematic features of wheelchair propulsion. *Journal of Biomechanics* 18: 423-429.

Schantz, O. 2003. Spectators at the Sydney 2000 Paralympics, a field study. In *14th international symposium in adapted physical activity, abstracts* (pp. 84-85). August 4-7, 2003, Seoul.

Schantz, O., and Gilbert, K. 1997. Misconstrued ideals: Media coverage of the 1996 Atlanta Paralympic Games—an analysis of German and French newspapers. In *Proceedings 11th international symposium in adapted physical activity, Active Living—Differently,* May 3-7, 1997, ed. D. Drouin, C. Lepine, and C. Simard (pp. 248-256). Quebec, PQ: Institute de readaptation en deficience physique de Quebec.

Schuman, S. 1979. Wheelchair frame modification. *Sports 'n Spokes* 4: 5-6.

Scruton, S. 1998. *Stoke Mandeville: Road to the Paralympics.* Aylesbury, England: Peterhouse Press.

Seaman, J.A. 1999. Physical activity and fitness for persons with disabilities. *President's Council on Physical Fitness and Sports Research Digest* 3 (9).

Shapiro, J. 1993. *No pity: People with disabilities forging a new civil rights movement.* New York: Random House.

Shephard, R.J. 1990. *Fitness in special populations.* Champaign, IL: Human Kinetics.

Sherrill, C. 1986. Social and psychological dimensions of sports for disabled athletes. In *Sport and disabled athletes,* ed. C. Sherrill (pp. 21-33). Champaign, IL: Human Kinetics.

Sherrill, C. 1990. Psychosocial status of disabled athletes. In *Problems in motor control,* ed. G. Reid (pp. 339-364). Amsterdam: North-Holland.

Sherrill, C. 1993. Paralympics 1992: Excellence and challenge. *Palaestra* 9: 25-42.

Sherrill, C. 1997. Disability, identity and involvement in sport and exercise. In *The physical self: From motivation to well-being,* ed. K.R. Fox (pp. 257-286). Champaign, IL: Human Kinetics.

Sherrill, C., ed. 2001a. *Adapted physical activity, recreation and sport: Cross-disciplinary and lifespan.* 6th ed. St. Louis: McGraw-Hill.

Sherrill, C. 2001b. Gender concerns in integration, development and recruitment of female athletes with a disability. In *New horizons in sport for athletes with a disability, proceedings of the international Vista '99 conference,* Cologne, Germany, August 28-September 1, 1999, ed. G. Doll-Tepper, M. Kroner, and W. Sonnenschein (pp. 631-642). Oxford, England: Meyer & Meyer Sport.

Sherrill, C., Adams-Mushett, C., and Jones, J. 1986. Classification and other issues in sports for blind, cerebral palsied, les autres, and amputee athletes. In *Sport and disabled athletes,* ed. C. Sherrill (pp. 113-130). Champaign, IL: Human Kinetics.

Sherrill, C., and DePauw, K.P. 1997. History of adapted physical activity and education. In *History of exercise and sport science,* ed. J.D. Massengale and R.A. Swanson (pp. 39-108). Champaign, IL: Human Kinetics.

Sherrill, C., Pope, C., and Arnhold, R. 1986. Sport socialization of blind athletes. *Journal of Visual Impairment and Blindness* 80 (5): 740-744.

Sherrill, C., and Rainbolt, W.J. 1986. Sociological perspectives of cerebral palsy sports. *Palaestra* 4 (2): 21-26, 50.

Sherrill, C., and Rainbolt, W.J. 1987. Self-actualization profiles and able-bodied and cerebral palsied female athletes. *Abstracts of research papers.* 1987 AAHPERD convention. Reston, VA: American Alliance for Health, Physical Education, Recreation and Dance.

Sherrill, C., Rainbolt, W.J., Montelione, T., and Pope, C. 1986. Sport socialization of blind and cerebral palsied elite athletes. In *Sport and disabled athletes,* ed. C. Sherrill (pp. 189-196). Champaign, IL: Human Kinetics.

Shogan, D. 1998. The social construction of disability: The impact of statistics and technology. *Adapted Physical Activity Quarterly* 15: 269-277.

Siekman, A., Chesney, D., and Axelson, P. 1999. Design of a universal canoe seating system. In *Proceedings of the RESNA 1999 annual conference,* ed. S. Sprigle (pp. 266-268). Arlington, VA: RESNA Press.

Skrotsky, K. 1983. Gait analysis in cerebral palsied and nonhandicapped children. *Archives of Physical Medicine and Rehabilitation* 64: 291-295.

Smith, A.W. 1990. A biomechanical analysis of amputee athlete gait. *International Journal of Sport Biomechanics* 6: 262-282.

Smith, A.W., Smith, L., Fraser, C., and Grebert, J. 1988. Biomechanical analyses of amputee athlete gait. In *The athlete maximising participation and minimising risk,* ed. M. Torode (pp. 123-132). Sydney: Cumberland College of Health Sciences, Australian Sports Federation.

Snow, R. 2001. *Pushing forward: A memoir of motivation.* Dubuque, IA: Kendall/ Hunt.

Snyder, E.E. 1984. Sport involvement for the handicapped: Some analytical and sensitizing concepts. *ARENA Review* 8: 16-26.

Soeder, M. 1995. Empowerment, rehabilitation or freak show: Sports for the disabled and the socialization of young people with disabilities. In *Quality of life through adapted physical activity and sport—conference proceedings,* ed. I. Morisbak (pp. 46-59). Omslag, The Netherlands: BB Grafisk.

Songster, T. 1986. The Special Olympics sport program: An international sport program for mentally retarded athletes. In *Sport and disabled athletes,* ed. C. Sherrill (pp. 73-80). Champaign, IL: Human Kinetics.

South Australian Sport and Recreation Association of People with Integration Difficulties (SASRAPID). 2004. www.sasrapid.com.au/philosophy/philosophy.

Special Olympics, Inc. n.d.a. Aquatics. www.specialolympics.org/Special+Olym pics+Public+Website/English/Coach/Sports_Offered/Aquatics.htm (accessed November 4, 2003).

Special Olympics, Inc. n.d.b. Athletics. www.specialolympics.org/Special+Olym pics+Public+Website/English/Coach/Sports_Offered/Athletics.htm (accessed November 4, 2003).

Special Olympics, Inc. n.d.c. Badminton. www.specialolympics.org/Special+Olym pics+Public+Website/English/Coach/Sports_Offered/Badminton.htm (accessed November 3, 2003).

Special Olympics, Inc. n.d.d. Basketball. www.specialolympics.org/Special+Olym pics+Public+Website/English/Coach/Sports_Offered/Basketball.htm (accessed November 6, 2003).

Special Olympics, Inc. n.d.e. Bocce. www.specialolympics.org/Special+Olympics+ Public+Website/English/Coach/Sports_Offered/Bocce.htm (accessed November 2, 2003).

Special Olympics, Inc. n.d.f. Bowling. www.specialolympics.org/Special+Olym pics+Public+Website/English/Coach/Sports_Offered/Bowling.htm (accessed November 4, 2003).

Special Olympics, Inc. n.d.g. Cross country skiing. www.specialolympics.org/ Special+Olympics+Public+Website/English/Coach/Sports_Offered/ Cross+Country+Skiing.htm (accessed November 3, 2003).

Special Olympics, Inc. n.d.h. Cycling. www.specialolympics.org/Special+Olym pics+Public+Website/English/Coach/Sports_Offered/Cycling.htm (accessed November 1, 2003).

Special Olympics, Inc. n.d.i. Divisioning. www.specialolympics.org/Special+O lympics+Public+Website/English/Coach/Divisioning/default.htm (accessed November 9, 2003).

Special Olympics, Inc. n.d.j. Equestrian. www.specialolympics.org/Special+Olym pics+Public+Website/English/Coach/Sports_Offered/Equestrian.htm (accessed November 1, 2003).

Special Olympics, Inc. n.d.k. Figure skating. www.specialolympics.org/Special+ Olympics+Public+Website/English/Coach/Sports_Offered/Figure+Skating.htm (accessed November 2, 2003).

Special Olympics, Inc. n.d.l. Floor hockey. www.specialolympics.org/Special+ Olympics+Public+Website/English/Coach/Sports_Offered/Floor+Hockey.htm (accessed November 4, 2003).

Special Olympics, Inc. n.d.m. Football. www.specialolympics.org/Special+Olym pics+Public+Website/English/Coach/Sports_Offered/Football.htm (accessed November 5, 2003).

Special Olympics, Inc. n.d.n. Golf. www.specialolympics.org/Special+Olympics+ Public+Website/English/Coach/Sports_Offered/Golf.htm (accessed November 7, 2003).

Special Olympics, Inc. n.d.o. Gymnastics. www.specialolympics.org/Special+Olym pics+Public+Website/English/Coach/Sports_Offered/Gymnastics.htm (accessed November 7, 2003).

Special Olympics, Inc. n.d.p. Powerlifting. www.specialolympics.org/Special+Olym pics+Public+Website/English/Coach/Sports_Offered/Powerlifting.htm (accessed November 8, 2003).

Special Olympics, Inc. n.d.q. Rollerskating. www.specialolympics.org/Special+ Olympics+Public+Website/English/Coach/Sports_Offered/Rollerskating.htm (accessed November 3, 2003).

Special Olympics, Inc. n.d.r. Sailing. www.specialolympics.org/Special+Olym pics+Public+Website/English/Coach/Sports_Offered/Sailing.htm (accessed November 5, 2003).

Special Olympics, Inc. n.d.s. Snowboarding. www.specialolympics.org/Special+ Olympics+Public+Website/English/Coach/Sports_Offered/Snowboarding.htm (accessed November 4, 2003).

Special Olympics, Inc. n.d.t. Snowshoeing. www.specialolympics.org/Special+ Olympics+Public+Website/English/Coach/Sports_Offered/Snowshoeing.htm (accessed November 4, 2003).

Special Olympics, Inc. n.d.u. Softball. www.specialolympics.org/Special+Olym pics+Public+Website/English/Coach/Sports_Offered/Softball.htm (accessed November 4, 2003).

Special Olympics, Inc. n.d.v. Speed skating. www.specialolympics.org/Special+ Olympics+Public+Website/English/Coach/Sports_Offered/Speed+Skating.htm (accessed November 3, 2003).

Special Olympics, Inc. n.d.w. Table tennis. www.specialolympics.org/Special+ Olympics+Public+Website/English/Coach/Sports_Offered/Table+Tennis.htm (accessed November 2, 2003).

Special Olympics, Inc. n.d.x. Team handball. www.specialolympics.org/Special+ Olympics+Public+Website/English/Coach/Sports_Offered/Team+Handball.htm (accessed November 4, 2003).

Special Olympics, Inc. n.d.y. Tennis. www.specialolympics.org/Special+Olym pics+Public+Website/English/Coach/Sports_Offered/Tennis.htm (accessed November 5, 2003).

Special Olympics, Inc. n.d.z. Volleyball. www.specialolympics.org/Special+Olym pics+Public+Website/English/Coach/Sports_Offered/Volleyball.htm (accessed November 4, 2003).

Spoke-tacular. 2003, March. *Sports 'n Spokes* 29 (2).

Squires, J. 1987. Classification: Can the best means to the fairest end be found? *Palaestra* 3 (4): 45-48.

Steadward, R.D. 1980. Analysis of wheelchair sport events. In *Proceedings of the first international medical congress on sports for the disabled,* ed. H. Natvig (pp. 184-192). Oslo, Norway: Royal Ministry of Church and Education, State Office for Youth and Sports.

Steadward, R.D. 1987. Advance in knowledge related to disabled athletes. *CAHPER/ ACSEPL Journal* 5 (53): 36-38.

Steadward, R.D. 1990. International Paralympic Committee. *IFAPA Newsletter.* Berlin: International Federation of Adapted Physical Activity.

Steadward, R.D., Nelson, E.R., and Wheeler, G.D. 1994. *Vista '93—The outlook.* Edmonton, AB: Priority Printing.

Steadward, R.D., and Peterson, C. 1997. *Paralympics: Where heroes come.* Altona, MB: DW Friesens.

Steadward, R.D., and Walsh, C. 1986. Training and fitness programs for disabled athletes: Past, present and future. In *Sport and disabled athletes,* ed. C. Sherrill (pp. 3-19). Champaign, IL: Human Kinetics.

Steadward, R.D., Wheeler, G.D., and Watkinson, E.J., eds. 2003. *Adapted physical activity.* Edmonton, AB: University of Alberta Press.

Stein, J.U. 1983. Bridge over troubled waters—Research and recommendations for relevance. In *Adapted physical activity,* ed. R.L. Eason, T.L. Smith, and F. Caron (pp. 189-198). Champaign, IL: Human Kinetics.

Stein, J.U. 1986. International perspectives: Physical education and sport for participants with handicapping conditions. In *Sport and disabled athletes,* ed. C. Sherrill (pp. 51-64). Champaign, IL: Human Kinetics.

Stevens, T. 1998. Ted Stevens Olympic & Amateur Sports Act, USCA 2205 et seq.1998. http://home.earthlink.net/~albatrossyc/amateuract.html

Stewart, D.A. 1985. Silently succeeding: How to become a better coach of deaf athletes. *Coaching Review* 8: 30-33.

Stewart, D.A. 1987. Social factors influencing participation in sport for the deaf. *Palaestra* 4 (3): 22-28, 50.

Stewart, D.A. 1990. Global dimensions of World Games for the Deaf. *Palaestra* 6: 32-35, 43.

Stewart, D.A. 1991. *Deaf sport: The impact of sports within the Deaf community.* Washington, DC: Gallaudet University Press.

Stewart, D.A. 1993. Participating in deaf sport: Characteristics of deaf spectators. *Adapted Physical Activity Quarterly* 10: 146-156.

Stewart, D.A., and Ammons, D. 2001. Future directions of the Deaflympics. *Palaestra* 3: 45-49.

Stewart, D.A., McCarthy, D., and Robinson, J. 1988. Participation in deaf sport: Characteristics of deaf sport directors. *Adapted Physical Activity Quarterly* 5: 233-244.

Stewart, D.A., Robinson, J., and McCarthy, D. 1991. Participation in deaf sport: Characteristics of elite deaf athletes. *Adapted Physical Activity Quarterly* 8 (2): 136-145.

Stewart, N. 1981. The value of sport in the rehabilitation of the physically disabled. *Canadian Journal of Applied Sport Sciences* 6 (4): 166-167.

Stotts, K.M. 1985. Health maintenance: Paraplegic athletes and nonathletes. *Archives of Physical Medicine and Rehabilitation* 67: 109-114.

Strike, S.C., and Wells, J. 2003. A kinematic analysis of a trans tibial amputee in the take off of a vertical jump. In *Proceedings, 13th international symposium in adapted physical activity,* July 3-7, 2001, ed. M. Dinold, G. Gerber, and T. Reinelt (pp. 466-471). Vienna: Manz Verlag Schleicher.

Strohkendl, H. 1986. The new classification for wheelchair basketball. In *Sport and disabled athletes,* ed. C. Sherrill (pp. 101-112). Champaign, IL: Human Kinetics.

Strohkendl, H. 2001. Implications of sports classification systems for person with disabilities and consequences for science and research. In *New horizons in sports for athletes with a disability, proceedings of the international Vista '99 conference,* Cologne, Germany, August 28-September 1, 1999, ed. G. Doll-Tepper, M. Kroner, and W. Sonnenschein (pp. 281-301). London: Meyer & Meyer Sport.

Suggs, W. 2004. Varsity with an asterisk. *Chronicle of Higher Education,* February 13, A35-37.

Szyman, R. 1980. The effect of participation in wheelchair sports. Unpublished doctoral dissertation, University of Illinois at Urbana-Champaign.

Taylor, A.W., McDonnell, E., and Brassard, L. 1986. The effect of an arm ergometer training programme on wheelchair subjects. *Paraplegia* 24: 105-114.

Taylor, A.W., McDonnell, E., Royer, D., Loiselle, R., Luch, N., and Steadward, R. 1979. Skeletal muscle analysis of wheelchair athletes. *Paraplegia* 17: 456-460.

Theberge, N. 1985. Toward a feminist alternative to sport as a male perspective. *Quest* 37: 193-202.

Thiboutot, A., Smith, R.W., and Labanowich, S. 1992. Examining the concept of reverse integration: A response to Brasile's new perspective on integration. *Adapted Physical Activity Quarterly* 9: 283-292.

Thiboutot, T. 1986. Classification: Time for change. *Sports 'n Spokes* 11: 42-44.

Tiessen, J.A. 1997. *The triumph of the human spirit: The Atlanta paralympic experience.* Oakville, ON: Disability Today Publishing Group.

United States Olympic Committee. 1989. *USOC constitution and by-laws.* Colorado Springs, CO: Author.

United States Olympic Committee. 1993. *1993 United States Olympic Committee fact book.* Colorado Springs, CO: Author.

United States Olympic Committee constitution. 2001. www.olympic-usa.org (accessed May 23, 2002).

United we stand. 1988. *International Fund Sports Disabled.* Arnhem, The Netherlands: Author.

U.S. Architectural and Transportation Barriers Compliance Board. 2002. www.access-board.gov.

USCPAA. n.d. *United States Cerebral Palsy Athletic Association.* Kingston, RI: Author.

Valliant, P.M., Bezzubyk, I., Daley, L., and Asu, M.E. 1985. Psychological impact of sport on disabled athletes. *Psychological Reports* 3 (56): 923-929.

van Hal, L., Rarick, G.L., and Vermeer, A. 1984. Sport for the mentally handicapped. Haarlem, The Netherlands: Uitgeverij de Vrisesborch.

Vanlandewicjk, Y. 2003. Scientific support for elite athletes with a disability: A plea for international cooperation. Paper presented at the 2003 ISAPA, Seoul.

Vanlandewijck, Y., Spaepen, A., Daly, D., and Theisen, D. 2001. Understanding handrim wheelchair propulsion. In *New horizons in sports for athletes with a disability, proceedings of the international Vista '99 conference,* Cologne, Germany, August 28-September 1, 1999, ed. G. Doll-Tepper, M. Kroner, and W. Sonnenschein (pp. 205-221). London: Meyer & Meyer Sport.

Vermeer, A. 1986. *Sports for the disabled.* Haarlem, The Netherlands: Uitgeverij de Vrisesborch.

Vinton, D.A., Hawkins, D.E., Pantzer, B.D., and Farley, E.M. 1978. *Camping and environmental education for handicapped children and youth.* Washington, DC: Hawkins.

Von Selzam, H. 2001. Paralympic and Olympic games—separate or together? In *New horizons in sports for athletes with a disability, proceedings of the international Vista '99 conference,* Cologne, Germany, August 28-September 1, 1999, ed. G. Doll-Tepper, M. Kroner, and W. Sonnenschein (pp. 583-597). London: Meyer & Meyer Sport.

Wall, A.E. 1990. Fostering physical activity among Canadians with disabilities. *Journal of Physical Education, Recreation and Dance* 61: 52, 54, 56.

Walsh, C.M. 1986. The effect of pushing frequency on the kinematics of wheelchair sprinting. Unpublished master's thesis, University of Alberta.

Walsh, C.M., Holland, L.J., and Steadward, R.D. 1985. *Get fit: Aerobic exercises for the wheelchair user.* Edmonton, AB: University of Alberta (Research and Training Centre for the Physically Disabled).

Walsh, C.M., Marchiori, G.E., and Steadward, R.D. 1986. Effect of seat position on maximal linear velocity in wheelchair sprinting. *Canadian Journal of Applied Sport Sciences* 11: 186-190.

Wang, W., and DePauw, K.P. 1991. Early sport socialization of Chinese disabled athletes. Paper presented at 1991 International Symposium on Adapted Physical Activity, Miami.

Wantanabe, K.T., Cooper, R.A., Vosse, A.J., Baldini, F.D., and Robertson, R.N. 1992. Training practices of athletes who participated in the National Wheel-chair

Athletic Association training camps. *Adapted Physical Activity Quarterly* 9 (3): 249-260.

Wanzel, R., Gibeault, H., and Tsarouhas, A. 2001. Marketing sport for persons with a disability. In *New horizons in sports for athletes with a disability, proceedings of the international Vista '99 conference,* Cologne, Germany, August 28-September 1, 1999, ed. G. Doll-Tepper, M. Kroner, and W. Sonnenschein (pp. 851-873). London: Meyer & Meyer Sport.

Weiss, M., and Curtis, K. 1986. Controversies in medical classification of wheelchair athletes. In *Sport and disabled athletes,* ed. C. Sherrill (pp. 93-100). Champaign, IL: Human Kinetics.

Wells, C.L., and Hooker, S.P. 1990. The spinal injured athlete. *Adapted Physical Activity Quarterly* 7: 265-285.

West, J., ed. 1991. *The Americans with Disabilities Act: From policy to practice.* New York: Milbank Memorial Fund.

Wheeler, G. 2001. Ethical issues in the paralympics—what is right and what is fair? In *New horizons in sports for athletes with a disability, proceedings of the international Vista '99 conference,* Cologne, Germany, August 28-September 1, 1999, ed. G. Doll-Tepper, M. Kroner, and W. Sonnenschein (pp. 395-433). London: Meyer & Meyer Sport.

Whitaker, G., and Molstead, S. 1988. Role modeling and female coaches. *Sex Roles* 18: 555-566.

Wicks, J.R., Oldridge, N.G., Cameron, B.J., and Jones, N.L. 1983. Arm cranking and wheelchair ergometry in elite spinal cord-injured athletes. *Medicine and Science in Sports and Exercise* 15: 224-231.

Williams, T. 1994. Disability sport socialization and identity construction. *Adapted Physical Activity Quarterly* 11: 14-31.

Wirta, R.W., Golbranson, F.L., Mason, R., and Calvo, K. 1990. Analysis of below-knee suspension systems: Effect on gait. *Journal of Rehabilitation Research* 27 (4): 385-396.

Wolff, E.A., and Hums, M.A. 2003, October. Sport without disability: Understanding the exclusion of athletes with a disability. Paper presented at the Annual Conference of the North American Society for Sociology of Sport, Montreal, PQ, Canada.

Women's Sports Foundation. 2003. Cheri Blauwet breaks NYC marathon course record. www.women'ssportsfoundation.org (accessed November 14, 2003).

Wong, K.M., Chizinsky, K., MacLeod, S.T., Wright, W.E., Axelson, P.A., and Chesney, D.A. 1998. Trails web site with universal access information. In *Proceedings of the RESNA 1998 annual conference,* ed. S. Sprigle (pp. 358-360). Arlington, VA: RESNA Press.

Woodman, L. 1988. Coaching advances for athletes with disabilities. *NICAN Networking* 1 (2): 1-2.

World Curling Federation. 2003. Wheelchair curling. www.wheelchaircurling.ch/EN/rc.htm (accessed November 7, 2003).

World Health Organization. 2002. *International classification of functioning, disability and health.* Geneva: Author. www3.who.int/icf/icftemplate.cfm.

Wright, J., and Cowden, J. 1986. Changes in self-concept and cardiovascular endurance of mentally retarded youths in a Special Olympics swim training program. *Adapted Physical Activity Quarterly* 3: 177-183.

Wyness, G.B. 1984. Strategic reminders for effective event management. *Athletic Business* 8: 72-77.

York, S., and Kimura, I. 1986. An analysis of basic construction variables of racing wheelchairs used in the 1984 International Games for the Disabled. *Research Quarterly for Exercise and Sports* 58: 16-20.

Zwiren, L., and Bar-Or, O. 1975. Responses to exercise of paraplegics who differ in conditioning level. *Medicine and Science in Sports and Exercise* 7: 94-98.

index

Note: The italicized *f* and *t* following page numbers refer to figures and tables, respectively.

H

Hansen, R. 243
Hart, R. 191
Hartel, L. 38, 263
Hasbrook, C.A. 252
Haslacher, D. 157*t*
hearing aids 204*f*
hearing-impaired athletes 38, 97-99, 177,
    187-188, 260
Hedrick, B. 246
Hedrick, S.R. 246, 263
Higgs, C. 168, 247, 248, 249
Hippocrates 23
historical perspectives on research 55-57
historical perspectives on sport 29-32,
    34-35
historical treatment of persons with dis-
    abilities 22-25, 26-29
history of disability sport
    international disability sport 37-44
    research 55-57
    trends and milestones 57-59, 270, 277-
        287
    United States disability sport 45-55
hockey 141*t*, 145, 326
Holmes, C. 158*t*
Hong Kong 128-129
Hopf, Y. 158*t*
horseback riding 34-35, 87, 149, 191
Huebner, C. 52

I

iceberg profile 165
images of disability sport 271, 273
inclusion and integration
    barriers to 13-14
    legislation on 47-49, 50
    three issues in 242-244, 246
    trends 29, 271
Individuals with Disabilities Education Act
    (IDEA) 47, 48*t*
injuries
    common 184-185, 186*f*
    contraindications to exercise 200*t*
    prevention of 187*t*
    treatment considerations 185, 187-190
Intellectual Disability, International Sports
    Federation for Persons with (INAS-
    FID) 71-72
intellectual impairments 71-72, 96-97, 176,
    262

intensity of exercise 194
intercollegiate and interscholastic athletic
    programs 110-112
International Blind Sports Association
    (IBSA) 42-43, 61, 62, 68-70, 78*t*
International Committee of Sports for the
    Deaf (CISS) 38, 43, 61, 63, 64, 74, 76,
    78*t*
International Coordinating Committee of
    the World Sports Organizations 43,
    67, 76-77
international disability sport
    history of 37-39, 42-44
    organizations 64-77, 305-310
International Ex-Servicemen's Wheelchair
    Games 104
International Olympic Committee (IOC)
    39, 43, 44, 63*t*, 64, 66, 67, 77
International Paralympic Committee
    (IPC) 43-44, 56, 57, 61-62, 63*t*, 64-68,
    77, 274
international perspectives 115-116. *See
    also* world view
international ski and sport associations
    301-303
international sport event planning 233,
    235-236
International Sports Federation for Per-
    sons with Intellectual Disability
    (INAS-FID) 71-72
International Sports Organization for the
    Disabled (ISOD) 39, 42, 43, 61-62, 63,
    70, 72-74, 78*t*
International Stoke Mandeville Wheelchair
    Sports Federation (ISMWSF) 38-39,
    63, 72, 78*t*
international structure for disability sport
    61-64
Iran 40-42
Itard, J.M. 26, 27

J

Jackson, R.W. 223, 224
Japan 129-130
Jones, J.A. 213
journal resources 196, 197*t*-198*t*, 349-351
judo 141*t*, 151

K

Kane, M.J. 253
Kanner, L. 27

Karen P. DePauw, PhD, is vice provost for graduate studies and dean of the graduate school at Virginia Tech in Blacksburg, Virginia. She has been involved with disability sport since 1981 and was on the original United States Olympic Committee's (USOC) Committee on Sports for the Disabled, serving on that committee for 12 years. She also served on the USOC Task Force on Disability and was a member of the Organizing Committee for the 1996 Paralympic Congress in Atlanta, Georgia. Dr. DePauw has served as president of the International Federation on Adapted Physical Activity (IFAPA). She is a member of the American Alliance for Health, Physical Education, Recreation and Dance (AAHPERD); American College of Sports Medicine; National Association for Physical Education in Higher Education (NAPEHE); National Consortium on Physical Education and Recreation for Handicapped (NCPERH); and North American Federation for Adapted Physical Activity. She also serves on the editorial board of *Adapted Physical Activity Quarterly.* Dr. DePauw enjoys playing golf, cycling, and traveling in her spare time.

Susan J. Gavron, PED, is associate professor emeritus at Bowling Green State University in Bowling Green, Ohio. She has had a lifelong involvement with people and disabilities in a variety of program formats, including teaching, camping, and sport.

Dr. Gavron has been involved in research of elite athletes with disabilities at the national and international levels. She participated in the research advisory group for the USOC Committee on Sports for the Disabled. She also has extensive programming experience in physical education and leisure for individuals with disabilities. She has received numerous awards for her work and service to the state of Ohio. Recently retired, Dr. Gavron is a firefighter and first responder and enjoys photography, fishing, and reading in her leisure time.

*You'll find
other outstanding adapted
physical activity resources at*

www.HumanKinetics.com

In the U.S. call

1-800-747-4457

Australia................................ 08 8277 1555
Canada 1-800-465-7301
Europe...................... +44 (0) 113 255 5665
New Zealand................... 0064 9 448 1207

HUMAN KINETICS
The Information Leader in Physical Activity
P.O. Box 5076 • Champaign, IL 61825-5076 USA